## Services Liberalization in the EU and the WTO

Both in WTO law and EU law there is a dichotomy between liberalization based on market access and targeting domestic regulation. Consequently, both regimes share the problem of distinguishing national measures impairing market access and those that do not have such effect. Looking at the provision of services, a cornerstone of EU substantive law, in the EU and the WTO, this book offers a comprehensive evaluation of the current legal status quo on transnational services provision at a global level. Based on thorough analysis of both EU and WTO law, policymakers are provided with concrete proposals for fostering the consistency and effectiveness of the current regime. A final chapter discusses possible approaches to regulation such as home state rule, host state rule and mutual recognition from a comparative perspective. Written by a highly respected author, this is essential reading for EU internal market specialists and WTO law scholars alike.

**Marcus Klamert** is a member of the Legal and Constitutional Service of the Austrian Federal Chancellery and a lecturer at the Vienna University of Economics and Business.

Cambridge Studies in European Law and Policy

This series aims to produce original works that contain a critical analysis of the state of the law in particular areas of European Law and set out different perspectives and suggestions for its future development. It also aims to encourage a range of work on law, legal institutions and legal phenomena in Europe, including 'law in context' approaches. The titles in the series will be of interest to academics; policymakers; policy formers who are interested in European legal, commercial, and political affairs; practising lawyers including the judiciary; and advanced law students and researchers.

Books in the series

*EU Enlargement and the Constitutions of Central and Eastern Europe*
Anneli Albi

*Social Rights and Market Freedom in the European Constitution: A Labour Law Perspective*
Stefano Giubboni

*The Constitution for Europe: A Legal Analysis*
Jean-Claude Piris

*The European Convention on Human Rights: Achievements, Problems and Prospects*
Steven Greer

*European Broadcasting Law and Policy*
Jackie Harrison and Lorna Woods

*The Transformation of Citizenship in the European Union: Electoral Rights and the Restructuring of Political Space*
Jo Shaw

*Implementing EU Pollution Control: Law and Integration*
Bettina Lange

*The Evolving European Union: Migration Law and Policy*
Dora Kostakopoulou

*Ethical Dimensions of the Foreign Policy of the European Union: A Legal Appraisal*
Urfan Khaliq

*The European Civil Code: The Way Forward*
Hugh Collins

*State and Market in European Union Law*
Wolf Sauter and Harm Schepel

*The Ethos of Europe: Values, Law and Justice in the EU*
Andrew Williams

*The European Union's Fight Against Corruption: The Evolving Policy Towards Member States and Candidate Countries*
Patrycja Szarek-Mason

*The Lisbon Treaty: A Legal and Political Analysis*
Jean-Claude Piris

*New Governance and the Transformation of European Law: Coordinating EU Social Law and Policy*
Mark Dawson

*The Limits of Legal Reasoning and the European Court of Justice*
Gerard Conway

*International Trade Disputes and EU Liability*
Anne Thies

*Referendums and the European Union: A Comparative Enquiry*
Fernando Mendez, Mario Mendez, Vasilki Triga

*Services Liberalization in the EU and the WTO: Concepts, Standards and Regulatory Approaches*
Marcus Klamert

# Services Liberalization in the EU and the WTO

## Concepts, Standards and Regulatory Approaches

Marcus Klamert

CAMBRIDGE
UNIVERSITY PRESS

CAMBRIDGE
UNIVERSITY PRESS

University Printing House, Cambridge CB2 8BS, United Kingdom

Cambridge University Press is part of the University of Cambridge.

It furthers the University's mission by disseminating knowledge in the pursuit of education, learning and research at the highest international levels of excellence.

www.cambridge.org
Information on this title: www.cambridge.org/9781107034594



First published 2015

Printed in the United Kingdom by Clays, St Ives plc

*A catalogue record for this publication is available from the British Library*

*Library of Congress Cataloguing in Publication data*
Klamert, Marcus, author.
Services liberalization in the EU and the WTO : concepts, standards and regulatory approaches / Marcus Klamert.
pages cm – (Cambridge studies in European law and policy)
Includes bibliographical references and index.
ISBN 978-1-107-03459-4 (hardback)
1. Service industries–Law and legislation–European Union countries. 2. Foreign trade regulation–European Union countries. 3. International and municipal law–European Union countries. 4. World Trade Organization. 5. Foreign trade regulation. 6. Service industries–Law and legislation. I. Title.
KJE6819.K53 2014
343.2408′7–dc23
2014032248

ISBN 978-1-107-03459-4 Hardback

# Contents

# Series editors' preface

Services liberalization is just as much a hot potato within the European Union as it is within the WTO. In this work Marcus Klamert offers a stimulating examination of how the EU and the WTO have coped with market liberalization and with the development of regulatory standards. His analysis almost recalls the perceived relationship between the United Kingdom and the United States (two nations divided by a common language). While the EU and WTO regimes display manifest differences, the language of market access, discrimination, justification and harmonization can be seen as being hewn from the same roots. This work seeks to lift the veil of ignorance about these similarities and to encourage more cross-fertilization than has hitherto occurred.

Klamert argues that the EU should take cues from WTO law to permit clarification of the non-discrimination standard in EU law, just as in relation to double burdens, lessons should be learned in the other direction. His analysis of the EU's Services Directive exposes some real weaknesses, yet also in some respects a close relationship between the EU and WTO approaches.

This is a book that is a welcome addition to the *Cambridge Studies in European Law and Policy* series: it is challenging, and is a timely reminder that the development of EU law and policy does not take place in a vacuum; internal and external developments cannot ignore one another, and the solutions that are adopted in order to reach a minimum agreement in the Council are not always the most desirable; a heads in the sand approach on the part of policymakers is rarely productive. With this in mind, this work offers a challenge to look at matters differently.

Laurence Gormley
Jo Shaw

# Preface

This book has been a long time in the making. It dates back to a research project conducted at the Europainstitute of the Vienna University for Economics and Business, which received funding from the Austrian Science Fund (FWF) and concluded in 2009. While the project was mainly focused on the Services Directive, which at that time had caused a lot of debate, now that several years have passed this book has a much broader perspective. The Services Directive and its impact on the services regime in the EU remains an important issue. The leitmotiv of this book, however, is the discussion of legal principles that are pertinent both in the EU and the WTO, such as the various prohibitions of discriminatory measures, the approach to domestic regulation, the concept of market access, and in general the balance struck between market regulation and regulatory autonomy within the two legal systems.

This book is not a textbook on the GATS, nor is it a textbook on EU services law. While we do need to lay the relevant groundwork by expounding some of the key rules of both regimes, some of the issues that are commonly found in more comprehensive books about the GATS or about EU services law might therefore be missing here. Another word of caution is warranted: the parts of the book on the GATS might not in all respects conform to the orthodox way in which this regime is commonly described. This is not meant as heresy, but also as an attempt to lay the aforementioned groundwork with regard to the GATS in a way that should be more accessible than is often the case. Instead of providing a complete picture of the GATS and EU services law, this book thus aims at laying bare the regulatory approaches adopted under each system, how they relate to each other, what differences exist, where we can find analogies, and on which issues there can be a cross-fertilization between the two systems. Another objective of this book is to make the regulatory concepts used in either regime more accessible, and to make the actual degree of sectoral coverage of either regime more transparent.

A thorough comparative study of EU law and WTO law in the pertinent area would necessitate an examination that goes beyond a purely legal analysis, to also cover economic and technical aspects. We will limit ourselves to the legal perspective and will only refer to an economic view where necessary. Hence, while our assessment might not capture all aspects of the relationship between EU and WTO law, it should produce some important findings about the levels and modalities of integration in the EU and the WTO both from a comparative perspective and in absolute terms. While there is one chapter that is thoroughly comparative, comparative aspects will be considered and dealt with throughout this book. Thus, to give one example, an issue such as the overlap between the GATS and the GATT is not dealt with in Chapter 1 on the GATS, but is discussed in Chapter 3 on EU services law, where similar problems exist between the rules applying to goods and to services, respectively.

We are grateful to a number of people who have contributed throughout the course of this project in different ways. We thank Armin Hatje and Robert Adlung for having dedicated their time and expertise as peer reviewers for the FWF research project, to the participants of a conference in Vienna in 2009 where we benefited from discussions with some of the most eminent scholars in the field, especially on the Services Directive, and to Roman Puff for being an invaluable organizational support.

We are indebted to Sanam Haghighi, who has written first drafts of parts of some chapters. Georg Adler has gracefully agreed to contribute to Chapter 7 on the implementation of the Services Directive. Kathrin Blanck-Putz has been so kind as to contribute to one section in Chapter 3 and Chapter 8. Last but not least, Stefan Griller not only initiated the original FWF project grant and was a dedicated project leader until its termination, but also thereafter has been actively engaged with the writing of this book.

Any opinion expressed in this book is the personal opinion of the author and the contributors and does not represent the opinion of the Austrian Chancellery or the European Commission.

Case law and literature has been considered up to January 2014.

# Table of case law

## WTO Dispute Settlement Bodies

## Other international courts



## Court of Justice of the European Union

127/73, *BRT* v. *SABAM* [1974] ECR 313 116
T-289/03, *BUPA et al* v. *Commission* [2008] ECR II-81 115, 170
C-442/02, *CaixaBank France* v. *Ministère de l'Économie, des Finances et de l'Industrie* [2004] ECR I-8961 133–134
C-390/99, *Canal Satélite Digital SL* v. *Adminstración General del Estado, and Distribuidora de Televisión Digital SA (DTS)* [2002] ECR I-607 101, 106, 295
C-60/00, *Mary Carpenter* v. *Secretary of State for the Home Department* [2002] I-6279 82, 84
C-386/04, *Centro di Musicologia Walter Stauffer* [2006] ECR I-8203 91
C-212/97, *Centros Ltd gegen Erhvervs-og Selskabsstyrelsen* [1999] ECR I-1459 22, 82, 83
C-300/98, *Christian Dior* and C-392/98 *Assco Gerüste* [2000] ECR I-11307 60
C-83/01P, C-93/01P and C-94/01P, *Chronopost SA, La Poste and French Republic* v. *Union française de l'express (Ufex), DHL International, Federal express international (France) SNC and CRIE SA* [2003] ECR I-6993 119
C-194/94, *CIA Security* [1996] ECR I-2201 207, 208
C-94/04 and C-202/04, *Federico Cipolla* v. *Rosaria Fazari, née Portolese and Stefano Macrino and Claudia Capoparte* v. *Roberto Meloni* [2006] ECR I-11421 195
C-320/03, *Commission* v. *Austria* [2005] ECR I-9871 145, 207
C-147/03, *Commission* v. *Austria (Conditions of Access to University Education)* [2005] ECR I-5969 145, 147, 148, 151, 275
C-257/05, *Commission* v. *Austria ('Kesselprüfstelle')* [2006] ECR I-134 195
C-53/08, *Commission* v. *Austria (Notaries)* [2011] ECR I-4309 111
C-161/07, *Commission* v. *Austria (Self-certification)* [2008] ECR I-10671 91
C-2/90, *Commission* v. *Belgium* [1992] ECR I-4431 94
C-355/98, *Commission* v. *Belgium* [2000] ECR I-1221 90, 137
C-577/10, *Commission* v. *Belgium (Self-employed Service Providers)* [2012] not yet published in the Official Journal 94
220/83, *Commission* v. *France* [1986] ECR 3663 137
C-381/93, *Commission* v. *France* [1994] ECR I-5145 80
C-265/95, *Commission* v. *France* [1997] ECR I-6959 207
C-264/03, *Commission* v. *France* [2005] ECR I-8831 125
C-89/09, *Commission* v. *France (Laboratories)* [2010] ECR I-12941 97
270/83, *Commission* v. *France ('Avoir Fiscal')* [1986] ECR 273 82
C-159/94, *Commission* v. *France (EDF)* [1997] ECR I-5815 116
C-34/98, *Commission* v. *France (Social Security)* [2000] ECR I-995 93, 142
29/84, *Commission* v. *Germany* [1985] ECR 1661 242
C-131/88, *Commission* v. *Germany* [1991] ECR I-825 235
C-493/99, *Commission* v. *Germany* [2001] ECR I-8163 90
C-490/04, *Commission* v. *Germany* [2007] ECR I-6095 195

# Table of materials

## WTO materials

## EU materials

# Introduction

Since its conception after the Second World War, the General Agreement on Tariffs and Trade (GATT) has always aspired to create a multilateral framework that would regulate international trade and stimulate commerce. This, it is believed, would raise standards of living and progressively develop the economies of the contracting parties. Until today, the objective of having trade flow as freely as possible has remained at the core of the ambitions of the World Trade Organization (WTO). Hence, the WTO's efforts circle around trade and any activity that would affect trade. However, dealing with barriers to the access of services to markets has also engaged domestic regulatory policies and domestic legal systems more than is the case with products. With the General Agreement on Trade in Services (GATS), this has meant a move away from traditional conceptions of sovereign relations in international trade. The liberalization of services trade has thus been claimed to be 'hardly the GATT world of shallow integration but a different world of ever deepening integration and globalization ... negotiations center entirely on what were considered domestic policies and even institutional infrastructure, quite alien in terms of GATT tradition'.[1] This has brought matters that were once exclusively within the national domain within the reach of international rule-making.

The overarching regulatory objectives underpinning the European Union and the WTO are clearly quite different. The WTO agreements do not aim at establishing a common market, a customs union or even a free trade area, while the EU is all of that. The WTO is not as openly

[1] S. Ostry, 'Globalization and the World Trading System: the Deeper Integration Policy Agenda', in Canadian Bar Association and Department of Justice Canada, 14th International Trade Law Seminar, 1996.

seeking deregulation of national law as the EU, which has a fitting arsenal of legal principles to achieve this end. Nonetheless, WTO law is built on the same aim and the same philosophy of free trade as has inspired the EU.[2] This analogy goes beyond the well-known fact that what is now Article 28 Treaty on the Functioning of the European Union (TFEU) – the key provision in Union law on the prohibition of quantitative restrictions – was modelled on the GATT. The EU is 'a child of the GATT, a regional integration agreement based on non-discrimination and market access among a number of regionally linked participants'.[3] It has, however, always professed much broader ambitions and has become increasingly preoccupied with matters not (or not exclusively) related to trade, finding expression in the shedding of the central 'E' to become the EC with the Maastricht Treaty, and then the EU with the Lisbon Treaty. The Treaty explicitly refers to European integration as 'the process of creating an ever closer union among the peoples of Europe'. Article 3 Treaty on European Union (TEU) does not only speak of the objective of establishing an internal market, but also mentions peace, freedom, security and justice without internal frontiers, the fight against social exclusion and discrimination, solidarity among its Member States, and the safeguarding of cultural heritage.

At its conception, the GATS was claimed to be one of the major achievements of the Uruguay Round of negotiations and one of the most important legal frameworks for liberalizing trade in services at the multilateral level. Governments were called upon to guarantee 'some' access to their markets by foreign services or service suppliers. The goal of establishing rules in the sector of services at the multilateral level was believed to contribute to the development of the world economy, with success in this area sought by (1) expanding trade under conditions of transparency and progressive liberalization, and (2) promoting economic growth, thus following the same reasoning as the WTO system as a whole. While service sectors per se do not contribute directly to economic growth, as they seek to contribute to increasing the quantity and productivity of capital and labour inputs, they are claimed to have a 'facilitating role'. In other words, the growth of services is deemed 'an

[2] P.-C. Müller-Graff, 'Protectionism or reasonable national regulation?', in S. Griller (ed.), *At the Crossroads: The World Trading System and the Doha Round* (Vienna, New York: Springer, 2008), pp. 147–67 at p. 150.

[3] M. Cremona, 'Neutrality or discrimination? The WTO, the EU and external trade', in G. de Búrca and J. Scott (eds.), *The EU and the WTO: Legal and Constitutional Issues* (Oxford and Portland, OR: Hart Publishing, 2002), pp. 151–84 at pp. 151–2.

important determinant of overall economic growth and development'.[4] The EU has been described as an initially defensive actor at the birth of the GATS, being fearful of having to compromise on its agricultural policy.[5] The European Commission is said to have been a key agent for enhancing the role of the EU in the negotiations, largely motivated by institutional self-interest.[6]

In the EU, services had a slow start within the rules governing the common market. For a long time the freedom to provide services had been considered only subsidiary to the other fundamental freedoms. It gained importance and attention in correspondence with the increasing share of the service sector in the economies of the Member States.[7] As has been noted in the context of the EU Services Directive,[8] 'the production of a car requires many service inputs such as design, marketing, technical analysis and sales, while the sale of the car requires services such as finance, insurance and training'.[9] Therefore, as trade in goods might depend on the degree of market power that is exercised by domestic trade and distribution sectors, an absence of competition in the domestic service sector can serve as an effective import barrier against goods. This links market access conditions for goods with the structure of the domestic service sector. Conversely, services liberalization can provide a boost for the trade in goods,[10] and 'actions taken

[4] See in general, B. Hoekman, 'Liberalizing trade in services: a survey' (2006) Working Paper Series 4030, World Bank, Washington DC, https://openknowledge.worldbank.org/handle/10986/9004.

[5] J. A. Marchetti and P. C. Mavroidis, 'The genesis of the GATS (General Agreement on Trade in Services)' (2011) 22(3) *The European Journal of International Law* 689–721 at 695.

[6] Marchetti and Mavroidis, 'The genesis of the GATS', 696.

[7] See V. Hatzopoulos, *Regulating Services in the European Union* (Oxford University Press, 2012), pp. vii–viii; and V. Robertson, *Perspectiven für den grenzüberschreitenden Dienstleistungshandel: Das EU-Dienstleistungsrecht und sein Verhältnis zum GATS* (Baden-Baden: Nomos, 2012), pp. 32–6.

[8] Directive 2006/123/EC of the European Parliament and the Council of 12 December 2006 on services in the internal market, OJ 2006 No. L376/36. The Services Directive, unlike the GATS, does not apply to goods. See Rec. 76 of Directive 2006/123/EC.

[9] See C. Barnard, 'Unravelling the Services Directive' (2008) *Common Market Law Review* 323–94 at 335.

[10] See also J. F. Francois, and I. Wooton, 'Market structure, trade liberalization, and the GATS' (2001) 17(2) *European Journal of Political Economics* 389–402 at 402. See also J. F. Francois, and I. Wooton, 'Market structure and market access' (2008) World Bank Policy Research Working Paper No. 4151, http://ssrn.com/abstract=965604. They argue that the trade volume effect of a tariff reduction in the goods sector depends on the underlying trade volume and hence on the degree of competition in the domestic distribution sector. To some extent, therefore, tariff reductions may simply lead to a

in services markets can affect competition in goods markets and vice versa'.[11] Therefore, in regulating the market, it is important to consider fully this interaction in order to ensure that one set of regulations does not undermine the other. At the same time, the inherent overlap between goods and services regulation does not necessarily undermine the coherence of the overall framework, but they may rather be mutually reinforcing.

It has been argued for the EU that because of the more diverse nature of services regulations, the more complex objectives involved and the involvement of sub-state or non-state entities, private measures are more readily tackled by the Court of Justice in the field of services than in the field of goods.[12] As also noted by Hatzopoulos, 'services regulations rarely concern the service itself; instead they fulfil the conditions that the service providers should themselves fulfil (qualifications, authorizations, entry into registers, deontology rules, provider's liability) or the circumstances under which the providers may offer their services (opening hours and days, location, price-fixing, access subject to a devolution system etc.).'[13] In other words, services rules are not of a technical, but rather of a social, environmental and qualification-related nature.[14] While this may have been argued for the EU, it equally holds for the WTO.

Our fundamental premise is therefore that both in WTO law and in EU law there is a dichotomy between a regulatory model based on market access on the one hand, and one aimed at domestic regulation on the other hand. This refers to the fact that, as a matter of principle, both the GATS and the EU subject measures that affect market access to more scrutiny than measures that do not concern market access. Moreover, because of this approach, both regimes share the dilemma of how to distinguish 'benign' domestic measures from 'problematic' ones. This places the problem of balancing the autonomy of Member

greater exercise of market power by the domestic distribution sector and vice versa, 'nullifying expected direct benefits from tariff reductions in export markets'.

11 See B. Hoeckman and P. A. Maeserlin, 'Liberalizing trade in services: reciprocal negotiations and regulatory reform', in P. Sauvé and R. Stern (eds.), *GATS 2000: New Directions in Services Trade Liberalization* (Washington DC: Brookings, 2000), pp. 487–508 at p. 91.

12 V. Hatzopoulos, 'Forms of mutual recognition in the field of services', in I. Lianos and O. Odudu (eds.), *Regulating Trade in Services: Trust, Distrust and Economic Integration* (Cambridge University Press, 2012), pp. 59–98 at p. 61.

13 Hatzopoulos, 'Forms of mutual recognition in the field of services', p. 63.

14 See Hatzopoulos, 'Forms of mutual recognition in the field of services', p. 65.

States with the need and mandate to liberalize at the core of both regimes, informing the fiercest debates in WTO and EU law alike.[15] Such a common regulatory goal pursued by each regime and a shared 'regulatory DNA' suggests that we cannot simply consider EU law in general and EU law on services in particular as fundamentally different from WTO law. For instance, the *Keck* doctrine, introduced by the Court of Justice to address the aforementioned distinction, has been deemed to represent 'a "bending" of the EC towards the National Treatment rationale of the GATT'.[16] Therefore, we submit that an effort to search for further analogies between the two regimes is not entirely fanciful and we are therefore not 'comparing the incomparable'.

These analogies have of course not gone unnoticed in the past. However, a sizable amount of comparative analysis to this date has focused on the nature of the 'necessity test' under WTO law, and to the transfer of the proportionality principle as applied in the EU common market to the GATT[17] and the GATS.[18] We will show that it verges on denial to ignore the variety of concepts and terms – the 'common legal vocabulary'[19] – that feature prominently in both regimes. We will show

[15] See W. Weiß, 'GATS and domestic regulation: a threat to democracy?', in S. Griller (ed.), *At the Crossroads: The World Trading System and the Doha Round* (Vienna, New York: Springer, 2008), pp. 369–83 at p. 371, on the domestic regulation making 'GATS particularly sensitive for democracy concerns as the national regulatory autonomy comes under greater scrutiny'.

[16] J. H. H. Weiler, 'Epilogue: Towards a Common Law of International Trade', in J. H. H. Weiler (ed.), *The EU, the WTO, and the NAFTA* (Oxford University Press, Collected Courses of the Academy of European Law, 2001), pp. 201–32 at 230.

[17] See Müller-Graff, 'Protectionism or reasonable national regulation?', p. 150.

[18] See the discussion at M. Krajewski, *National Regulation and Trade Liberalization in Services: The Legal Impact of the General Agreement on Trade in Services (GATS) on National Regulatory Autonomy* (The Hague: Kluwer, 2003), pp. 141–5. However, for a notable exception, see the profound comparison of the approach to (de)regulating tax measures within the EU and the WTO by Weiler, 'Epilogue', especially at pp. 204–16. See also D. J. Neven and J. Weiler, 'One bad apple? A comment on Japan – Measures Affecting the Importation of Apples – AB-2003-4', in D. Horovitz, D. Moulis and D. Steger (eds.), *Ten Years of WTO Dispute Settlement* (London: International Bar Association, 2007), pp. 235–57, drawing analogies between the WTO Agreement on Sanitary and Phytosanitary Measures and the *Dassonville* case law of the ECJ on targeting non-discriminatory, non-protectionist measures.

[19] See the rallying call for a better mutual understanding among the lawyers dealing with the two systems by J. H. H. Weiler, 'Cain and Abel: Convergence and Divergence in International Trade Law', in Joseph H.H. Weiler (ed.), *The EU, the WTO, and the NAFTA* (Oxford University Press, Collected Courses of the Academy of European Law, 2001), pp. 1–4 at 1.

that experiences in the EU such as with the delimitation between market access and domestic regulation might be instructive for the path that should be taken by the WTO. At the same time, in the WTO the debate on the various forms of discrimination in particular seems to have been more fully explored than in the EU. Here, it is EU law that might take some cues from WTO law. Note that WTO and EU law differ in one important and obvious respect. The EU services regime has only recently been modified in a fundamental manner with the entry into force of the Services Directive 2006/123/EC.[20] This reformed area of EU law might thus require some time before we are fully able to judge its effects and effectiveness. In contrast, the GATS and the negotiations for which it should provide the forum are effectively stalled by the demise of the Doha Round of negotiations under the umbrella of the WTO.

Distinguishing the dichotomies between a prohibition of discrimination and the more intrusive prohibition of non-discriminatory national measures on the one hand, and market access regulation and (equally intrusive) domestic regulation on the other hand, might be faulted for overly simplifying a very complex and casuistic regime. However, they arguably serve as an appropriate frame under which to assess the Services Directive, and are also useful when comparing the GATS with the EU law regime. In addition to the parallels between EU law and WTO law, on which we will draw in this book, we will also take account of the differences. When comparing the ways through which the EU and the GATS deal with the services sector, it is apposite to highlight the rationale behind different regulatory approaches chosen for similar goals and objectives pursued in both systems. On the other hand, when the goals pursued by lawmakers differ yet similar outcomes are achieved, it is apposite to determine why each system has failed or succeeded in attaining those objectives. When, finally, there are both dissimilar goals and dissimilar outcomes for the regimes examined, these contrasts and differences may not only disclose important facts about the systems themselves, but may also pave the way for identifying the strengths and weaknesses of each system.

In Chapter 1 we will provide a discussion of the structure and basic principles of the GATS, including its effect on the national laws of its

[20] Directive 2006/123/EC of the European Parliament and the Council of 12 December 2006 on services in the internal market, OJ 2006 No. L376/36.

members. Where appropriate, we will already make some cross-references to the situation in the EU. As mentioned, we will not always follow an orthodox pattern when describing the GATS.

Chapter 2 will deal with the relationship between the EU and the WTO on several accounts. We will analyse differences in the organizational structure of both systems, their respective capacities to set standards and the functioning of their adjudication regimes. We will also specifically discuss the effect of WTO law within the EU legal order, as well as give an overview of the EU's commitments undertaken and offered under the GATS.

Chapter 3 will sketch the fundamentals of the Treaty freedom to provide services and the Treaty freedom of establishment, without yet taking into account the rules of the Services Directive 2006/123/EC. This chapter also discusses the delimitations between the two mentioned freedoms and other fundamental freedoms in EU law, as well as the EU regime on what will broadly be called public services.

In Chapter 4 the regulatory principles underlying EU law on services and establishments such as the concepts of discrimination, restrictions and market access will be analysed in greater depth. Thus the current state of affairs of integrating the common market in services will be presented from a different perspective and with a higher degree of abstraction than in Chapter 3.

This is followed by Chapter 5, where we show the diverse ways in which the regulation of different service sectors in the EU is approached. This will be shown to range from minimum harmonization and mutual recognition to a combination of soft law and case law, such as with respect to the 'regulation' of services of general economic interest.

Chapter 6 will then address the Services Directive 2006/123/EC in detail, laying particular focus on the screening mechanisms and the variety of instruments foreseen to regulate different kinds of measures pertaining to services and establishments respectively. This chapter will also include an assessment of the ways the Services Directive interacts with the pre-existing Treaty regime, and of the implications for the fragmentation of the EU services regime both from a substantive and a sectoral perspective.

Chapter 7 will discuss the implementation of the Services Directive in the EU Member States, where the points of single contact and the key liberalizing provision for services in particular have raised difficult issues.

Finally, Chapter 8 will bring together several threads from previous chapters in examining the diverse approaches, concepts and regulatory standards that exist in EU law and WTO law on services.

# 1 WTO law on services: a starter kit

## 1.1 Introduction

The GATS forms Annex 1B to the Marrakesh Agreement on the WTO and entered into force on 1 January 1995. As a multilateral WTO agreement, Members are obliged to accede to it. Its creation was largely at the behest of the United States in order to protect its interests in an area where it had comparative advantages. Marchetti and Mavroidis have explained that it actually was the threat that new barriers to trade would be set up, mainly by developing countries, to counter the opening of foreign markets such as in financial services and telecoms through technology that prompted the USA to drive the GATS forward.[1] In the meantime, a number of developing countries have closed the gap and now account for a considerable amount of international trade in services.[2]

The target of the GATS is trade restrictions set up by the parties other than tariffs such as under the GATT. To achieve this end, the GATS primarily offers the prescription of market access and the prohibition of discrimination, which in WTO language is called national treatment.[3] It has been claimed that the GATS is not about the 'deregulation' of national markets, and that national rules applying to services or service

[1] J. A. Marchetti and P. C. Mavroidis, 'The genesis of the GATS (General Agreement on Trade in Services)' (2011) 22(3) *The European Journal of International Law* 689–721 at 692.

[2] See M. J. Trebilcock, R. Howse, and A. Eliason, *The Regulation of International Trade*, 4th edn (London and New York: Routledge, 2013), p. 473.

[3] Arts. XVI and XVII GATS.

providers after the crossing of the border remain the prerogative of the Members.[4] In 'official' language:

> Rather, the Agreement explicitly recognizes governments' right to regulate, and introduce new regulations, to meet national policy objectives and the particular need of developing countries to exercise this right.[5]

However, there is also the provision on domestic regulation in Article VI GATS, which specifically concerns this sphere of national regulatory autonomy.

In contrast to the GATT, profound liberalization in the GATS is subject to specific commitments by the WTO Members. Article XX GATS obliges WTO Members to submit a schedule of specific commitments according to defined services sectors. WTO Members can decide autonomously which concessions in which sectors they want to enter into. These commitments take the form of binding (scheduled) promises to all other Members either to grant market access or not to discriminate in a specific services sector or sub-sector. If a sector is so committed, this is binding on the respective WTO Member in the sense of providing a guaranteed minimum standard awarded to foreigners. Treatment that is more favourable is subject to the Most Favoured Nation principle (MFN) pursuant to Article II:1 GATS, requiring each Member to extend this treatment immediately and unconditionally to services and service suppliers of any other Member, unless this right is expressly excluded.

The GATS works only as a framework agreement for negotiating these specific and detailed obligations among the Members. Without such bilateral negotiations on services under the GATS, even the MFN principle is not able to work its magic as it does under GATT. The reason for this is that, despite its general application irrespective of specific (scheduled) commitments of Members, it requires bilateral deals on the liberalization of the trade in services to enter into effect. Only on these grounds are the best access conditions that have been conceded to one country multilateralized and thus automatically extended to all other WTO Members.

In the rest of this chapter, we will take a closer look at the way GATS liberalizes trade in services and at the tools that it provides for Members to commit to this end. Note that we do not aim at offering

[4] C. Herrmann, W. Weiß and C. Ohler, *Welthandelsrecht*, 2nd edn (Munich: Beck, 2007), p. 384.

[5] See www.wto.org/english/tratop_e/serv_e/cbt_course_e/c1s2p1_e.htm.

a full analysis of all aspects related to the GATS. Instead, our focus in this book is on structural, systematic questions. This means, among other things, that we will not discuss Part V of the GATS on dispute settlement and Part VI on rules of origin. Wherever apposite, we will point out regulatory or conceptual differences to EU law. The commitments and the current offer of the EU in the framework of the GATS will be assessed later in this book. We will start by briefly recapping the history of the GATS and the current state of liberalization under its umbrella.

## 1.2 Status of negotiations under the GATS

The initial goal of the GATS was the gradual opening up of services markets over time, acknowledging that 'liberalization of trade in services cannot be achieved overnight and that not every country can move at the same pace'.[6] All Members have pledged to enter into new rounds of negotiations and achieve progressive liberalization.[7] However, it is commonly understood that the GATS has produced only meagre results beyond a 'locking in' of the liberalization status quo that had already been achieved at the time of its adoption.[8] Progress has been achieved in the area of telecommunication services and financial services only through the negotiation of separate agreements in these sectors, as will be discussed later.

The latest, and not yet concluded, Doha Round of trade negotiations was launched in 2000 and envisaged further trade liberalization. After the Uruguay Round, this goal apparently constituted a significant progress in itself. In March 2001 Guidelines and Procedures

[6] G. Feketekuty, 'Assessing and improving the architecture of GATS', in P. Sauvé and R. Stern (eds.), *GATS 2000: New Directions in Services Trade Liberalization* (Washington DC: Brookings, 2000), pp. 85–111.

[7] Art. XIX(1) GATS.

[8] Trebilcock *et al.*, *The Regulation of International Trade*, p. 486 with further references; Herrmann *et al.*, *Welthandelsrecht*, p. 384 and p. 398. But see the Disciplines on Telecommunications, discussed specifically in Chapter 2. A notable exception is the accession of new parties where 'phase-in commitments', constituting 'promises' of future negotiated liberalization, are more frequent. See R. Adlung, 'Services liberalization from a WTO/GATS perspective: in search of volunteers' (2009) Staff Working Paper ERSD 6, who mentions the case of China, whose accession schedule of 2001 subjected 60 per cent of all committed sectors to phase-in commitments, which were to be implemented within six years at most.

for the Services Negotiations were adopted by the Council for Trade in Services.[9] According to these Guidelines, rule-making negotiations in the areas of subsidies, government procurement and domestic regulation should be concluded before those on specific commitments. The Ministerial Conference in Doha of November 2001 confirmed the Guidelines with initial requests to be submitted within a set deadline. This and subsequent deadlines have passed without much progress on effective liberalization offers. Indeed, the request-and-offer process in services abated before the Ministerial Conference in Cancún in 2003.

The Hong Kong Ministerial Declaration of December 2005 proclaimed very ambitious and detailed objectives in its Annex C. Among others, it foresaw plurilateral request–offer negotiations in addition to bilateral ones, mode-specific objectives and an emphasis on increased clarity and certainty in scheduling. Final draft schedules were to be tabled by October 2006. Such rounds of plurilateral negotiations were conducted in 2006 but were suspended the same year due to disputes on agricultural and non-agricultural market access (NAMA). They were resumed later but never produced any sizeable results, and a prepared report by the Council for Trade in Services was not endorsed at the Mini-Ministerial Meeting in July 2008.[10]

Services negotiations, and negotiations in other areas under the Doha Development Agenda, picked up steam in April 2011, when the Chairman of the Council for Trade in Services submitted a report to the Trade Negotiations Committee on the achievements and remaining gaps in the services negotiations. Of the main areas in these negotiations that were identified, namely market access, domestic regulation, GATS rules and the implementation of LDC modalities, only with regard to the latter did the WTO Ministerial Conference in December 2011 adopt a waiver that allows WTO members to deviate from their MFN obligation in order to provide preferential treatment to services and service suppliers from least-developed countries.

[9] WTO, Council for Trade in Services, Guidelines and Procedures for the Negotiations on Trade in Services, adopted by the Special Session of the Council for Trade in Services on 28 March 2001, S/L/93, 29 March 2001.

[10] Four delegations refused to go any further than agreed in Annex C of the Hong Kong Ministerial Declaration. See WTO, Council for Trade in Services, Special Session, Elements Required for the Completion of the Services Negotiations, Report by the Chairman, TN/S/34, 28 July 2008.

There are several reasons why the Doha Round has so far not produced substantial offers on services.[11] One structural problem with the GATS is that Members have not listed their restrictions on market access in full, rendering the picture and thus the basis for negotiations incomplete.[12] Another problem is that transparency of domestic measures is in general wanting. This information would be especially important to providers and recipients of services since, as already mentioned, domestic regulation and not tariffs are the issue here.[13] However, despite Article III GATS, which requires Members to publish promptly 'all relevant measures of general application which pertain to or affect the operation of this Agreement', records on notifications are poor.[14] Other reasons for the modest results achieved so far are that negotiations are held up by negotiations on other issues in the Doha Round, such as agriculture and NAMA, the lack of legal certainty with regard to the 'bite' of rules in the GATS on areas such as domestic regulation, technical ambiguities such as the delimitation between the different modes of service supply discussed later, and lack of pressure on the part of industry because markets are already quite open, in particular.[15] Finally, it has also been suggested that countries are extremely reluctant to open their markets to the temporary movement of workers and thus labour migration.[16]

## 1.3 The architecture of the GATS

### *1.3.1 General obligations and specific commitments*

Understanding the interplay between general obligations and specific commitments is crucial for comprehending the legal system of the GATS. The superficial distinction is that general obligations apply irrespective of whether Members have agreed to make specific commitments.

[11] See Adlung, 'Services liberalization from a WTO/GATS perspective', 13.

[12] Herrmann *et al.*, *Welthandelsrecht*, p. 401.

[13] Herrmann *et al.*, *Welthandelsrecht*, p. 397.

[14] Adlung, 'Services liberalization from a WTO/GATS perspective', 4.

[15] See M. Krajewski, 'Services trade liberalisation and regulation: new developments and old problems', in C. Herrmann and J. P. Terhechte (eds.), *European Yearbook of International Economic Law* (Heidelberg, New York: Springer, 2009), pp. 153–78 at pp. 167–9; E. Kessie, 'The Doha Development Agenda at the crossroads: what are the remaining obstacles to the conclusion of the round: Part II', in C. Herrmann and J. P. Terhechte (eds.), *European Yearbook of International Economic Law* (Heidelberg: Springer, 2011), pp. 403–15 at pp. 407–8.

[16] K. Jones, *The Doha Blues: Institutional Crisis and Reform in the WTO* (Oxford University Press, 2010), p. 43.

MFN, provided under Part II GATS entitled 'General Obligations and Disciplines', is the most important general obligation and it applies both in the absence of specific commitments by Members, as well as where a Member has scheduled specific commitments.

Other important rules in the GATS pertain exclusively to specific commitments by Members. Market access and national treatment are provided in Part III of the GATS, which has the title 'Specific Commitments'. The title of Part III of the GATS thus might be seen as a misnomer. After all, this part is not concerned with the scheduling of specific commitments, and thus with specific commitments themselves, but with the rules applying to them.

The rules on domestic regulation under Article VI GATS, in contrast, are more difficult to understand when looking at the system provided by the GATS. According to the GATS, domestic regulation belongs under *general* obligations in Part II. This would suggest, following the logic of the GATS, that Article VI GATS applies to specific commitments by Members as well as in cases where a Member has not scheduled such commitments. However, Article VI GATS contains four distinct elements of regulation, discussed in more detail later, of which not all are general in the meaning used for MFN. These elements are the following:

(1) Article VI:2 GATS requires Members to provide for administrative review, irrespective of whether there are specific commitments by Members;
(2) Article VI:1, VI:3 and VI:5 provide for rules applying in cases where Members have scheduled commitments;
(3) Article VI:4 GATS regulates the creation of a body of rules on domestic regulation, called disciplines, for specific service sectors;[17]
(4) Article VI:5 GATS provides for a standstill period if specific commitments exist but there are not yet any disciplines.

Only the part of Article VI mentioned under point (1) is therefore truly general in the sense of the MFN principle. With the provisions mentioned under point (2), matters are already more difficult. It has been argued that their inclusion under Part II can only be explained by the fact that they apply unconditionally to all sectors for which a Member

[17] See WTO, Council for Trade in Services, Decision on Disciplines Relating to the Accountancy Sector, adopted on 14 December 1998, S/L/63, 15 December 1998.

has scheduled commitments, instead of only relating to a specific concession in a specific service sector.[18] However Article VI:5 GATS bears no resemblance to a general obligation because it expressly locks its application to the existence of specific commitments.

There are also other provisions in GATS prescribing two different standards of scrutiny, depending on whether specific commitments have been inscribed for a sector or whether Members have not so committed themselves. Article III GATS on the one hand requires Members to notify all measures relevant under GATS in general. However, according to this provision Members must also regularly notify the Council for Trade in Services and cooperate with other Member States on any measures that significantly 'affect trade in services covered by its specific commitments'.[19] The same combination of reference to general obligations and specific obligations can also be found in Article VIII GATS on anti-competitive practices and in Article IX GATS on business practices.

We will therefore discuss MFN only under the heading 'general obligation'. Domestic regulation and the other rules mentioned will be dealt with separately to highlight their two-pronged character. When these rules apply only to sectoral commitments, we will refer to them as 'specific obligations', using language that cannot be found in the GATS, but which in our opinion is conducive to better displaying the regulatory structure of the Agreement.[20]

### 1.3.2 *Reference papers, annexes and disciplines*

An additional instrument to schedules foreseen by the GATS are reference papers. Article XVIII GATS allows Members to schedule 'additional commitments' beyond market access and national treatment. A reference paper is a list of such commitments for a specific sector. They are outside formal schedules because they hold no binding value unless they are inscribed in the schedules of commitments by Members. They are meant, however, to serve as a 'reference' for negotiations on the liberalization of trade in a certain sector. The only existing reference paper is on telecommunications, already mentioned above and further

[18] See E. Vranes, *Trade and the Environment: Fundamental Issues in International Law, WTO Law and Legal Theory* (Oxford University Press, 2009), p. 463.

[19] Enquiry points for requests from other Members have to be established, as well as contact points for developing country service suppliers according to Art. IV GATS.

[20] An alternative terminology would be 'conditional general obligations', as opposed to the unconditional general obligation of MFN.

discussed in Chapter 2. However, the EU has proposed another such paper on the postal and courier sector in its latest GATS offer.[21]

An annex differs in effect from a reference paper in that it has universal coverage among the Members.[22] According to Article XXIX GATS, the provisions of an annex constitute an integral part of the GATS. The most important case is the Annex on Article II (MFN) Exemptions. Another important annex is the Annex on Telecommunications. Nineteen Members[23] established a Negotiating Group on Basic Telecommunications, and in 1997 sixty-nine Members[24] finally made commitments, that were attached as an Annex to the Fourth Protocol of the GATS,[25] and that were later endorsed by more WTO Members.[26] The USA had a predominant role in this context, having already partially liberalized its national telecommunications market.[27] For this reason, the US law distinction between basic and value-added telecommunications services, with which many other Members including the (then) EC Member States were unacquainted, was adopted in the WTO, with much liberalization being confined to the latter category.[28] However, the Annex does not provide a distinct rule on the liberalization of

21 European Communities, Attachment E, TN/S/W/26, Reference paper on postal and courier services, pp. 387–8.

22 M. E. Footer and C. George, 'The General Agreement on Trade in Services', in P. F. J. Macrory, A. E. Appleton and M. G. Plummer (eds.), *The World Trade Organization: Legal, Economic and Political Analysis* (New York: Springer, 2005), pp. 799–953 at p. 901.

23 The twelve members of the (then) EC were counted as one.

24 The fifteen members of the EU were counted as one.

25 WTO, Fourth Protocol to the General Agreement on Trade in Services, WTO S/L/20, 30 April 1996.

26 WTO, Council for Trade in Services, Special Session, Communication from the European Communities and its Member States, Conditional Revised Offer, TN/S/O/EEC/Rev.1, 29 June 2005, p. 388.

27 M. Bronckers, *A Cross-section of WTO Law* (London: Cameron May, 2000), p. 104. Under pressure from the US government, the monopolist AT&T had acceded to divestiture into a new AT&T and seven regional Bell operating companies.

28 At the time of negotiations, the proportion of value-added services in the overall telecommunications industry was small. It was thus easier by far for Member States to make commitments in this respect than to open the basic telecommunications markets, which, according to many Member States, would have entailed great risks for established stakeholders. See K. Cameron, 'Telecommunications and audio-visual services in the context of the WTO: today and tomorrow', in D. Geradin and D. Luff (eds.), *Global Convergence in Telecommunications and Audio-Visual Services* (Cambridge University Press, 2004), pp. 21–33 at p. 22. It is no wonder that at the end of the Uruguay Round more than fifty countries granted market access in respect of value-added services whereas hardly any step forward was taken in respect of basic telecommunications. See also Marchetti and Mavroidis, 'The genesis of the GATS', 718.

telecommunication services or networks. Its main purpose lies in the concretization of various provisions of the GATS and the completion of services by horizontal commitments.[29] The Annex applies to all services on which a Member State has given a specific commitment. Thus, if a Member State has made commitments for insurance services, every provider of the service X is allowed to establish, operate or supply telecommunications transport networks or services for the insurance sector. The core provision of the Annex is Section 5. It is a specification of Article XVI GATS on market access, granting reasonable and non-discriminatory access to and the use of public telecommunications transport networks[30] and services for all service suppliers. In *Mexico–Telecoms*, Mexico was found in breach of Section 5 because it failed to grant such access to US suppliers.[31]

Four provisions in GATS provide a mandate to conduct negotiations on four distinct issues. Article X:1 GATS foresees negotiations on emergency safeguard measures, Article XIII:2 GATS on government procurement and Article XV:1 GATS on subsidies. The GATS is therefore said to have an agenda for further liberalization built into its architecture. However, nothing substantial has been produced on these three counts to date.[32] The above-mentioned Article VI:4 GATS calls for the creation of disciplines on domestic regulation. Disciplines need to be integrated into the GATS by making corresponding commitments under either market access or national treatment.[33] So far, only Disciplines on Domestic Regulation (DDR) in the Accountancy Sector have been drafted by the Working Party on Professional Services – the predecessor to the Working Party on Domestic Regulation – and were approved

[29] See Art. 1 of the Annex on Telecommunications: 'Accordingly, this Annex provides notes and supplementary provisions to the Agreement.'

[30] It does not address the ownership structure, i.e. whether the telecommunications service concerned is in private or public ownership, but solely the target group, namely that the service is rendered to the public generally. It entails any telecommunications transport service required by a Member State to be offered to the public. The supply of telegraph, telephone or telex services, inter alia, are covered. See Art. 3 para. b of the Annex on Telecommunications. 'Network' is defined as the infrastructure that permits telecommunications between and among defined points. The Annex does not apply to cable or broadcast distribution of radio or television programming; they are explicitly excluded from its scope. See Art. 2 para. b of the Annex on Telecommunications.

[31] See WTO Panel Report, *Mexico–Measures Affecting Telecommunications Services (Mexico–Telecoms)*, WT/DS204/R, adopted 1 June 2004, para 8.1.

[32] See Krajewski, 'Services trade liberalisation and regulation', pp. 169–71.

[33] Herrmann *et al.*, *Welthandelsrecht*, p. 411.

by the Services Council in December 1998.[34] WTO Members have also drafted general DDR, which we will discuss later.

## 1.4 Scope of application of the GATS

### *1.4.1 Substantive coverage*

According to Article I:1, the GATS applies to measures by Member States 'affecting trade in services'. This is the central trigger for the applicability of the GATS. It must be understood in broad terms, capturing a wide array of national measures irrespective of their form and the level at which they are taken within a state. The GATS also covers measures by non-governmental bodies exercising delegated powers.[35] Private measures, however, are not covered. The provision of services under the GATS comprises the entire economic process starting with the production, the supply, the marketing, the selling, the actual provision of the service, to the consumption by the recipient.[36]

The term services, and in particular trade in services as understood by the GATS, covers all services 'with the exception of services supplied in the exercise of governmental authority'.[37] As stipulated by Article I:3(c), these encompass 'any service which is supplied neither on a commercial basis, nor in competition with one or more service suppliers'. In the WTO context, such as in the EU, formerly well-established boundaries separating public from private services are constantly evolving, producing overlaps and hybrid forms of service provision that are difficult to classify. Thus the ongoing process of transferring public functions to the private sector through privatization and liberalization policies has resulted in uncertainty as to the scope of application of legal exceptions such as Article I:3(b) and (c) GATS. For the legal exception to apply under the GATS regime, the relevant conditions concerning the commercial basis of a service and its competitive nature must be fulfilled cumulatively. This is supported by Article VIII GATS, which deals with monopolies and exclusive service suppliers. The mere existence of this Article confirms that the drafters of the GATS acknowledged the possibility of

[34] Disciplines Relating to the Accountancy Sector, S/L/63.

[35] Art. I:3(ii).

[36] See Art. XXVIII(b) and (c).

[37] Art. I:3(b) GATS. Moreover, as set out in the WTO, GATS, Annex on Air Transport Services, measures affecting air traffic rights and services directly related to their exercise are also explicitly excluded from the GATS.

service provision by governmental organizations or public entities that do not fall under Article I:3(b) and (c), because they provide services either on a commercial basis or in competition with another supplier. We discuss the equivalent to these services in EU law in Chapter 3 and compare the two regimes in Chapter 8 later in this book.

### 1.4.2 *Sectoral coverage*

Although the Members did not agree on an exhaustive list of services to be covered, a 'Services Sectoral Classification List' was developed during the negotiations based on the UN Central Product Classification System (CPC), which classifies services by sector and sub-sector.[38] While the use of this list is not mandatory, most WTO Members have referred to it in scheduling their commitments. The CPC in some instances also provides the definition of a particular service, such as with financial services.[39]

Services covered under the GATS are commonly classified as twelve core service sectors, which are further subdivided into around 160 subsectors. The core sectors are:

- business services (including professional services and computer services);
- communication services;
- construction and related engineering services;
- distribution services;
- educational services;
- environmental services;[40]
- financial services (including insurance and banking);
- health-related and social services;

[38] GATT Secretariat, Services Sectoral Classification List, MTN.GNS/W/120, 10 July 1991.

[39] For example, the UN Central Product Classification System defines the financial and related services, real estate services and rental and leasing services by categorizing them into various groupings (financial intermediation, insurance and auxiliary services, leasing or rental services without operator) and defines each sub-grouping, for example insurance services, into classes of life insurance and pension services, etc. and the classes into sub-classes.

[40] See M. Cossy, 'Environmental services and the General Agreement on Trade in Services (GATS): legal issues and negotiating stakes at the WTO', in C. Herrmann and J. P. Terhechte (eds.), *European Yearbook of International Economic Law* (Heidelberg, Vienna: Springer, 2011), pp. 239–63; R. Adlung, 'GATS commitments on environmental services: "hover through the fog and filthy air"?', in T. Cottier, O. Nartova and S. Z. Bigdeli (eds.), *International Trade Regulation and the Mitigation of Climate Change* (Cambridge University Press, 2009), pp. 274–80.

- Tourism and travel-related services;
- Recreational, cultural and sporting services;
- Transport services;
- Other services not included elsewhere.

As the last point *per definitionem* refers to any service not covered by the foregoing categories, this classification must be read as providing for comprehensive coverage.[41] It is also meant to exclude double entries. Thus, if a specific service falls under a certain sector, this assignation is conclusive.[42] A general exception exists for 'public services' according to Article I:3(b), as mentioned above.[43]

For the GATT, it has been decided that any legal definition of the scope of a Member's commitment in a specific service should be based on the CPC description of the sector and the activities it covers.[44] This would mean that the CPC 'authoritatively interprets the scope of national commitments'.[45] However, it has been countered that the CPC classification has disadvantages because its static scheme might not cover a number of services that are being traded today, and because it will not cover a range of new services that might be traded tomorrow.[46] Nevertheless, the mere fact that it defines what a specific sector consists of assists countries in relying on a standard set of services while scheduling their commitments. Note, however, that more elaborate and specific rules can be found in sectors such as financial services or telecommunications, discussed later in this chapter.

### *1.4.3 The modes of supply covered*

Pursuant to Article I:2 GATS, there are four categories of services covered, namely cross-border supply, foreign consumption, commercial presence and provision of service through transfer of a natural person.

[41] But see the sector-specific exception under the GATS Annex on Air Transport Services.

[42] WTO Appellate Body Report, *United States–Measures Affecting the Cross-Border Supply of Gambling and Betting Services (US–Gambling)*, WT/DS285/AB/R, adopted 20 April 2005, para. 180.

[43] See also Chapter 8.

[44] See the WTO Panel Report, *European Communities–Regime for the Importation, Sale and Distribution of Bananas (EC–Bananas III)*, Complaint by the United States, WT/DS27/R/USA, adopted 25 September 1997, para. 7.289.

[45] See M. Matsushita, T. J. Schoenbaum and P. C. Mavroidis, *The World Trade Organization: Law, Practice and Policy* (Oxford University Press, 2003), p. 236.

[46] See A. Mattoo and S. Wunsch-Vincent, 'Preempting protectionism in services: the GATS and outsourcing', Publication of Peter G. Peterson Institute for International Economics, January 2004, 25.

Hence, services in the GATS are defined in terms of four categories of transactions, and not by the nature of the activities concerned. We will now discuss this in more detail.

- **Mode 1 – cross-border services** are supplied from the territory of one Member into the territory of any other Member. Focus is placed on the 'act' undertaken by the supplier falling within the ambit of Article XXVIII(j), (k), (l), (m) and (n).[47] Thus the service supplier must be a natural or a legal person constituted under the laws of a GATS Member. This means that the presence of the supplier in another country is not required.[48] Article XXVII GATS also mentions that benefits of the GATS will be denied to a service supplier that is a juridical person but is not a service supplier of another Member, or that is a service supplier of a Member to which the denying Member does not apply the WTO Agreement. Mode 1 pertains to consultancy or market research services, medical advice via the telephone or the Internet, or distance training. Telecommunications is another major application for this mode of supply.[49]
- **Mode 2 – consumption abroad** relates to services provided in the territory of one Member to a recipient of another Member. This covers, inter alia, tourists, students and patient mobility. It works only one way as Members may regulate their own recipients, but not those of other Member States.[50] Service consumers are defined as 'any person' who receives or uses the service. The nationality of the recipient thus is irrelevant.[51]

[47] This Article defines persons as any natural person or juridical person. In defining natural persons, nationality or permanent residency is referred to, and in defining juridical persons, their establishment under applicable law.

[48] See especially the WTO Panel Report, *Mexico–Telecoms*, WT/DS204/R, adopted 1 June 2004.

[49] WTO Panel Report, *Mexico–Telecoms*, WT/DS204/R, para. 7.40 *et seq.* (e.g. call back, calling cards). See Bronckers, *A Cross-section of WTO Law*, p. 112.

[50] WTO, Council for Trade in Services, Guidelines for the Scheduling of Specific Commitments under the GATS, adopted on 23 March 2001, S/L/92, 28 March 2001, p. 9.

[51] Compare this to the definition of service recipients in Art. 4(3) of the Services Directive 2006/123/EC of the European Parliament and the Council of 12 December 2006 on services in the internal market, OJ 2006 No. L376/36, covering 'any natural person who is a national of a Member State or who benefits from rights conferred upon him by Community acts, or any legal person as referred to in Article 48 of the Treaty and established in a Member State, who, for professional or non-professional purposes, uses, or wishes to use, a service'.

- **Mode 3 – commercial presence** means that services are provided by a supplier of one Member through locally established affiliates, subsidiaries or a representative office in the territory of any other Member. Thus the GATS covers foreign direct investments both by way of establishment of legal persons abroad or by virtue of a permanent establishment without such personality.[52] Legal persons benefiting from Mode 3 concessions must conduct an actual economic activity in their state of foundation or residence and must be foreign-owned.[53]
- **Mode 4 – presence of natural persons** covers services supplied by a supplier of one Member through the presence of 'natural persons of a Member in the territory of any other Member'. This concerns independent suppliers such as consultants, health workers or employees of a service supplier such as a consultancy firm, hospital or a construction company.[54]

Under EU law, neither commercial presence nor the posting of workers comes under the Treaty regime on services *stricto sensu*. Commercial presence falls under the freedom of establishment and the posting of workers is regulated by secondary law. Thus the GATS covers more disparate situations than the services regime in EU law.[55] As we shall discuss, however, Directive 2006/123/EC now regulates both established service providers and non-established service providers under the title 'Services Directive'.[56]

On the other hand, neither Mode 3 nor Mode 4 cover employed workers in the meaning of the Union law concept of free movement of workers.[57] The Council for Trade in Services has explicitly stated that the distinction between 'temporary' and 'permanent' residency, as mentioned

[52] See the definition in Art. XXVIII(d).

[53] Herrmann *et al.*, *Welthandelsrecht*, p. 393. See the discussion in EU law on letterbox companies benefiting from the freedom of establishment in the wake of Case C-212/97, *Centros* [1999] ECR I-1459. See Chapter 3.

[54] The latter case is known under EU law as posting of workers and is governed as such by the eponymous Directive 96/71/EC of the European Parliament and the Council of 16 December 1996 concerning the posting of workers in the framework of the provision of services, OJ 1997 No. L18/1. See Chapter 5 on this and other related secondary EU law.

[55] See P. Eeckhout, 'Constitutional concepts for free trade in services', in G. de Búrca and J. Scott (eds.), *The EU and the WTO: Legal and Constitutional Issues* (Oxford and Portland, OR: Hart Publishing, 2002), pp. 211–35 at pp. 221–2, on the ramifications of this difference.

[56] Directive 2006/123/EC, OJ 2006 No. L376/36.

[57] See Herrmann *et al.*, *Welthandelsrecht*, p. 391.

in the GATS, should be dealt with by WTO Members themselves.[58] Labour movement was never intended to become a focal point of liberalization under the GATS. The reason for this is that it would rather serve the interests of developing countries, where there is comparatively cheaper labour than in countries such as the USA. Consequently, an Annex 1B exempts 'measures affecting natural persons seeking access to the employment market' and 'measures regarding citizenship, residence or employment on a permanent basis'.[59] Only with regard to the question of citizenship is Union law similarly limited, leaving the decision to award national citizenship to the discretion of the Member States. This means that the conferral of Union citizenship, which is accessory to national citizenship, depends on the Member States.[60]

The different modes presented above give rise to issues of delimitation, which we will briefly address later in the context of scheduling. However, suffice it to note here that this delimitation is far more relevant under the GATS than under EU law, where there is a similar distinction in the doctrine, yet where this has little impact on decisions by the Court of Justice. On the other hand, the different modes make no difference for the assessment of a national measure under either regime.[61] Thus, both under GATS and EU law, it does not matter whether a measure only affects market access in one specific services mode or, rather, applies to all forms of rendering services.[62] In EU law this is due to the broad definition of restrictions, which does not distinguish between different modes and which is discussed in the next chapter.[63]

[58] See WTO, Council for Trade in Services, Conclusion of the SubCommittee on Services concerning measures relating to the entry and stay of natural persons, S/C/M/1, 1 March 1995, para. 6.

[59] GATS, Annex 1B on movement of natural persons supplying services under the agreement. See Trebilcock *et al.*, *The Regulation of International Trade*, p. 481.

[60] See Art. 20(1) TFEU.

[61] But see the discussion in Case C-212/08, *Zeturf* [2011] ECR I-5633, paras. 80–3, on whether the national legislation applies in the same way to horse race betting online and to such betting through traditional channels, and on whether the restriction on the freedom to provide services should be assessed from the point of view of the restrictions placed on the entire sector concerned.

[62] See, however, the debate on establishing likeness in WTO law, where differences in the modes has been one criterion discussed. See later in this chapter.

[63] See Case C-384/93, *Alpine Investments* [1995] ECR I-1141, where it was not decisive that the pertinent restriction only concerned cross-border services (cold calling). In *US–Gambling*, WT/DS285/AB/R the contested laws in some US states equally only concerned a Mode 1 type of regulation (online gambling). The only decisive issue, at

## 1.5 The Most Favoured Nation principle

Article II:1 GATS requires each Member to 'accord immediately and unconditionally to services and service suppliers of any other Member treatment no less favourable than that it accords to like services and service suppliers of any other country'. This prohibits any formal (*de jure*) and material (indirect, factual, de facto) discrimination between like services or like service suppliers.[64] The criterion with open, direct or *de jure* discrimination is nationality, and the GATS protects not only services but also service suppliers from discrimination based on it.[65] Discrimination is not only examined by comparing the treatment of other WTO Members, but also by comparing the treatment accorded by Members to third countries. This MFN obligation seeps through the entire Agreement and its Annexes, and reappears in different wording in a number of other provisions.[66]

It is difficult to establish from the dispute settlement practice what precisely amounts to likeness for the purposes of Article II:1 GATS (and also for Article XVII GATS discussed later). The Panel statement that suppliers are like 'to the extent that [they] provide like services'[67] speaks both for a linkage between the likeness of suppliers and the likeness of services, and at the same time for a certain circularity in argumentation.[68] It has been suggested that the following factors for determining likeness under the GATS be adopted: (a) service's end user in a given market; (b) consumer habits and preferences regarding the services or the service supplier; (c) characteristics of the service or the service supplier; and (d) the classification and description of the service in the UN CPC system.[69] We will return to likeness in Chapter 8 in the context of a more comprehensive discussion of discrimination.

least before the Appellate Body, was whether this prohibition came under one of the listed prohibited national measures.

[64] WTO Appellate Body Report, *EC–Bananas III*, WT/DS27/AB/R, para. 233. See Trebilcock *et al.*, *The Regulation of International Trade*, pp. 76–80.

[65] W. Zdouc, 'WTO dispute settlement practice relating to the General Agreement on Trade in Services', in F. Ortino and E.-U. Petersmann (eds.), *The WTO Dispute Settlement System 1995–2003* (The Hague: Kluwer, 2004), pp. 381–420 at p. 386.

[66] See Footer and George, 'The General Agreement on Trade in Services', pp. 827–8.

[67] WTO Panel Report, *EC–Bananas III*, WT/DS27/R/USA, paras. 7.322 and 7.346. See also Vranes, *Trade and the Environment*, pp. 458–9.

[68] See the complex differentiations made by Vranes in *Trade and the Environment*, pp. 459–61.

[69] F. Ortino, *Basic Legal Instruments for the Liberalisation of Trade: A Comparative Analysis of EC and WTO Law* (Oxford and Portland, OR: Hart Publishing, 2004).

The MFN obligation applies to all Members for any sector falling under the GATS, and to any measure affecting trade in services. However, Member States may schedule exemptions to the MFN principle in the Annex on Article II Exemptions. Such exemptions had to be claimed by the Members at the time of acceptance of the GATS, or in case of later accession to the GATS at that time. Among others, their duration must be limited to ten years and they are necessarily subject to negotiation in subsequent negotiation rounds, and in addition are reviewed regularly.[70] Around eighty Members have made use of this instrument to opt out of one of the foremost principles in WTO law, mainly to exempt regional trade preferences. Sectors that are very often included are the transportation sector, audio-visual services and financial services, as we will also see later by example of the EU schedule.

## 1.6 Specific commitments

### *1.6.1 Scheduling*

Achieving the objectives of the GATS depends on the extent and the nature of sector-specific commitments made by individual Members.[71] Article XX GATS thus obliges WTO Members to submit a schedule of specific commitments according to the different sectors mentioned above. Schedules form 'an integral part' of the Agreement. The so-called positive listing approach enables each WTO Member to decide autonomously on the level of concessions it wants to enter into.[72] As a result, the level of liberalization under GATS is extremely uneven between the Members, with commitments ranging from a handful of sectors to several dozen sectors. If a Member has not scheduled anything, it must be deemed unbound, unless there is conclusive reason to assume otherwise based on the Member's other commitments.[73]

The rules on modifying or withdrawing specific commitments are provided in Article XXI GATS. Thus concessions may be changed, although subject to compensation. This compensation must consist in

[70] Art. 6 of the Annex on Article II-Exemptions.

[71] See Matsushita *et al.*, *The World Trade Organization*, p. 246.

[72] In combination with the fact that once such commitment has been made for a sector, the sector is supposed to be fully liberalized unless limitations are scheduled, the GATS approach has also been called 'hybrid'. See Footer and George, 'The General Agreement on Trade in Services', p. 857.

[73] See WTO Appellate Body Report, *US–Gambling*, WT/DS285/AB/R, paras. 158 *et seq*. See Herrmann *et al.*, *Welthandelsrecht*, p. 407.

more far-reaching commitments elsewhere that 'endeavour to maintain a general level of mutually advantageous commitments not less favourable to trade'. Compensatory adjustments are subject to MFN. Where there is no agreement, Article XXI:3(a) GATS foresees arbitration between the parties.[74]

National schedules of commitments contain at least eight entries per sector, comprising the commitments on market access and national treatment concerning the four modes of supply. Additional commitments not falling under either market access or national treatment can be listed under a third category reserved for 'licensing and qualification requirements and technical standards' pursuant to Article XVIII GATS.[75] Full commitments without limitation are labelled as 'none' in the schedules. The preservation of full regulatory autonomy in applying market access restrictions or discriminatory measures is inscribed as 'unbound'.

Commitments may be either horizontal, thus applying across all scheduled sectors, or on a sectoral basis. Horizontal commitments apply to trade in services in all scheduled service sectors unless otherwise stated. They oblige a Member either not to limit market access or not to discriminate against other WTO Members. Alternatively, they constitute binding statements on limitations of market access or national treatment. Under Article XI GATS, Members are required to allow international transfers and payments for current transactions relating to specific commitments.[76] Limitations of commitments entered into national schedules must refer either to market access and national treatment or to licensing requirements, qualification requirements and technical standards.

[74] See WTO, Council for Trade in Services, Procedures for the Implementation of Article XXI of the General Agreement on Trade in Services (GATS) (Modification of Schedules), adopted on 19 July 1999, S/L/80, 29 October 1999, and WTO, Council for Trade in Services, Procedures for the Certification of Rectifications or Improvements to Schedules of Specific Commitments, adopted on 14 April 2000, S/L/84, 18 April 2000, on detailed procedures for the modification of schedules pursuant to Art. XXI GATS.

[75] Such additional commitments have been undertaken in the telecommunications sector by around sixty Members by virtue of the Telecoms Reference Paper by the Negotiating Group on basic telecommunications, 24 April 1996. See S. Lester and B. Mercurio, *World Trade Law: Text, Materials and Commentary* (Oxford and Portland, OR: Hart Publishing, 2008), p. 629.

[76] See fn. 8 to Art. XVI, which further regulates the ability to restrict capital movements in sectors where specific commitments on cross-border trade and commercial presence have been scheduled.

Scheduled limitations on market access are guarantees of minimum treatment and do not prevent the award of more favourable treatment.[77] Limitations of the MFN obligation, in contrast, must be listed in the respective Annex and not in the schedules themselves. Similarly, the obligation under Article VI:1 GATS on the reasonable, objective and impartial administration of measures of general application cannot be exempted in the national schedules. In the same vein, measures justified under the exceptions pursuant to Article XIV GATS, discussed further below, or those aimed to ensure the stability and integrity of the financial services sector, do not require separate scheduling.

National measures that are impairing market access and are at the same time discriminatory, and could thus be scheduled both under Articles XVI and XVII GATS, must be inscribed under market access.[78] Non-discriminatory national measures such as professional qualification requirements, insurance requirements regarding certain professions or tax measures, do not require scheduling, since they neither affect market access nor fall under national treatment.[79]

### *1.6.2 Market access*

Article XVI GATS prohibits the following six types of restrictions:

(a) The number of service suppliers such as through monopolies for government labour exchange agency services. This also includes a prohibition of so-called ‘zero-quotas’, which denotes the absolute prevention of market access;[80]
(b) The value of service transactions or assets;
(c) The number of operations or the quantity of output;
(d) The number of natural persons supplying a service, such as by means of annual quotas for foreign medical practitioners;
(e) The type of legal entity or joint venture;
(f) The participation of foreign capital.[81]

[77] Footer and George, ‘The General Agreement on Trade in Services’, p. 847.

[78] Art. XX:2. On the exact meaning of this provision on the relationship between Arts. XVI and XVII GATS see the discussion at J. Pauwelyn, ‘Rien ne va plus? Distinguishing domestic regulation from market access in GATT and GATS’ (2005) *World Trade Review* 131–70 at 150.

[79] See Footer and George, ‘The General Agreement on Trade in Services’, p. 847.

[80] Herrmann *et al.*, *Welthandelsrecht*, p. 399.

[81] Together with point (a), this is especially important in telecommunications where markets have often been protected by restrictions on licenses and investments.

Most of these measures are non-discriminatory and mainly take the form of monopolies, quotas or economic needs tests, as shown later in Chapter 2 by example of the schedules of the EU.[82] Only the limitation on foreign capital is *per definitionem* discriminatory against providers from other states.[83]

Thus, if a Member has committed a specific mode under a specific sector by inscribing 'none' in its national schedule, and has not at the same time foreseen limitations, it is prohibited to undertake the measures listed above.[84] However, should a Member cabin its commitment by also scheduling limitations to market access, it is not curtailed in the nature or in the number of such limitations. Examples of commonly scheduled limitations on market access are:

- licence requirements such as for a new restaurant based on an economic needs test;
- nationality requirements for suppliers of services;
- restrictions on broadcasting time available for foreign films;
- requirements for companies to establish subsidiaries.[85]

The GATS Scheduling Guidelines provide that minimum requirements should not be inscribed under Article XVI GATS.[86] The *US–Gambling* case has raised the issue whether the pertinent measure in this case, namely the prohibition of online gambling, could be considered as such a minimum requirement.[87] We would argue that the instructions in the Guidelines refer to regulatory measures that require certain minimum standards from providers in order to be allowed to provide certain services. Thus such requirements should give providers the chance to qualify if they adopt higher standards than the minimum threshold required by a Member. If the cross-border mode were considered a minimum requirement that should not be inscribed under Article XVI GATS, this would mean that the commercial presence mode would be considered as having a higher standard. We would submit that such

[82] See Art. XVII:2.

[83] See Pauwelyn, 'Rien ne va plus?', 149; Vranes, *Trade and the Environment*, p. 466. Note that sometimes also point (e) is qualified as discriminatory.

[84] In contrast, as discussed below, discriminatory measures prohibited under national treatment in Art. XVII GATS are not predetermined by GATS.

[85] See Guidelines for the Scheduling of Specific Commitments under the GATS, S/L/92, p. 5.

[86] Guidelines for the Scheduling of Specific Commitments under the GATS, S/L/92, para. 11.

[87] For a different perspective, see Pauwelyn, 'Rien ne va plus?', 162.

ranking of the different modes of supply cannot have been intended with the concept of minimum requirements.

### 1.6.3 *National treatment*

National treatment under Article XVII GATS concerns the discrimination of like services or service suppliers of another Member. The text of the first three paragraphs of Article XVII GATS is worth quoting in full:

> In the sectors inscribed in its Schedule, and subject to any conditions and qualifications set out therein, each Member shall accord to services and service suppliers of any other Member, in respect of all measures affecting the supply of services, treatment no less favourable than that it accords to its own like services and service suppliers.
>
> A Member may meet the requirement of paragraph 1 by according to services and service suppliers of any other Member, either formally identical treatment or formally different treatment to that it accords to its own like services and service suppliers.
>
> Formally identical or formally different treatment shall be considered to be less favourable if it modifies the conditions of competition in favour of services or service suppliers of the Member compared to like services or service suppliers of any other Member.

Footnote 10 to the first paragraph of Article XVII GATS states that specific commitments under this Article 'shall not be construed to require any Member to compensate for any inherent competitive disadvantages which result from the foreign character of the relevant services or service suppliers'.

Article XVII GATS sets out a four-tier test of consistency that requires the examination of whether (1) a national treatment commitment was made in respect of the service sector concerned, (2) the measure at issue 'affects' trade in services, (3) the foreign and domestic services and service suppliers are 'like services or service suppliers', and (4) whether the foreign services or service suppliers are granted treatment no less favourable.[88] Diebold has argued that the principle of non-discrimination consists of a comparator clause calling for a comparison between market actors and a comparison between the treatments

[88] See P. Van den Bossche and W. Zdouc, *The Law and Policy of the World Trade Organization: Text Cases and Materials* (Cambridge University Press, 2013), p. 406. See also F. Ortino, 'The principle of non-discrimination and its exceptions in GATS: selected legal issues', in M. Andenas and K. Alexander (eds.), *The World Trade Organization and Trade in Services* (Nijhoff: Brill, 2008), pp. 173–206 at p. 175.

accorded to them.[89] The former would require identifying the relevant *tertium comparationis*, which would be done differently throughout international economic law.[90] Note that the 'comparator clause' would be a misnomer in the context of EU law and also most national laws. The *tertium comparationis* does not need to be positively stated in legal texts; it is inherent in any discrimination standard because there can only be discrimination when equal matters are treated unequally (or unequal matters equally).[91] However, this language can be explained by the fact that precisely such a clause permeates the WTO agreements in the form of the criterion of likeness.[92] We will also discuss the *tertium comparationis* in the context of EU law in Chapter 3 and from a comparative perspective in Chapter 8.

Treatment, as under MFN in Article II GATS, must be 'no less favourable' in the sense of not modifying 'the conditions of competition' to the detriment of foreign services or service suppliers. There is a wealth of discussion on the meaning of likeness in WTO law in general, to which we do not aim to contribute here.[93] Thus pertinent questions are whether the same classification indicates likeness, whether the likeness of suppliers has some bearing on the likeness of services and whether services must be rendered in the same mode to qualify as alike.[94]

[89] N. Diebold, 'Standards of non-discrimination in international economic law' (2011) 60(4) *International and Comparative Law Quarterly* 831–65 at 834.

[90] Diebold, 'Standards of non-discrimination in international economic law', 835.

[91] See also J. H. H. Weiler, 'Law, culture, and values in the WTO: gazing into the crystal ball', in D. Bethlehem *et al.* (eds.), *The Oxford Handbook of International Trade Law* (Oxford University Press, 2009), pp. 750–72 at p. 764.

[92] W. J. Davey, 'Non-discrimination in the World Trade Organization: the rules and exceptions', in Académie De Droit International (ed.), *Collected Courses of the Academy of International Law* (Leiden, Boston: Martinus Nijhoff, 2011), pp. 182–430 at p. 301, recalling that the term like product may mean different things in different contexts of WTO law.

[93] See the discussion in Trebilcock *et al.*, *The Regulation of International Trade*, pp. 168–71. Even in cases under GATT, the findings on the likeness of products by the dispute settlement bodies have been controversial. See J. Scott, 'Mandatory or imperative requirements in the EU and the WTO', in C. Barnard and J. Scott (eds.), *The Law of the Single European Market: Unpacking the Premises* (Oxford and Portland, OR: Hart Publishing, 2002), pp. 269–93 at p. 284. On the fact that an analysis of likeness has been completely missing, see WTO Appellate Body Report, *European Communities–Regime for the Importation, Sale and Distribution of Bananas*, WT/DS27/AB/R, adopted 25 September 1997. See also Eeckhout, 'Constitutional concepts for free trade in services', p. 232.

[94] '[t]o the extent that entities provide "like" services, they are like service suppliers'. See the WTO Panel Report, *European Communities–Regime for the Importation, Sale and Distribution of Bananas (EC–Bananas III) – Recourse to Article 21.5 of the DSU by the European*

As with Article II GATS, Article XVII GATS on national treatment targets both formal and material discrimination.[95] Treatment in a formally identical way is thus not decisive. What matters is to provide for equal opportunities to compete. Residency requirements are stated as examples of de facto discrimination.[96]

Article XVII GATS does not contain an exhaustive list of discriminatory measures prohibited once a Member has committed itself under a specific sector and mode. Therefore, and in the absence of limitations, *any* form of discrimination would be barred. However, the limitations to such an unconditional prohibition of discrimination that can lawfully be scheduled are no less exhaustive than under Article XVII GATS on market access. Examples for such possible limitations are:

- subsidies reserved to nationals;[97]
- discriminatory tax measures;
- other financial measures such as higher licence fees for non-residents;
- nationality requirements or residency requirements for agents, managers or foreign bank employees, or for the receipt of licences, licensing and qualification requirements such as for mountain guides or ski instructors or lawyers (e.g. that they must be graduates of national universities);
- registration requirements such as for law firms to market their services or for foreign companies in general or for certain activities such as certification services;
- authorization requirements for loans, bank subsidiaries, foreign directors of banks;
- technology transfer/training requirements for foreign service suppliers (e.g. that they must use and transfer appropriate and advanced technology and managerial experience, or that they must train locals);

*Communities*, WT/DS27/RW/EEC, 12 April 1999, unadopted; and WTO Panel Report, *Canada–Certain Measures Affecting the Automotive Industry*, WT/DS139/R, WT/DS142/R, adopted 19 June 2000, where it was explicitly stated that 'to the extent that the service suppliers concerned supply the same services, they should be considered "like" for the purpose of this case'. See e.g. Footer and George, 'The General Agreement on Trade in Services', pp. 849–51.

[95] See Davey, 'Non-discrimination in the World Trade Organization', p. 259.

[96] Guidelines for the Scheduling of Specific Commitments under the GATS, S/L/92, p. 6.

[97] Discriminatory subsidies not scheduled as a limitation on national treatment must be brought into conformity with above described Art. XV GATS.

- local content requirements;
- restrictions on ownership of property.[98]

Should a measure be discriminatory but be permitted by the limitations scheduled under Article XVII GATS on national treatment, it is important to note that it might nevertheless be found to violate Article XVI GATS on market access.

### *1.6.4 Conclusion*

Discrimination, as a regulatory 'evil' under the GATS, is thus fought by the instrument of MFN when it concerns differential treatment awarded to third states, and by the instrument of commitments on market access and national treatment when it is meted out to foreign service providers or service recipients. The latter instruments, however, require that Members schedule commitments on either national treatment or market access.

## 1.7 Exemptions from the GATS

### *1.7.1 General exemptions*

Article XIV GATS allows WTO Members to take measures necessary to attain certain exhaustively stated policy concerns. These national regulatory objectives are:

- the protection of public morals or public order;
- the protection of human, animal or plant life or health;
- the compliance with laws or regulations that are not inconsistent with the GATS, including those relating to (i) fraud and contractual default, (ii) privacy and confidentiality and (iii) safety;
- the imposition or collection of direct taxes provided this is inconsistent with Article XVII on national treatment (i.e. discriminatory);
- the avoidance of double taxation when otherwise inconsistent with Article II on MFN.

The condition of a violation of GATS required by the last two exceptions is also a general condition for the application of the other grounds of justification. Thus only when GATS obligations or commitments have

[98] See Guidelines for the Scheduling of Specific Commitments under the GATS, S/L/92, pp. 16–18.

been breached by a Member may Article XIV GATS be invoked as a defence.

The other general prerequisite of successfully raising any of the listed exemptions is that 'such measures are not applied in a manner which would constitute a means of arbitrary or unjustifiable discrimination between countries where like conditions prevail, or a disguised restriction on trade in services'. In other words, the application of the exemptions must be 'reasonable'.[99] This is referred to as the *chapeau* of Article XIV GATS and, technically, must be examined prior to assessing the applicability of any of the stated policy reasons. It has been noted by Cremona that the way this prohibition of discrimination in Article XIV GATS (and Article XX GATT) is applied by the WTO Appellate Body (AB), namely as an obligation to balance the right of a Member to invoke an exception on the one hand, and the rights of other Members under substantive provisions such as on the prohibition of quotas on the other hand, contrasts the approach under EU law where policy interests of Member States are weighed against the policy objective of the Treaty to establish a common market.[100]

The only decision in WTO settlement practice where Article XIV GATS has (unsuccessfully) been appealed is *US–Gambling*. There the AB made clear that the interpretation of this provision in the GATS has to be in analogy with the 'sister' provision of Article XX GATT, as concerning the burden of proof standard, the necessity test and the handling of the *chapeau*.[101] Under the GATT, the appropriate level of protection in a concrete case 'is a prerogative of the Member concerned'.[102] A matter to be assessed by the Dispute Settlement Body (DSB) is whether a WTO-consistent or less inconsistent alternative measure to the measure in violation of the GATT is 'reasonably available'.[103] This is the so-called 'new necessity test', which, above all, seems to entirely exempt *indispensable* national measures from scrutiny and assesses only such measures as are 'necessary' to a lesser degree.[104] Thus an alternative measure

99 WTO Appellate Body Report, *US–Gambling*, WT/DS285/AB/R, para. 367 *et seq*. See also WTO Appellate Body Report, *United States–Standards for Reformulated and Conventional Gasoline*, WT/DS2/AB/R, adopted 20 May 1996, p. 22.

100 See M. Cremona, 'Neutrality or discrimination?' at pp. 156–7.

101 See Vranes, *Trade and the Environment*, p. 483.

102 Vranes, *Trade and the Environment*, p. 331, with references from dispute settlement.

103 WTO Appellate Body Report, *Korea–Measures Affecting Imports of Fresh, Chilled and Frozen Beef*, WT/DS161/AB/R, WT/DS169/AB/R, adopted 10 January 2001, para. 164.

104 Vranes, *Trade and the Environment*, pp. 340–1. Vranes is critical of this approach in dispute settlement practice at 342–5. For a similar 'double standard' derived from

may be found not to be reasonably available where it is merely theoretical in nature, where it imposes an undue burden on the Member, or where it would not preserve the right to achieve the desired level of protection.[105] In general, if the respondent has made a prima facie case that the challenged measure is necessary, which means that it is 'significantly closer to the pole of "indispensable" than to the opposite pole of simply "making a contribution to"', the measure is deemed necessary.[106] We will discuss later how this may be considerably more sophisticated a test than in EU law, but that the basic mechanism is very similar.[107]

As mentioned, services and in particular trade in services as understood by the GATS, cover relevant activities in any sector, however 'with the exception of services supplied in the exercise of governmental authority'.[108] According to Article I:3(c) GATS, these encompass 'any service which is supplied neither on a commercial basis, nor in competition with one or more service suppliers'. As found in *Canada–Dairy*, the 'essence of government' is that it enjoys the effective power to regulate, control or supervise individuals, or otherwise restrain their conduct, through the exercise of lawful authority.[109] Article 1(b) of the Annex on Financial Services defines services supplied in the exercise of governmental authority among others as 'other activities conducted by a public entity for the account or with the guarantee or using the financial resources of the Government'. Article 5(c) of the Annex defines a 'public entity' as 'an entity owned or controlled by a Member, that is principally engaged in carrying out governmental functions or activities for governmental purposes'. While being restricted to the sector of financial services, the Annex forms a part of the GATS,[110] and can thus guide us in the interpretation of Article I:3(b) GATS. We would

a concept of necessity in an entirely different context, see the interpretation of the principle now codified in Art. 3(2) TFEU by M. Klamert and N. Maydell, 'Lost in exclusivity: implied non-exclusive external competences in Community law' (2008) *European Foreign Affairs Review* 493–513.

105 WTO Appellate Body Report, *US–Gambling*, WT/DS285/AB/R, para. 308.

106 WTO Appellate Body Report, *US–Gambling*, WT/DS285/AB/R, para. 310.

107 See Chapter 3.

108 Art. I:3(b) GATS. Moreover, as set out in the Annex on Air Transport Services, measures affecting air traffic rights and services directly related to their exercise are also explicitly excluded from the GATS.

109 WTO Appellate Body Report, *Canada–Measures Affecting the Importation of Milk and the Exportation of Dairy Products*, WT/DS103/AB/R, WT/DS113/AB/R, adopted 27 October 1999, para. 97.

110 Art. XXIX GATS.

therefore argue that governmental authority in the GATS refers to a claim of legitimacy (lawful authority) and that any linkage to commercial activities is explicitly excluded. Conversely, we would argue that service activities undertaken by governmental authorities on commercial terms escape the exemption stipulated in Article I:3(b) and (c) and are thus covered by the GATS. This exemption will be further discussed in Chapter 8 in comparison with the corresponding exemption under EU law.

### *1.7.2 Exemptions from MFN*

Pursuant to Article V GATS, WTO Members can enter into economic integration agreements (EIAs) under the condition that such agreements have 'substantial sectoral coverage' and abolish 'substantially all discrimination' between the parties to the agreement.[111] Moreover, the overall level of trade barriers must not be raised in respect of third WTO states by virtue of such agreement. These conditions are to be assessed in the broader context of a possible wider process of economic integration between the Members concerned. In Chapter 2 we will discuss what this exemption means with respect to the EU.

In respect of the participation of developing countries in such agreements, Article V:3 GATS allows for a flexible application of the above-mentioned criteria. Should commitments be withdrawn in the course of such agreement, Article V:5 GATS requires the negotiation of appropriate compensation in accordance with Article XXI GATS.[112] Article V:7 GATS provides for an elaborate notification and reporting obligation on EIAs vis-à-vis the Council for Trade in Services and working parties set up by it, with the possibility of the Council issuing recommendations to the parties based on such reports. Article V bis GATS contains a similar provision relating to agreements on labour markets integration. These are exempted from MFN if the citizens involved are exempted from requirements concerning residency and work permits.

Article VII GATS allows the Members to enter into international agreements on the recognition of standards or criteria for the authorization, licensing or certification of services suppliers, including on the

[111] See C. Herrmann, 'Bilateral and regional trade agreements as a challenge to the multilateral trading system' (2008/09) EUI Working Papers LAW 10–12.

[112] Among other situations, this can arise when the legal regime established is more restrictive than the prior regime of a participating country. This was the case with Estonia when it became a Member of the EU in 2004.

recognition of education or experience obtained, requirements met, or licenses or certifications granted in a particular country.[113] As this exception must not constitute a means of discrimination or a disguised trade restriction, other WTO Members may also enter into the regime.

Article XIII GATS exempts the procurement of 'services purchased for governmental purposes' from both MFN and the rules on market access and national treatment. Multilateral negotiations, which this provision mandates in exchange, have shown few results to date. The Plurilateral Agreement on Government Procurement so far has been concluded by only a limited number of more developed Members.

## 1.8 Domestic regulation

### *1.8.1 The background*

Within the GATT there is a distinction between measures imposed at the border, that is market access measures, and measures affecting imports as they enter the market. Border measures are normally custom duties and similar charges imposed at the border, which are regulated by Article II and Article XI of the GATT, whereas domestic regulations, such as internal taxation or internal regulations in the form of safety regulations, and so on are covered by Article III GATT. The distinction between these two measures in the GATT is clear: market access measures in the form of quantitative restrictions are in principle prohibited, but domestic regulations are only prohibited if they are discriminatory. Hence, Members largely keep their regulatory autonomy under the latter set of measures within the GATT. Only in some instances, such as with the Agreement on Sanitary and Phytosanitary Measures (SPS Agreement) and the Agreement on Technical Barriers to Trade (TBT Agreement), did they wish to reduce their regulatory autonomy and expanded measures on domestic regulation beyond non-discrimination to cover measures that are more restrictive than necessary.

In contrast, as mentioned in the introduction, trade in services is not commonly hampered by tariffs or other restrictions taking effect at the border.[114] Instead, nearly everything in the GATS concerns domestic regulation when this is understood as national regulatory measures

[113] The connected notification duty is only poorly complied with. See Adlung, 'Services liberalization from a WTO/GATS perspective'.

[114] See Krajewski, 'Services trade liberalisation and regulation', pp. 161–2.

affecting trade in services.[115] However, as has been explained, WTO Members felt more at ease 'committing to the elimination or reduction in tariffs and quantitative import restrictions than tying their hands in the politically more sensitive field of domestic regulation'.[116] Thus the GATS does contain a provision on domestic regulation that contrasts quite sharply with the rules on market access and national treatment and is fairly complex. We will now discuss Article VI GATS and its relation to the other core substantive rules in the GATS.

### 1.8.2 *Article VI GATS*

Article VI:1 GATS contains a duty of 'fairness' with respect to sectors with specific commitments. As already mentioned, Member States are required to 'ensure that all measures of general application affecting trade in services are administered in a reasonable, objective and impartial manner'. Article VI:2(a) GATS requires each Member to ensure the objective and impartial judicial review of administrative decisions affecting trade in services.[117] This obligation applies irrespective of whether Member States have scheduled commitments.[118] In a similar vein, Article VI:3 GATS obliges Members to decide on applications for authorizations required for the supply of a service on which a specific commitment has been made within a reasonable period. Article VI:6 GATS provides, again with regard to sectors where specific commitments have been undertaken, that Members shall provide for adequate procedures to verify the competence of professionals of other Members.

The most interesting part of Article VI is its fourth paragraph. Article VI:4 has the following wording:

> With a view to ensuring that measures relating to qualification requirements and procedures, technical standards and licensing requirements do not constitute unnecessary barriers to trade in services, the Council for Trade in Services shall … develop any necessary disciplines. Such disciplines shall aim to ensure that such requirements are, inter alia:
>
> (a) based on objective and transparent criteria, such as competence and the ability to supply the service;
>
> (b) not more burdensome than necessary to ensure the quality of the service;

[115] See Feketekuty, 'Assessing and improving the architecture of GATS', pp. 90–1.

[116] Pauwelyn, 'Rien ne va plus?', 131.

[117] However, this does not require a Member to change its constitutional structure or the nature of its legal system.

[118] Vranes, *Trade and the Environment*, p. 463.

(c) in the case of licensing procedures, not in themselves a restriction on the supply of the service.

Based on this mandate, the already mentioned Working Party on Domestic Regulation was established. Disciplines need to be integrated into the GATS by making corresponding commitments under either Article XVII or XVIII. In other words, they are only applicable to such Members who have scheduled specific commitments in the sector concerned.[119] A core feature of disciplines is their focus on non-discriminatory regulations that are not subject to scheduling under Articles XVI and XVII GATS. In contrast, measures relating to licensing, qualifications and technical standards that discriminate (formally or in fact) between foreign and domestic suppliers would need to be scheduled as national treatment limitation in the sectors where GATS commitments have been made. It has been argued that the potential of this provision hinges on the notion of necessity also provided in Article XIV GATS and discussed below.[120]

Pending the entry into force of the aforementioned draft disciplines, Article VI:5(a) GATS seeks to ensure that regulatory requirements (licensing and qualification requirements, and technical standards) do not 'nullify or impair' specific commitments:

In sectors in which a Member has undertaken specific commitments, pending the entry into force of disciplines developed in these sectors pursuant to paragraph 4, the Member shall not apply licensing and qualification requirements and technical standards that nullify or impair such specific commitments in a manner which:

(i) does not comply with the criteria outlined in subparagraphs 4(a), (b) or (c); and
(ii) could not reasonably have been expected of that Member at the time the specific commitments in those sectors were made.

This latter criterion suggests that only new national measures may come under this provision.[121] Despite its broad application to national non-discriminatory measures, the ambit of this standstill obligation is rather limited due to the host of conditions attached to it by Article VI:5 GATS.

[119] Lester and Mercurio, *World Trade Law*, p. 605 on the disciplines on accountancy.
[120] Lester and Mercurio, *World Trade Law*, p. 605.
[121] Herrmann, *et al.*, *Welthandelsrecht*, p. 412; Vranes, *Trade and the Environment*, p. 465.

### *1.8.3 The relation to specific commitments*

#### 1.8.3.1 The interplay between 'market access' and national treatment under the GATT

The interplay between market access and national treatment for specific commitments under the GATS is not fully comparable to what could be seen as the equivalent under the GATT. The GATT distinguishes between measures affecting the 'importation' of products, which are regulated in Article XI GATT on quantitative restrictions, and those affecting 'imported products', which are dealt with under Article III GATT on national treatment.[122] With services, such distinction between customs measures and domestic regulation is much less relevant since, as mentioned, barriers to the trade in services are rarely put up at the border.

This difference explains why, under the GATT, quantitative restrictions imposed at the border are analysed separately from national treatment. In other words, a domestic regulation applying equally to an imported foreign product and a domestic product is not only subject to Article XI GATT on quantitative restriction, but is also covered by Article III GATT on national treatment.[123] Hence, the distinction between measures operating at the border and purely domestic measures is clear-cut.[124] If a measure is found to comply with Article III GATT but also indirectly to restrict imports, Article XI GATT should not apply. In other words, under the GATT there is a clear line between market access and domestic regulation.[125] Thus the French ban on products containing asbestos was examined under Article III GATT because it did not primarily target imports, irrespective of the fact that it might also have had an incidental effect on the number of imports of such products.[126]

In an unadopted report in the *US–Tuna* case, it was argued that Article III only applies to measures that regulate the physical characteristics of the restricted product; however, they would not apply to measures that regulate the way in which the product was processed or produced.[127]

[122] See GATT Panel Report, *Canada–Administration of the Foreign Investment Review Act*, BISD 30S/140, adopted 7 February 1984, para. 5.14.

[123] See the Ad Note to Art. III.

[124] Arts. III and XI GATT respectively. See Pauwelyn, 'Rien ne va plus?', 142–5.

[125] But see Pauwelyn, 'Rien ne va plus?', 160, 167.

[126] WTO Appellate Body Report, *European Communities–Measures Affecting Asbestos and Asbestos-Containing Products (EC–Asbestos)*, WT/DS135/AB/R, adopted 5 April 2001.

[127] GATT Panel Report, *United States–Restrictions on Imports of Tuna*, 3 September 1991, not adopted, BISD 39S/155, DS21/R. This distinction has not been discussed prominently

Hence a domestic regulation on the harvesting of yellow fin tuna to reduce the incidental taking of dolphins could not be regarded as directly regulating the sale of tuna and could therefore not possibly affect tuna as a product. This view would entail that if a measure regulates the way the product is processed or produced, it would fall under Article XI GATT, irrespective of whether a domestic regulation was at issue.[128] This is an unresolved matter under the GATT, and it should not concern us further for present purposes. Suffice it to note that, in contrast, under the GATT no overlap exists between measures that would qualify as domestic regulation under the GATS on the one hand and measures that would qualify as affecting market access under the GATS on the other hand. Under the GATT, such measures are governed by Article III on national treatment, or by Article XI on quantitative restrictions.

### 1.8.3.2 The interplay of domestic regulation with national treatment and market access under the GATS

Under the broad understanding of domestic regulation under Article VI GATS, any Member regulation may come under its purview. In addition, domestic regulations may also be found to violate Article XVI GATS by quantitatively restricting market access to services and services suppliers. Recall that national measures prohibited under Article XVI GATS are inherently non-discriminatory, with the exception of the category 'limitations on the participation of foreign capital'. This means that the double nature of non-discriminatory measures under the GATS gives rise to issues of overlap/conflict especially between the market access provision of Article XVI GATS and the domestic regulation provision of Article VI GATS.[129] The only precaution that Members can take with regard to Article XVI GATS is to schedule their restrictions for committed services. This potential norm conflict is addressed by Article XX:2 GATS, which orders that measures must be scheduled under Article XVI GATS on market access in case of doubt. However, in spite of this clear provision in the GATS, it has been argued that Article XVI GATS should be read as a subcategory of Article XVII GATS and the scope of the former provision should be reduced to apply only

in the EU, where it is rather distinguished between product requirements and selling arrangments. See Chapter 4.

[128] See GATT Panel Report, *United States–Restrictions on Imports of Tuna*, BISD 39S/155, DS21/R, para. 5.14.

[129] See Vranes, *Trade and the Environment*, pp. 470–7.

Table 1.1 Domestic regulation = any national law or regulation

| Art XVI GATS (MA) | Art XVII GATS (NT) | Art VI GATS (DR) |
|---|---|---|
| must concern a committed sector | must concern a committed sector | (1) must concern a committed sector<br>(2) there are no disciplines |
| prohibited if a listed measure | prohibited if discriminatory | must not 'nullify or impair' |

to measures limiting the market access of foreign services or foreign providers.[130]

On the relation between Article XVI GATS and Article VI GATS, it has been argued that they should be considered as mutually exclusive rules.[131] In contrast, the Disciplines on Accountancy Services and the non-adopted Disciplines on Domestic Regulation, discussed in the next section and which concern non-discriminatory measures, resolve this potential overlap between the rules on market access and those on domestic regulation by giving priority to market access. Thus a measure does not fall within the scope of the Disciplines if it also comes under one of the categories listed in Article XVI GATS.

Table 1.1 summarizes the basic differences between market access, national treatment and domestic regulation in the GATS.

### *1.8.4 Disciplines on domestic regulation*

As mentioned, the Council adopted the Accountancy Disciplines in 1998. They contain powerful obligations, in wording that resembles concepts known from EU law. The Accountancy Disciplines concern national requirements concerning the accountancy sector on licensing, technical standards and qualifications. They prohibit 'unnecessary barriers to trade' and require Members to ensure that 'such measures are not more trade-restrictive than necessary to fulfil a legitimate objective'. In defining legitimate objectives, the Accountancy Disciplines mention the protection of consumers, the quality of the service, professional

[130] P. Mavroidis, 'Highway XVI re-visited: the road from non-discrimination to market access in GATS' (2007) *World Trade Review* 1–23.

[131] Pauwelyn, 'Rien ne va plus?'. See also Vranes, *Trade and the Environment*, pp. 467–8 on the mutually exclusive relationship between Art. VI(5) on domestic regulations and Art. XVII on market access by example of licensing and qualification requirements and technical standards.

competence and the integrity of the profession.[132] This list is non-exhaustive, yet could be understood to cover only public policy areas similar to those listed.[133]

Even when not adopting such expansive understanding of this provision in the Accountancy Disciplines, there is nothing comparable to be found in the draft DDR.[134] As already mentioned, the Working Party on Domestic Regulation has drafted these disciplines pursuant to its mandate conferred by Article VI:4 GATS. They would constitute the first fulfilment of the regulatory potential promised by Article VI:4 GATS, and would be the first substantial result coming out of the Working Party. The DDR would apply to 'measures by Members relating to licensing requirements and procedures, qualification requirements and procedures, and technical standards affecting trade in services'.[135] They would only apply in sectors where specific commitments are undertaken, and would not apply to measures subject to scheduling under Articles XVI or XVII GATS.[136] The draft provides for transparency and information obligations such as competent authorities, procedures relating to appeals or reviews of applications and the time frame for the processing of an application, and it contains an exemption for universal services.

As regards national licensing rules, the most promising part of the draft DDR from the perspective of the development of the GATS are the 'less trade restrictive means' requirements for licensing requirements. According to the draft, licensing procedures should be 'as simple as possible'. The prohibition, though only stated 'in principle', of not having to deal with more than one competent authority is strikingly similar to the obligation to set up points of single contact under

[132] WTO Council for Trade in Services, Disciplines on Domestic Regulation in the Accountancy Sector, 14 December 1998, s. 2.

[133] M. Krajewski, *National Regulation and Trade Liberalization in Services: The Legal Impact of the General Agreement on Trade in Services (GATS) on National Regulatory Autonomy* (The Hague: Kluwer, 2003), pp. 133, 144.

[134] P. Delimatsis, 'Determining the necessity of domestic regulations in services: the best is yet to come' (2008) *European Journal of International Law* 365–401 at 386, argues for a rebuttable presumption in favour of explicity listed objectives in analogy to Art. 2 Agreement on Technical Barriers to Trade.

[135] Licensing procedures signifies an extension of the explicit mandate in Art. VI:4. Including further measures is not condoned by the majority of Members. See Krajewski, *National Regulation and Trade Liberalization in Services*, p. 135.

[136] Neither is self-evident but both are defendable both from a systematic and a practical perspective. See Krajewski, *National Regulation and Trade Liberalization in Services*, pp. 138–40.

the EU Services Directive 2006/123/EC, discussed later in this book.[137] Similarly, the requirement set forth in the draft DDR to enable electronic applications and accept authenticated copies instead of originals bears a strong resemblance to provisions in Directive 2006/123/EC.[138]

On qualification requirements for the supply of a service, the draft DDR foresees obligations of mutual recognition requiring 'due consideration to relevant professional experience of the applicant as a complement to educational qualifications'. Deficiencies must be curable, among other means, through course work, examinations, training and work experience. Residency requirements shall play no role in recognizing qualification requirements. This constitutes an obligation of mutual recognition that does not exist in the body of the GATS, but which is already familiar from the Accountancy Disciplines.[139] As with licences, procedures on qualification requirements shall be 'as simple as possible and do not in themselves constitute a restriction on the supply of services'. As for the part on technical standards, it is notable that Members 'should take into account' relevant international standards 'except when such international standards or relevant parts would be an ineffective or inappropriate means for the fulfilment of national policy objectives'.

One of the most contentious issues in these negotiations is whether a necessity test should be included into the disciplines.[140] One of the proposals would stipulate that measures relating to licensing requirements and procedures, qualification requirements and procedures, and technical standards are based on objective and transparent criteria, such as competence and the ability to supply the service, are not more burdensome than necessary to ensure the quality of the service, and in the case of licensing procedures not in themselves a restriction on the supply of the service.[141]

[137] See Chapters 6 and 7.

[138] Directive 2006/123/EC, OJ 2006 No. L376/36.

[139] Note that such obligation is conspicuously missing in the part of the DDR on licensing. However, it calls to mind provisions in the TBT Agreement and the SPS Agreement. See Krajewski, *National Regulation and Trade Liberalization in Services*, p. 148.

[140] Progress Report by the Chairman of the Working Party on Domestic Regulation, S/WPDR/W/45, 14 April 2011, attached to the Report by the Chairman of the Council on Trade in Services to the Trade Negotiations Committee, TN/S/36, 21 April 2011.

[141] *Ibid.*, p. 40.

## 1.9 The effect of WTO law in national law

The relationship between the WTO agreements and the national laws of the WTO Members is governed by the umbrella Agreement establishing the WTO. Because of their nature as international and multilateral treaties, the WTO agreements fall under the scope of the Vienna Convention on the Law of Treaties (VCLT).[142] According to the VCLT, 'a party may not invoke the provisions of its internal law as justification for its failure to perform a treaty'.[143] This has to be seen in the context of Article 26 VCLT, which provides for the principle of *pacta sunt servanda*. The AB applied this principle in the *Brazil–Aircraft* case, where it found that 'a WTO Member's domestic law does not excuse that Member from fulfilling its international obligations'.[144]

The WTO Agreement goes a step further than the VCLT by specifying that Members have to ensure the *conformity* of laws and administrative procedures with 'obligations as provided in the annexed Agreements', such as the GATS.[145] The mere non-application of conflicting national laws will not suffice for compliance with WTO law. Member States are rather required proactively to bring their national law in line with WTO rules. In EU law there is a similarly resolute requirement for the rectification of national law that is in conflict with EU law. Article 4(3) TEU requires the Member States to take all measures necessary to fulfil their obligations under EU law, and to abstain from all measures that might undermine the effectiveness of EU law.[146] Based on this provision, the European Court of Justice (ECJ) has ruled that the direct effect of EU law does not release Member States from their obligation 'to remove any provisions incompatible with Community law from their domestic legal order'.[147] The reason for this is that the maintenance of such provisions gives rise to ambiguity, because it leaves individuals in a state of uncertainty as to the possibilities available to them of relying on Union law. This has been referred to as a duty to nullify the unlawful consequences of a breach of Union law.[148] To

[142] See Art. 1, which states that the VCLT only applies to agreements between states.

[143] Art. 27 VCLT.

[144] Appellate Body Report, *Brazil–Export Financing Programme for Aircraft–Recourse by Canada to Article 21.5 of the DSU*, WT/DS46/AB/RW, adopted 4 August 2000, para. 46.

[145] Art. XVI:4 Marrakesh Agreement Establishing the World Trade Organization, 1867 UNTS 154.

[146] On the effects of Article 4(3) TEU, see M. Klamert, *The Principle of Loyalty in EU Law* (Oxford University Press, 2014).

[147] Case 104/86, *Commission v. Italy (Recovery of Undue Payment)* [1998] ECR 1799, para. 12. Joined Cases C-231/06 to C-233/06, *Jonkman* [2007] ECR I-5149, paras. 37–41.

[148] Case C-201/02, *Wells* [2004] ECR I-723, para. 64.

this end, national authorities 'must in particular ensure that national law is changed so as to comply with Community law as soon as possible and that the rights which individuals derive from Community law are given full effect'.

There is no uniform approach to the effect of WTO law among WTO Members. The USA follows 'a purely dualistic approach'.[149] While the US Constitution provides that 'all Treaties made, or which shall be made, under the Authority of the United States, shall be the supreme Law of the Land',[150] this only applies to self-executing international agreements. In contrast, the direct effect of the WTO agreements and of decisions by the WTO dispute settlement bodies is commonly denied under US law.[151] Also in Japan, despite pronunciations on the due respect for international treaties and their prevalence over domestic law,[152] the direct effect of the GATT has been rejected for being insufficiently precise and unconditional.[153]

Supporters of a direct effect of WTO law have argued that it would serve as a countermeasure against protectionist domestic laws caused by asymmetries in national decision-making processes.[154] According to this view, by assuming an individual right to trade freely with foreigners, WTO law would be granted the 'quasi-constitutional' quality of a fundamental human right.[155] However, even taking such a view, countries with a monist tradition will not always directly apply WTO law, but will assess each case separately as to whether the provisions concerned are drafted in a sufficiently precise manner. Provisions with a clear 'programmatic nature' (e.g. negotiating programmes)

[149] Matsushita *et al.*, *The World Trade Organization*, p. 94.

[150] US Constitution, Art. VI, s. 2.

[151] The US Senate held that the Uruguay Round Agreements 'are not self executing and thus their legal effect in the United States is governed by implementing legislation'. See Matsushita *et al.*, *The World Trade Organization*, p. 93.

[152] Matsushita *et al.*, *The World Trade Organization*, pp. 99, 101, referring to Art. 98(2) of the Japanese Constitution.

[153] X. Zhang, 'Direct effect of the WTO Agreements: national survey' (2003) 9 *International Trade Law & Regulation* 35–46 at 40–4. Whether this non-invocability before Japanese courts applies only to the GATT or to all WTO agreements has not yet been clarified.

[154] E.-U. Petersmann, 'Rights and duties of states and rights and duties of their citizens', in U. Beyerlin *et al.* (eds.), *Recht zwischen Umbruch und Bewahrung: Festschrift für Rudolf Bernhardt* (Berlin: Springer, 1995), pp. 1087–128.

[155] T. Cottier and K. N. Schefer, 'The relationship between World Trade Organization law, national law and regional law' (1998) *Journal of International Economic Law* 83–122 at 93.

would therefore not be deemed self-executing.[156] A more cautious view of direct effect in relation to WTO law voices concerns about the lack of democratic participation during the treaty-making process, given that the parliaments of the Members only enter the scene with ratification. According to this view, each Member has to decide autonomously on awarding direct effect depending on the mode of treaty-making and the framework of domestic (particularly constitutional) law.[157]

The need for the above-mentioned strict standard of compliance in WTO law may be explained by its anaemic legal effect. This makes clarity and legal certainty, which such a strict standard of compliance helps to ensure, all the more important. Moreover, when provisions of national law allow for different interpretations, they must be construed in a manner to avoid a conflict with public international law.[158] For matters falling under EU competence, the ECJ has acknowledged this principle of consistent interpretation especially relating to the interpretation of secondary law.[159] However, national courts such as the Court of Cassation in France also apply this mode of interpretation as far as the wording of national law allows.[160]

## 1.10 Conclusion

The architecture of the GATS is difficult to access, which is one of the reasons why its potential for liberalizing services trade has so far not been exhausted. Moreover, its legal effect in the Member States is weak. However, most crucially, the thrust of the liberalizing power of the

[156] Cottier and Schefer, 'The relationship between World Trade Organization law', 89.

[157] See J. Jackson, 'Status of treaties in domestic legal systems: a policy analysis' (1992) 86 *American Journal of International Law* 315–19.

[158] See Van den Bossche and Zdouc, *The Law and Policy of the World Trade Organization*, p. 66.

[159] Particularly concerning the relationship between WTO law and EU law, inter alia Case C-135/93, *Spain* v. *Commission* [1995] ECR I-1651; Case C-83/94, *Leifer* [1995] ECR I-3231; Case C-89/99, *Schieving-Nijstad* [2001] ECR I-5851; Case C-53/96, *Hermès* [1998] ECR I-3603.

[160] For further evidence see S. Vogenauer, *Die Auslegung von Gesetzen in England und auf dem Kontinent: Eine vergleichende Untersuchung der Rechtsprechung und ihrer historischen Grundlagen* (Tübingen: Mohr Siebeck, 2000), vol. I, p. 284. The US Court of International Trade held in this context that 'absent express language to the contrary, a statute should not be interpreted to conflict with international obligations'. US Court of International Trade, *Hyundai Electronics Co* v. *United States*, 53 F. Supp 2d 1343 (1999).

GATS is contingent on specific commitments, which can either grant market access or national treatment, or both for a certain service. If specific commitments are made under the title market access in a Member's schedule (such as a commitment not to limit access for commercial presence by foreign hospital providers by inscribing 'none' in the respective schedule), the GATS only prohibits an exhaustive list of both discriminatory and non-discriminatory national measures. Since national treatment deals only with discriminatory measures, should a measure not be discriminatory and not constitute one of the measures prohibited by Article XVII GATS, it can only possibly be caught by Article VI GATS on domestic regulation. However, non-discriminatory measures under Article VI GATS are subjected to a lesser degree of scrutiny than barriers to market access restrictions under Article XVI GATS (as well as compared to discriminatory measures under Article XVII GATS). Under Article VI GATS, such measures would only be barred if relevant disciplines exist, which is the case only for the accountancy sector to date.

The instruments available in WTO law such as schedules, reference papers and annexes are rather different from those in EU law. While the draft Disciplines on Domestic Regulation would provide for far-reaching obligations similar to the EU Services Directive 2006/123/EC, especially as regards qualification requirements and a test of necessity, it does not seem likely that these disciplines will be adopted any time soon. In EU law on services there are no schedules of commitments, but the obligations imposed on the Member States by the Treaty are unconditional and apply to all sectors. As we will discuss in Chapter 3, EU law deregulates national markets by virtue of standards that have been developed by the Court of Justice. However, under EU law there is also a need to distinguish between discriminatory measures and non-discriminatory measures, since both are subject to a different regime on justifications.

We will return to some central issues touched upon in this chapter such as likeness and the non-discrimination standard in Chapter 8, where the regulatory standards and approaches in the EU and the WTO will be compared in a more structured form. In the following chapter, we will, among other things, examine the differences between the two regimes from the more 'constitutional' perspective, including their respective capacities to provide for negative and positive integration.

# 2 The relationship between the EU and the WTO: differentiation and participation

## 2.1 Introduction

EU law has a very different institutional setting compared to the WTO. EU law intervenes in the legal order of its Member States by directly commanding the disapplication of certain national measures deemed detrimental to trade within the Union.[1] Moreover, the European Parliament and the Council of Ministers adopt directives and regulations that either require the Member States to adapt their national laws, or that provide for directly effective rules detailing the core provisions of the Treaties. Services trade offers an apt illustration of how both Union Treaty (primary) law and Union directives (secondary law) can work together to (de)regulate a certain policy field. Since the adoption of the Services Directive 2006/123/EC[2] in 2006, EU law provides for two interlocked and mutually complementary regimes on services. Outside the scope of application of the Services Directive, the Treaty rules are the relevant source of rights and obligations in this field. Demarcating these two regulatory standards has become one of the foremost tasks in this area, which will be dealt with in detail later in this book.

There are thus seemingly irreconcilable differences between EU law and WTO law in respect of the means available to achieve their respective regulatory objectives. While the institutions of the WTO work 'in a bilateral, consensual way', Member States in the EU have transferred more sovereignty to the EU and thus its institutions, allowing them to

[1] For some of these effects, see in general M. Klamert, *The Principle of Loyalty in EU Law* (Oxford University Press, 2014), pp. 101–38 in particular.

[2] Directive 2006/123/EC of the European Parliament and the Council of 12 December 2006 on services in the internal market, OJ 2006 No. L376/36.

operate in a more interventionist, pro-active manner.[3] In this chapter we will, very briefly, explore some of the main differences between the architecture of the EU and the WTO, both in institutional and in substantive terms. However, we will at the same time demonstrate that nearly all of the 'big' issues in EU law, such as judicial activism and positive vs negative integration, also reverberate in the WTO. We will also discuss the competence of the EU in WTO matters, the WTO rules for determining the status of the EU as a non-state actor within the WTO, and the commitments undertaken by the EU under the GATS. Finally, we will deal with the area of competition law, which, as we will show, is one of the major dividing lines between the two regimes in substantive terms.

## 2.2 'Constitutional' differences between the EU and the WTO

### *2.2.1 'Law-making'*

The European Commission deregulates through its role as complainant in infringement proceedings, and re-regulates by virtue of its right of initiative for the passing of secondary law. In its role, the European Commission has no match in the purely intergovernmental WTO, which lacks a rule maker independent from its Members.[4] As regards services, Article VI:4 GATS does provide for a mandate for the Council for Trade in Services to develop 'disciplines' to prevent domestic regulations from constituting 'unnecessary barriers to trade in services'. For this purpose, as already mentioned, a Working Party on Domestic Regulation has been established and has been vested with a broad mandate for drafting rules on non-discriminatory national restrictions to trade in services. This Working Party in theory could pave the way for deeper inroads into WTO Members' regulatory autonomy. In practice, however, it has to date not produced any definite results, and even if such disciplines on domestic regulations were adopted, they would

[3] See C. Hsueh, 'Direct effect, the WTO compliance mechanism and protection for individuals: lessons from the EC' (2009) 4(2) *Asian Journal of WTO & International Health Law and Policy* 521–55 at 545, who criticizes the WTO for being a 'hybrid' of momentous substantive rules and an inappropriate institutional system.

[4] See also P.-C. Müller-Graff, 'Protectionism or reasonable national regulation?', in S. Griller (ed.), *At the Crossroads: The World Trading System and the Doha Round* (Vienna, New York: Springer, 2008), pp. 147–67 at p. 151.

require the unanimous approval by all Members to acquire immediate binding force.

The WTO cannot avail itself of secondary law in the same form as Union directives or regulations, which have come to play such a prominent role in the regulatory regime of the EU. There is only one WTO provision that comes strikingly close to secondary law in the sense of creating a legal obligation not by way of unilateral concessions by WTO Members, but by an act of a WTO institution. This is the Decision on Disciplines relating to the Accountancy Sector adopted by the Council for Trade in Services in 1998. According to this Decision, 'until the formal integration of these disciplines into the GATS, Members shall, to the fullest extent consistent with their existing legislation, not take measures which would be inconsistent with these disciplines'.[5] This could be taken to mean that even absent of the binding adoption of Disciplines as an Annex or at least as a Reference Paper, Members would be subject to a standstill obligation. However, the legal force of a WTO Council decision is not comparable to that of scheduled commitments. Only the latter are adjudicable in a dispute settlement procedure.

In the EU, this process of integrating the legal orders of the Member States by legal acts is often termed 'positive integration', as opposed to 'negative integration' engineered by prohibitions, such as discriminatory and restrictive measures. In the context of WTO law, such language is not entirely alien, yet has mainly been employed to qualify measures in regional trade agreements (RTAs) and their legality, especially under MFN.[6] Moreover, while the concept of 'harmonization' would seem quintessentially EU, where it refers to the approximation of Member State laws by means of passing directives and regulations, it has also appeared in the WTO context. There it has been defined 'as the process of making different regulations, principles, domestic laws and government policies substantially or effectively the same or similar'.[7] It

[5] See WTO, Council for Trade in Services, Decision on Disciplines Relating to the Accountancy Sector, adopted on 14 December 1998, S/L/63, 15 December 1998.

[6] See J. P. Trachtman, 'Toward open recognition? Standardization and regional integration under Article XXIV of GATT' (2003) 6(2) *Journal of International Economic Law* 459–92. However, Trachtman seems to assign 'positive integration' to the RTAs, while he deems national treatment and necessity under the SPS and TBT Agreements as 'judicially applied standards' of 'negative integration'. See *ibid.*, 462.

[7] G. Mayeda, 'Developing disharmony? The SPS and TBT Agreements and the impact of harmonization on developing countries' (2004) 7(4) *Journal of International Economic Law* 737–64 at 740; H. Zúñiga Schroder, *Harmonization, Equivalence and Mutual Recognition of Standards in WTO Law* (Alphen/Rijn: Kluwer Law International, 2011), p. 22.

has been argued that this instrument is found in the WTO in Article 3 of the SPS Agreement and Article 2.4–2.6 of the TBT Agreement.[8] This is reflected in the Report by the AB in *EC–Hormones* regarding import restrictions on hormone-treated meat from the USA, where it held as follows:

> In generalized terms, the object and purpose of Article 3 is to promote the harmonization of the SPS measures of Members on as wide a basis as possible, while recognizing and safeguarding, at the same time, the right and duty of Members to protect the life and health of their people. The ultimate goal of the harmonization of SPS measures is to prevent the use of such measures for arbitrary or unjustifiable discrimination between Members or as a disguised restriction on international trade, without preventing Members from adopting or enforcing measures which are both 'necessary to protect' human life or health and 'based on scientific principles', and without requiring them to change their appropriate level of protection.[9]

We should be clear, however, that what is referred to as harmonization in this Report corresponds to what is called 'negative' harmonization in the EU context. Thus it refers to the abolition of national obstacles to trade, but does not mean that there is harmonizing legislation in the WTO approximating the laws and regulations of the WTO Members in case such obstacles can be justified for reasons of public policy. In the WTO, therefore, as Weiler has put it, '[m]arket integration is inbuilt', since harmonization is not an option and that leaves justified, import-restricting measures untouched.[10] This difference can be further illustrated if we consider the different roles a principle such as non-discrimination can play in the EU and the WTO respectively. As has been argued, non-discrimination in the EU has a market-unifying, a regulatory and a constitutional role, of which the first corresponds to negative integration and the second to positive integration.[11] In the WTO, non-discrimination shares only the first of these three roles, while it is not constraining the executive discretion

[8] Zúñiga Schroder, *Harmonization, Equivalence and Mutual Recognition of Standards*, p. 21.

[9] WTO Appellate Body Report, *EC Measures Concerning Meat and Meat Products (Hormones)*, WT/DS26/AB/R, WT/DS48/AB/R, adopted 13 February 1998, para. 177.

[10] J. H. H. Weiler, 'Epilogue: Towards a common law of international trade', in J. H. H. Weiler (ed.), *The EU, the WTO, and the NAFTA* (Oxford University Press, Collected Courses of the Academy of European Law, 2001), pp. 201–32 at 215.

[11] See M. Cremona, 'Neutrality or discrimination? The WTO, the EU and External Trade', in G. de Búrca and J. Scott (eds.), *The EU and the WTO: Legal and Constitutional Issues* (Oxford and Portland, OR: Hart Publishing, 2002), pp. 151–84 at p. 159.

of WTO institutions, and does not have the status of a fundamental right.[12]

We therefore see that what is understood by harmonization might differ substantially between different regimes. However, this alone already illustrates that legal concepts exist in both the EU and the WTO that are superficially similar but, at a second glance, betray fundamental differences in the set-up of the two systems.

### *2.2.2 'Adjudication'*

The other motor of integration in the EU besides the Commission is the ECJ. It has the final power to review the legality of EU law and interpret the Treaties.[13] It has transformed and 'constitutionalized' Union law in ways too numerous to mention here.[14] Different from most national regimes, the *travaux préparatoires* to the original Treaties were never used as a guide to their interpretation, since they have never been published.[15] Instead, the ECJ places more emphasis on a systematic and a teleological interpretation. This is directly reflected by the importance of the principle of *effet utile* in Union law, which has served as the underlying rationale for pivotal EU law concepts such as direct effect and state liability.[16] Its legitimacy in expanding the effect and the scope of Union law, in the area of fundamental freedoms among others, has not been spared criticism.[17] In *Mangold*, for instance, the Court was accused of undermining its long-standing

[12] Cremona, 'Neutrality or discrimination?' On the lack of a regulatory role for non-discrimination in WTO law, we should, however, consider that there is not much legislative intervention possible in the WTO that might be in need of constraint.

[13] Art. 267 TFEU.

[14] See P. Craig and G. de Búrca, *EU Law: Texts and Materials*, 5th edn (Oxford University Press, 2011), p. 63; J. H. H. Weiler, 'The transformation of Europe' (1991) *The Yale Law Journal* 2403–83.

[15] See Craig and de Búrca, *EU Law*, p. 64. On the interpretation of secondary law, see M. Potacs, *Auslegung im öffentlichen Recht: Eine vergleichende Untersuchung der Auslegungspraxis des Europäischen Gerichtshofs und der österreichischen Gerichtshöfe des öffentlichen Rechts* (Baden-Baden: Nomos, 1994), pp. 136–42. However, it seems likely that recourse to the *travaux préparatoires* will become more compelling now, in view of the availability of documents from the Convention on the Future of the European Union, which is also relevant for the Lisbon Treaty. See F. C. Mayer, 'Art. 19 EUV', in E. Grabitz, M. Hilf and M. Nettesheim (eds.), *Das Recht der Europäischen Union* (Munich: Beck, 2011), para. 66.

[16] See Klamert, *The Principle of Loyalty in EU Law*, Chapter 13.

[17] Among others in the collection by G. Roth and P. Hilpold (eds.), *Der EuGH und die Souveränität der Mitgliedstaaten* (Stuttgart: Richard Boorberg, 2008).

denial of the direct effect of Union directives in disputes between private parties.[18] Moreover, the Court's argument here was based on a general principle of Union law on prohibiting discrimination on grounds of old age, whose existence in the Member States had been questioned.[19] However, its jurisprudence in most cases has been implicitly endorsed, in particular by the Council and the Parliament adopting secondary law codifying earlier case law of the Court.[20] The EU Services Directive is another example of this, because it adopts and builds on the general prohibition of restrictions developed by the Court of Justice, as we will discuss in Chapter 6.

The WTO dispute settlement system is remarkably effective compared to other international regimes, which is mainly due to the reverse consensus method in the DSB, which makes the rejection of AB awards very unlikely. The AB in the WTO has been deemed to possess de facto judicial supremacy because of this reverse consensus principle for adopting reports and because of its right to determine the boundaries of its jurisdiction within the WTO system.[21] It is noteworthy that the notion of *Kompetenz-Kompetenz* that is often referred to in order to describe the limits of EU competences is commonly and affirmatively used with regard to the powers of the DSB.[22] However, this might in practice mean no more than could also be said about the ECJ, namely that the DSB decides the limits of its own jurisdiction, and that it decides on admissibility. A difference would indeed be the greater autonomy of the DSB in deciding on its own procedure, explained, however, by the lack of such explicit rules in the WTO. Another procedural difference would be the greater reluctance of the DSB to find

18 See the literature cited by R. Streinz and C. Herrmann, 'Der Fall Mangold: eine "kopernikanische Wende im Europarecht"?' (2007) *Recht der Arbeit* 165–9, in fn. 2.

19 See Streinz and Herrmann, 'Der Fall Mangold', 165–9.

20 See the example discussed by D. Damjanovic, 'Annotation to Joined Cases C-22/08 & C-23/08, *Athanasios Vatsouras and Josif Koupatantze* v. *Arbeitsgemeinschaft (ARGE) Nürnberg* 900' (2010) *Common Market Law Review* 847–61.

21 See R. Howse and K. Nicolaïdis, 'Democracy without sovereignty: the global vocation of political ethics', in T. Broude and Y. Shany (eds.), *The Shifting Allocation of Authority in International Law: Considering Sovereignty, Supremacy and Subsidiarity – Essays in Honour of Professor Ruth Lapidoth* (Oxford and Portland, OR: Hart Publishing, 2008), pp. 163–91 at p. 179. *De jure*, the Ministerial Conference and the General Council are vested with the exclusive authority to interpret covered agreements pursuant to Art. IX of the WTO Agreement.

22 See I. Van Damme, 'Interpretation, jurisdiction, and applicable law', in D. Bethlehem, D. McRae, R. Neufeld and I. Van Damme (eds.), *The Oxford Handbook of International Trade Law* (Oxford University Press, 2009), pp. 298–343 at p. 307.

claims inadmissible.[23] As regards the effectiveness of the two systems of adjudication, it must be noted that both regimes foresee a two-tier sanctions regime. While there is a special sanctions claim under Article 260 TFEU that follows the infringement judgment under Article 258 TFEU in the EU,[24] applicants must submit a separate sanctions motion before the DSB. It is, however, an exaggeration to argue that that efficiency of the WTO enforcement mechanism is 'comparable perhaps to that of the European Court of Justice'.[25]

Awards by the DSB have so far created far less debate on their legitimacy, and have not spurred accusations of judicial activism of the magnitude as with the ECJ.[26] Some pertinent exceptions to this finding will be discussed below. At first sight, this history of greater restraint on the part of the DSB is not surprising in view of Article 3.2 of the Dispute Settlement Understanding (DSU), providing that recommendations and rulings of the DSB cannot 'add to or diminish the rights and obligations provided in the covered agreements'. This is extended to the Panels and the AB by Article 19.2 DSU.[27] There is no comparable safeguard clause in Union law, where Article 19 TEU merely states that the Court 'shall ensure that in the interpretation and application of the Treaties the law is observed'. Indeed, if the DSB has been criticized on a principled basis, this concerned what can be seen as procedural matters, such as the AB's *de novo* review of all legal issues, thereby denying deference to the Panel's assessment.[28]

[23] See on this, Van Damme, 'Interpretation, jurisdiction, and applicable law', pp. 312–13.

[24] See, however, the new Art. 260(3) TFEU introduced by the Lisbon Treaty, providing for a fast track procedure for the non-violation of directives.

[25] M. Cartland, G. Depayre and J. Woznowski, 'Is something going wrong in the WTO dispute settlement?' (2012) 46(5) *Journal of World Trade* 979–1015 at 985.

[26] See the overview by B. Swick and V. Gruben, 'Judicial activism and the WTO: the evolution of an unprecedented juridical institution', in D. Horovitz, D. Moulis and D. Steger (eds.), *Ten Years of WTO Dispute Settlement* (London: International Bar Association, 2007), pp. 93–112. For an attempt to conceptualize judicial activism in the international law context, see F. Zarbiyev, 'Judicial activism in international law: a conceptual framework for analysis' (2012) 3(2) *Journal of International Dispute Settlement* 247–78.

[27] See T. P. Stewart, 'Trade remedy actions by WTO members: a cause for concern or a reflection of improved market access?' (2013) 8(6) *Global Trade and Customs Journal* 159–63 at 163, warning against creating 'obligations or rights not contained in the documents' and from bringing 'a bias against users of trade remedies'.

[28] See Cartland *et al.*, 'Is something going wrong in the WTO dispute settlement?', 990–1, who otherwise seem to base their rhetorical question on the rather specific award under the Agreement on Subsidies and Countervailing Measures in WTO, Appellate Body Report, *United States–Definitive Anti-Dumping and Countervailing Duties on Certain Products from China*, WT/DS379/AB/R, adopted 25 March 2011.

One reason for this might be the comparably modest number of arbitral procedures under the GATT, and even more so under the GATS (when compared to the case load in the EU).[29] A second explanation, it is submitted, are the methods of interpretation used by the WTO DSB, which are markedly different from the methods employed by the ECJ.[30] While the latter, as mentioned, largely disregard the intentions of the drafters of the EU Treaties (the Member States), the interpretation of the WTO agreements is governed by the VCLT.[31] According to Article 31 VCLT, interpretation of treaties primarily has to respect their wording, context, object and purpose. Article 32 VCLT permits subsidiary and optional recourse to the preparatory work for a treaty.

Yet in dispute settlement practice, fidelity to the texts of the WTO Treaties has trumped any other of these rules of interpretation.[32] In addition, *travaux préparatoires* have been consulted much more readily than the VCLT would require.[33] This bears witness to an anxiety not to jeopardize the acceptance of dispute settlement awards, thereby acknowledging that they are a reflection of the finely balanced interests of the WTO Members concerned.[34] It has also been argued that the comparable deficit of legitimacy for filling gaps (lacunae) can be explained by the lack of a provision in WTO law corresponding to Article 267 TFEU on the jurisdiction of the ECJ.[35] This textual literalism has been assailed by Hudec in the context of the approach to domestic regulations and

[29] For a more general comparison of the Panels and the Appellate Body with the ECJ, see M. Matsushita, 'Some thoughts on the Appellate Body', in P. F. J. Macrory, A. E. Appleton and M. G. Plummer (eds.), *The World Trade Organization: Legal, Economic and Political Analysis* (New York: Springer, 2005), pp. 1389–403 at p. 1390. On the low level of dispute settlement activity, see also A. T. F. Lang, 'GATS', in D. Bethlehem *et al.* (eds.), *The Oxford Handbook of International Trade Law* (Oxford University Press, 2009), pp. 157–85.

[30] See Müller-Graff, 'Protectionism or reasonable national regulation?', pp. 172–4.

[31] See M. J. Trebilcock, R. Howse and A. Eliason, *The Regulation of International Trade*, 4th edn (London and New York: Routledge, 2013), p. 200.

[32] Trebilcock *et al.*, *The Regulation of International Trade*, p. 201. Cf. J. Bacchus, 'Appellators: the quest for the meaning of and/or', in D. Horovitz, D. Moulis and D. Steger (eds.), *Ten Years of WTO Dispute Settlement* (London: International Bar Association, 2007), pp. 19–40.

[33] Trebilcock *et al.*, *The Regulation of International Trade*, p. 202.

[34] Matushita, 'Some thoughts on the Appellate Body', p. 1397. An indication of this are frequent references to dictionaries that are almost non-existent in the ECJ's jurisprudence.

[35] See Hsueh, 'Direct effect', 544.

the aims and effects test discussed later in this book with the following words:

Developing an accepted and effective jurisprudence in this area requires a high degree of creativity in fashioning answers that provide a satisfactory balance. It is not encouraging to think that the Appellate Body has launched itself upon this delicate and sensitive task bound hand and foot to the words of an old, and often badly drafted, instrument.[36]

In spite of this very 'literalist' approach by the DSB when compared with the ECJ, seeking 'the shelter of the legal texts accepted by governments',[37] there have been occasions where WTO Members have expressed unprecedented and harsh criticism, such as with the award in the *EC–Bananas* dispute, where the AB found the GATS applicable despite protestation by the EU.[38] It has also been noted that the AB has 'recognised and emphasised the value of the principle of effectiveness as the underlying structure and justification of its interpretations'.[39] While applications of this principle in the WTO recall one particular aspect of *effet utile* that is so important in the EU, namely the *argumentum ad absurdum*,[40] the more transformative sides of this principle that are very familiar from EU law have not yet been applied to WTO law.[41]

It could be argued that the Appellate Body in *US–Gambling*, which is one of the few cases to date decided exclusively under the GATS, has shown a bit of the activist 'verve' commonly associated with the Court of Justice.[42] In 2003 Antigua and Barbuda had brought a

[36] R. E. Hudec, *Essays on the Nature of International Trade Law* (London: Cameron May, 1999), p. 375.

[37] Hudec, *Essays on the Nature of International Trade Law*, pp. 375–6.

[38] WTO Appellate Body Report, *European Communities–Regime for the Importation, Sale and Distribution of Bananas (EC–Bananas III)*, WT/DS27/AB/R, adopted 25 September 1997, para. 220.

[39] Van Damme, 'Interpretation, jurisdiction, and applicable law', p. 328.

[40] See WTO Appellate Body Report, *United States–Standards for Reformulated and Conventional Gasoline*, WT/DS2/AB/R, adopted 20 May 1996, para. 21.

[41] See Van Damme, 'Interpretation, jurisdiction, and applicable law', p. 329.

[42] WTO Appellate Body Report, *United States–Measures Affecting the Cross-Border Supply of Gambling and Betting Services (US–Gambling)*, WT/DS285/AB/R, adopted 20 April 2005. On the facts of this case see, among many others, D. Prévost, 'Services and public policy regulation in WTO law: the example of the US-Gambling case', in J. van de Gronden (ed.), *EU and WTO Law on Services: Limits to the Realisation of General Interest Policies within the Services Markets?* (The Hague: Kluwer, 2008), pp. 215–46. WTO Panel Report, *Mexico–Measures Affecting Telecommunications Services (Mexico–Telecoms)*, WT/DS204/R, adopted 1 June 2004, is also a GATS case but under the Agreement of Telecommunications.

complaint against the USA regarding measures by the latter's central, regional and local authorities affecting the cross-border supply of gambling and betting services. Antigua and Barbuda had claimed that the cumulative impact of the US measures prevented the supply of gambling and betting services from another WTO Member to the United States on a cross-border basis, and that they were therefore inconsistent with the US obligations under the GATS. Against the stated intent of the USA, the AB in this case interpreted the US schedules of commitments as applying to the pertinent gambling measures, thus laying the ground for a conviction of the USA under the GATS.[43] Moreover, the AB has been accused of disregarding the explicit wording of Article XVI GATS on market access in applying it to the US measure at hand.[44]

While we will revert to this decision later in this book, suffice it to note that the outcry it has caused in the literature arguably reveals the unease in the WTO with a DSB that refuses to adhere to the grammatical wording of treaty norms or fails to respect the clear intent of WTO Members. This leads us finally to another, possibly minor difference between the ECJ and DSB. The DSU does not foresee the rule of *stare decisis*. Whether traces of this rule exist in the WTO dispute settlement system has been a matter of scholarly debate for a long time.[45] A certain general effect has been affirmed with regard to AB awards.[46] The ECJ, in contrast, while equally not considering itself bound by a strict system of precedent, displays a very strong consistency in its case law, some important exceptions notwithstanding.[47]

[43] On this, the Appellate Body could point to the Guidelines on Scheduling by the WTO Secretariat, which made it abundantly clear that sloppy scheduling should be held against the respective Member.

[44] See J. Pauwelyn, 'Rien ne va plus? Distinguishing domestic regulation from market access in GATT and GATS' (2005) *World Trade Review* 131–70 at 164. See also Prévost, 'Services and public policy regulation', p. 243, who argues that the AB here seems to have followed in the footsteps of the EU and its prohibition of restrictions. However, she ignores the fact that in the EU harmonization can be imposed to replace domestic regulations, thus counteracting the deregulatory effect of the broad application of this prohibition, which is not the case in the WTO.

[45] See the references at A. Krallmann, 'WTO dispute settlement: the establishment of "binding guidance" by the Appellate Body in US Stainless Steel and recent dispute settlement rulings', in C. Herrmann and J. P. Terhechte (eds.), *European Yearbook of International Economic Law* (Heidelberg: Springer, 2011), pp. 417–46 at p. 425.

[46] See Krallmann, 'WTO dispute settlement', p. 420.

[47] See Craig and de Búrca, *EU Law*, p. 63.

### 2.2.3 *Effect in national law*

In Union law, deficiencies in compliance with its rules can be addressed with the principle of direct effect, which is granted to many of the most important provisions of Union law, such as the freedom of establishment and the freedom to provide services, discussed later in this book. If a norm has direct effect, this means that an individual can rely upon it vis-à-vis its state and vis-à-vis private persons, although it has not been (properly) implemented into national law. Hence, the principle of direct effect comprises two distinct aspects. First, it implies the application of an international law provision by a national authority. Second, it grants an individual the right to rely on such a rule. Note that the affirmation of the direct effect of WTO law does not necessarily answer the question of its precedence over national law. Such connection has been made for the law of the (at that time) European Economic Community by the ECJ in the landmark decision in *Costa* v. *ENEL* on the primacy of Community law, which had followed on the decision in *Van Gend en Loos* on the direct effect of then Community law.[48] Supremacy of EU law means that national law is set aside by a conflicting norm of EU law or by a conflicting objective of a Union directive under certain conditions.[49]

International agreements concluded by the EU form an integral part of Union law, which gives the Court the exclusive right to interpret them on matters such as whether a certain provision has direct effect within the Union.[50] Thus the other crucial difference between the effect of EU law and the effect of WTO law within national law besides supremacy is that *Van Gend* established the prerogative of the ECJ to decide

[48] For the full story, see, among many others, E. Stein, 'Lawyers, judges, and the making of a transnational constitution' (1981) *The American Journal of International Law* 1–27. J. H. H. Weiler, 'Law, culture, and values in the WTO: gazing into the crystal ball', in D. Bethlehem *et al.* (eds.), *The Oxford Handbook of International Trade Law* (Oxford University Press, 2009), pp. 750–72 at p. 754 has called this the 'drama of EC "constitutionalisation"'. Thus, while it may be the case that a provision has direct effect in WTO law, domestic law may nonetheless take priority.

[49] On the nature of supremacy, see among others Klamert, *The Principle of Loyalty in EU Law*, pp. 101–5.

[50] See P. Koutrakos, 'Interpretation of mixed agreements', in C. Hillion and P. Koutrakos (eds.), *Mixed Agreements Revisited: The EU and its Member States in the World* (Oxford and Portland, Oregon: Hart Publishing, 2010), pp. 116–37 at p. 123. See also F. Jacobs, 'Direct effect and interpretation of international agreements in the recent case law of the Court', in A. Dashwood and M. Maresceau (eds.), *Law and Practice of EU External Relations: Salient Features of a Changing Landscape* (Cambridge University Press, 2008), p. 13–33 at pp. 16–23.

about an EU law provision's direct effect, thereby deviating from public international law including WTO law, where this right lies with the Member States.[51] The ECJ thus grants EU primary and secondary law as well as provisions of international agreements concluded by the Union direct effect if they contain a clear and precise obligation, and are not subject to a condition to be applicable.[52] However, for WTO law these prerequisites are deemed wanting as a matter of principle by the ECJ,[53] a position that has been sharply criticized in the literature.[54] WTO law may only take effect in EU law for the review of the legality of Union secondary law if this law intends to implement a specific WTO law obligation or if the Union act makes a reference to a WTO provision.[55]

In contrast, international agreements not falling under Union competence, such as parts of so-called mixed agreements, 'belong' to the Member States and thus come under the jurisdiction of national courts.[56] Hence for matters in WTO agreements, which are concluded by the Member States, the respective national courts are in principle free to decide on their direct effect. This, however, does not apply to the interpretation of procedural, 'competence-neutral' provisions in mixed agreements.[57] This has been expounded by the Court in two preliminary rulings on Article 50 of the Agreement on Trade-Related Aspects of Intellectual Property Rights (TRIPS Agreement), which has

[51] B. de Witte, 'Direct effect, supremacy, and the nature of the legal order', in P. Craig and G. de Búrca (eds.), *The Evolution of EU Law* (Oxford University Press, 1999), pp. 177–213 at p. 181.

[52] Case C-12/86, *Demirel* [1987] ECR I-3719, para. 14.

[53] See recently Case C-307/99, *OGT* [2001] ECR I-3159, para. 25, where the Court pointed out that the provisions of the TRIPS Agreement are 'not such as to create rights on which individuals may rely directly before the courts by virtue of Community law'. See Case T-52/99, *T. Port* [2001] ECR II-981, para. 51: 'WTO rules are not in principle intended to confer rights on individuals'.

[54] See, among others, S. Griller, 'Judicial enforceability of WTO law in the European Union: Annotation to Case C-149/96, Portugal V. Council' (2000) 3(3) *Journal of International Economic Law* 441–72 at 441.

[55] See M. Matsushita, T. J. Schoenbaum and P. C. Mavroidis, *The World Trade Organization: Law, Practice and Policy* (Oxford University Press, 2003), p. 98, who call these situations the *Nakajima* doctrine and the *Fediol* doctrine after the cases where they appeared: Case C-68/89, *Nakajima* [1991] ECR I-2069, para. 31; Case C-70/87, *Fediol* [1989] ECR I-1781, paras. 19–22.

[56] C. Herrmann, W. Weiß and C. Ohler, *Welthandelsrecht*, 2nd edn (Munich: Beck, 2007), p. 76.

[57] According to Art. 50 TRIPS Agreement, judicial authorities of WTO Members have the authority to order prompt and effective provisional measures either to prevent the infringement of an intellectual property right from occurring, or to preserve relevant evidence for an alleged infringement.

been concluded by both the Union and the Member States. In *Hermès*, the ECJ held that 'where a provision can apply both to situations falling within the scope of national law and to situations falling within the scope of Community law, it is clearly in the Community interest that, in order to forestall future differences of interpretation, that provision should be interpreted uniformly, whatever the circumstances in which it is to apply'.[58]

Thus the effects of EU law within the regimes of its Member States are considerably different from the effects of WTO law within the legal orders of its Members. Direct effect is determined 'centrally' by the ECJ for the EU, and EU law is always superior to national law, setting it aside in case of conflict. This makes compliance less of an issue within the EU. For WTO law, however, direct effect is denied, whereas at least those parts of WTO law clearly within EU competence take precedence over national law of a Member State. Mixed EU agreements, of which the WTO agreements are a prime example, are the 'apotheosis' of the intricacies of the distribution of competence in the EU, to which we turn now.

## 2.3 The prerequisites and modalities of the participation of the EU in the WTO

### *2.3.1 Introduction*

In this section we will discuss several interrelated issues regarding the role of the EU within the WTO in general and related to the GATS in particular. First, we will deal with the status of the EU within the WTO, where it stands to benefit from derogation for RTAs. This question concerns both whether the EU is covered under this derogation in the first place, and if it is, whether it satisfies the requirements that have been established by the Court for being exempted mainly from MFN. Second, we will look at the 'constitutional' foundations for the EU's participation in the GATS, namely the pertinent distribution of competences for this matter. Here we will see that the internal allocation of power for participating in the GATS does not correspond to the practice of

[58] See Case C-53/96, *Hermès* [1998] ECR I-3603, para. 32. See also Case C-300/98, *Dior* and C-392/98 *Assco Gerüste* [2000] ECR I-11307, and recently, Case C-240/09, *Lesoochranárske* [2011] ECR I-1255. On this, see M. Klamert, 'Dark matter: competence, jurisdiction and the area largely covered by EU law – Comment on Lesoochranárske' (2012) *European Law Review* 340–50.

representation within the organs of the WTO. The combination of the issue of the status of the EU from the point of view of WTO law and the competence issue produces the question of attributability, thus the question whether the EU is responsible for the conduct of its Member States. We will also, in some detail but not exhaustibly, discuss the current commitments of the EU and some selected Member States under the GATS.

### *2.3.2 The EU and WTO derogations for regional trade agreements*

Regional trade agreements, as already mentioned in Chapter 1, are regulated by Article XXIV GATT and Article V GATS, where they are called agreements for 'economic integration' and 'trade liberalization' respectively.[59] As mentioned, pursuant to Article V GATS, WTO Members can enter into these agreements under the condition that such agreements have 'substantial sectoral coverage' and abolish 'substantially all discrimination' between the parties to the agreement.[60] There is no dispute settlement practice on Article V GATS, so guidance must be gained from the practice with regard to the corresponding provision in the GATT. According to the AB award in *Turkey–Textiles*, Article XXIV GATT can only exempt measures that are 'necessary' for the establishment of a customs union or a free trade agreement from MFN. Without this exemption, other WTO Members could demand MFN with regard to the privileges granted between the members of such customs union or free trade zone.

In the words of the AB, Article XXIV can justify a measure that is inconsistent with other GATT provisions only under two conditions that must be met cumulatively:

> First, the party claiming the benefit of this defence must demonstrate that the measure at issue is introduced upon the formation of a customs union that fully meets the requirements of sub-paragraphs 8(a) and 5(a) of Article XXIV. And, second, that party must demonstrate that the formation of that customs union would be prevented if it were not allowed to introduce the measure at issue.[61]

With regard to the EU, two general problems present themselves here. First, does the exception under Article XXIV GATT, or more pertinently

[59] We will also stick with the term regional trade agreements (RTA) for the GATS.

[60] See Chapter 1.

[61] Appellate Body Report, *Turkey–Restrictions on Imports of Textile and Clothing Products*, WT/DS34/AB/R, adopted 19 November 1999, DSR 1999:VI, 2345, para. 58.

under Article V GATS, also concern RTAs that go beyond a free trade zone, which the EU undoubtedly does? Were the EU decisively more than what is meant under Article V GATS, it would have to be treated as one party for the purposes of the GATS. In this case, the relations between its members would be exempt from MFN without any further assessment of the criteria under Article V GATS, but would be subject to national treatment (NT).[62] However, both the EU and the WTO seem to consider the EU to be covered by these derogation rules, witness of which opinion are corresponding notifications by the EU and its pleading in *Turkey–Textiles*.[63] This is also consistent with the fact that under some GATS modes it is not the EU that has scheduled commitments but the individual Member States, as we will discuss below.[64] Thus the criteria must also apply in principle to agreements under Article V GATS.

This leads to the question of the standard of 'necessity' in the sense of *Turkey–Textiles* that would apply to national measures in this context.[65] Here it could be argued that the broader wording of Article V GATS, which is not limited to specific forms of integration models, supports a more extensive interpretation of this provision. It would not make much sense to apply the strict standard suitable for customs unions and free trade agreements, since this would have the effect of blocking any measure under such 'deeper' RTA from the start. The standard of necessity would have to take account of the specifics of the EU, namely its institutional self-perception as a supranational, partly political union. Thus, provided that the EU benefits from the general exemption under Article V in the first place, it would be free to introduce new measures in violation of the GATS, if these measures were necessary for the establishment of an economic union/single market.

[62] This seems to be what is meant by C. Herrmann, 'Bilateral and regional trade agreements as a challenge to the multilateral trading system' (2008/09) EUI Working Papers LAW 13.

[63] For a discussion of such 'political exception', see L. Bartels, 'The legality of the EC mutual recognition clause under WTO law' (2005) 8(3) *Journal of International Economic Law* 691–720.

[64] When Herrmann, 'Bilateral and regional trade agreements', 13, proffers that applying the WTO obligations directly to an RTA 'would pose no specific problems with regard to the European Community, which is a WTO Member in its own right anyway', this might therefore ignore the fact that the modalities of participation are more complex under the GATS.

[65] For mutual recognition regimes under the GATT, see the analysis by Bartels, 'The legality of the EC mutual recognition clause under WTO law'.

### *2.3.3 EU competence and representation*

In its Opinion on the Agreement Establishing the World Trade Organization, the ECJ clarified that 'the modes of supply of services referred to by GATS as "consumption abroad", "commercial presence" and the "presence of natural persons" are not covered by the exclusive Union competence for the common commercial policy'.[66] Thus the only area under the GATS covered by ex-Article 133 EC was the cross-border provision of services, corresponding to Mode 1 of the GATS.[67] Consequently, the GATS was concluded by the (then) EC and the (then) EC Member States in the form of a mixed agreement.[68]

Mixity, however, was only facultative since the WTO agreements did not require the participation of the Member States. Thus, already prior to the amendments of the provisions on the Common Commercial Policy by the Lisbon Treaty, in theory the WTO agreements in their entirety could have been concluded by the Union alone.[69] Moreover, one could have argued that this demarcation of competence had already been changed to the detriment of the Member States with the passing of the EU Services Directive, which arguably has pre-empted the rights of the Member States to enter into international agreements in the whole field of services.[70]

The Lisbon Treaty has now brought explicit, if perhaps only theoretical, change. Under the amended Article 207 TFEU (ex-Article 133 EC), it has substantially extended the competence of the EU for Common Commercial Policy to cover 'changes in tariff rates, the conclusion of tariff and trade agreements relating to trade in goods and services, and the commercial aspects of intellectual property, foreign direct investment, the achievement of uniformity in measures of liberalisation,

[66] Opinion 1/94, *Agreement Establishing the World Trade Organization* [1994] ECR I-5267, para. 47.

[67] On these modes, see Chapter 1.

[68] Herrmann *et al.*, *Welthandelsrecht*, pp. 69ff. See Art. XI:1 WTO Agreement. On mixed agreements, see the contributions in C. Hillion and P. Koutrakos (eds.), *Mixed Agreements Revisited: The EU and its Member States in the World* (Oxford and Portland, OR: Hart Publishing, 2010).

[69] See M. Klamert and N. Maydell, 'Lost in exclusivity: implied non-exclusive external competences in Community law' (2008) *European Foreign Affairs Review* 493–513. See also S. Griller and K. Gamharter, 'External trade: is there a path through the maze of competences?', in S. Griller and B. Weidel (eds.), *External Economic Relations and Foreign Policy in the European Union* (Vienna, New York: Springer, 2002), pp. 65–112 at pp. 81–4.

[70] M. Klamert and N. Maydell, 'Rechtsfragen der impliziten Außenkompetenz der EG illustriert am Beispiel der Dienstleistungsrichtlinie und der Minimum Platform on Investment' (2008) 4 *Europarecht* 589–602.

export policy and measures to protect trade such as those to be taken in the event of dumping or subsidies'.[71] Given that this competence does now also cover agreements on foreign direct investments (FDIs), it is commonly held that the scope of 'trade in services' in Article 207(1) TFEU is now in line with the scope of the GATS, also covering commercial presence.[72] Formally, therefore, all matters dealt with by the WTO including the GATS in its entirety now fall under the exclusive competence of the EU, which could conclude the WTO agreements on its own as a result. However, this would require that the Member States renounce their participation in the WTO, which seems unlikely.[73]

In spite of the above-mentioned lack of competence of the EU (before the Lisbon Treaty) for all modes under the GATS except of Mode 1, in practice the Member States coordinate their position and the European Commission also speaks in their name at almost all WTO meetings and on almost all WTO matters, including on the full range of modes covered by the GATS.[74] This strong role of the Commission dates back to the negotiations of the GATS, where it has been described as a key player, even though at that stage the exact distribution of competences had not been clarified by the ECJ.[75] Where the EU exercises its right to vote, it has the number of votes equal to the number of its Members that are parties to the WTO.[76] The uniform representation of the EU and its Member States by the European Commission also extends to dispute settlement proceedings. Irrespective of whether claims were brought against an individual EU Member State, against the EU and the

[71] The treaty-making powers of the EU under the common commercial policy had already been broadened by the Nice Treaty, although to unclear effect. See J. Wouters, D. Coppens and B. de Meester, 'The European Union's external relations after the Lisbon Treaty', in S. Griller and J. Ziller (eds.), *The Lisbon Treaty: EU Constitutionalism without a Constitutional Treaty* (Vienna, New York: Springer, 2008), pp. 143–203 at p. 170.

[72] See Wouters *et al.*, 'The European Union's external relations', p. 171. The competence for investment-related treaties, however, remains ambigious under the Lisbon Treaty. See *ibid.*, pp. 171–3.

[73] See R. Streinz, C. Ohler and C. Herrmann, *Der Vertrag von Lissabon zur Reform der EU*, 2nd edn (Munich: Beck, 2008), p. 151.

[74] See www.wto.org/english/thewto_e/countries_e/european_union_or_communities_popup.htm. See also Herrmann *et al.*, *Welthandelsrecht*, p. 71; P. Van den Bossche and W. Zdouc, *The Law and Policy of the World Trade Organization: Text Cases and Materials* (Cambridge University Press, 2013), p. 138.

[75] J. A. Marchetti and P. C. Mavroidis, 'The genesis of the GATS (General Agreement on Trade in Services)' (2011) 22(3) *The European Journal of International Law* 689–721 at 705.

[76] See Art. IX:1 WTO Agreement. A footnote states that the number of votes must never exceed the number of EU Member States.

Member States concerned, or only against the EU, it was always the EU that defended before the DSB.[77] In practice, therefore, the conduct of the Member States is attributed to the EU.[78]

### 2.3.4 *EU commitments*

There are no uniform commitments binding all EU Member States, but partly concurring and partly diverging commitments made by individual Member States. This does not contribute to the readability of the EU schedule, nor does it make the role of the EU in the WTO regime very transparent. Moreover, it is somewhat misleading to read on the WTO services database website concerning the EU as a WTO Member that 'sometimes references are made to the specific member States, particularly where their laws differ'.[79] In reality, reference is almost always made to the individual Member States, as will be shown when we later discuss the schedule of commitments and the offer for amending this schedule of the EU.

The EU submitted its current schedule of commitments in 2006, comprising the national schedules for all twenty-five EU Member States at that time (including the schedules for the ten acceding countries of 2004).[80] Prior to the enlargement in 2003, the EU Member States had completely separate schedules, which, technically, are still in force. The Consolidated Schedule of 2006 was renegotiated and certified according to the procedure required by Article XXI GATS. The acceding EU Member States thereby scheduled modifications of their previous individual schedules and the EU provided for compensation.[81] The three Member States that had joined the EU in 2005 (Austria, Finland and Sweden) also modified their schedules on this occasion.[82] This 2006 schedule, however, will only enter into force 'on a date to be specified

[77] See Van den Bossche and Zdouc, *The Law and Policy of the World Trade Organization*, p. 171.

[78] See Bartels, 'The legality of the EC mutual recognition clause under WTO law', 691.

[79] See http://tsdb.wto.org/default.aspx.

[80] WTO, Council for Trade in Services, Communication from the European Communities and its Member States, Draft Consolidated GATS Schedule, S/C/W/273, 9 October 2006.

[81] See WTO, Trade Policy Review Body, Trade Policy Review, Report by the Secretariat, European Communities, WT/TPR/S/214, 2 March 2009, p. 134.

[82] See WTO, Committee on Regional Trade Agreements, Factual Presentation, Enlargement of the European Union to 25 Member States (Services), Report by the Secretariat, Revision, WT/REG170/8/Rev.1, 1 May 2009, p. 20. Austria, for instance, removed its commitments on space transport and compensated by removing a horizontal limitation on investments.

by the European Communities and its Member States'.[83] In addition and in the meantime, the EU has launched negotiations in order to certify a consolidated schedule also including Bulgaria and Romania, which acceded to the EU in 2007.[84] Finally, the EU had already tabled a revised conditional offer for modifications of its commitments within the ongoing negotiations in June 2005.[85]

As regards horizontal commitments in the 2006 schedules,[86] there is a uniform carve-out on market access within Mode 3 for public utilities subject to monopolies or exclusive rights.[87] In addition, widespread restrictions on corporate form and nationality or residence requirements for founders and managing directors are scheduled for the establishment of legal persons in the Union. Foreign subsidiaries may be discriminated against across all sectors. Market access and national treatment are heavily constrained in investment-related matters such as portfolio investments, where France and Poland in particular put up barriers for foreign participation and real estate purchases with widespread permission requirements.

On the recognition of foreign diplomas, the schedule clarifies that EU directives on this do not apply to nationals of third countries and recognition in regulated professions 'remains within the competence of each Member State'. The bulk of commitments by EU Member States under the GATS relate to 'regulated professions' such as lawyers, tax advisors and doctors. These services are centrally governed by Directive 2005/36/EC[88] and corresponding specific secondary law for the legal profession in Union law.[89] Thus Union law in this respect is comprehensive and requires a clear delimitation from the GATS.

[83] WTO, Trade in Services, Certification, Schedule of Commitments, The European Communities and its Member States, S/L/286, 18 December 2006. This status quo *in limbo* is only poorly reflected on the official services gateway of the WTO.

[84] WTO, Report by the Secretariat, European Communities, WT/TPR/S/214, p. 134.

[85] WTO, Council for Trade in Services, Special Session, Communication from the European Communities and its Member States, Conditional Revised Offer, TN/S/O/EEC/Rev.1, 29 June 2005.

[86] For more details see also WTO, Enlargement of the EU, WT/REG170/8/Rev.1, pp. 21–2.

[87] See M. Cossy, 'Environmental services and the General Agreement on Trade in Services (GATS): legal issues and negotiating stakes at the WTO', in C. Herrmann and J. P. Terhechte (eds.), *European Yearbook of International Economic Law* (Heidelberg, Vienna: Springer, 2011), pp. 239–63 at pp. 251–2.

[88] Directive 2005/36/EC of the European Parliament and the Council of 7 September 2005 on the recognition of professional qualifications, OJ 2005 No. L255/22.

[89] See Chapter 8.

Finally, market access of natural persons both for entry into the EU and temporary stay in an EU Member State is subject to a wide but only slightly differing variety of conditions set up by individual Member States. Here WTO scheduling distinguishes the categories of intra-corporate transfers (ICT), contractual service suppliers (CSS) and business visitors (BV). The latter category is further divided in 'service sellers' and employees of foreign legal persons engaged in the establishment of commercial presence within the Union. In EU terminology, these latter cases may partly fall within the category of 'posted workers' or are not regulated specifically under EU law. Disparate commitments of Member States in these categories make this part of the EU schedule an especially cumbersome read.

A variety of different constellations is also scheduled on MFN exemptions.[90] Most exemptions concern special treaty regimes of one or several EU Member States with third states, such as in the transport sector, with former colonies, or international agreements of the EU with third countries such as the 'Bilaterals' with Switzerland. Culture and audio-visual services are also largely exempted from the obligation to award MFN.[91]

As regards sectoral commitments, we will restrict our analysis to the tourism, health and construction sectors. The most important mode with regard to 'tourism and travel related services', subcategory 'A. Hotels, Restaurants and Catering (CPC 641, 642, 643)',[92] is commercial presence. Here most EU Member States have committed to open their markets fully. For Spain, Greece and Portugal, as recipients of investment in this sector, limitations have been scheduled in order to protect areas of particular historic and artistic interest. Italy, which is in a similar situation, imposes an economic needs tests on bars, cafes and restaurants.

Within the category of 'health services and social services', subcategory 'A. Hospital Services', patient mobility falls under consumption abroad (Mode 2). Most Member States grant full market access and national treatment for recipients of hospital services from other WTO Members (inscribed 'none').[93] On Mode 3, most (eighteen) EU Member

90 One sector for all Member States, all sectors for one Member State, etc.

91 This is not surprising in view of the fact that the only sector the EU had wanted to exclude from liberalization during the Uruguay Round negotiations was audio-visual services. See Marchetti and Mavroidis, 'The genesis of the GATS', 716.

92 This is excluding catering in the transport services sector except in Austria, Hungary, Finland and Sweden.

93 Exceptions are Cyprus, Czech Republic, Finland, Malta, Sweden and Slovakia.

States have scheduled a variety of limitations to market access for foreign providers. Throughout, the number of beds and/or heavy equipment is made subject to an economic needs test. On national treatment in Mode 3, only ten Member States have refused to either make any binding commitments or have scheduled limitations. In contrast, nearly all Member States have refused concessions under Mode 4 (presence of natural persons). This means that foreign doctors, nurses or midwives will find it difficult to enter an EU Member State, and will likely be discriminated against at a later stage.

The construction sector falls under the classification 'construction and related engineering services'.[94] Most EU Member States have not scheduled limitations for market access through commercial presence. Greece imposes a nationality condition for managers of construction companies; Italy and Portugal have a reservation to grant exclusive rights for the construction, maintenance and management of highways. With market access and national treatment in Mode 4, it must be borne in mind that this does not cover employed persons, and therefore does not concern construction workers, in particular. This explains why the schedule, in this respect, is not very elaborate and mainly concerned with managers and posted technicians. France, in particular, makes the temporary entry of posted[95] technicians subject to a long list of conditions, such as a limited work permit, requirement of a work certificate, proof of agreement to the transfer and an economic needs test. Other sectors where EU Member States have scheduled substantial commitments are professional services, educational services, environmental services such as sewage and sanitation services,[96] financial and banking services, and recreational services including tour guides and travel agencies.

The EU and its Member States submitted the current initial offer in 2004, already based on the Consolidated Schedules of 2006 discussed above, which, as mentioned, have not yet entered into force. In general, the initial offer in many respects would lead to a harmonization of the commitments by the individual Member States. Thus the horizontal commitments for the above-mentioned categories of persons

[94] However, in this area many Member States have carved out certain subsectors from the application of their commitments.

[95] 'The technician is an employee of a juridical person within the territory of another Member and is transferred to a commercial presence in FR which has a contract with that juridical person.'

[96] See Cossy, 'Environmental services and the GATS, pp. 245–8.

under Mode 4 are now largely uniform for all Member States (only with the exception of Cyprus), thereby replacing the previous opaque list. In other parts of the current offer, such as on retailing services (department stores) commitments, the limitations to the commitments on market access are now drafted as joint limitations. This, however, is largely a technical change. Substantial new sectoral commitments are offered for telecommunications both concerning market access and national treatment, as well as by incorporating the Reference Paper on Telecommunications as additional commitments pursuant to Article XVIII GATS. Moreover, there are new commitments in the offer on maritime transport and related services, ground handling, hairdressing, beauty services and spa services. In contrast, with regard to construction and health (hospital) services discussed above, the EU proposes no new, substantial modifications. Very few changes are offered on MFN exemptions. We have already noted that the EU has proposed a reference paper on postal services, which is annexed to the EU offer.

Thus, despite the uniformity of representation within the WTO, which overcomes the competence quagmire, EU Member States maintain their individual and diverging commitments under the GATS. This is reflected both by their horizontal commitments and by their specific commitments in the current EU schedule.

In the following section we will discuss one area of substantive law that illustrates a fundamentally different standard of review in a core aspect of market liberalization, namely the battle against the abuse of market power.

## 2.4 A structural divide: competition law

In almost all respects and sectors, the competition rules of the WTO lag behind those of the EU both in terms of breadth and bite. With regard to subsidies by WTO Members, MFN applies as well as any specific commitments such as on national treatment.[97] In addition, Article XV GATS calls on Member States to enter into negotiations on disciplines in this matter, and exchange information on existing subsidies. However, not much has happened on either account since the creation of the

[97] See B. de Meester, 'The global financial crisis and government support for banks: what role for the GATS?' (2010) 13(1) *Journal Of International Economic Law* 27–63. The WTO Agreement on Subsidies and Countervailing Measures is limited to the trade in goods.

Agreement.[98] Under Article VIII:2 GATS on monopolies and exclusive service suppliers, Members must prevent monopoly suppliers active in sectors other than those where they hold the monopoly and where the Member has scheduled specific commitments from abusing their position and acting inconsistently with such commitments.[99] Article IX GATS on business practices requires WTO Members to consult with each other, upon request, in order to end any practices other than those covered by Article VIII GATS that impair competition and, therefore, negatively affect trade in services.

The GATS does not therefore provide a competition regime in parallel with its rules on market access and national treatment. Considerations of market power and universal service obligations are only poorly served by these WTO instruments. Under the GATS, emphasis rather lies on allowing foreign participation in domestic services markets and on preventing any type of discrimination once the providers operate in the markets. Thus the focus is on the permission of foreign participation in the market, without an increase in the degree of competition allowed to occur in the market.[100] Imposing competition rules and creating greater accountability on the part of regulators for the economic impact of regulations on markets and competition would require the WTO 'to analyze regulatory proposals from an economic policy perspective', creating a responsibility for regulators to justify the imposition of a new set of rules and regulations.[101] Some states within the WTO believe that such rules would further contribute to trade liberalization

[98] See www.wto.org/english/thewto_e/whatis_e/tif_e/agrm6_e.htm. See also Trebilcock *et al.*, *The Regulation of International Trade*, p. 499.

[99] A monopoly supplier under the GATS is defined as an entity established formally or de facto to be the sole supplier of a service in a Member State. See Art. XXVIII(h) GATS. This, however, does not include natural monopolies without governmental intervention. Herrmann *et al.*, *Welthandelsrecht*, p. 408.

[100] P. Low and A. Mattoo, 'Is there a better way? Alternative approaches to liberalization under GATS', in P. Sauvé and R. Stern (eds.), *GATS 2000: New Directions in Services Trade Liberalization* (Washington DC: Brookings, 2000), pp. 449–72.

[101] This would call for a more competition-oriented approach to GATS negotiations, assessing the real value of commitments by Members by considering the underlying regulatory and market structures. See G. Feketekuty, 'Competition policy and the WTO: implications or recent developments in the services sector', Paper prepared for the Third Symposium on Competition Policy and the Multilateral Trading System, Geneva, April 1999. See also G. Feketekuty and R. A. Rogowsky, 'The scope, implication and economic rationale of a competition-oriented approach to future multilateral trade negotiations', in S. Arndt and C. Milner, *The World Economy: Global Trade Policy* (London: Blackwell Publishers, 1996), 167–81 at pp. 171.

and thus to the objective of the WTO.[102] However, there is a deep-felt resistance among many WTO Members to using the WTO as a forum to harmonize competition policies.[103]

In contrast, Article 101 TFEU prohibits agreements and concerted practices that affect trade between Member States and 'which have as their object or effect the prevention, restriction or distortion of competition within the internal market'. Article 102 TFEU prohibits any abuse of a dominant position within the internal market or in a substantial part of it.[104] These competition law rules, as a matter of principle, also apply within the area of the regulation of services in the EU. By virtue of these rules in an area of de facto exclusive competence of the Union, which is directly enforced by the European Commission, there is a constant assault against collusion and abuse of monopoly power in the EU. This helps service providers to secure not only market access but also their fair share of competition once having entered the national market. It should, however, be noted that competition rules and free movement rules in the EU operate fairly independently of each other.[105]

What the WTO shares with the EU is that neither regime forces a government to privatize service industries or provides a general rule requiring the abolition of monopolies. EU law does not oblige the dismantling of monopolies; it rather prevents the creation of new ones by a merger control policy and prevents the abuse of monopoly power

[102] See especially the contribution of Canada on 'Competition policy considerations in the GATS Negotiations', Paper for public consultation, June 2001.

[103] See R. Howse, 'Importing regulatory standards and principles into WTO dispute settlement: the challenge of interpreting the GATS Arrangements on Telecommunications', in I. Lianos and O. Odudu (eds.), *Regulating Trade in Services: Trust, Distrust and Economic Integration* (Cambridge University Press, 2012), pp. 445–69 at p. 448.

[104] This may concern the following practices: imposing unfair purchase or selling prices or other unfair trading conditions; limiting production, markets or technical development to the prejudice of consumers; applying dissimilar conditions to equivalent transactions with other trading parties, thereby placing them at a competitive disadvantage; or making the conclusion of contracts subject to acceptance by the other parties of supplementary obligations that, by their nature or according to commercial usage, have no connection with the subject of such contracts.

[105] See Directive 2006/123/EC of the European Parliament and the Council of 12 December 2006 on services in the internal market, OJ 2006 No. L376/36, Rec. 8, stating that the freedom of establishment and free movement of services apply only 'to the extent that the activities in question are open to competition, so that they do not oblige Member States either to liberalize services of general economic interest or to privatize public entities'.

under Article 102 TFEU. For the same reason, the Services Directive also purports not to deal 'with the abolition of monopolies providing services nor with aids granted by Member States'.[106] Article 106 TFEU, discussed in the following chapter, exempts public service suppliers from the competition rules. Similarly, the GATS does not curtail the existence of monopolies or exclusive service suppliers.[107] Article VIII:1 GATS subjects them to granting MFN treatment and to specific commitments, should they have been entered into by the WTO Member concerned.[108] Pursuant to Article VIII:4 GATS, Members are obliged to report the granting of new monopoly rights in a sector subject to specific commitments to the Council for Trade in Services. This is then treated as modification of schedules under Article XXI GATS.

There are also some analogies between the WTO and the EU in the regulation of the telecommunication sector. This sector has been tackled in the mid-1980s both in the EU and at the beginning of the Uruguay Round (in 1986).[109] The result in the WTO is the Reference Paper on Telecommunications annexed to the GATS, which outlines the most severe violations of competition rules. The reference paper annexed to the Agreement on Basic Telecommunications states that anti-competitive practices in telecommunications, such as cross-subsidization, using information obtained from competitors with anti-competitive results or not making available to other services suppliers necessary technical information about essential facilities, should be prevented. These are the most acute restrictions in this sector that could distort competition and lessen liberalization. Through such new regulation, governments are obliged to take and maintain appropriate measures for preventing major suppliers from engaging in anti-competitive practices with respect to foreign competitors active

[106] See Art. 1(3) Directive 2006/123/EC. The latter of course alludes to the state aids regime under Article 107 TFEU.

[107] See also M. Burri-Nenova and S. Z. Bigdeli, 'Commentary of GATS Article IX Business Practices' (2008) SSRN Working Paper Series. See also the specific reference to competition policy in the TRIPS Agreement, which allows countries to take steps such as compulsory licensing when they can show that an anti-competitive abuse has occurred.

[108] This is a general obligation, since it applies across the board and not only when a Member has listed specific commitments.

[109] Until the Uruguay Round, states controlled the national telecommunication operators and only coordinated technical standards, such as the frequency spectrum. See M. Bobjoseph, *The WTO Agreements on Telecommunications* (Berne/Frankfurt/Brussels: Peter Lang, 2003), p. 27.

in their country.[110] This listing is exceptional in WTO law, which usually does not aim at regulating competition in the Member's domestic markets.

The EU Framework Directive[111] provides the corresponding regulatory framework in the EU. The central notion here is significant market power (SMP).[112] SMP is not necessarily the equivalent to a qualification as a major supplier under the GATS Annex.[113] A major supplier is defined in the Reference Paper as a provider that has power on the relevant market that materially affects the terms of participation of prospective competitors in respect of price and supply because it can exercise control over essential facilities or over the use of its position in the market. To qualify as a major supplier, it is sufficient to exert power, for example from a neighbouring market.[114] Thus a provider may have SMP under EU law, while not being a major supplier under the WTO rules. There is, however, an express linkage between the EU and the WTO regulatory regime. The EU Access Directive[115] provides in its Article 8(3) that national authorities may impose SMP restrictions in order to comply with international commitments, such as under WTO law. Meeting the requirements laid down in EU law is not required under the Access Directive.[116] This provision thus serves the convergence between the concept of major supplier in WTO law and of SMP in EU law.

[110] See also WTO Panel Report, *Japan–Measures Affecting Consumer Photographic Film and Paper*, WT/DS44/R, adopted 22 April 1998. The Report reveals how the initial problems in the non-violation cases could intensify in the context of newly emerging areas, such as the GATS and competition policies.

[111] Directive 2002/21/EC of the European Parliament and the Council of 7 March 2002 on a common regulatory framework for electronic communications networks and services, OJ 2002 No. L108/33.

[112] See Art. 14(2): 'An undertaking [that] ... enjoys a position equivalent to dominance, that is to say a position of economic strength affording it the power to behave to an appreciable extent independently of competitors, customers and ultimately consumers.'

[113] See M. Bronckers, *A Cross-section of WTO Law* (London: Cameron May, 2000), p. 124.

[114] Anti-competitive practices can originate from a single major supplier or from several jointly or collusively acting undertakings. See L. B. Sherman, '"Wildly enthusiastic" about the first multilateral agreement on trade in telecommunications services' (1991) 51 *Federal Communications Law Journal* 61–110 at 77.

[115] Directive 2002/19/EC of the European Parliament and the Council of 7 March 2002 on access to, and interconnection of, electronic communications networks and associated facilities, OJ 2002 No. L108/7

[116] M. Bronckers and P. Larouche, 'Telecommunications services', in P. F. J. Macrory, A. E. Appleton and M. G. Plummer (eds.), *The World Trade Organization: Legal, Economic and Political Analysis* (New York: Springer, 2005), pp. 989–1040 at p. 1025.

## 2.5 Conclusion

The relation between the WTO and the EU is a complex one, on several distinct accounts. First, the competence situation, especially with regard to the GATS, is intricate and, after the Lisbon Treaty, the official delimitation no longer reflects the law. Second, the effect of WTO law within the EU and its Member States is a hostage of this complexity, with intricate case law with regard to the right to interpret procedural provision in the TRIPS Agreement and direct effect within the EU. Third, the scheduling practice of the EU under the GATS is as complex as the EU competence regime, and the (non-)application of the exemption for regional trade organizations betrays the difficulty of dealing with this fact. In contrast to these legal conundrums, from a practical perspective the participation of the EU in the WTO can be described as smooth and coordinated.

While the WTO and the EU may seem very different especially in institutional terms, we have shown that in WTO law there is also a discourse in terms of harmonization, effectiveness and judicial activism, concepts very much associated with the special nature of EU law. We have, however, explained that these superficial parallels hide fundamental differences in terms of the power to provide for both negative and positive integration.

We have suggested that the main difference between the WTO and the EU regime in substantive terms is the entirely different set-up of competition rules. The objectives of the WTO and of the EU in this respect are very similar. However, the instruments used in the two regimes are radically different. While a powerful, comprehensive and obligatory regime has been established in the EU, and arguably has been one of the great successes of European economic integration, such a competition law regime is lacking in the WTO. Despite its relevance, the Reference Paper on Telecommunications annexed to the GATS does not establish a comprehensive competition law regime for the WTO.[117] This compounds the other differences at a constitutional level, such as the WTO's law-making capacity and the strength of the dispute resolution system discussed above.

[117] D. Luff, 'Current international trade rules relevant to telecommunications services', in D. Geradin and D. Luff, *Global Convergence in Telecommunications and Audio-Visual Services* (Cambridge University Press, 2004), pp. 34–51 at p. 46.

# 3 EU primary law on services: fundamentals and delimitations

*Marcus Klamert and Kathrin Blanck-Putz*

## 3.1 Introduction

While the Lisbon Treaty has remodelled EU law in a number of areas, it has not modified the rules on services and establishments.[1] This means that the Court of Justice will continue to shape this area of EU law, as it has done in the past by handing down more than 600 cases since the beginnings of the EEC.[2] Some of this case law will be discussed in this chapter, while the most important development at the level of secondary law, the Services Directive, will be discussed separately in Chapters 5 and 6.

As mentioned above, the definition of services in EU law has always been narrower compared to the GATS. Under EU law, the provision of services by means of a commercial presence falls under the freedom of establishment. While the similarities between this area and the freedom to provide services outweigh their differences,[3] both the Lisbon Treaty and the Services Directive regulate establishments and services separately. We therefore need to deal with issues of the convergence of the rules for the two areas in EU law, while delimiting their scope

Kathrin Blanck-Putz, Team Leader, DG MARKT, European Commission, Brussels.

1 Article 49 TFEU on establishments and Article 56 TFEU on services have been adopted without any change in wording.

2 See V. Hatzopoulos, 'The Court's approach to services (2006–2012): from case law to case load?' (2013) 50 *Common Market Law Review* 459–502 at 460, who however notes that the role of the Court has been reduced to that of a casuistic problem-solver, leaving the development of the area to the legislator. See *ibid.*, 501.

3 See H. Jarass, 'A unified approach to the fundamental freedoms', in M. Andenas and W.-H. Roth (eds.), *Services and Free Movement in EU Law* (The Hague: Kluwer, 2002), pp. 141–62 at pp. 141ff.

from other fundamental freedoms.[4] The justification regime will be discussed for both freedoms together, as well as issues of proportionality and the test of equivalence.

In this chapter we will also discuss the rules in EU law on what can be called public services, comprising both services delivered by official authority and services of general economic interest, of which the latter is an especially complex and multi-layered legal regime, short-cutting the freedoms with state aid and public procurement law.

## 3.2 Fundamentals

### *3.2.1 The regulatory standard and establishments*

The freedom of establishment guarantees the right of legal persons defined by Article 54 TFEU and of nationals of a Member State to carry out a stable and continuous economic activity in one or more Member States. Subject to the exceptions and conditions discussed below, the freedom of establishment applies to all types of self-employed activity taken up and pursued within any other Member State, thus covering both primary and secondary establishments (agencies, branches or subsidiaries).[5] Article 49 TFEU has the following wording:

> Within the framework of the provisions set out below, restrictions on the freedom of establishment of nationals of a Member State in the territory of another Member State shall be prohibited. Such prohibition shall also apply to restrictions on the setting-up of agencies, branches or subsidiaries by nationals of any Member State established in the territory of any Member State.
>
> Freedom of establishment shall include the right to take up and pursue activities as self-employed persons and to set up and manage undertakings, in particular companies or firms within the meaning of the second paragraph of Article 54, under the conditions laid down for its own nationals by the law of the country where such establishment is effected, subject to the provisions of the Chapter relating to capital.

The freedom 'covers all measures which permit or even merely facilitate access to another Member State and the pursuit of an economic activity in that State'.[6] This includes the ancillary rights for the applicant and

[4] See e.g. Case C-55/94, *Gebhard* [1995] ECR I-4165, or Case C-384/93, *Alpine Investments* [1995] ECR I-1141, where the Court seemed to make declarations of principle applying equally to all three freedoms (i.e., the right of establishment and the free movement of services and workers).

[5] See Case C-55/94, *Gebhard* [1995] ECR I-4165, para. 23.

[6] See Case C-411/03, *SEVIC* [2005] ECR I-10805, para. 18.

his family of entry into and residence in the host country, as well as the right to remain in the territory of a Member State after having been self-employed there.[7] It affects not only national rules and practices relating directly and specifically to the pursuit of the economic activity, but also all rules 'relating to the various general facilities which are of assistance in the pursuit of those activities'.[8]

Article 49(1) TFEU prohibits 'restrictions on the freedom of establishment'. As with services and discussed below, the Court initially held this prohibition to apply only to discriminatory Member State measures,[9] and this approach has been supported in particular by the wording of Article 49(2) TFEU ('under the conditions laid down for its own nationals by the law of the country where such establishment is effected').[10] The expansion in case law from a regulatory model focusing on discriminatory measures to adopting a broader model targeting restrictions occurred more recently in the area of establishments than with services. Since the 1996 judgment in *Gebhard*, the 'restrictions approach' has been the settled standard of review as regards non-discriminatory national measures.[11]

While the freedom to provide services prohibits *any* national rule that would undermine its qualification as service provision ('very negation') by de facto transforming the activity into one constituting an establishment (authorization, registration etc.), measures by Member States on establishments are scrutinized less intensively.[12] The key

[7] See Directive 2004/38/EC of the European Parliament and the Council of 29 April 2004 on the right of citizens of the Union and their family members to move and reside freely within the territory of the Member States, OJ 2004 No. L158/77, pp. 77–123.

[8] Case 63/86, *Commission* v. *Italy (Re Housing Aid)* [1988] ECR 29, para. 14. This includes the right to purchase, exploit and transfer real and personal property and the right to obtain loans and, most importantly, to have access to the various forms of credit.

[9] Including indirect discriminations. See Case 107/83, *Ordre des avocats au Barreau de Paris* v. *Onno Klopp* [1984] ECR 2971, para. 22.

[10] See Case 107/83, *Klopp* [1984] ECR 2971, para. 17.

[11] Case C-55/94, *Gebhard* [1995] ECR I-4165. See P. Craig and G. de Búrca, *EU Law: Texts and Materials*, 5th edn (Oxford University Press, 2011), pp. 774–5. For a different perspective see J. L. Hansen, 'Full circle: is there a difference between the freedom of establishment and the freedom to provide services?', in M. Andenas and W.-H. Roth (eds.), *Services and Free Movement in EU Law* (The Hague: Kluwer, 2002), pp. 197–210 at p. 197ff.

[12] Case C-205/84, *Commission* v. *Germany (Insurance Cases)* [1986] ECR-3755, para. 52; Case C-101/94, *Commission* v. *Italy* [1996] ECR I-2691, para. 31; Case C-287/10, *Tankreederei* [2010] ECR I-14233, para. 10, on making the grant of a tax credit for investments subject to the condition that the investments in question be made in an establishment situated in national territory, that they be intended to remain there on

section in *Gebhard*, which notably does not make specific reference to the freedom of establishment, is worth quoting:

> It follows, however, from the Court's case-law that national measures liable to hinder or make less attractive the exercise of fundamental freedoms guaranteed by the Treaty must fulfil four conditions: they must be applied in a non-discriminatory manner; they must be justified by imperative requirements in the general interest; they must be suitable for securing the attainment of the objective which they pursue; and they must not go beyond what is necessary in order to attain it.[13]

The Court specified that such restrictive effects may arise 'where, on account of national legislation, a company may be deterred from setting up subsidiary entities, such as permanent establishments, in other Member States and from carrying on its activities through such entities'.[14] This has been decided with respect to an Italian rule requiring operators from other Member States to have a fully paid up capital of a minimum of EUR 10 million in order to carry out the activities of assessment, verification and collection of certain Italian local authority revenue.[15] The *Yellow Cab* case has brought an important clarification with respect to authorization requirements imposed on foreign companies.[16] After stating that the requirement of a seat or another establishment in the territory of the host Member State cannot logically constitute a restriction, the Court held that such requirement for the period *before* authorization has been granted 'has a dissuasive effect'.[17]

a permanent basis and that they be physically used in that territory. See J. Snell and M. Andenas, 'Exploring the outer limits: restrictions on the free movement of goods and services', in M. Andenas and W.-H. Roth (eds.), *Services and Free Movement in EU Law* (The Hague: Kluwer, 2002), pp. 69–140 at p. 80; V. Hatzopoulos and U. Do, 'The case law of the ECJ concerning the free provision of services: 2000–2005' (2006) 43 *Common Market Law Review* 923–91 at 956.

[13] Case C-55/94, *Gebhard* [1995] ECR I-4165, para. 37. See recently Case C-400/08, *Commission* v. *Spain (Shopping Centers)* [2011] ECR I-1915, paras. 65–71, mentioning among other things that the legislation would restrict the localities available for new establishments and impose limits on the sales areas for which such a licence could be obtained, would license new establishments only in so far as there was no effect on existing small traders, and would impose unfavourable procedures.

[14] Joined Cases C-357/10 to C-359/10, *Duomo* [2012] not yet published in the Official Journal, para. 35. Case C-384/08, *Attanasio Group* [2010] ECR I-2055, paras. 43 and 44 and the case law cited, and Case C-148/10, *DHL International* [2011] ECR I-8543, para. 60.

[15] Joined Cases C-357/10 to C-359/10, *Duomo* [2012] not yet published in the Official Journal.

[16] Case C-338/09, *Yellow Cab* [2010] ECR I-3297.

[17] Case C-338/09, *Yellow Cab* [2010] ECR I-3297, paras. 36–40.

In addition to EU nationals, the freedom of establishment extends to all nationals of the European Economic Area.[18] The Treaty provisions on establishment have been found directly applicable by the Court in its decision in *Reyners*.[19]

### 3.2.2 *The regulatory standard with services*

Article 56(1) TFEU provides that 'restrictions on freedom to provide services within the Union shall be prohibited in respect of nationals of Member States who are established in a Member State other than that of the person for whom the services are intended'. Service providers or recipients are natural persons or legal persons legally established in one of the Member States of the Union, requiring a permanent economic infrastructure within a Member State.[20] Article 57 TFEU defines services being 'normally provided for remuneration, in so far as they are not governed by the provisions relating to freedom of movement for goods, capital and persons'. In particular, services include (a) activities of an industrial character; (b) activities of a commercial character; (c) activities of craftsmen; and (d) activities of the professions. Article 57 TFEU continues:

> Without prejudice to the provisions of the Chapter relating to the right of establishment, the person providing a service may, in order to do so, temporarily pursue his activity in the Member State where the service is provided, under the same conditions as are imposed by that State on its own nationals.

As mentioned, Article 56 TFEU has initially been construed as a prohibition of both directly and indirectly discriminatory measures by a Member State.[21] The Court then also proceeded to apply it to non-

[18] See Arts. 31–35 of the Agreement on the European Economic Area, OJ 1994 L 1/1; and in particular the EEA Joint Committee, Decision No. 190/1999 of 17 December 1999, OJ 2001, L74/26; and EEA Joint Committee, Decision No. 191/1999 of 17 December 1999, OJ 2001, L74/29. The same holds true for Swiss nationals based on the agreement of free movement between the EU and its fifteen (old) Member States on the one side and the Swiss Confederation on the other side, which took effect as of 1 June 2002. See the Agreement between the European Community and its Member States, of the one part, and the Swiss Confederation, of the other, on the free movement of persons, OJ 2002 No. L114/468, pp. 6–63. It is supplemented by a protocol extending free movement to the ten new EU Member States while providing for transitional safeguard measures. The protocol on the extension of free movement to the new Member States and the improved safeguard measures was approved by 56 per cent of Swiss voters during a popular vote held on 25 September 2005.

[19] Case 2/74, *Reyners* [1974] 631, para. 10.

[20] This also includes state-run and public enterprises.

[21] See among others Case 33/74, *van Binsbergen* [1974] ECR 1299, para. 10.

discriminatory measures, irrespective of whether such restriction is put up by the host Member State or by the state of origin of the service provider.[22] The leading case for this is *Säger* on the requirement of having a lawyer's licence to provide patent renewal services in Germany, where the Court held as follows:

> It should first be pointed out that Article [49] of the Treaty requires not only the elimination of all discrimination against a person providing services on the ground of his nationality but also the abolition of any restriction, even if it applies without distinction to national providers of services and to those of other Member States, when it is liable to prohibit or otherwise impede the activities of a provider of services established in another Member State where he lawfully provides similar services.[23]

Moreover, Article 56 TFEU has been held to preclude the application of national rules 'which have the effect of making the provision of services between Member States more difficult than the provision of services purely within a Member State'.[24] In other cases, the Court spoke of obstacles 'liable to prohibit, to impede or to render less advantageous the activities of a provider of services established in another Member State in which he lawfully provides similar services'.[25] In the *Peñarroja* case this concerned registers of court translators considered likely to influence the choice made by the courts on whom to appoint, even when selection from the registers was not mandatory.[26] In other cases the Court referred to the attractiveness of the exercise of the freedom, or to the discouragement from providing services.[27] Thus measures are qualified as restrictions if they either 'prohibit, impede or render less

[22] C-384/93, *Alpine Investments* [1995] ECR I-1141, para. 30. See also J. L. Da Cruz Vilaça, 'On the application of Keck in the field of free provision of services', in M. Andenas and W.-H. Roth (eds.), *Services and Free Movement in EU Law* (Oxford University Press, 2003), pp. 25–40 at p. 29.

[23] Case C-76/90, *Säger* [1991] ECR I-4221, para. 12. See also Joined Cases C-403/08 and C-429/08, *Football Association Premier League* [2011] ECR I-9083, para. 85; Joined Cases C-357/10 to C-359/10, *Duomo* [2012] not yet published in the Official Journal, para. 36.

[24] Joined Cases C-357/10 to C-359/10, *Duomo* [2012] not yet published in the Official Journal, para. 36. See also Case C-381/93, *Commission* v. *France* [1994] ECR I-5145, para. 17; Case C-250/06, *United Pan-Europe Communications* [2007] ECR I-11135, para. 30; Joined Cases C-155/08 and C-157/08, *X and Passenheim-van Schoot* [2009] ECR I-5093, para. 32; Case C-287/10, *Tankreederei* [2010] ECR I-14233, para. 15.

[25] Joined Cases C-372/09 and C-373/09, *Peñarroja* [2011] ECR I-1785, para. 50.

[26] Joined Cases C-372/09 and C-373/09, *Peñarroja* [2011] ECR I-1785, paras. 52–3.

[27] Case C-287/10, *Tankreederei* [2010] ECR I-14233, para. 15; Case C-330/07, *Jobra* [2008] ECR I-9099, paras. 15 and 17 respectively.

attractive' the exercise of the freedom.[28] While these can be seen as codes for different 'degrees of restrictiveness', to which we will return later in this book, Enchelmaier has shown that, from the case law of the Court, no conclusions can be drawn on the basis of these different formulae.[29]

With respect to the modes of providing respectively of receiving services, the jurisprudence of the Court has undergone the same development from the strong adherence to the black letter of the Treaty in early case law to an increasingly expansive stance. Thus, with the judgment in *Luisi and Carbone*, service recipients both in the home state as well as in the host state (e.g. tourist services, medical services) were covered by the freedom.[30] The decision in *Koestler* on banking and insurance services brought what in EU law are called correspondence services into the scope of Article 56 TFEU.[31] These are the same as cross-border services under Mode 1 in the GATS, and have subsequently been the basis of Court judgments on TV broadcasting,[32] telecommunication services[33] and advertising.[34] On online gambling services the Court held that Article 56 TFEU applies even when the provider makes use of intermediaries established in the Member State of the service recipients,[35] or makes use only of computer support services in the host Member State.[36]

Article 56 TFEU also covers situations in which both the service provider and the recipient cross the border where the service will then be rendered. This is treated as a distinct category in EU law (in contrast to the GATS), and the classic example is a tourist guide accompanying a group of tourists into another Member State.

[28] Case C-565/08, *Commission* v. *Italy (Maximum Fee Tariffs)* [2011] ECR I-2101, para. 45.

[29] S. Enchelmaier, 'Always at your service (within limits): the ECJ's case law on Article 56 TFEU (2006–11)' (2011) 36 *European Law Review* 615–50 at 618–30.

[30] Joined Cases 286/82 and 26/83, *Luisi and Carbone* [1984] ECR 377, para. 10. In the Court's view the extended scope of application constituted the 'necessary corollary' of the narrow wording of Art. 50(3) Treaty establishing the European Community (EC) in order to fulfil the objective of 'liberalizing all gainful activity'.

[31] Case 15/78, *Koestler* [1978] ECR 1971, para. 3.

[32] Case 155/73, *Sacchi* [1974] ECR 409, para. 6.

[33] Case C17/00, *De Coster* [2001] ECR I-9445.

[34] Case C-405/98, *Gourmet* [2001] ECR I-1795. See also Directive 2000/31/EC of the European Parliament and the Council of 8 June 2000 on certain legal aspects of information society services, in particular electronic commerce, in the internal market, OJ 2000 No. L178/1.

[35] Case C-243/01, *Gambelli* [2003] ECR I-13031, para. 58.

[36] Case C-347/09, *Dickinger* [2011] ECR I-8185, para. 37.

The rights enacted in Article 56 TFEU can be relied upon by the provider or by the recipient individually, and they are directly effective.[37] In its controversial decision in *Carpenter*, the Court further stretched the scope of application to the partner of a service provider, arguing that any separation would be detrimental not only to their family life, but would also render the right of the service provider ineffective.[38] Moreover, the Court extended the personal scope of application to the recipient claiming privileges emanating from the Union freedom on behalf of the provider. This is of particular importance for employers of so-called posted workers.[39]

### *3.2.3 Some specifics on companies*

With regard to companies, Article 54 TFEU provides:

> Companies or firms formed in accordance with the law of a Member State and having their registered office, central administration or principal place of business within the Union shall, for the purposes of this Chapter, be treated in the same way as natural persons who are nationals of Member States.

As mentioned, any company has the right to carry out its business in another Member State by forming an agency, branch or subsidiary. The 'connecting factor with the legal system of a particular State'[40] is the location of a company's registered office, its central administration, its principal place of business, or another presence operated by the company's own staff.[41]

The general prohibition of restrictions under Article 49 TFEU also prohibits discriminatory tax treatment. Thus any tax provision differentiating between companies registered in the host state and those registered in another Member State runs counter to Article 49 TFEU.[42] In *Sodemare* the Court held that non-discriminatory restrictions regarding the legal form of a company incorporated in another Member State violate Article 49 TFEU.[43] Furthermore, in the seminal *Centros* judgment host states were precluded from denying registration of a branch or agency of a company validly incorporated in another Member State,

[37] Case 33/74, *van Binsbergen* [1974] ECR 1299, para. 27.

[38] See Case C-60/00, *Carpenter* [2002] I-6279, para. 39.

[39] See Case C-58/98, *Corsten* [2000] ECR I-7919; Case C-294/97, *Eurowings* [1999] ECR I-7447.

[40] Case C-212/97, *Centros* [1999] ECR I-1459, para. 20.

[41] Case C-205/84, *Commission* v. *Germany (Insurance Cases)* [1986] ECR-3755, para. 21.

[42] Case 270/83, *Commission* v. *France ('Avoir Fiscal')* [1986] ECR 273, para. 22.

[43] Case C-70/95, *Sodemare* [1997] ECR I-3395, para. 33.

irrespective of whether the undertaking's objective was solely to circumvent the more rigid and costly incorporation rules of the host state.[44] In its *Daily Mail* decision the Court put this broad interpretation of the freedom of establishment into perspective. It found the Treaty not applicable to a situation where a change of primary establishment involves a transfer of a company's central management and control to another Member State, while retaining the status as company incorporated under the legislation of the first Member State.[45] Consequently, Member States enjoy much more regulatory leeway regarding primary establishments, as they may prevent entities incorporated under national law from moving their main seat to another Member State. They have, in contrast, little or even no discretion at all to refuse a foreign-incorporated company to set up any legally permitted form of secondary establishment on their territory.

Finally, in *Überseering* the Court decided on the question of a foreign-incorporated entity's legal capacity. It concluded that the host state is required to fully recognize the legal capacity of a company incorporated in another Member State and exercising its freedom of establishment, which includes its right to be party to legal proceedings.[46] The Court held that the application of Articles 49 and 50 TFEU is not impaired by the fact that the company does not conduct any actual business in the country of incorporation and that it was set up in that country only for the purpose of establishing itself in the second country where its main, or even entire, business is to be carried out. The same holds true if this procedure was employed only in order to circumvent national legislation.[47]

[44] Case C-212/97, *Centros* [1999] ECR I-1459, para. 30.

[45] Case 81/87, *Daily Mail* [1988] ECR 5483, para. 25.

[46] Case C-208/00, *Überseering* [2002] ECR I-9919, para. 94.

[47] All this has raised considerable controversy in literature and uncertainty in practice as to the compatibility of the so-called 'real seat theory' with the freedom of establishment. It is commonly distinguished between the 'real seat doctrine' and the 'incorporation doctrine' in order to determine the laws applicable to a company when it has links to more than one jurisdiction. On this see among others K. Baelz and T. Baldwin, 'The end of the real seat theory (Sitztheorie): the European Court of Justice decision in Ueberseering of 5 November 2002 and its impact on German and European company law' (2002) 3 *German Law Journal*, available at www.germanlawjournal.com/index.php?pageID=11&artID=214; N. Rothe, 'Freedom of establishment of legal persons within the European Union: an analysis of the European Court of Justice decision in the Überseering case' (2004) *American University Law Review* 1103–41.

### 3.2.4 *Constitutive elements*

#### 3.2.4.1 Introduction

The Court of Justice, in its case law, developed some constitutive elements for the freedom of establishment and the freedom to provide services to apply. However, most of these criteria are in a state of flux, especially when they were originally used to demarcate the scope of application of the one freedom from the other, or when they were initially cabining the scope of the freedoms altogether. Both freedoms are concerned with self-employed persons, thus their taking-up and pursuit of any (generally gainful) economic activity while assuming all the risks and responsibilities linked to the business enterprise. The blurring of the borders between the freedom of establishment and the freedom to provide services can be seen in the context of 'a more economic approach to services'.[48] Instead of applying formal criteria such as duration and remuneration, it should be decisive on whether the activity requires more profound regulation. As mentioned, this has produced case law where the Court has applied both Articles 49 and 56 TFEU when examining national restrictions affecting self-employed activity within the Union.[49] However, this does not allow for the conclusion that all differences between the two freedoms have been foregone.[50]

#### 3.2.4.2 Inter-state element

In its early case law the Court emphasized the requirement of a transborder element for the freedom to provide services to apply.[51] This test has been relaxed in cases such as *Alpine Investment*, and the existence of virtual or future service recipients has been deemed sufficient.[52] Similarly, the Court showed a tendency to accept that cross-border mobility may only be a mere possibility, and that a service may be available only in order to fulfil the inter-state test, even if the service

[48] See Hatzopoulos, 'The Court's approach to services (2006–2012)', 464.

[49] Joined Cases C-357/10 to C-359/10, *Duomo* [2012] not yet published in the Official Journal, para. 33. See Hatzopoulos and Do, 'The case law of the ECJ', 30ff.

[50] For further details see, Hansen, 'Full circle', pp. 197–209.

[51] See Case 52/79, *Debauve* [1980] ECR 833, para. 9.

[52] Case C-384/93, *Alpine Investments* [1995] ECR I-1141, para. 22. This argument was further developed in the highly controversial *Carpenter* judgment. See Case C-60/00, *Carpenter* [2002] I-6279, para. 30. See V. Hatzopoulos, 'Recent development of the case law of the ECJ in the field of free movement of services 1994–2000' (2000) *Common Market Law Review* 43–82, 58.

provider and service recipient are situated within the same Member State.[53] At the same time, however, the Court drew a line with regard to purely hypothetical service cases.[54] In the *Duomo* case and in other case law, the Court argued that companies from other Member States (other than Italy) might be interested in pursuing the service activities on issue in this case, even though the actual case had concerned only Italian companies.[55] It seems that such interest would have to be 'inconceivable' in order to fall short of the inter-state requirement.[56] It also argued, rather disingenuously, that the admission of the case was necessary in the event that national law required the referring court to give national companies the same rights that foreign companies would derive from EU law.[57] Moreover, it held that provisions or concepts taken from Union law should be interpreted uniformly, irrespective of the circumstances in which they apply.[58]

According to Article 49 TFEU, any restriction with regard to 'nationals of a Member State in the territory of another Member State' is prohibited. In its case law the Court showed some tendency to accept reliance on the freedom of establishment by nationals to challenge restrictions of their home country, provided there is a genuine factual element transcending a purely national setting.[59] Lawful residence and vocational training obtained in another Member State, for instance,

[53] See Joined Cases C-51/96 and C-191/97, *Deliège* [2000] ECR I-2549, para. 59. See also Hatzopoulos, 'The Court's approach to services (2006–2012)', 472, on the public procurement case law.

[54] See Case C-215/03, *Oulane* [2005] ECR I-1215.

[55] Joined Cases C-357/10 to C-359/10, *Duomo* [2012] not yet published in the Official Journal, para. 27. See also Case C-448/98, *Guimont* [2000] ECR I-10663, para. 21; Case C-6/01, *Anomar* [2003] ECR I-8621, para. 39; Case C-451/03, *Servizi Ausiliari* [2006] ECR I-2941, para. 29; Case C-384/08, *Attanasio Group* [2010] ECR I-2055, paras. 23 and 24; and Joined Cases C-570/07 and C-571/07, *Pérez and Gómez* [2010] ECR I-4629, paras. 39 and 40. See AG Cruz Villalón in Joined Cases C-357/10 to C-359/10, *Duomo* [2012] not yet published in the Official Journal, para. 36.

[56] See Case C-470/11, *SIA Garkalns* [2012] not yet published in the Official Journal, para. 21. For an interesting analogy with the *Dassonville* formula ('actually or potentially'), see Enchelmaier, 'Always at your service', 618. However, a difference might be that this formula does not decide on admissibility, in contrast to the inter-state element.

[57] Joined Cases C-357/10 to C-359/10, *Duomo* [2012] not yet published in the Official Journal, para. 28; Case C-327/12, *SOA* [2013] not yet published in the Official Journal, para. 49. But see Case C-245/09, *Omalet* [2010] ECR I-3771, where this was denied because the Belgian Constitutional Court had found that internal and external situations were not comparable. Critical of this case law is also Enchelmaier, 'Always at your service (within limits)', 617.

[58] Case C-522/12, *Tevfik* [2013] not yet published in the Official Journal, para. 28.

[59] Case C-19/92, *Kraus* [1993] ECR I-1663, para. 15.

sufficed to constitute a cross-border element rendering Union law applicable.[60]

### 3.2.4.3 Economic activity/remuneration

Economic activity comprises any work that is 'genuine and effective and not such as to be regarded as purely marginal and ancillary'.[61] This definition includes, among other things, gainful activities of professional or semi-professional sportsmen or sportswomen,[62] as well as commercial activities performed by members of religious communities, if the services rendered by the community to its members constitute the indirect quid pro quo for genuine and effective work.[63]

It is generally deemed to apply to any economic activity within the ambit of the Treaty that is provided for consideration.[64] This remuneration must normally be agreed upon between the provider and the recipient of the service.[65] It has thus been broadly construed by the Court to include sports activities,[66] cultural services such as those of tourist guides[67] and broadcasting services.[68] Particular difficulties arise with regard to services remunerated by the state. As regards educational services, the Court differentiated according to the means of financing.[69] Hence privately remunerated schools or institutions may qualify as service providers, whereas publicly financed education is not covered by Article 56 TFEU.[70]

Similarly, it has proven difficult to draw a clear line between publicly and privately remunerated services in the field of health services.[71] The

[60] See e.g. Case 114/78, *Knoors* [1979] ECR 399, para. 24; Case 204/87, *Bekaert* [1988] ECR 2029, para. 12; Case C-61/89, *Bouchoucha* [1990] ECR I-3551, para. 13; Case C-19/92, *Kraus* [1993] ECR I-1663, para. 15.

[61] See Case C-196/87, *Steymann* [1988] ECR 6159, para. 13.

[62] See Case C-415/93, *Bosman* [1995] ECR I-4921, para. 73 with further references.

[63] Case C-196/87, *Steymann* [1988] ECR 6159, para. 14.

[64] Case 36/74, *Walrave* [1974] ECR 1405, para. 4.

[65] Joined Cases C-372/09 and C373/09, *Peñarroja* [2011] ECR I-1785, para. 37. See also Case C-355/00, *Freskot* [2003] ECR I-5263, paras. 54 and 55, and Case C-169/08, *Presidente del Consiglio dei Ministri* [2009] ECR I-10821, para. 23.

[66] Joined Cases C51/96 and C-191/97, *Deliège* [2000] ECR I-2549.

[67] Case C-198/89, *Commission* v. *Greece (Tourist Guides)* [1991] ECR I-727, para. 7.

[68] See among others Case 155/73, *Sacchi* [1974] ECR 409, para. 6.

[69] Case 263/86, *Humbel* [1988] ECR 5365, paras. 17–19.

[70] See the summary of the case law of the Court on this in Rec. 34 of Directive 2006/123/EC of the European Parliament and the Council of 12 December 2006 on services in the internal market, OJ 2006 No. L376/36.

[71] It is now undisputed that health services fall under the scope of Article 56 TFEU. See Joined Cases C-286/82 and 26/83, *Luisi and Carbone* [1984] ECR 377, para. 16 and

Court extended the traditional definition of remuneration as a 'consideration for the service in question ... normally agreed upon between the provider and the recipient of the service'[72] to include triangular situations such as in the social security sector,[73] and even indirect remuneration such as through sponsorship and TV broadcasting deals.[74] It, moreover, adopted a similar position with regard to services due to be rendered some decades later as with payments for old-age pensions.[75] As a matter of principle, it does not distinguish between care provided in a hospital environment (*intra mural*) and care provided outside such an environment (*extra mural*).[76] However, the Court has found that treatment in the former situation may be subject to prior authorization in the home state of the services recipient, based on the public interest in maintaining a balanced medical and hospital service for the entire population.[77] Such authorization procedure must comply with requirements of transparency, timeliness and legal protection. Moreover, it may not be refused for treatment that would be excluded for purely national reasons, nor if the patient cannot be given the treatment within the time normally necessary for obtaining the treatment in the Member State of residence, taking into account the actual and prospective state of health of the patient concerned.[78] In contrast, this authorization requirement does not apply to non-hospital treatment in another Member State. For this, patients are entitled to reimbursement of costs based on the tariffs of their home state.[79] Directive 2011/24/EU has recently codified this

C-159/90, *Grogan* [1991] ECR I-4685, para. 18; The Court does not differentiate between individual national health security systems: see Case C-157/99, *Smits and Peerboms* [2001] ECR I-5473, para. 55. See, among others, A. Dawes, '"Bonjour Herr Doctor": national healthcare systems, the internal market and cross-border medical care within the European Union' (2006) 33(2) *Legal Issues of Economic Integration* 167–82.

72 See Case 263/86, *Humbel* [1988] ECR 5365, para. 17.

73 See among other Case C-157/99, *Smits and Peerboms* [2001] ECR I-5473.

74 Joined Cases C-51/96 and C-191/97, *Deliège* [2000] ECR I-2549; Case C-157/99, *Smits and Peerboms* [2001] ECR I-5473.

75 Case C-136/00, *Danner* [2002] ECR I-8147; Case C-422/01, *Ramstedt* [2003] ECR I-6817.

76 Case C-368/98, *Vanbraekeland* [2001] ECR I-5363, para. 41, Case C-490/09, *Commission* v. *Luxemburg (Laboratory Costs)* ECR [2011] I-247, para. 34.

77 Case C-158/96, *Kohll* [1998] ECR I-1931, para. 50; Case C-56/01, *Inizan* [2003] ECR I-2403, para. 56.

78 See Case C-372/04, *Watts* [2006] ECR I-4325, para. 114 while drawing on Case C-157/99, *Smits and Peerboms* [2001] ECR I-5473, para. 82 and Case C-385/99, *Müller-Fauré* [2003] ECR I-4509, para. 83.

79 See Case C-372/04, *Watts* [2006] ECR I-4325, paras. 113 *et seq.*

complex case law.[80] It makes authorization the rule and provides an exhaustive list of reasons for refusing authorization.[81]

### 3.2.4.4 Permanence/duration

The third 'classic' criterion for finding the freedom to provide services applicable is the duration of the economic activity and has lost its importance over the years. In *Gebhard* the Court agreed with the argument put forward by AG Léger that the temporary nature of the activities 'has to be determined in the light, not only of the duration of the provision of the service, but also of its regularity, periodicity or continuity'.[82] This may include service providers availing themselves of some permanent infrastructure in the host state without necessarily triggering the applicability of Article 49 TFEU.[83] Duration is therefore not decisive for distinguishing the provision of services from the freedom of establishment.[84] This creates a more flexible legal background for applying the pertinent freedom, which is aptly expressed by the Court in the *Schnitzer* case with the following words:

[80] Directive 2011/24/EU of the European Parliament and the Council of 9 March 2011 on the application of patients' rights in cross-border healthcare, OJ 2011 No. L88/45. See S. de la Rosa, 'The Directive on Cross-border Healthcare or the art of codifying complex case law' (2012) 49 *Common Market Law Review* 15–46.

[81] Art. 8(6) Directive 2011/24/EU lists unacceptable patient-safety risks, a substantial safety hazard for the general public, serious and specific concerns relating to the respect of standards and guidelines on quality of care and patient safety by the healthcare provider, and that healthcare can be provided domestically within a time limit which is medically justifiable.

[82] Case Case C-55/94, *Gebhard* [1995] ECR I-4165, para. 27. See also Opinion of AG Léger in Case C-55/94, *Gebhard* [1995] ECR I-4165, paras. 31 *et seq.*

[83] Case Case C-55/94, *Gebhard* [1995] ECR I-4165, para. 27.

[84] It is interesting to note that in the proposal for the Directive on the recognition of professional qualifications the Commission was ready to accept a quantitative definition. Any cross-border provision of services not exceeding a maximum time limit of sixteen weeks per year was proposed to fall within the ambit of Art. 56 EC. See European Commission, Proposal on a Directive on the recognition of professional qualifications, COM(2002)119, Art. 5(2). However, this limitation has been dropped in the final version which solely requires the service provider to pursue its action 'on a temporary and occasional basis'. See Art. 5 Directive 2005/36/EC of the European Parliament and the Council of 7 September 2005 on the recognition of professional qualifications, OJ 2005 No. L255/22. The second paragraph also states that 'the temporary and occasional nature of the provision of services shall be assessed case by case, in particular in relation to its duration, its frequency, its regularity and its continuity'.

> Thus, services within the meaning of the Treaty may cover services varying widely in nature, including services which are provided over an extended period, even over several years, where, for example, the services in question are supplied in connection with the construction of a large building. Services within the meaning of the Treaty may likewise be constituted by services which a business established in a Member State supplies with a greater or lesser degree of frequency or regularity, even over an extended period, to persons established in one or more other Member States, for example the giving of advice or information for remuneration.[85]

Thus 'no provision of the Treaty affords a means of determining, in an abstract manner, the duration or frequency beyond which the supply of a service or of a certain type of service in another Member State can no longer be regarded as the provision of services within the meaning of the Treaty'.[86]

The prerequisite for the application of the freedom of establishment, that it should entitle persons 'to participate, on a stable and continuous basis'[87] in the economic life of another Member State, has therefore taken on a qualitative rather than a temporal connotation. In other words, permanence primarily equates with permanent integration into the host state's economy, either through creating a sole place of business in the host state or by founding secondary establishments. This does not necessarily require the physical presence of a natural person, but may be fulfilled by means of setting up and managing undertakings, or even by assuming financial control of a company established in another Member State giving a person definite influence over the company's decisions and allowing them to determine its activities.[88] The same holds true with regard to merger activities between a foreign company and an undertaking incorporated at the national level.[89] It may also be done by means of an office managed by a person who is independent but authorized to act on a permanent basis for the operator, such as with an agency.[90]

[85] Case C-215/01, *Schnitzer* [2003] ECR I-14847, paras. 30 and 31.

[86] Case C-171/02, *Commission* v. *Portugal (Private Security Firms)* [2004] I-5645, para. 26. See also Case C-208/07, *von Chamier-Glisczinski* [2009] ECR I-6095, para. 74; Case C-97/09, *Schmelz* [2010] ECR I-465, para. 42; and Case C-359/10, *Duomo* [2012] not yet published in the Official Journal, para. 32.

[87] Case C-55/94, *Gebhard* [1995] ECR I-4165, para. 25.

[88] Case C-251/98, *Baars* [2000] ECR I-2787, para. 22.

[89] See Case C-411/03, *SEVIC* [2005] ECR I-10805.

[90] Case C-347/09, *Dickinger* [2011] ECR I-8185, para. 35; Joined Cases C-316/07, C-358/07 to C-360/07, C-409/07 and C-410/07, *Stoß* [2010] ECR I-8069, paras. 59 and 60.

## 3.3 The justification regime

### 3.3.1 Introduction

Article 49 TFEU on establishments applies the same regime on justifications for national measures as does Article 56 TFEU on services discussed below. Discriminatory measures are commonly held to be subject only to the express Treaty derogations, whereas non-discriminatory measures may be justified by a broader list of mandatory requirements.[91] However, we will show that this distinction is shrouded in ambiguity, and increasingly undermined by developments in case law. We will also discuss the proportionality test and the test of equivalence, which can be seen as an element of proportionality, but should also be seen in the greater frame of mutual recognition.

### 3.3.2 General (treaty-based) justifications

Pursuant to Articles 52 and 62 TFEU, both discriminatory and non-discriminatory Member State measures in the fields of services and establishments may be justified by three specific reasons:[92]

> The provisions of this Chapter and measures taken in pursuance thereof shall not prejudice the applicability of provisions laid down by law, regulation or administrative action providing for special treatment for foreign nationals on grounds of public policy, public security or public health.

Any such measure must constitute an indispensable condition for attaining the mentioned objectives.[93] In the same vein, these three explicit grounds of justification must be interpreted narrowly,[94] although Member States have some discretion with regard to public policy and security.[95]

[91] See N. Maydell, 'The Services Directive and existing community law', in F. Breuss, G. Fink and S. Griller (eds.), *Services Liberalisation in the Internal Market* (Vienna, New York: Springer, 2008), pp. 21–124 at p. 56 with further references.

[92] See also Case C-158/96, *Kohll* [1998] ECR I-1931, para. 31; Joined Cases C-357/10 to C-359/10, *Duomo* [2012] not yet published in the Official Journal, para. 39; Case C-212/08, *Zeturf* [2011] ECR I-5633, para. 37; and Case C-347/09, *Dickinger* [2011] ECR I-8185, para. 42.

[93] See also Case C-222/95, *Parodi* [1997] ECR I-3899, para. 31; Case C-493/99, *Commission* v. *Germany* [2001] ECR I-8163, para. 19.

[94] Case C-260/89, *ERT* [1991] ECR I-2925; Case C-355/98, *Commission* v. *Belgium* [2000] ECR I-1221; Case C-398/95, *SETTG* [1997] ECR I-3091, para. 23.

[95] Case 41/74, *Van Duyn* [1974] ECR 1337, paras. 18 and 19.

The public policy ground demands that there is a genuine and sufficiently serious threat to a fundamental interest of society.[96] Under the public health ground falls the objective of maintaining a balanced medical and hospital service open to all, in so far as such an objective contributes to the attainment of a high level of health protection.[97] Economic policy considerations cannot qualify as justification within the public policy context as stipulated in Article 52 TFEU.[98] Thus the generation of levies on the proceeds of authorized gambling can only be an ancillary beneficial consequence and not the substantive justification for a restrictive policy on gambling.[99] Moreover, the Court held that the administrative inconvenience of having to supervise more operators than would be active under a monopoly cannot justify restrictions.[100]

However, pursuant to Article 106 TFEU, specific exemptions from the applicability of the Treaty are granted with regard to services of general economic interest, as discussed below.

### 3.3.3 *Specific (case law-based) justifications*

Non-discriminatory measures can be justified by 'overriding requirements of the general interest'.[101] This legal construct, not expressly enshrined in the Treaty, has been developed by the ECJ in close analogy to the system of express justifications just mentioned.[102] So far the Court has recognized more than twenty (non-exhaustive) overriding requirements.[103] Note that the specific reasons of justification tend to

[96] Joined Cases 115/81 and 116/81, *Adoui* [1982] ECR 1665, para. 8; Case C-268/99, *Jany* [2001] ECR I-8615, para. 59; Case C-161/07, *Commission* v. *Austria (Self-certification)* [2008] ECR I-10671, para. 35.

[97] See Joined Cases C-357/10 to C-359/10, *Duomo* [2012] not yet published in the Official Journal, para. 43; Case C-158/96, *Kohll* [1998] ECR I-1931, para. 50.

[98] See Case C243/01, *Gambelli* [2003] ECR I-13031, para. 61; Case C-153/08 *Commission* v. *Spain* [2009] ECR I-9735, para. 43; Case C-212/08, *Zeturf* [2011] ECR I-5633, para. 52; Case C-109/04, *Kranemann* [2005] ECR I-2421, para. 34; Joined Cases C-72/10 and C-77/10, *Costa* [2012] not yet published in the Official Journal, para. 59.

[99] Case C-212/08, *Zeturf* [2011] 5633, para. 52; Case C275/92, *Schindler* [1994] ECR I-1039, para. 60, and Case C-67/98, *Zenatti* [1999] ECR I-7289, para. 36.

[100] Case C-212/08, *Zeturf* [2011] ECR I-5633, para. 52; Case C-386/04, *Stauffer* [2006] ECR I-8203, para. 48; Case C-318/07, *Persche* [2009] ECR I-359, para. 55.

[101] We will use the terms 'mandatory requirements', 'objective justifications', 'imperative requirements', 'justifications' and 'derogations' interchangeably, as does, apparently, the ECJ. See Craig and de Búrca, *EU Law*, p. 800; C. Barnard, *The Substantive Law of the EU*, 3rd edn (Oxford University Press, 2010), p. 166.

[102] This was acknowledged for the free movement of services in Case C-222/95, *Parodi* [1997] ECR I-3899, para. 19, among others.

[103] The number of requirements counted depends on the systematization approach used. See S. O'Leary and J. Fernández-Martín, 'Judicially-created exceptions to the

be applied uniformly with regard to all freedoms.[104] Thus in the *Gambelli* case, the national measure was examined for justification under both Article 49 and Article 56 TFEU without differentiating between the two regimes.[105]

In the *Gouda* case the Court acknowledged the application of the following public interest requirements:[106]

- professional rules intended to protect recipients of the service;
- the protection of intellectual property;
- the protection of workers;
- consumer protection;
- the conservation of the national historic and artistic heritage; and
- the widest possible dissemination of knowledge of the artistic and cultural heritage of a country.

Other case law (without claiming to give the complete picture) has invoked the following justifications:

- the integrity of the legal system;[107]
- the independence of accountant services;[108]
- the independence of lawyers concerning professional secrecy obligations;[109]
- maintaining the good reputation of the financial sector;[110]
- the protection of the stability of the securities market;[111]
- the protection of the quality of manufacturing and processing services;[112]
- the integrity of the flow of trade;[113]

free provision of services', in M. Andenas and W.-H. Roth (eds.), *Services and Free Movement in EU Law* (The Hague: Kluwer, 2002), pp. 163–96 at pp. 170–1.

104 Hatzopoulos and Do, 'The case law of the ECJ', 963.

105 Case C-243/01, *Gambelli*, [2003] ECR I-13031. See Hatzopoulos and Do, 'The case law of the ECJ', 963–4, who present an even more general argument based on Case C-322/01, *DocMorris* [2003] ECR I-14887, which concerned services and goods.

106 Case C-288/89, *Gouda* [1991] ECR I-4007, para. 14.

107 Case C-3/95, *Reisebüro Broede* [1996] ECR I-6511.

108 Case C-106/91, *Ramrath* [1992] ECR I-3351.

109 Case C-309/99, *Wouters* [2002] ECR I-1577.

110 Case C-384/93, *Alpine Investments* [1995] ECR I-1141.

111 Case C-101/94, *Commission* v. *Italy* [1996] ECR I-2691.

112 Case C-58/98, *Corsten* [2000] ECR I-7919.

113 Joined Cases C-34/95, C-35/95, C-36/95, *De Agostini* [1997] ECR I-3843.

- the protection of the social system;[114]
- road traffic safety;[115]
- safety of maritime transport in ports;[116]
- environmental protection;[117]
- the imposition of public service obligations in connection with the granting of a licence;[118]
- the protection of fundamental rights;[119]
- the protection of litigants and the sound administration of justice;[120]
- the protection of the recipients of services in general[121] and of recipients of gambling services in particular;[122]
- the risk of seriously undermining the financial balance of the social security system;[123]
- town and country planning;[124] and
- the effective collection of tax.[125]

Whether the protection of public authorities against possible non-performance by the concession-holder qualifies as another overriding reason in the general interest remained unclear in *Duomo*.[126]

While Member States relying on an overriding reason in the public interest must demonstrate that its legislation is appropriate and necessary to attain the objective pursued, they are not required to 'prove, positively, that no other conceivable measure could enable that objective to be attained under the same conditions'.[127]

[114] Case C-275/92, *Schindler* [1994] ECR I-1039; C-124/97, *Läärä* [1999] ECR I-6067; Case C-67/98, *Zenatti* [1999] ECR I-7289; Case C-159/90, *Grogan* [1991] ECR I-4685.

[115] Case C-249/00, *Commission* v. *Netherlands* [2003] ECR I-7485, para. 67.

[116] Case C-266/96, *Corsica Ferries* [1998] ECR I-3949.

[117] Case C-451/99, *Cura Anlagen* [2002] ECR I-3193; Case C-384/08, *Attanasio Group* [2010] ECR I-2055, para. 50

[118] Case C-205/99, *Analir* [2001] ECR I-1271; Joined Cases C-430/99, *Sea-Land Service and* C-431/99, *Nedlloyd Lijnen* [2002] ECR I-5235.

[119] Case C-112/00, *Schmidberger* [2003] ECR I-5659, paras. 71–4.

[120] Joined Cases C-372/09 and C-373/09, *Peñarroja* [2011] ECR I-1785, para. 55.

[121] Case C-327/12, *SOA* [2013] not yet published in the Official Journal, para. 61.

[122] C-347/09, *Dickinger* [2011] ECR I-8185, para. 44; Joined Cases C-316/07, C-358/07 to C-360/07, C-409/07 and C-410/07, *Stoß* [2010] ECR I-8069, para. 74.

[123] Case C-490/09, *Commission* v. *Luxemburg (Laboratory Costs)* ECR [2011] I-247, para. 43 with further references.

[124] Case C-400/08, *Commission* v. *Spain (Shopping Centers)* [2011] ECR I-1915, para. 74

[125] Case C-34/98, *Commission* v. *France (Social Security)* [2000] ECR I-995.

[126] Joined Cases C-357/10 to C-359/10, *Duomo* [2012] not yet published in the Official Journal, paras. 40–2.

[127] Case C-400/08, *Commission* v. *Spain (Shopping Centers)* [2011] ECR I-1915, para. 75.

### 3.3.4 *Convergence of the justification regime*

While initially only non-discriminatory measures could be justified by overriding requirements of the general interest, the Court increasingly applied these justifications in combination with the Treaty-based derogations mentioned above to discriminatory measures.[128] This concerns cases where the Court fails to distinguish whether the measure is discriminatory or non-discriminatory,[129] cases where the nature of the measure was not expressly stated and national measures that have been falsely qualified as non-discriminatory.[130] In recent case law we can observe that the Court, countering explicit claims by the Commission to treat certain measures as discriminatory, relies on objective differences between different categories of service providers to avoid such qualification.[131] This development can also be observed under the free movement of goods in EU law, where the restrictions standard with the full list of justifications has been applied to national measures that would normally have been considered discriminatory.[132]

The protection of the environment in particular has frequently been invoked as an 'extra-statutory' justification, in addition to the three derogations provided for under Article 52 TFEU. This has led to pleas by Advocates General in favour of granting environmental protection as a justification for cases of direct discrimination as a matter of principle. The Court has, however, never explicitly taken up such proposition.[133] Nevertheless, environmental protection as sort of a 'higher level' public

[128] Hatzopoulos and Do, 'The case law of the ECJ', 961–2.

[129] Barnard, *The Substantive Law of the EU*, p. 86, has thus accused the Court of having 'conveniently overlooked the fact' that a rule was directly discriminatory in allowing recourse to mandatory requirements.

[130] Case C-158/96, *Kohll* [1998] ECR I-1931. There, however, the justification was claimed to fall under public health. See also Case C-118/96, *Safir* [1998] ECR I-1897; Case C-302/97, *Konle* [1999] ECR I-3099. See O'Leary and Fernández-Martín, 'Judicially-created exceptions', p. 172; and Jarass, 'A unified approach to the fundamental freedoms', p. 157.

[131] Case C-577/10, *Commission* v. *Belgium (Self-employed Service Providers)* [2012] not yet published in the Official Journal, paras. 48–9.

[132] Case C-67/97, *Bluhme* [1998] ECR I-8033, para. 19. See also the cases mentioned by Barnard, *The Substantive Law of the EU*, p. 86. See Case C-114/97, *Commission* v. *Spain* [1998] ECR I-6717, para. 43; J. Scott, 'Mandatory or imperative requirements in the EU and the WTO', in C. Barnard and J. Scott (eds.), *The Law of the Single European Market: Unpacking the Premises* (Oxford and Portland, OR: Hart Publishing, 2002), pp. 269–93 at pp. 270–5.

[133] Case C-2/90, *Commission* v. *Belgium* [1992] ECR I-4431. Cf. the cases mentioned and the account by Craig and de Búrca, *EU Law*, p. 675.

interest will reappear in our discussion on the relationship between the Services Directive and the Treaty regime later in this book.

Convergence in the realm of justification takes on another form as well. Cases of open discrimination such as the requirement of an establishment for service providers have already been justified by a reason not found in Article 52 TFEU.[134] This of course also depends on how wide one casts the net on discrimination. Thus *Schindler* was a case where the Court argued that national legislation that prohibits the holding of specific lotteries in a Member State would not be discriminatory and could therefore be justified by the protection of consumers and the maintenance of order in society.[135]

### 3.3.5 *Proportionality*

The principle of proportionality applies to any justification put forward by a Member State. The Court requires that a restriction of free movement must be suitable, necessary and reasonable. Suitability is met when a national measure pursues one of the mentioned objectives.[136] In EU law, this test is generally relaxed, as it is under WTO law, where a measure is already found suitable when it makes a contribution to achieving the regulatory objective.[137] According to more recent case law, however, this objective must be attained 'in a consistent and systematic manner'.[138] What this pertains to precisely has so far remained unclear, but it already seems to apply to the suitability stage. While this test has for some time been reserved for gambling cases, where different games of chance were not regulated equally,[139] it is now also

[134] Case C-204/90, *Bachmann* [1992] ECR I-249; Case C-484/93, *Svensson and Gustavsson* [1995] ECR I-3955, paras. 15–16. However, as this reason is the cohesion and integrity of the tax system, these cases should not be generalized.

[135] See Case C-275/92, *Schindler* [1994] ECR I-1039, paras. 49–51,where foreign providers were not found to be in a comparable situation. See O'Leary and Fernández-Martín, 'Judicially-created exceptions', pp. 177–9, who speak of an indistinctly applicable measure that only became discriminatory in the course of the proceeding.

[136] Case C-124/97, *Läärä* [1999] ECR I-6067, para. 31.

[137] See E. Vranes, 'Der Verhältnismäßigkeitsgrundsatz: Herleitungsalternativen, Rechtsstatus und Funktionen' (2009) 47(1) *Archiv des Völkerrechts* 1–35 at 20.

[138] See Joined Cases C-357/10 to C-359/10, *Duomo* [2012] not yet published in the Official Journal, para. 42; Case C-169/07, *Hartlauer* [2009] ECR I-1721, para. 55, Case C-384/08, *Attanasio Group* [2010] ECR I-2055, para. 51; and Case C-212/08, *Zeturf* [2011] ECR I-5633, para. 57.

[139] See Joined Cases C-316/07, C-358/07 to C-360/07, C-409/07 and C-410/07, *Stoß* [2010] ECR I-8069, paras. 88–107 regarding a public monopoly on bets on sporting competitions and lotteries as opposed to the rules applying to other games of chance.

applied in other constellations. Thus in *Hartlauer*, the Austrian law on hospitals was faulted on these grounds because it did not treat dental group practices equally with outpatient dental clinics.[140] There is thus an element of suitability where the Court looks at how Member States choose to regulate a broader field and whether burdens are distributed unevenly between operations or regions. The long 'dormant' first step of the proportionality test thus seems to have now gained in 'bite' and might prove irritating for national regulatory autonomy.

The second element of analysis means that the measure at issue must not exceed what is necessary to achieve the pursued objective.[141] In other words, less restrictive means to achieve either the general or the specific reasons of justification must not be available.[142] This assessment has been relaxed in particular with regard to restrictions on the operation of gambling and betting services in the common market. Thus the Court decided that the Member States are 'in principle free to set the objectives of their policy on games of chance and, where appropriate, to define in detail the level of protection sought'.[143] This may include the right to grant exclusive rights to a single entity, rationalized with the greater and more effective regulatory oversight of such entity.[144] Such holders of monopolies may be subjected to a number of specific restrictions, such as minimum capitalization and the location of their registered office.[145] While, as already mentioned, financial considerations must not be the real aim of a restrictive policy, but can only be regarded as an incidental beneficial consequence, the assessment of a Member State's motivation to maximize tax revenues is regularly deferred to the national courts.[146]

The third requirement of reasonableness or *stricto sensu* proportionality is an often-neglected element of the proportionality test and is rarely operated by the Court. Only in comparably few cases is a test of the adequacy of a measure in light of the reason of justification actually

[140] See Case C-169/07, *Hartlauer* [2009] ECR I-1721, para. 63.

[141] Case C-205/84, *Commission* v. *Germany (Insurance Cases)* [1986] ECR-3755, para. 33.

[142] See Case C-3/95, *Reisebüro Broede* [1996] ECR I-6511, para. 28; Joined Cases C-369/96 and C-376/96, *Arblade* [1999] ECR I-8453, para. 35.

[143] Case C-347/09, *Dickinger* [2011] ECR I-8185, para. 47.

[144] Case C-347/09, *Dickinger* [2011] ECR I-8185, paras. 48–9; Joined Cases C-316/07, C-358/07 to C-360/07, C-409/07 and C-410/07, *Stoß* [2010] ECR I-8069, paras. 81–3, and Case C-212/08 *Zeturf* [2011] ECR I-5633, para. 41.

[145] Case C-347/09, *Dickinger* [2011] ECR I-8185, paras. 70–81.

[146] Case C-347/09, *Dickinger* [2011] ECR I-8185, para. 54–66.

applied.[147] It has been shown by Vranes that foregoing this third tier of the proportionality test means that, from a choice of equally suitable measures, the most lenient one would always prevail.[148] With gambling, the Court has in contrast allowed a margin of discretion for the national authorities to determine, 'in accordance with their own scale of values', what is required in order to ensure consumer protection and the protection of society.[149] Similarly, discretion is allowed to the Member States in the areas of public health and road safety.[150] In the latter context, the Court also, in a more general vein, stated that 'it is not essential, with regard to the proportionality criterion, that a restrictive measure laid down by the authorities of a Member State should correspond to a view shared by all the Member States concerning the means of protecting the legitimate interest at issue'.[151] With reference to public interest objectives in the area of road safety, the Court continued:

> Whilst it is true that it is for a Member State which relies on an imperative requirement to justify a restriction within the meaning of the EC Treaty to demonstrate that its rules are appropriate and necessary to attain the legitimate objective being pursued, that burden of proof cannot be so extensive as to require the Member State to prove, positively, that no other conceivable measure could enable that objective to be attained under the same conditions.[152]

In *US–Gambling* the application of Article XIV GATS displayed a very similar mechanism.[153] It is for a responding party to make a prima facie case that its measure is necessary, without, however, having to establish in the first instance that this is the case. Only if the complaining party raises a WTO-consistent alternative measure must the responding party demonstrate why its challenged measure nevertheless remains

[147] W. Frenz, *Handbuch Europarecht: Europäische Grundfreiheiten* (Heidelberg: Springer, 2004), vol. I, p. 202. See also Hatzopoulos, 'The Court's approach to services (2006–2012)', 497–9, who refers to 'true proportionality control' or 'external proportionality control'.

[148] Vranes, 'Der Verhältnismäßigkeitsgrundsatz', 31.

[149] Case C-347/09, *Dickinger* [2011] ECR I-8185, para. 45; Joined Cases C-316/07, C-358/07 to C-360/07, C-409/07 and C-410/07, *Stoß* [2010] ECR I-8069, para. 76.

[150] See Case C-89/09, *Commission* v. *France (Laboratories)* [2010] ECR I-12941, paras. 42 and 82 for public health, and Case C-518/06, *Commission* v. *Italy (Motor Insurance)* [2009] ECR I-3491, para. 84.

[151] Case C-518/06, *Commission* v. *Italy (Motor Insurance)* [2009] ECR I-3491, para. 83.

[152] Case C-518/06, *Commission* v. *Italy (Motor Insurance)* [2009] ECR I-3491, para. 84.

[153] For a different perspective, see Hatzopoulos, 'The Court's approach to services (2006–2012)', 476.

necessary in light of that alternative, such as by showing that the proposed alternative is not reasonably available.[154]

### *3.3.6 The test of equivalence*

The host Member State is obliged to examine whether the envisaged national restrictive measure is not already imposed by the home Member State. More precisely, a general interest lawfully served by an overriding requirement only exists 'in so far as that interest is not protected by the rules to which the person providing the services is subject in the Member State in which he is established'.[155] In other words, 'it is incompatible with the freedom to provide services to make a provider subject to restrictions for safeguarding the public interest in so far as that interest is already safeguarded by the rules to which the provider is subject in the Member State where he is established.'[156] In a double burden constellation, the home state thus retains a quasi-regulatory, extraterritorial role. We will refer to this as the test of equivalence or the *Säger* test.

Thus tests passed in the home state, licences and qualifications obtained must be 'accorded their proper value and duly taken into account'.[157] In the *Peñarroja* case the Court held that this 'must be properly carried out by the national authorities in accordance with a procedure which complies with the requirements of EU law concerning the

[154] WTO Appellate Body Report, *United States–Measures Affecting the Cross-Border Supply of Gambling and Betting Services (US–Gambling)*, WT/DS285/AB/R, adopted 20 April 2005, paras. 310–11.

[155] Case C-76/90, *Säger* [1991] ECR I-4221, para. 15. See AG Kokott in Case C-514/03, *Commission* v. *Spain (Private Security)* [2006] ECR I-963, paras. 75–86. See among others Case 279/80, *Webb* [1981] ECR 3305, para. 20; Case C-180/89, *Commission* v. *Italy (Tourist Guides)* [1991] ECR I-709, para. 18. On this and the forerunner Joined Cases 110 and 111/78, *van Wesemael* [1979] ECR 35, see J. Snell, 'Free movement of services and the Services Directive: the legitimacy of the case law', in J. van de Gronden (ed.), *EU and WTO Law on Services: Limits to the Realisation of General Interest Policies within the Services Markets?* (The Hague: Kluwer, 2008), pp. 31–54 at pp. 37–8.

[156] Case C-288/89, *Gouda* [1991] ECR I-4007, para. 13; Case 279/80, *Webb* [1981] ECR 3305, para. 17; Joined Cases C-369/96 and C-376/96, *Arblade* [1999] ECR I-8453, paras. 34 and 35; Case C-347/09, *Dickinger* [2011] ECR I-8185, para. 94. See also W.-H. Roth, 'The European Court of Justice's case law in the freedom to provide services: is Keck relevant?', in M. Andenas and W.-H. Roth (eds.), *Services and Free Movement in EU Law* (The Hague: Kluwer, 2002), pp. 1–24 at p. 3; M. Klamert, 'Of empty glasses and double burdens: approaches to regulating the services market à propos the implementation of the Services Directive' (2010) *Legal Issues of Economic Integration* 111–32.

[157] Joined Cases C-372/09 and C-373/09, *Peñarroja* [2011] ECR I-1785, para. 58; Case C-340/89 *Vlassopoulou* [1991] ECR I-2357, para. 16.

effective protection of the fundamental rights conferred on EU citizens and, in particular, with Article 47 of the Charter of Fundamental Rights of the European Union'.[158] This means that all such decisions must be subject to judicial review, and must state reasons as to whether the qualifications obtained and recognized in other Member States have been properly taken into account.[159] In *Commission* v. *Portugal (Construction)* concerning a system of prior authorization of all construction undertakings operating for longer than one year, the Court held that such a scheme 'precludes the possibility of account being duly taken of equivalent obligations to which such an undertaking is subject in the Member State of establishment or of the verifications already carried out in that regard by the authorities of that Member State'.[160]

Again, with regard to the gaming and betting sector, this test of equivalence has been qualified by the Court. Thus the Court held that 'no duty of mutual recognition of authorisations issued by the various Member States can exist in the current state of European Union law' in this field.[161] This, the Court argued, is because of the absence of harmonization at EU level and in view of the substantial differences between the objectives pursued, and the different levels of protection sought by the legislation of the various Member States.[162] In this area, therefore, the Court pays tribute to the 'system of protection' chosen by a Member State, which is allowed to differ from that adopted by another Member State. This may be rationalized by considering that cross-border services such as online gambling are fundamentally different from other modes of services provision. On the other hand, divergent systems of regulation with regard to companies within the Union have not prevented an entity duly established in one Member State from also acquiring the right to establish itself in another Member State, as discussed above. We doubt, however, whether the case law in this specific area, where as also explained previously the proportionality test proper is only applied with qualification, should be viewed as indication of a general negation of mutual recognition, even when some statements in these cases were made in quite general wording.[163]

[158] Joined Cases C-372/09 and C-373/09, *Peñarroja* [2011] ECR I-1785, para. 62.
[159] Joined Cases C-372/09 and C-373/09, *Peñarroja* [2011] ECR I-1785, para. 62.
[160] Case C-458/08, *Commission* v. *Portugal* [2010] ECR I-11599, para. 101.
[161] Case C-347/09, *Dickinger* [2011] ECR I-8185, para. 96; Joined Cases C-316/07, C-358/07 to C-360/07, C-409/07 and C-410/07, *Stoß* [2010] ECR I-8069, para. 112.
[162] Case C-347/09, *Dickinger* [2011] ECR I-8185, para. 99.
[163] Such as concern is voiced by Hatzopoulos, 'The Court's approach to services (2006–2012)', 493–7.

Notably, in a recent case on the requirement that for the advertising of foreign gaming establishments the level of protection against the risk of gaming in the other Member State must be in essence 'of a level equivalent' to that which is guaranteed in the host Member State, the Court held that this would only be disproportionate if the rules of the other Member State would have to be identical.[164] This also militates in favour of the principled application of mutual recognition in this area.

Hatzopoulos and Do have argued that this principle of equivalence is a part of the proportionality test under the general prohibition of restrictions.[165] We will discuss later in Chapter 6 whether this view can still be upheld after the adoption of the Services Directive. Somewhat differently, Hatzopoulos himself has argued that the principle of mutual recognition constitutes 'the reverse of the principle of proportionality: the host State legislation will not be deemed necessary, and thus proportional, if its regulatory objective is sufficiently secured by the rules of the home State'.[166] We would submit that the test of equivalence either already applies at the qualification stage, such as in the above-mentioned *Säger* case, where the Court did not conduct a proper proportionality test, or that it is an element of the second tier of the proportionality test, such as in *Commission* v. *Portugal (Construction)*.[167] The close connection between mutual recognition and proportionality has also been noted by Weiler, who has called the former 'a very conservative and fully justified application of the principle of proportionality'.[168] We will return to the test of equivalence and mutual recognition more generally in Chapter 8.

164 Case C-176/11, *HIT* [2012] not yet published in the Official Journal, paras. 31–2.

165 Hatzopoulos and Do, 'The case law of the ECJ', 981, and V. Hatzopoulos, *Regulating Services in the European Union* (Oxford University Press, 2012), pp. 232–4.

166 V. Hatzopoulos, 'Forms of mutual recognition in the field of services', in I. Lianos and O. Odudu (eds.), *Regulating Trade in Services: Trust, Distrust and Economic Integration* (Cambridge University Press, 2012), pp. 59–98 at p. 76. But contrast this with *ibid.*, p. 8, where it is considered 'a part of the proportionality test of the host State's restrictive measures'.

167 See Case C-458/08, *Commission* v. *Portugal* [2010] ECR I-11599, para. 100.

168 J. H. H. Weiler, 'Epilogue: Towards a common law of international trade', in J. H. H. Weiler (ed.), *The EU, the WTO, and the NAFTA* (Oxford University Press, Collected Courses of the Academy of European Law, 2001), pp. 201–32 at p. 221.

## 3.4 Relationship with the other freedoms

### 3.4.1 *Introduction*

The non-exhaustive list of activities in Article 57 TFEU indicates the services that should be covered by the freedom to provide services. In addition, the wording of Article 57 TFEU suggests the area of services to have merely residual character.[169] As mentioned above, however, the Court in its more recent case law such as *Schnitzer* abandoned any reference to such residual character of the freedom.[170] The rules on services are only disregarded if they are 'entirely secondary' and may be considered together with another freedom.[171] If this is not the case, both freedoms will be applied. As we will see, this may even lead to the de facto residual application of the free movement of capital in relation to the freedom to provide services.

In general, the line between services and the free movement of workers is one that is relatively easy to draw. A worker is defined as an employed natural person, whereas a service provider is self-employed. The only borderline cases are posted workers. These are workers from one Member State sent to another EU Member State while remaining employed by a company in the first state. The close relationship between the freedom to provide services and the category of posted workers was emphasized by the Court in *Finalarte*, where it described posted workers as 'workers employed by a business established in one Member State who are temporarily sent to another Member State to provide service [and] do not, in any way, seek access to the labour market in that second State if they return to their country of origin or residence after completion of their work'.[172] This delimitation has been resolved by secondary law. Directive 96/71/EC regulating this category of workers is discussed later in this book.[173]

[169] 'in so far as they are not governed by the provisions relating to freedom of movement for goods, capital and persons'.

[170] See Hatzopoulos, 'The Court's approach to services (2006–2012)', 465.

[171] See Case C-275/92, *Schindler* [1994] ECR I-1039, para. 22; Case C-390/99, *Canal Satélite* [2002] ECR I-607, para. 31; Case C-71/02, *Karner* [2004] ECR I-3025, para. 46; Case C-36/02, *Omega* [2004] ECR I-9609, para. 26; and Case C-233/09, *Dijkman* [2010] ECR I-6649, para. 33; Case C-137/09, *Josemans* [2010] ECR I-13019, para. 50. See Hatzopoulos, 'The Court's approach to services (2006–2012)', 466.

[172] Joined Cases C-49/98, C-50/98, C-52/98 to C-54/98 and C-68/98 to C-71/98, *Finalarte* [2001] ECR I-7831, paras. 22–3.

[173] Directive 96/71/EC of the European Parliament and the Council of 16 December 1996 concerning the posting of workers in the framework of the provision of services, OJ 1997 No. L18/1

In the following sections, we will delimit the scope of application of the freedom to provide services from the free movement of capital, and from the freedom of establishment, for which the Services Directive in particular has provided new impetus. We will also discuss the relationship between the free movement of goods and the freedom to provide services, and will in this frame also make comparisons to the situation under WTO law, where similar issues exist.

### *3.4.2 Services and establishments*

Service providers pursue an intangible activity and provide non-physical output. Establishments, in contrast, can be distinguished by those set up to provide services such as medical services, financial services or accommodation and catering services by means of an establishment on the one hand, and those using an establishment to trade in goods such as by setting up a branch of a department store on the other hand. The Treaty does not differentiate between the two categories of establishments in terms of legal protection or the scope of application of Article 49 TFEU. However, it does distinguish between the regulatory treatment of non-established service providers, which we will also refer to as service providers *stricto sensu*, and that of established service providers. The basic difference is that a service provider is not forced to integrate in the host state. An established operator, in contrast, must adhere strictly to all professional and business-related rules in the host country.

The divergence of regulation of services and establishments is also reflected by Directive 2005/36/EC, which distinguishes between the mutual recognition of professional qualifications for service providers in Title II, and their recognition for established service providers in its Title III.[174] While the services part of the Directive grants full access to the market of the host state without the need for the recognition of qualifications,[175] with establishments the mutual recognition of professional titles requires compensatory measures,[176] certain periods of practical experience in the home state, or the minimum harmonization of training requirements.[177]

[174] Directive 2005/36/EC, OJ 2005 No. L255/22.

[175] However, the Directive imposes some information and documentation obligations on the service provider when entering the host state for the first time. See Art. 7 Directive 2005/36/EC.

[176] Art. 14 Directive 2005/36/EC.

[177] See further Chapter H.

Table 3.1 Fragmentation of the EU regime of services and establishments

| Services *stricto sensu* | Established service providers | Other establishments |
|---|---|---|
| Chapter IV Services Directive | Chapter III Services Directive | Article 49–55 TFEU |

Finally, this difference is also reflected by the (pre-Lisbon) Services Directive. As we shall discuss in detail in the following chapter, the Directive applies to services as defined by Article 57 TFEU as well as to services provided by means of an establishment.[178] Both are subject to separate and diverging substantive rules, with a number of mainly administrative provisions applying across the board. The non-services-related aspects of the regulation of establishments under Article 49 TFEU are excluded from the scope of the Services Directive. Thus established providers of goods (the department store mentioned above) are subject to a different regime than established service providers. Suffice to note here that, as a result, three different legal regimes with regard to services and establishments currently apply, as shown in Table 3.1.[179] As we shall also see below, this is only the tip of the iceberg as far as the fragmentation of the regulation of services in EU law is concerned.

Thus it is not yet justified to speak of a legal regime encompassing all (economic) service activities and dismantling the classic distinction between services and establishments.[180] The Services Directive brings about convergence only in the sense that it provides for some mainly procedural and administrative regulation applying both to services *stricto sensu* and to established service providers. However, it continues to treat services and establishments differently. This has been demonstrated by the Opinion of the Advocate General in the *Duomo* case, who considered the Services Directive applicable (which opinion was not followed by the Court in this case) and consequently went to

[178] Directive 2006/123/EC, Chapters III and IV.

[179] As will be explained in Chapter 8, this becomes more complex when accounting for the areas exempt from the Services Directive, which continue to fall under the Treaty regime.

[180] See Hatzopoulos and Do, 'The case law of the ECJ', 928.

great lengths to distinguish the scope of application of the parts of the Directive on services and establishments respectively, and thus also the scope of Articles 49 and 56 TFEU.[181]

Against this background, the question arises whether it is reconcilable with the fundamental right to equal treatment in EU law to provide for different rules between established service providers and established providers of goods. It may be appropriate to treat service providers differently from establishments, because the latter entail a much greater integration into the territory and thus the legal order of the host Member State. This may justify stricter requirements for establishments compared to a merely temporary provision of services in the host state. However, this reasoning is less convincing with regard to established service providers on the one hand, and establishments not operating in the services sector on the other hand. Both may be integrated in the legal order of the host state to an equal degree, while the only difference is what is being traded from the basis of the establishment.

As already explained, under WTO law established service providers fall under commercial presence (Mode 3) under the GATS, while other established traders of goods are governed by the GATT. Thus these two kinds of establishments come under very different legal regimes. In WTO law, however, there is no principle comparable to Article 18 TFEU, which prohibits citizens from being treated unequally. Thus, without such overarching principle of equality, there can be no discussion as to whether the different treatment of establishments and commercial presence respectively violates WTO law.

With EU law, the answer, it is submitted, lies in the delimitation between goods and services. If these two tradables can be distinguished from each other in the sense of requiring a different set of rules for objective reasons, this would also affect the equality assessment. This distinction we will address in the following section.

### 3.4.3 *Goods and services*

In its early case law, the ECJ drew a basic dividing line between Articles 34 and 56 TFEU based on the idea that goods have material form,

[181] Joined Cases C-357/10 to C-359/10, *Duomo* [2012] not yet published in the Official Journal, paras. 32–4. However, he argued that, since no freedom was secondary to the other, the case should be examined under both regimes. The solution suggested by the AG based on proportionality avoided an assessment of the conflict between Arts. 9 and 16 Directive 2006/123/EC, discussed in Chapters 6 and 8.

whereas services are intangible in nature.[182] According to this view, rules on goods and on services are mutually exclusive. In order to identify which set of rules applies in a given situation, the ECJ regularly sought to identify the predominant activity under consideration, treating the other effects as purely ancillary.[183]

Scenarios where issues of delimitation have arisen are the production and provision of energy such as electricity and gas, broadcasting[184] and leasing.[185] With regard to the latter, the Court held in *Omega* that

> where a national measure affects both the freedom to provide services and the free movement of goods, the Court will, in principle, examine it in relation to just one of those two fundamental freedoms if it is clear that, in the circumstances of the case, one of those freedoms is entirely secondary in relation to the other and may be attached to it.[186]

Should the predominance either of the free movement of goods or the freedom to provide services be impossible to establish, the latter freedom has often been deemed subsidiary to the former in this constellation. Hence the Court held that marketing and sales activities for goods carried out by the owner of these goods do not fall within the scope of Article 56 TFEU.[187]

We would argue that this approach could be generalized with regard to 'hybrid' enterprises that are engaged both in the production and in the distribution of products. Any cross-border sales activity for products owned or self-produced by such companies, therefore, should follow the rules applying to the product. An example would be a bakery producing in one Member State and selling its products in another Member State through a subsidiary. The distribution activity should be seen as an extension of the production activity, and should thus be assessed under the free movement of goods. On the other hand, with the marketing of non-alcoholic beverages and food in coffee shops the services element was considered predominant to the supply of the product itself.[188]

[182] Case 155/73, *Sacchi* [1974] ECR 409, paras. 6 and 7.

[183] See Case C-275/92, *Schindler* [1994] ECR I-1039; Case C-97/98, *Jägerskiöld* [1999] ECR I-7319.

[184] See Case 155/73, *Sacchi* [1974] ECR 409, paras. 6 *et seq*; Case C-17/00, *De Coster* [2001] ECR I-9445, para. 37.

[185] Case C-451/99, *Cura Anlagen* [2002] ECR I-3193, para. 18.

[186] Case C-36/02, *Omega* [2004] ECR I-9609, para. 26 with further references to relevant case law.

[187] Case C-239/90, *Boscher* [1991] ECR I-2023, paras. 9 and 10.

[188] Case C-137/09, *Josemans* [2010] ECR I-13019.

In contrast, with regard to the qualification of lotteries, the Court held that the mere 'importation and distribution of objects [here lottery tickets] are not ends in this business in themselves and their sole purpose is to enable residents of the member States, where those objects are imported and distributed, to participate in the lottery'.[189] The Court argued that such participation is because remuneration is paid for the services provided by the operator of the lottery and, hence, that the weight lies more on the services aspect of the activity than on the goods aspect. Consequently, the Treaty provisions on services were held applicable in this case and not ex Article 30 EC on the free movement of goods.

Finally, in the specific circumstances of the *Canal Satélite* case, the Court adopted yet another approach and applied the rules on goods and services simultaneously.[190] It held that national legislation 'which makes the marketing of apparatus, equipment, decoders or digital transmission and reception systems for television signals by satellite and the provision of related services by operators of conditional-access services subject to a prior authorisation procedure restricts both the free movement of goods and the freedom to provide services'.[191] The Court thus abandoned the sequential analysis applied in cases such as *Gourmet*[192] for a combined assessment of compatibility of national measures with the freedoms at issue.[193] This has implications for the justifications Member States may invoke in such a constellation.

In WTO law, this question of the applicability of the GATT or of the GATS has a far greater import. There, an overlap of the services regime and the goods regime has been considered inevitable, and the GATT and the GATS are not considered mutually exclusive agreements.[194] In the 1997 *Canada–Periodicals* case, the GATT has been given prevalence in a constellation involving differential treatment of advertising in

[189] See Case C-275/92, *Schindler* [1994] ECR I-1039, para. 22. See also Case C-418/02, *Praktiker* [2005] ECR I-5873, para. 39, where the Court explains that the concept of 'services within the meaning of the Directive includes services provided in connection with retail trade in goods'.

[190] Case C-390/99, *Canal Satélite* [2002] ECR I-607, para. 33.

[191] Case C-390/99, *Canal Satélite* [2002] ECR I-607, para. 43/1.

[192] See e.g. Case C-405/98, *Gourmet* [2001] ECR I-1795.

[193] See the annotation of this case by M. Dougan, 'Annotation of Case C-390/99, *Canal Satelite Digital* [2002] ECR I-607 and Case C-159/00, *Sapod Audicv EcoEmballages* [2002] ECR I-5031' (2003) 40 (1) *Common Market Law Review* 193–218 at 197.

[194] The WTO Panel reports have revealed that the goods and services sectors overlap is inevitable. See WTO Panel Report, *Canada–Certain Measures Concerning Periodicals,*

periodicals that seemed to have at least as much relation to services as to trade in goods.[195] However, in later cases the WTO adjudicating bodies have shown little consistency in applying delimitation criteria between measures falling under the GATS and those coming under the GATT.[196] It has been suggested solving any potential regulatory conflict by reliance on whether a measure primarily regulates and/or affects goods or services.[197] It has also been suggested that cases where none of the national measures can be qualified as being only marginal should be resolved by considering the type of conflict at issue.[198]

This shows that both in EU law and in WTO law there are no straightforward solutions to the question of how to demarcate the scope of the goods regime from the services regime. Both regimes display a tendency to apply a rule of predominance, while at the same time accepting that the regulation of services and goods may overlap and that both regimes may be applied simultaneously. However, as with the relationship between services and establishments discussed above, the stakes are much higher in WTO law. It potentially makes a huge difference if a measure falls under the GATT or under the GATS, or under both regimes.

Under EU law, the differences between the regulation of services and goods are more subtle. However, this has changed with the adoption of the Services Directive, which provides for a much more elaborate regime on services than exists in the field of goods. Moreover, as I will discuss below, there is a fundamental distinction concerning the (de)regulation of Member State rules on goods and services

WT/DS31/R and Corr.1, adopted 30 July 1997, para. 5.18. See Panel Report, *European Communities – Regime for the Importation, Sale and Distribution of Bananas (EC–Bananas III)*, WT/DS27/R/USA, Complaint by the United States, para. 7.283; WTO Appellate Body, *EC–Bananas III*, WT/DS27/AB/R, paras. 220–1.

195 WTO Panel Report, *Canada–Periodicals*, WT/DS31/R, pp. 18–22.

196 See E. Vranes, 'The overlap between GATT and GATS: a methodological mate' (2009) *Legal Issues of Economic Integration* 215–38 at 224–6. See also A. T. F. Lang, 'GATS', in D. Bethlehem *et al.* (eds.), *The Oxford Handbook of International Trade Law* (Oxford University Press, 2009), pp. 157–85 at pp. 180–1, questioning the soundness of awards finding any vertically integrated company to be at the same time a potential service supplier.

197 See Vranes, 'The overlap between GATT and GATS', 230.

198 See Vranes, 'The overlap between GATT and GATS', 231–6, who distinguishes between a conflict between a scheduled permission in the GATS with a prohibition in the GATT, between an implicit permission under either agreement with a prohibtion under the other agreement, and between justified measures under either agreement.

respectively following the *Keck* jurisprudence. This is the application of a less strict standard of review for certain national measures affecting the trade in goods, which has not been adopted for the area of services.

### 3.4.4 *Services and capital*

Initially, the rules governing capital movements in the EU were less peremptory than those in other areas. Moreover, the direct effect of the Treaty provisions on capital was not established before the mid-1990s.[199] This entailed that pertinent cases have frequently been assessed under the capital regime together with other Treaty freedoms, or only under other freedoms.[200] Since then, a growing body of case law under the free movement of capital has emerged.[201] However, because of the limited substantive scope of the rules on capital movements and the formerly only residual nature of the services rules, it was often difficult to draw a dividing line between these two freedoms. Particularly with regard to enforcement actions, the Court often considered the whole spectrum of Treaty freedoms, each from a different perspective, instead of addressing overlaps.[202]

There is, however, one fundamental difference between the Treaty provisions governing the free movement of capital as compared to all other freedoms including the freedom to provide services. While the objective of the freedom to provide services is to bestow rights on nationals of EU Member States,[203] the free movement of capital equally extends to third countries. Thus any company established outside the EU can rely on the free movement of capital, but not on the freedom to provide services.[204] Note that the definition of capital in this context does not encompass 'current payments' relating to financial trans-

[199] See Case C-416/93, *Bordessa* [1995] ECR I-361, para. 34; Joined Cases C-163, 165 and 250/94, *Sanz de Lera* [1995] ECR I-4821, paras. 41–7.

[200] See Case C-484/93, *Svensson* [1995] ECR I-3955, para. 19; Case C-118/96, *Safir* [1998] ECR I-1897, para. 35; Case C-410/96, *Ambry* [1998] ECR I-7875, para. 40.

[201] See L. Flynn, 'Coming of age: the free movement of capital case law 1993–2002' (2002) 39 *Common Market Law Review* 773–805.

[202] See Case C-279/00, *Commission* v. *Italy (Temporary Labour Agencies)* [2002] I-1425, paras. 37 and 38.

[203] Opinion 1/94, *Agreement Establishing the World Trade Organization* [1994] ECR I-5267, para. 81.

[204] See Case C-452/04, *Fidium Finanz* [2006] ECR I-9521, para. 25, where, as mentioned, the breach of Art. 63 TFEU was not examined after negating a breach of Art. 56 TFEU.

actions linked to trade in goods and services between residents of a Member State and the rest of the world.

Financial operations are often intimately linked to the services sector, such as the acquisition of shares in non-domestic companies or the granting of loans. This is also reflected by Article 58(2) TFEU, pursuant to which 'the liberalisation of banking and insurance services connected with movements of capital shall be effected in step with the progressive liberalisation of movement of capital'. AG Tesauro has proposed some parameters of distinction in his opinion in the *Safir* case that are strongly reminiscent of the above-discussed criteria on the goods–services nexus.[205] According to AG Tesauro, the rules on the free movement of capital shall apply with regard to any measure that directly restricts the transfer of capital by rendering it impossible or more difficult. In contrast, any measure that only indirectly restricts the movement of capital and primarily constitutes a non-monetary restriction on the freedom to provide services shall be subject to Article 56 TFEU. Only if a national measure simultaneously restricts services and the movement of capital should both provisions apply in conjunction.[206] Note that AG Tesauro here still assumed a residual nature of the rules on services, a view revised in the meantime, as explained above.

## 3.5 Public services

### 3.5.1 *Introduction*

The debate on public services is framed by the growing importance attached to non-economic values within the internal market.[207] Public services are 'deemed to be in the general economic interest, or even more broadly, in the general interest of a country/society'.[208] The concept of public services is not officially used in Union law, although

[205] Opinion of AG Tesauro in Case C-118/96, *Safir* [1998] ECR I-1897.

[206] Opinion of AG Tesauro in Case C-118/96, *Safir* [1998] ECR I-1897, para. 17.

[207] See T. Prosser, 'Competition law and public services: from single market to citizenship rights? (2005) 11(4) *European Public Law* 543–63; J. Baquero Cruz, 'Beyond competition: services of general interest and European Community law', in G. de Búrca (ed.), *EU Law and the Welfare State: In Search of Solidarity* (Oxford University Press, 2005), pp. 169–212; M. T. Karayigit, 'The notion of services of general economic interest revisited' (2009) 15(4) *European Public Law* 575–95.

[208] See R. Adlung, 'Public services and the GATS' (2006) 9(2) *Journal of International Economic Law* 455–85 at 456.

it has been claimed that it should be.[209] The corresponding term in Union law is probably 'services of general interest' (SGI), at least when one refers to the above-mentioned broader meaning of public services that also encompasses general public interests.[210] Given this meaning, SGI would comprise the narrower concepts of services of general economic interest (SGEI) and of non-economic services of general interest (NESGI).[211] The concept of NESGI comprises services that lack any market relevance in economic terms, such as national education and statutory social security schemes.[212] Moreover, it can also refer to traditional state prerogatives such as the police, justice or diplomatic service, which we will discuss below under the name given to them in the TFEU, namely services in public authority.

In Chapter 5 on the different approaches to regulating and liberalizing the Union market in services, we will discuss how the playing field with regard to public services is determined by a combination of soft law and case law. There we will also discuss the various legal concepts that have been introduced into this debate.[213] In the following section, we will focus on the complex rule-exemption regulatory regime applicable to SGEI in EU law. We will start, however, with a brief outline of the Treaty exemption for services rendered in official authority.

### *3.5.2 Services in official authority*

Article 51 TFEU provides that the rules governing the freedom of establishment shall not apply 'so far as any given member State is concerned,

[209] On the notion of public services, see P. Bauby, 'From Rome to Lisbon: SGIs in primary law', in E. Szyszczak *et al.* (eds.), *Developments in Services of General Interest* (The Hague: TMC Asser, Springer, 2011), pp. 19–36 at pp. 20–2.

[210] U. Neergaard, 'Services of general economic interest: the nature of the beast', in M. Krajewski, U. Neergaard and J. van de Gronden (eds.), *The Changing Legal Framework for Services of General Interest in Europe: Between Competition and Solidarity* (The Hague: TMC Asser, Kluwer, 2009), pp. 17–50 at p. 28, has argued that the difference between SGEI and public services is similar to the difference between public interest and general interest: it is unclear if there is any.

[211] It may seem strange to distinguish SGI from NESGI when one could have left it at the dichotomy between SGI and SGEI. However, according to the Commission's Green Paper of 2003, the notion of SGI is derived 'in Community practice' from that of SGEI and covers both market and non-market services.

[212] With regard to national education systems, the Court explained that a Member State, 'in establishing and maintaining such a system, is not seeking to engage in gainful activity, but is fulfilling its duties towards its own population in the social, cultural and educational fields. Secondly, the system in question is, as a general rule, funded from the public purse.' See Case C-109/92, *Wirth* [1993] ECR I-6447, para. 15.

[213] Neergaard, 'Services of general economic interest', p. 18.

to activities which in that State are connected, even occasionally, with the exercise of official authority'. This provision is extended to the chapter on services by virtue of Article 62 TFEU.[214] Union law lacks any clear definition of 'official authority', leaving its interpretation to the Court. While reference is primarily made to the interpretation at national level,[215] the concept and scope of official authority is determined from the point of view of Union law. Constituting an exception to the fundamental freedoms, the Court held that it must be 'interpreted in a manner which limits its scope to what is strictly necessary to safeguard the interests it allows the Member States to protect'.[216] In addition, the scope of Article 51 TFEU is limited to activities that 'in themselves are directly and specifically connected with the exercise of official authority'.[217] The Court has thus adopted a restrictive stance in response to repeated attempts by Member States to exempt the services provided by certain professions such as lawyers,[218] traffic accident experts,[219] commissioners of insurance companies[220] or private security guards.[221] These activities were not deemed to be covered by the exception because they were deemed auxiliary or preparatory to the exercise of official authority, they left the providers' discretionary and decision-making powers intact, or because they did not involve the exercise of decision-making powers, powers of constraint or powers of coercion.[222] Thus, most recently, activities of public notaries were not qualified as the exercise of official authority.[223]

On the other hand, in its landmark *Reyner* case, the Court of Justice clarified that Article 51 TFEU relates to specific activities, and not to

[214] Art. 45(4) TFEU contains a similar public service exception with regard to the free movement of workers. It is, however, only relevant to jobs in public administration and is thus not applicable to private firms or self-employed persons.
[215] See Case C-53/08, *Commission* v. *Austria (Notaries)* [2011] not yet published in the Official Journal.
[216] See Case C-53/08, *Commission* v. *Austria (Notaries)* [2011] not yet published in the Official Journal, para. 83 and the case law cited.
[217] Case C-53/08, *Commission* v. *Austria (Notaries)* [2011] not yet published in the Official Journal, para. 84 and the case law cited.
[218] Case 2/74, *Reyners* [1974] 631.
[219] Case C-306/89, *Commission* v. *Greece* [1991] ECR I-5863.
[220] Case C-42/92, *Thijssen* [1993] ECR I-4047.
[221] Case C-283/99, *Commission* v. *Italy* [2001] ECR I-4195.
[222] Case C-53/08, *Commission* v. *Austria (Notaries)* [2011] not yet published in the Official Journal, para. 85 with references to previous case law.
[223] Case C-53/08, *Commission* v. *Austria (Notaries)* [2011] not yet published in the Official Journal, para. 119.

whole professions.[224] Consequently, it did not exempt an entire profession, unless the entire activity was dedicated to the exercise of official authority, such as with judges or prosecutors, or unless the activity under consideration was so closely tied to the other activities that they would form a coherent whole that cannot be separated.[225] In other words, Article 51 TFEU applies not to the profession or institution within which a specific service is supplied as such, but to the service itself.[226]

### *3.5.3 Services of general economic interest*

#### 3.5.3.1 Introduction

The creation of the common market has been characterized by continuous efforts to strike a balance between Member State interventions that are liable to cause market distortions on the one hand, and an unobstructed internal market driven by competition on the other hand. Thus, since the early 1990s the European Commission has increasingly insisted on finding a compromise between accomplishing public services on the one hand, and the promotion of market access and liberalization on the other hand.[227] The gradual opening and regulation of large network industries such as electricity, gas, telecommunication, transport or postal services reflects the Union's ambition not only to integrate such general interest services into the common market, but also to strike a balance between competition law and an autonomous approach to an EU concept of public services. The underlying objectives of this endeavour are to ensure the provision of high quality services at affordable prices, to protect competitors against cross-subsidies for non-public services and to minimize costs for the public budgets.

Whereas details on the regulation of SGEI are complex, of which we will give a taste below, the general legal issues underlying the regime on SGEI in the Union are fairly straightforward. First, private undertakings are sometimes given special or even exclusive rights by a state. This raises the problem of the conditions under which Member States decide which undertaking is entrusted with such obligations, thus raising issues of public procurement. Second, SGEI are services rendered for

[224] Case 2/74, *Reyners* [1974] 631, para. 47.

[225] Case 2/74, *Reyners* [1974] 631, para. 47.

[226] Art. 58(1) TFEU, however, generally exempts services in the transportation sector from the freedom to provide services, and Art. 58(2) TFEU provides for specific regulations with regard to the banking and insurance sector.

[227] See Case C-302/94, *British Telecommunications plc* [1996] ECR I-6417, para. 34.

remuneration.[228] At the same time, however, they are services provided at an economic loss by undertakings. In order to re-establish a situation of economic equilibrium, private actors rendering SGEI are granted compensation, which opens a flank for the EU state aid regime.[229]

In the following section we will explore the complex interplay between competition law, state aid rules and public procurement with respect to SGEI.

#### 3.5.3.2 The basic rule for the conferral of special or exclusive rights

Pursuant to Article 106(1) TFEU, 'in the case of public undertakings and undertakings to which Member States grant special or exclusive rights', Member States shall not violate the Treaty and in particular the rule on non-discrimination in Article 18 TFEU and the competition rules in Articles 101 to 109 TFEU. This means that undertakings to which Member States grant special or exclusive rights are considered equivalent to public undertakings, irrespective of whether they are publicly or privately owned.[230] Thus, although Article 106(1) TFEU acknowledges the existence of undertakings benefiting from special or exclusive rights, these rights must be assessed in the light of different rules of the Treaty.[231] As such, Article 106(1) TFEU does not produce any independent effect unless read in conjunction with the relevant Treaty rules.[232] This is reflected by the Court's case law, which regularly examines the application of Article 106(1) TFEU in conjunction with alleged infringements of the four freedoms as well as with regard to a violation of the rules on competition.

[228] See Case 263/86, *Humbel* [1988] ECR 5365, para. 17; Case C-157/99, *Smits and Peerboms* [2001] ECR I-5473, para. 56.

[229] In its Green Paper on services of general interest the Commission differentiates between five ways of financing PSOs: (i) direct financial support through the state budget; (ii) special or exclusive rights; (iii) contribution by market participants; (iv) tariff averaging; and (v) solidarity-based financing. See European Commission, Green Paper on Services of General Interest, COM (2003)270, para. 4.2.

[230] See Art. 2 Commission Directive 2000/52/EC of 26 July 2000 on the transparency of financial relations between Member States and public undertakings, OJ 2000 No. L193/75.

[231] Case C-202/88, *France* v. *Commission (Telecommunication Terminals Equipment)* [1991] ECR I-1223, summary para. 2.

[232] See Case C-295/05, *Asemfo* [2007] ECR I-2999, para. 40. See T. Bekkedal, 'Article 106 TFEU is dead. Long live Article 106 TFEU!', in E. Szyszczak *et al.* (eds.), *Developments in Services of General Interest* (The Hague: TMC Asser, Springer, 2011), pp. 61–102 at p. 63 and pp. 78–9.

The concept of special rights that is mentioned in Article 106 TFEU differs from the concept of exclusive rights in that the former are mostly granted to a limited number of undertakings by public authorities. In this case, the act of conferral is generally considered to be based on subjective considerations and it does not necessarily abide by the principles of proportionality, non-discrimination and objectivity.[233] Exclusive rights, in contrast, establish a dominant influence by means of conferring a monopoly on an individual beneficiary in order to carry out a specific activity nationwide or in a particular geographic area.[234] These special and exclusive rights have been defined in secondary law as rights granted 'by way of any legislative, regulatory or administrative provision ... and which substantially affects the ability of other undertakings to carry out such activity on the same territory under substantially equivalent conditions'.[235] It follows that it is not solely the activity pursued that establishes the existence of exclusive or special rights, but it has to be assessed on a case-by-case basis whether these rights give their holders any substantial advantage over their potential competitors. As a rule, such an advantage will not be assumed to exist if the rights obtained have been awarded based on 'objective, proportional and non-discriminatory criteria'.[236]

### 3.5.3.3 The exception for public services

Article 106(2) TFEU lays down the conditions under which public and private undertakings entrusted with the operation of SGEI by discharging so-called public service obligations (PSOs) may exceptionally be exempt from the Treaty rules. Thus, according to this provision, 'undertakings entrusted with the operation of services of general economic

233 See also Art. VIII:5 GATS.

234 See among others Case C-320/91, *Corbeau* [1993] ECR I-2533; Case C-475/99, *Ambulanz Glöckner* [2001] ECR I-8089, paras. 23 and 24. In other words, an indefinable group of beneficiaries do not qualify as holders of exclusive rights under the Treaty. An exclusive right might be entrusted by different legal instruments such as public contracts or regulations including licences, concessions or quota agreements. See G. Davies, 'What does Article 86 actually do?', in M. Krajewski, U. Neergaard and J. van de Gronden (eds.), *The Changing Legal Framework for Services of General Interest in Europe: Between Competition and Solidarity* (The Hague: TMC Asser Press, Cambridge University Press, 2009), pp. 51–67 at p. 57, who has argued that Art. 106(1) TFEU does not add anything to the application of Art. 4(3) TEU in conjunction with competition law.

235 Directive 2004/17/EC of the European Parliament and the Council of 31 March 2004 coordinating the procurement procedures of entities operating in the water, energy, transport and postal services sectors, OJ 2004 No. L134/1.

236 Rec. 25 Directive 2004/17/EC.

interest or having the character of a revenue-producing monopoly shall be subject to the rules contained in the Treaties, in particular to the rules on competition.' This shall only apply, however, 'in so far as the application of such rules does not obstruct the performance, in law or in fact, of the particular tasks assigned to them'. Moreover, the development of trade 'must not be affected to such an extent as would be contrary to the interests of the Union'.

PSOs refer to obligations which 'the undertaking in question, if it were considering its own commercial interests, would not assume or would not assume to the same extent or under the same conditions'.[237] PSOs are discharged by the state based on a general interest criterion, such as the interest to provide quantitatively and geographically unlimited services that respond to a need that is common to the whole population or the interest to be supplied throughout a territory. These kinds of PSO are called universal service obligations (USOs).[238] USOs have played an important role in telecommunications, electricity, gas, transport and postal services, and partly also in public service broadcasting,[239] waste management, water supply and wastewater treatment.[240]

The mandate to discharge PSOs can result from a Member State's autonomy to define what it considers to be a PSO under Article 106(2) TFEU. Alternatively, it may be based on a specific authorization or obligation provided in harmonization directives, which require Member States to guarantee universal service, to protect vulnerable customers or to contribute to achieving objectives in the field of environmental protection.[241] PSOs are imposed through an act of public authority,

[237] See Art. 2(1) of Regulation 1191/69 on action by Member States concerning the obligations inherent in the concept of a public service in transport by rail, road and inland waterway, OJ 1969 No. L156/1.

[238] Such USO, however, is not a prerequisite for the existence of a PSO. See Case T-289/03, *BUPA* [2008] ECR II-81, paras. 179, 186. Compared to USOs, PSOs may serve additional, strategic purposes such as the security of supply, (energy) efficiency and environmental protection. See also J. Davies and E. Szyszczak, 'Universal service obligations: fulfilling new generations of services of general economic interest', in E. Szyszczak *et al.* (eds.), *Developments in Services of General Interest* (The Hague: TMC Asser, Springer, 2011), pp. 155–77.

[239] European Commission, Communication on services of general interest in Europe, COM(2000)580, OJ 2001 No. C17/4, Annex II, Definition of Terms.

[240] USOs typically involve universal coverage and uniform pricing requirements, which are often imposed simultaneously. See Communication on SGI, COM(2000)580, Annex II.

[241] Secondary EU law provisions may constitute specific interpretations of Article 106(2) TFEU authorizations when they provide for exclusive lists of potential categories of

which may include legislative or regulatory instruments, a contract or an instruction.[242] In this, Member States must comply with EU procurement rules as regards the selection of service providers. In its case law, the Court consistently held that the imposition of PSOs, whether or not linked to a public service contract, has to be necessary, proportionate to the aim pursued and based on objective, non-discriminatory criteria that must be known in advance.[243] This refers primarily to the conditions laid down in the EU public procurement directives.[244] The requirement for a selection procedure for certain authorizations is also stipulated in the Services Directive.[245]

Article 106(2) TFEU has been the focus of much discussion, which we will not revisit here.[246] However, we will come back to this provision in Chapter 8. The relevance of Article 106(2) TFEU for SGEI has been undermined by case law that denies the existence of an undertaking in the meaning of Articles 101 and 102 TFEU in cases on national

PSO, limiting the room for manoeuvre for Member States in implementing these obligations. See e.g. Art. 3(8) Directive 2003/54/EC of the European Parliament and the Council of 26 June 2003 concerning common rules for the internal market in electricity, OJ 2003 No. L176/37. See also M. Krajewski, 'Universal service provisions in international agreements of the EU', in E. Szyszczak *et al.* (eds.), *Developments in Services of General Interest* (TMC Asser, Springer, 2011), pp. 231–50 at p. 235.

242 See C-159/94, *Commission* v. *France (EDF)* [1997] ECR I-5815, para. 65. See, among others, Case 127/73, *SABAM* [1974] ECR 313; Case 155/73, *Sacchi* [1974] ECR 409; Case 66/86 *Ahmed Saeed Flugreisen* [1989] ECR 803; Case C-179/90, *Merci Convenzionali Porto di Genova* [1991] ECR I-5889; Case C-320/91, *Corbeau* [1993] ECR I-2533; Case C-242/95, *GT-Link A/S* v. *De Danske Statsbaner* (DSB) [1997] ECR I-4449; Case C-67/96, *Albany International* [1999] ECR I-5751; Case C-340/99, *TNT Traco* [2001] ECR I-4109; Case C-475/99, *Ambulanz Glöckner* [2001] ECR I-8089. See also Directive 2006/123/EC, Rec. 70. See European Commission, Non-Paper, Services of general economic interest and state aid, 12.11.2002, paras. 62 *et seq.*

243 See Case C-205/99, *Analir* [2001] ECR I-1271, para. 40.

244 See Directive 2004/18/EC of the European Parliament and the Council of 31 March 2004 on the coordination of procedures for the award of public works contracts, public supply contracts and public service contracts, OJ 2004 No. L134/114; Directive 2004/17/EC of the European Parliament and the Council of 31 March 2004 coordinating the procurement procedures of entities operating in the water, energy, transport and postal services sectors, OJ 2004 No. L134/1.

245 See Art. 12 Directive 2006/123/EC. See also J. van de Gronden, 'The EU and WTO law on free trade in services and the public interest: towards a framework directive on Services of General Economic Interest?', in J. van de Gronden (ed.), *EU and WTO Law on Services: Limits to the Realisation of General Interest Policies within the Services Markets?* (The Hague: Kluwer, 2008), pp. 247–80 at p. 258, who writes of 'public procurement-like procedures'.

246 See W. Sauter, 'Services of general economic interest and universal service in EU law' (2008) 2 *European Law Review* 167–93 at 186–8. For criticism of the use of this provision, see Davies, 'What does Article 86 actually do?', pp. 58–62.

social security systems on the one hand, and by case law denying the existence of state aid under certain conditions on the other hand.[247] Whereas we will discuss the former cases in Chapter 8, in the following section we will deal with the state aid exception introduced by the *Altmark* case.

#### 3.5.3.4 The exception from the exception and the *Altmark* criteria

Undertakings entrusted with PSOs may be entitled to receive appropriate economic compensation for the supplementary costs they incur by providing services at a loss. Such compensation is intended to ensure performance of the services under conditions of economic equilibrium.[248] However, according to Article 107 TFEU, 'any aid granted by a Member State or through State resources in any form whatsoever which distorts or threatens to distort competition by favouring certain undertakings or the production of certain goods shall, in so far as it affects trade between Member States, be incompatible with the internal market.' For a long time the approach by the Commission and in case law on whether public compensation for PSOs would constitute an 'advantage' in the sense of Article 107(1) TFEU was inconsistent, displaying frequent and unexpected conceptual shifts.[249]

It was not until its landmark decision in the *Altmark* case in 2003 that the ECJ established four procedural and substantive conditions that must be satisfied cumulatively in order to exempt a compensatory measure from the scope of the state aid regime, and thus from any notification requirement.[250] These conditions are that (1) the beneficiary must be entrusted with a clearly defined PSO, (2) compensation must be

[247] See M. Krajewski, *Grundstrukturen des Rechts öffentlicher Dienstleistungen* (Heidelberg: Springer, 2011), p. 87.

[248] In its Green Paper on SGI, COM (2003)270, para. 4.2, the Commission distinguishes between five ways of financing PSOs.

[249] See Case T-106/95, *FFSA* [1997] ECR II-229, and Case C-53/00, *Ferring* [2001] ECR I-9067. Proponents of the so-called state aid approach could be distinguished from those advocating the so-called compensation approach. See E. Szyszczak, 'Cases: financing services of general economic interest' (2004) 67(6) *Modern Law Review* 982–1011 at 983; N. Fiedziuk, 'Towards a more refined economic approach to services of general economic interest' (2010) 16(2) *European Public Law* 271–88.

[250] Case C-280/00, *Altmark Trans* [2003] ECR I-7747. J. van de Gronden, 'Social services of general interest and EU law', in E. Szyszczak *et al.* (eds.) *Developments in Services of General Interest*, Legal Issues of Services of General Interest (The Hague: TMC Asser, 2011), pp. 123–51 at p. 141, has called the latter element the great advantage of *Altmark*.

calculated in an objective and transparent matter,[251] (3) compensation must not exceed what is necessary to indemnify for the costs incurred, and (4) the beneficiary has to be chosen either by public tender or by awarding compensation which must not exceed the costs of a well-run undertaking that is adequately equipped to meet necessary public service requirements. Thus it can be said that there is no qualification as state aid unless there is over-compensation relative to the costs that an efficient company would have incurred.[252] The fourth *Altmark* criterion represents a preference for establishing a direct and manifest link between financing granted and the general interest duties imposed through a public service contract concluded with an undertaking in accordance with public procurement rules.[253]

[251] On the centrality of transparency in this context, see M. Krajewski, 'Conclusion', in M. Krajewski, U. Neergaard, and J. van de Gronden (eds.), *The Changing Legal Framework for Services of General Interest in Europe: Between Competition and Solidarity* (The Hague: TMC Asser, Kluwer, 2009), pp. 500–1.

[252] The benchmarking exercise in *Altmark* is principally aimed at the objectives of efficiency and transparency by cementing and clarifying established case law in the first and third condition, and by introducing new standards in the second and fourth condition. See among others the annotation to the case by Szyszczak, 'Cases: financing services of general economic interest', 982–1011; F. Louis and A. Vallery, 'Ferring revisited: the Altmark case and state financing of public service obligations' (2004) 27(1) *World Competition* 53–74 at 68ff. The fear that this approach would deprive Art. 106(2) TFEU of its effect has been proven wrong by subsequent Commission practice. See e.g. Commission Decision 2004/339/EC of 15 October 2003 on the measures implemented by Italy for RAI SpA, OJ 2004 No. L119/1, para. 99. *Altmark* has been said to adopt a hybrid between a compensation and a quid pro quo approach. C. Bovis, 'Financing services of general interest in the EU: how do public procurement and state aids interact to demarcate between market forces and protection?' (2005) *European Law Journal* 79–109 at 168.

[253] See M. Krajewski, 'Conclusion', in M. Krajewski, U. Neergaard, and J. van de Gronden (eds.), *The Changing Legal Framework for Services of General Interest in Europe: Between Competition and Solidarity* (The Hague: TMC Asser, Kluwer, 2009), pp. 499–506 at p. 501; Bovis, 'Financing services of general interest', 96; G. Skovgaard Olykke, 'The definition of a contract under Article 106 TFEU', in E. Szyszczak *et al.* (eds.), *Developments in Services of General Interest* (TMC Asser, Springer, 2011), pp. 103–20 at pp. 103–20. Conversely, the absence of a call for tender in the field of public service provision does not mean that there is a case of state aid. See also European Commission, Staff Working Document, FAQ concerning the application of public procurement rules to social services of general interest, SEC(2007)1514, para. 2.11. Note that the Court has also accepted the direct award of contracts to 'in-house' entities in cases such as C-107/98, *Teckal* [1999] ECR I-8121. On this see W. Frenz and P. Schleissing, 'The never ending story of "in-house" procurement', in M. Krajewski, U. Neergaard and J. van de Gronden (eds.), *The Changing Legal Framework for Services of General Interest in Europe: Between Competition and Solidarity* (The Hague: TMC Asser, Kluwer, 2009), pp. 171–87.

While public tender procedures may inject a certain degree of competition into the process of financing public services, some doubts remain. It seems questionable whether a tender procedure can really reflect the capacity of entrusted companies and private undertakings to compete effectively. The market price revealed by a public procurement procedure may not necessarily determine whether subsequent state funding will be excessive.[254] Moreover, the discharge of public services involves subjective elements, which risk additionally affecting legal certainty. This concerns the concept of reasonable profit and the option to draw a (hypothetical) comparison of entrusted undertakings with private markets or competitors. The approach at issue also refers to the nature and procedural quality of acts underlying public compensation of public services instead of on their effects.[255] On the other hand, a more subtle approach to measuring over-compensation risks becoming too complex. It might therefore be preferable to accept certain imprecision for the sake of a maximum degree of transparency in the relationship between Member States and undertakings entrusted with SGEI.

In *Altmark* the Court acknowledged that open tender procedures might not fit all circumstances and sectors. Therefore, the alternative is for the SGEI provider to prove not only that it incurred costs in discharging PSOs, but that these costs equal those incurred by any other 'typical' or 'ideal' undertaking entrusted with a similar set of services. We would submit that this finding is based on the misleading assumption that the compensation of public services is generally placed into a competitive setting. This does not hold water in scenarios where no market exists for the service under consideration, so that any comparison with private competitors becomes purely hypothetical.[256] Moreover, under the second alternative for fulfilling the fourth *Altmark* condition, comparison is required with how a private undertaking would act under similar circumstances. However, this misreads the motivation for entrusting undertakings with PSOs. While a private actor is generally driven by the objective of maximizing its revenue, the financing of SGEI strives to satisfy public interests that would otherwise not be

[254] Such an appraisal depends upon whether the public contract has been awarded with reference to the lowest price or whether additional factors have been taken into consideration in order to choose the most economically advantageous offer.

[255] See C-6/97, *Italy* v. *Commission (Tax Credit)* [1999] ECR I-2981, para. 11; Case T-288/97, *Regione autonoma Friuli Venezia Giulia* [1999] ECR II-1871, para. 46.

[256] See Joined Cases C-83/01P, C-93/01P and C-94/01P, *Chronopost* [2003] ECR I-6993.

catered to by private entities, precisely because of their lack of commercial profit. Thus the economic ratio behind private investors on the one hand, and that behind actors entrusted with the performance of SGEI on the other hand, cannot be validly compared.

*Altmark* raised the issue of what should apply if a Member State fails to fulfil the above-stated criteria.[257] As mentioned, before *Altmark* the case law was rather inconsistent. Consequently, the Commission presented the so-called Monti Package on financing SGEI, consisting of Decision 2005/842 and the Community framework.[258] However, this regime had the weakness that it was limited in scope, exempting medium-sized and large enterprises below a certain threshold of compensation and turnover.[259] The Framework clarified that Article 106(2) TFEU applies to measures not fulfilling the *Altmark* criteria.[260] The criterion of over-compensation was central to obtaining Commission clearance under the Monti Package.[261] In December 2011 this package was replaced by the Almunia Package, comprising four instruments clarifying basic concepts, providing exemption from the notification obligation for certain categories of SGEI, setting conditions for large compensation amounts, and providing of a de minimis rule for state aid given to undertakings.[262]

[257] See O. Lynskey, 'The application of Article 86(2) EC to measures which do not fulfil the Altmark criteria' (2007) 30(1) *World Competition* 153–68 at 158ff.

[258] Community framework for state aid in the form of public service compensation, OJ C 297, 29.11.2005, 4–7. On this see, among others, J.-M. Thouvenin, 'The Altmark case and its consequences', in M. Krajewski, U. Neergaard and J. van de Gronden (eds.), *The Changing Legal Framework for Services of General Interest in Europe: Between Competition and Solidarity* (The Hague: TMC Asser, Kluwer, 2009), pp. 103–15 at pp. 113–14.

[259] Compensation not exceeding EUR 30m per year granted to undertakings with an annual turnover of less than EUR 100m. In contrast, no financial threshold was set with regard to the funding of hospitals and social housing undertakings carrying out SGEI.

[260] European Commission, Communication on the application of State aid rules to public service broadcasting, OJ 2001 No. C320/5. The Framework covered all sectors with the exception of transport and public service broadcasting without a threshold.

[261] See the Commission Directive 2006/111/EC of 16 November 2006 on the transparency of financial relations between Member States and public undertakings as well as on financial transparency within certain undertakings, OJ 2006 No. L318/17. The requirements as to the selection method and efficiency-related concerns introduced by the Court in the fourth *Altmark* condition thus have not found entrance into the Monti Package.

[262] See N. Fiedziuk, 'Putting services of general economic interest up for tender: reflections on applicable rules' (2013) 50 *Common Market Law Review* 87–114 at 91–2.

## 3.6 Conclusion

This chapter has shown that the EU law regime on services suffers from some 'horizontal' issues such as on the appropriate standard for the proportionality test. Here, suitability seems to have stepped out of the shadow of the second tier of the principle by scrutinizing the inherent logic of national regulatory choices under a 'consistent and systematic' test. With the justifications regime, the level of convergence both between the different freedoms as well as between the regimes for discriminatory and non-discriminatory measures has been shown. The justification with environmental interests of the Member States in particular seems to transcend these borders.

The EU law on services also betrays some 'sectoral' intricacies, such as the very complex regime on SGEI, where private investors are referred to in order to justify exemptions from the market rules. We have also noted the subtle and not so subtle deviations from the 'normal' standards of examination that apply to gambling services. In this area especially, the principle that equivalent requirements must be recognized by the host state, granting the home state a quasi-regulatory role in a double burden constellation, is largely defunct. Thus, while the Court preaches consistency to the Member States qua proportionality, its own record on this count is rather poor.

We have also made comparisons to WTO law, not only as regards the proportionality test, where we have found similarities with the burden of proof imposed, but also with regard to the delimitation between the goods and the services regimes, which proves difficult both in EU and WTO law. In EU law, we have seen that despite some tendencies of convergence between the regimes on services and establishments in case law, this has been countered by the divergent regimes adopted in the Services Directive, subjecting services and establishments to three different legal regimes. Moreover, we have shown that established providers of goods are subject to a different regime to that covering established service providers, raising issues of equal treatment.

In the next chapter we will discuss more generally mould the way Union law approaches the regulation by Member States of national markets. Here, the legal development of the rules regarding *all* four fundamental freedoms underwent a series of tectonic shifts.

# 4 Deconstructing EU law on services and establishments

## 4.1 Introduction

Case law allows us to identify two perspectives from which the freedom of establishment and the free movement of services may be analysed. The first is based on an assessment of the sort of national measures the freedoms are targeting. This refers to the application of the freedoms not only to discriminatory Member State measures, but also to non-discriminatory Member State measures (restrictions). With this legal development by the Court, the intensity of the interference by Union law with national regulatory autonomy has been drastically increased. Second, we will discuss the Union regime as essentially balancing the imposition of market access for foreign providers and service recipients on the one hand, and levelling the playing field for those persons when they are already operating within the market of another Member State. This is thus the analogy to the distinction under WTO law between national treatment and domestic regulation.[1]

As we will show, there is little consistency on this in case law, and even less can we find an openly declared adherence by the Court to either of the two models of deregulating the common market. These analytical instruments might therefore be faulted for overly simplifying a very complex and casuistic regime. Nonetheless, we consider this analytical framework useful for assessing various aspects of the interplay between EU primary law, the Services Directive and WTO law. While the focus of this study is on services offered by both established and non-established providers, in this chapter we will also refer to the

[1] We will sometimes also refer to the latter approach in the EU law context as 'domestic regulation'. The reason for this is one of perspective only. It should not be taken to imply any more pronounced analogies with the scope of Article VI GATS.

Union law regime on the trade in goods for reasons of comparison and because there is a discussion about adopting key principles from this regime for the area of services.

We will therefore start by examining the dichotomy between a discrimination standard and a restrictions standard, followed by an examination of the dichotomy between a domestic regulation standard and a market access standard. Moreover, we will discuss two complex issues closely related to these principles of regulation. The first concerns the standard of review applying to certain selling arrangements in the goods context and the question of whether this is or could be applied in the area of services. Finally, we will analyse more closely the concept of discrimination as employed under EU law and show that this, on close inspection, has become a very confusing matter.

## 4.2 Some initial thoughts on deconstructing the regulatory standards

### *4.2.1 Discriminatory measures and restrictions*

The ECJ examines cases based on whether national laws and regulations discriminate against products or persons from other Member States. Other cases explore whether a national measure constitutes an 'obstacle', 'impediment', 'hindrance' or 'restriction' to the exercise of the freedom at issue. Thus there is a dichotomy between a discrimination standard and a restrictions standard in the case law of the Court. In the doctrine, this has been discussed under the terms 'fundamental freedoms vs. fundamental rights',[2] and it has been insinuated that the latter should be the reserve of the Member States.[3] The key question with this standard is, therefore, whether a national regulatory measure discriminates foreign market participants or whether a measure is 'neutral' in its application.

As we will see, the difficulty with this distinction is how far to cast the net of the anti-discrimination rule. Clearly, open discrimination is always covered; it is easy to detect and not a huge problem in practice after all the years of market integration. Indirect discrimination,

[2] 'Fundamental rights' is a rather misleading translation of the German and Austrian concept of '*Grundrechte*' which includes, e.g., the constitutional right to freely choose one's profession.

[3] T. Kingreen, 'Fundamental freedoms', in A. von Bogdandy and J. Bast (eds.), *Principles of European Constitutional Law* (Oxford and Portland, OR: Hart Publishing, 2005), p. 571.

in contrast, is a much thornier category and, as we will see, excruciatingly difficult to distinguish from measures affecting market access in those cases where such standard has played a role. Moreover, the definition of 'restriction' or the synonymous terms quoted above have a very opaque side to them. They not only differentiate measures that are not discriminatory, but also comprise the idea that not all national measures must necessarily constitute an obstacle to Union trade.

The trade-off between the discrimination standard and the restrictions standard concerns the extent of remaining regulatory autonomy of the Member States. If the Treaty is broad enough to cover national laws and regulations with no open or indirect intent to discriminate, then such national measures are, in principle, subject to the scrutiny of the ECJ. It has been remarked that, for this very reason, the restrictions standard has been a mixed blessing for the Court. On the one hand, it has bolstered the Court's jurisdiction and, thus, its standing. On the other hand, this extension spawned an onslaught of cases brought before the Court in the hope of overcoming national measures considered restrictive.[4] Attempts to somehow mitigate the restrictions standard have led to some of the most complex and ambiguous developments in case law in this area. On the one hand, this concerns the *Keck* strand of jurisprudence in the free movement of goods; on the other hand, it concerns a variety of judgments in the other freedoms that are even harder to classify. At the same time, it is evident that the restrictions standard is more conducive to the ending of trade-preventing or trade-reducing national practices.

The possible approaches to liberalizing trade in services in the EU from a perspective of a dichotomy between a restrictions and a discrimination standard is summarized in Table 4.1.

In the services context it has been claimed that 'the *Säger* market access test became the principle frame for analysis in nearly all cases after *Kraus* other than those concerning refusal of entry/deportation and direct discrimination'.[5] This is somewhat misleading in its reference to market access since it insinuates that the Court is employing

[4] See M. Poiares Maduro, 'Harmony and dissonance in free movement', in M. Andenas and W.-H. Roth (eds.), *Services and Free Movement in EU Law* (The Hague: Kluwer, 2002), pp. 41–68 at pp. 47–8.

[5] C. Barnard, *The Substantive Law of the EU: The Four Freedoms*, 3rd edn (Oxford University Press, 2010), p. 279.

Table 4.1 Discrimination standard versus restrictions standard

| Discrimination standard | Restrictions standard | Combined standard I |
|---|---|---|
| Only targets discriminatory measures | Targets both discriminatory and non-discriminatory measures | Targets both discriminatory and non-discriminatory measures |
| Closed list of justifications | Open list of justifications for all measures | Closed list of justifications for discriminatory and open list for non-discriminatory measures |

a full-out market access standard when it is still applying a combined standard.[6] The statement is, however, correct in the sense that the Court is increasingly applying Article 56 TFEU to non-discriminatory national measures and that it subjects both restrictions and indirect discriminations to the open list of justification, as discussed in Chapter 3. The services regime can even claim the title of 'first mover' in this respect.[7] As a regulatory model, this has become known as the principle of 'general prohibition on restrictions'.[8]

Notably, a true shift in the jurisprudence from the discrimination to the restrictions model would presuppose the consistent handling of discriminatory cases as restrictions, and their justification by the open list of mandatory requirements following the *Cassis* case law[9] (see column 2 of Table 4.1). Applying the restrictions standard to *all* cases would therefore lead to the complete irrelevance of the express Treaty justifications. This has not happened either with goods or with services on a large scale. In the goods area, while some cases represent a substitution in the sense described, they are still a minority.[10] What can also be observed with services, instead, is the *addition* of the restrictions model to the still-existing discrimination standard (the 'combined standard I' column in Table 4.1). Most discriminatory measures are still qualified as such, and the grounds for justifying them remain limited to the express derogations; this has been seen even in more recent, post-*Säger*

[6] See Table 4.2.

[7] Case 33/74, *Van Binsbergen* [1974] ECR 1299.

[8] See AG Stix-Hackl in Case C-452/04, *Fidium Finanz* [2006] ECR I-9521, para. 109; Case C-264/03, *Commission* v. *France* [2005] ECR I-8831, para. 66.

[9] Case 120/78, *Rewe-Zentral AG* [1979] ECR 649.

[10] Case C-204/90, *Bachmann* [1992] ECR I-249; Case C-484/93, *Svensson and Gustavsson* [1995] ECR I-3955, paras. 15–16.

cases.[11] The discrimination standard and the restrictions standard thus co-exist with services in EU law.[12]

### *4.2.2 Market access and domestic regulation*

The second analytical perspective as regards the way Union law limits the Member States' ability to regulate markets is to focus, on the one hand, on measures imposed by a Member State affecting the access of a product or service provider to its market, or, on the other hand, to target national measures restricting the activities of the retailers of products or providers of services once they have imported the goods, crossed the border, transferred the service or set up an establishment.

The thought underlying this distinction is either to concentrate exclusively on measures that prevent products or actors from other Member States from entering the market, or to reach further into the core of the territorial sphere of the Member State. The focus here lies less on the deregulation of national regimes; instead, the aim is to integrate Member State markets.[13] This regulatory choice between market access and domestic regulation has also been discussed under the terms 'market access rights vs. market design rights'.[14]

As with the discrimination/restrictions nexus, a regulatory concept based on market access may be exclusive of any other qualification. In such case, a national measure would either affect market access or would be market access-neutral (see column 2 in Table 4.2). Alternatively, the market access model could be 'merged' with the domestic regulation model. In this case, only non-discriminatory measures are examined in light of their effect on market access, and a separate justifications regime is applied to discriminatory measures (the combined standard II in column 3 of Table 4.2). It can thus be misleading to speak of a market access standard without any further specification, since this could refer to either the second or the third column in Table 4.2.

[11] Case C-250/95, *Futura Participations* [1997] ECR I-2471; Case C-446/03, *Marks & Spencer* [2005] ECR I-10837.

[12] W.-H. Roth, 'The European Court of Justice's case law in the freedom to provide services: is Keck relevant?', in M. Andenas and W.-H. Roth (eds.), *Services and Free Movement in EU Law* (The Hague: Kluwer, 2002), pp. 1–24 at pp. 6 and 14.

[13] Roth, 'The European Court of Justice's case law', p. 10. See also the system described by C. Barnard and S. Deakin, 'Market access and regulatory competition', in C. Barnard and J. Scott (eds.), *The Law of the Single European Market: Unpacking the Premises* (Oxford and Portland, OR: Hart Publishing, 2002), pp. 197–224 at pp. 204–13.

[14] Kingreen, 'Fundamental freedoms', p. 571.

Table 4.2 Market access versus domestic regulation standard

| Domestic regulation standard | Market access standard | Combined standard II |
|---|---|---|
| Targets both discriminatory and non-discriminatory measures | Targets discriminatory and non-discriminatory measures only when they affect market access | Targets discriminatory measures; targets non-discriminatory measures only when they affect market access |
| Open list of justifications for all or only for non-discriminatory measures | Open list of justifications for all measures | Closed list of justifications for discriminatory measures; open list for non-discriminatory measures |

## 4.3 The trouble with *Keck*

### 4.3.1 *Introduction*

The *Keck* case law and its progeny has been a constant preoccupation of the doctrine since its inception. It is not my intention to revisit the discussion on it in detail. However, some comments on a meta level are appropriate. First, there are without doubt many ways to conceptualize the case law of the Court, even if it were a consistent one by its own standards, which it is not. Second, most of the important contributions dealing with *Keck* and/or the standards for review with regard to restrictions have adopted either the perspective of market access or of discrimination and have on both accounts shed light on some aspects of the case law. However, the more fundamental problem underpinning this case law requires us to look at market access and discrimination together. As we shall see, this is also how we must understand the case law, that is as an amalgam of both standards.

It has been suggested that the relationship between indirect discrimination, direct discrimination and restrictions should be framed in the following terms.[15] Discriminatory measures have been said to impose a *different burden in law and in fact*. They differentiate to the detriment of operators from a Member State other than the one making the rule. Restrictive measures, conversely, can be represented to impose the *same burden in law and in fact*. Thus there is a burden but it is non-discriminatory. Between these two opposites, indirect discrimination takes the middle ground. Its regulatory impact on operators in the common market corresponds to imposing the *same burden in law but a different burden*

[15] See Barnard, *The Substantive Law of the EU*.

*in fact*. While we do not agree that this conceptualization is always helpful, we will refer to it below, not least because it is also sometimes used by the Court.

### 4.3.2 *The double rule exception in* Keck *and* Gourmet

Under the free movement of goods, the Court introduced a complicated double rule exception regime for the application of Article 34 TFEU in *Keck* and *Gourmet*.[16] This was meant to address the litigation frenzy directed against national measures in the wake of *Dassonville*.[17] The Court decided to consider some *non*-discriminatory measures as so undisruptive to free trade in the Union that they are per se qualified as not being restrictive and thus do not require justification. It held that national laws and regulations would not constitute measures having equivalent effect to quantitative restrictions if they are certain selling arrangements. The term certain selling arrangements has been given a broad reading in the literature, encompassing 'other types of market regulation rules which do not regulate the characteristics of a product but simply govern the conditions and methods of sale or other marketing circumstances'.[18] In other words, certain selling arrangements would be 'provisions concerning inter alia the place and time of sale of certain products and advertising of those products as well as certain marketing methods'.[19] Note that certain selling arrangements, as the most 'harmless' type of domestic regulation under the goods regime, remain within the scope of application of the Treaty because they are subject to the discrimination standard of scrutiny. In contrast, a Member State law or regulation is caught by Article 34 TFEU when it affects the characteristics or the content of a product ('product requirement').[20]

In *Gourmet*, a case on a Swedish prohibition on the advertising of alcoholic beverages, the Court added an exception to this exception from the general prohibition of measures having equivalent effect under the free movement of goods.[21] Selling arrangements would also be qualified as restrictions if they have 'a particular effect on the cross-

[16] Joined Cases C-267 and 268/91, *Keck and Mithouard* [1993] ECR I-6097; Case C-405/98, *Gourmet* [2001] ECR I-1795.

[17] Case 8/74, *Dassonville* [1974] ECR 837. See Poiares Maduro, 'Harmony and dissonance in free movement', p. 52.

[18] Poiares Maduro, 'Harmony and dissonance in free movement', p. 55.

[19] Case C-71/02, *Karner* [2004] ECR I-3025, para. 38.

[20] But see the 'borderline' cases: Case C-368/95, *Familiapress* [1997] ECR I-3689, and Case C-470/93, *Mars GmbH* [1995] ECR I-1923.

[21] Case C-405/98, *Gourmet* [2001] ECR I-1795.

border supply of advertising space, given the international nature of the advertising market in the category of products to which the prohibition relates'.[22]

Thus, if a Member State measure qualifies as a certain selling arrangement, it does not need to be justified by mandatory requirements of the public interest, because it is not caught by the freedom. Only if it is discriminatory must it be justified under the express derogations of Article 36 TFEU. This places the treatment of certain selling arrangements under the combined standard II in Table 4.2. The treatment of product requirements, in contrast, comes under the combined standard I in Table 4.1. This regime – created by the ECJ for the sake of clarification(!) – has given cause for criticism.[23] Not only is the distinction between certain selling arrangements and product requirements intricate in some cases, it is also often cumbersome to find out when market access is affected.[24]

Especially from a WTO perspective, a 'rule of reason' standard is often referred to when writing about the goods regime in EU law. Thus Ortino has argued that the 'rule of reason' doctrine fully elaborated in *Cassis* brings national measures outside of the scope of the Treaty.[25] In his words, 'if an indistinctly applicable measure is necessary to satisfy "mandatory requirements", that measure falls outside the scope of application of Article 28 altogether.'[26] However, this is a misrepresentation of the general prohibition of restrictions under the goods regime. Measures qualifying as having such equivalent effect come within the scope of the Treaty irrespective of whether they are eventually justified and deemed proportional. Such statement of an exemption of certain measures from the scope of the Treaty can only be made with

[22] Case C-405/98, *Gourmet* [2001] ECR I-1795, para. 39

[23] See, among others, C. Barnard, 'Fitting the remaining pieces into the goods and persons jigsaw?' (2001) 26 *European Law Review* 35–59 at 42, calling it an 'unnecessary straightjacket'; and Poiares Maduro, 'Harmony and dissonance in free movement', p. 54, note 52.

[24] P. Craig and G. de Búrca, *EU Law: Texts and Materials*, 5th edn (Oxford University Press, 2011), pp. 664–5; Barnard, 'Fitting the remaining pieces into the goods and persons jigsaw?', 55–7.

[25] Case 120/78, *Rewe-Zentral AG* [1979] ECR 649. See F. Ortino, *Basic Legal Instruments for the Liberalisation of Trade: A Comparative Analysis of EC and WTO Law* (Oxford and Portland, OR: Hart Publishing, 2004), p. 392. See H. Zúñiga Schroder, *Harmonization, Equivalence and Mutual Recognition of Standards in WTO Law* (Alphen/Rijn: Kluwer Law International, 2011), p. 157.

[26] Ortino, *Basic Legal Instruments for the Liberalisation of Trade*, p. 393.

respect to certain selling arrangements in the sense of the *Keck* case law. It is equally misleading if it is implied that in *Keck* the Court would have employed a proportionality review that was somehow different from the one in *Cassis*.[27] The proportionality test under the *Keck* regime is not different from the proportionality review of measures that do not fall under the certain selling arrangements/product requirements classification.

### 4.3.3 *Which regulatory standard does* Keck *represent?*

We would argue that a lot of the discussion on the meaning of the part in *Keck* referring to an imposition of the same burden 'in law and in fact' has its roots in a failure clearly to separate the discrimination/restrictions discourse from the domestic regulation/market access discourse. In *Keck* the Court arguably referred to the former dichotomy up to paragraph 16, where it argued that national measures would fall under (what is now) Article 34 TFEU if they affect foreign products differently 'in fact' and/or 'in law':

> By contrast, contrary to what has previously been decided, the application to products from other Member States of national provisions restricting or prohibiting certain selling arrangements is not such as to hinder directly or indirectly, actually or potentially, trade between Member States within the meaning of the *Dassonville* judgment ... so long as those provisions apply to all relevant traders operating within the national territory and so long as they affect in the same manner, in law and in fact, the marketing of domestic products and of those from other Member States.[28]

This corresponds to a perspective that looks at whether measures operate to the particular detriment of foreigners.[29] This is the language of indirect discrimination, as we have explained above.

In contrast, with paragraph 17 in the *Keck* judgment the Court switched to a discourse in terms of market access:[30]

> Provided that those conditions are fulfilled, the application of such rules to the sale of products from another Member State meeting the requirements laid down by that State is not by nature such as to prevent their access to the

[27] Case 120/78, *Rewe-Zentral* [1979] ECR 649. Zúñiga Schroder, *Harmonization, Equivalence and Mutual Recognition of Standards*, p. 159.

[28] Joined Cases C-267 and 268/91, *Keck and Mithouard* [1993] ECR I-6097, para. 16.

[29] See C-237/94, *O'Flynn* [1996] ECR I-2617.

[30] See the annotation by C. Lang, 'Annotation of the *DocMorris* case' (2005) *Common Market Law Review* 189–204 at 194–5.

market or to impede access any more than it impedes the access of domestic products.[31]

The problem is that indirectly discriminatory measures that are more detrimental to foreigners than to nationals might at the same time affect the willingness and ability of the foreigner to access the respective market. This can be illustrated by example of the prohibition of certain resale modes. If a Member State prohibits online selling completely for certain products, how must this be qualified? When foreigners can only effectively enter the market when they sell their products online, it is an indirect discrimination as defined above, imposing a different burden in fact that is particularly detrimental to foreigners. At the same time, however, it can be seen as impairing market access for foreigners since they need to use distance selling to be able to enter the market.

We would suggest seeing paragraph 17 of *Keck* as an extension of the second leg of paragraph 16. In *Ker-Optika* on a Hungarian prohibition on the selling of contact lenses via the Internet, after a rendition of *Keck*, the Court inquired whether the measure concerned 'applies to all relevant traders operating within the national territory and whether it affects in the same manner, in law and in fact, the selling of domestic products and the selling of those from other Member States'.[32] Affirming the first criterion, the Court continued in clear market access language.[33] This collapses paragraphs 16 and 17 into two tests: discrimination and market access.

*Keck* and its progeny are therefore problematic for using the language of discrimination when at the same time they are about market access. We would suggest that this explains the general difficulty in the literature with the post-*Keck* case law also regarding the other freedoms.[34] Take the *DocMorris* case, which concerned a national prohibition for the online resale of certain pharmaceuticals.[35] In this case the Advocate General relied on a market access discourse in line with the reasoning

[31] Joined Cases C-267 and 268/91, *Keck and Mithouard* [1993] ECR I-6097, para. 17.

[32] Case C-108/09, *Ker-Optika* [2010] ECR I-12213, para 52.

[33] Case C-108/09, *Ker-Optika* [2010] ECR I-12213, para 54: 'It is clear that the prohibition on selling contact lenses by mail order deprives traders from other Member States of a particularly effective means of selling those products and thus significantly impedes access of those traders to the market of the Member State concerned.'

[34] See E. Spaventa, 'Annotation to Case C-442/02, Caixa-Bank France v. Ministère de l'Économie, des Finances et de l'Industrie' (2005) 42(4) *Common Market Law Review* 1151–68 at 1159–61.

[35] Case C-322/01, *DocMorris* [2003] ECR I-14887.

in paragraph 17 of *Keck*. The Court, however, argued in terms of discrimination relying on paragraph 16 of *Keck*. Both came to the same conclusion, qualifying the national regulation as a measure having equivalent effect.[36] As long as the *Keck* jurisprudence is conceived as being about discrimination, it does not provide the adequate conceptual framework for addressing borderline cases such as *DocMorris*. The unease expressed by Wilsher with regard to the discrimination language used by the Court is therefore comprehensible.[37] However, the solution to this cannot be to tailor the discrimination standard to the case law by moulding the test required under a genuine discrimination standard to the standards applied by the Court, as suggested by Wilsher, but to accept that what is applied is something other than such discrimination standard *stricto sensu*.[38]

## 4.4 The market access–domestic regulation dichotomy in EU services law

### 4.4.1 *The application of* Keck *to services*

The *Keck* and *Gourmet* case law has not been adopted for the field of services by the Court.[39] In *Alpine Investments*, which was the first services judgment addressing this issue, the ECJ refused to extend the *Keck* jurisprudence to the field of application of Article 56 TFEU, distinguishing

[36] See Lang, 'Annotation of the *DocMorris* case', 201–3.

[37] D. Wilsher, 'Does Keck discrimination make any sense? An assessment of the non-discrimination principle within the European Single Market' (2008) 33 *European Law Review* 3–22 at 20: '"market access" practice is being cloaked in discrimination language.'

[38] For a different perspective, see Wilsher, 'Does Keck discrimination make any sense?', 10, who has even proffered that *Dassonville* has been about indirect discrimination.

[39] See C. Calliess, 'Europäischer Binnenmarkt und europäische Demokratie: von der Dienstleistungsfreiheit zur Dienstleistungsrichtlinie – und wieder Retour?' (2007) *Deutsches Verwaltungsblatt* 336–46 at 338 with further German references. Contrary to the law on services, as laid down above, there has not even been a discussion on transposing the *Keck* doctrine to establishments. Nonetheless, Member State measures may well be classified according to their impact on the exercise of the freedom of establishment, which may 'bite' either up front prior to or coincident with establishment, or may impose burdens at a later stage. The first category includes, e.g., qualification and registration requirements. The latter category includes rules on what the established actor may lawfully do in the host Member State and what the establishment must adhere to in order to be allowed to maintain its activities there.

the case from *Keck* on the facts.[40] This has prompted a debate in the literature whether that refusal represented a complete and definite rejection, or whether it implies the potential application of the *Keck* principles depending on the circumstances.[41] The former reading of the case law is arguably supported by the Court's refusal in *Bosman* to transpose the *Keck* principles to the field of the free movement of workers and the freedom of establishment.[42] Moreover, the Court did not follow the explicit invitation by AG Tizzano in *CaixaBank* to confirm a *Keck*-friendly reading of its previous case law.[43]

It is, however, interesting to note that in case law on the free movement of capital, when Member States tried to defend 'golden-sharish' rules[44] by invoking *Keck*, the Court did enter into this discourse, holding that these measures would constitute restrictions because 'they affect the position of a person acquiring a shareholding as such and are thus liable to deter investors from other Member States from making such investments and, consequently, affect access to the market'.[45] It is also noteworthy that on these occasions the Court referred to *Alpine Investments* when rendering the *Keck* doctrine.[46]

It has been argued that certain selling arrangements should be translated into the services context as Member State rules on quality and as the very act of the provision of the service.[47] It has also been proposed to frame the pertinent problem in terms of national rules that

[40] Case C-384/93, *Alpine Investments* [1995] ECR I-1141, para. 36: 'is not analogous to the legislation concerning selling arrangements held in Keck and Mithouard'.

[41] See among others J. L. Da Cruz Vilaça, 'On the application of Keck in the field of free provision of services', in M. Andenas and W.-H. Roth (eds.), *Services and Free Movement in EU Law* (Oxford University Press, 2003), pp. 25–40; Roth, 'The European Court of Justice's case law', pp. 1–24; both with numerous further references.

[42] Case C-415/93, *Bosman* [1995] ECR I-4921, para. 103, arguing with the incomparability of these areas.

[43] Opinion of AG Tizzano in Case C-442/02, *CaixaBank* [2004] ECR I-8961.

[44] The right of veto over certain general assembly resolutions, the exemption enjoyed by the Portuguese State from the 5 per cent voting ceiling and the right to appoint a director, in the event that the state has voted against the nominees successfully elected as directors.

[45] See, e.g., Case C-543/08, *Commission* v. *Portugal (Golden Shares)* [2010] ECR I-11241, para. 68.

[46] Case C-543/08, *Commission* v. *Portugal (Golden Shares)* [2010] ECR I-11241, para. 67.

[47] Calliess, 'Europäischer Binnenmarkt', 338 ('Regelungen der nationalen Qualitäts- und Tätigkeitskontrolle'). Calliess has claimed that the Court applied the *Keck* analogy in *Alpine Investments*. For a different perspective and classification, see Roth, 'The European Court of Justice's case law', pp. 15–16. Barnard, *The Substantive Law of the EU*, pp. 243–5, doubts that *Keck*-like principles do not apply equally to the free movement of persons.

merely structure the market, or, in other words, merely reduce the 'economic attractiveness' of exercising a freedom in a Member State.[48] (Non-discriminatory) rules of this nature should only be caught by Article 56 TFEU if they impede market access.[49] Such rules of the game are national laws and regulations that primarily pertain to commercial activities, and only have an indirect effect on other, private activities. Examples would include labour laws, environmental protection rules or consumer laws, as well as rules on shop opening hours, marketing and pricing.

Classifications such as these might give rise to the same concerns regarding the clarity of such categories as under the goods regime. Moreover, in general the adoption of the *Keck* concept of certain selling arrangements for services could also be seen as detrimental to Member State autonomy for the following reason. As explained, it would mean that certain national rules would only be subjected to the discrimination/market access standard. Conversely, however, it would entail that there would also be the equivalent of product requirements in the field of services. Product requirements, however, do not have the same 'benefit of the doubt' of not being disruptive to trade in the EU.[50] Thus those Member State measures that would *not* qualify as the services equivalent to certain selling arrangements would automatically be subjected to the full restrictions standard. Contrast this with the present situation, where, in theory, non-discriminatory Member State laws and regulations of any nature can escape the scope of Article 56 TFEU altogether, as we will discuss below.

There are examples in the services case law, discussed below, where certain national measures are subjected to a reduced standard of scrutiny. Thus, under Articles 49 and 56 TFEU there has also been case law that exempted certain non-discriminatory national measures from the prohibition of restrictions.[51] This, however, is not (openly) based on considerations of market access. Moreover, these measures are not classified in analogy to *Keck*, or in any other manner. We would proffer that the flexibility of such a regime outweighs the small degree

[48] AG Tizzano in C-442/02, *CaixaBank* [2004] ECR I-8961, paras. 45, 58.

[49] AG Tizzano in C-442/02, *CaixaBank* [2004] ECR I-8961, paras. 45, 58.

[50] See Barnard, *The Substantive Law of the EU*, p. 155.

[51] See also J. Snell, 'Freedom to provide services in the case law and in the Services Directive: problems, solutions, and institutions', in U. Neergaard, R. Nielsen and L. Roseberry (eds.), *The Services Directive: Consequences for the Welfare State and the European Social Model* (Copenhagen: Djof, 2008), pp. 171–97 at p. 187.

of legal clarity that might be gained with a classification of services regulations.

However, it is also correct to question the rationale for the existing diverging approach to achieving the trade-off between the freedoms and national sovereignty.[52] Applying the concept of certain selling arrangements or not applying this regime may result in differences in treatment that again raise doubts with respect to a regime's compliance with the principle of equality. This can be illustrated by national rules on advertising. If they are reviewed in a goods context such as in the *Gourmet* case, they may require justification only if they are discriminatory or they impair market access. Similar measures in the context of services would be considered restrictions and need to be justified irrespective of whether they have an effect on market access.[53]

### *4.4.2 Recital 9 Services Directive*

At this point it is apposite to discuss one aspect of the Services Directive, more fully examined later in this book. Recital 9 Services Directive excludes requirements that 'do not specifically regulate or specifically affect the service activity but have to be respected by providers in the course of carrying out their economic activity in the same way as by individuals acting in their private capacity'. It has been argued that Recital 9 should be understood to reflect the distinction between selling arrangements and product requirements discussed above.[54] This would entail that the rules mentioned in Recital 9, such as road traffic and land planning rules, only constitute restrictions/requirements if they are discriminatory. If they are not discriminatory, they will not be caught by the Services Directive. However, this analogy to the free movement of goods is problematic for several reasons.

First, as explained, the Court has not adopted the *Keck* categories for services. The Directive, so understood, would therefore modify the current EU services regime in an important aspect. We would argue that it is unlikely, even given the poor drafting standards of the Services Directive, that such an important alteration would be hidden in a Recital. Second, the Recital makes a point about rules that 'do not specifically regulate or specifically affect the service activity but have

[52] AG Maduro in Cases C-158 and 159/04, *Alfa Vita* [2006] ECR I-8135, paras. 33, 51.

[53] See Da Cruz Vilaça, 'On the application of Keck', p. 39.

[54] C. Barnard, 'Unravelling the Services Directive' (2008) *Common Market Law Review* 323–94 at 338–9.

to be respected by providers in the course of carrying out their economic activity in the same way as by individuals acting in their private capacity'. This implies an exemption for such Member State laws that affect commercial and private activities equally. However, this would be a novel rationale for exempting non-discriminatory Member State measures from the scope of application of Union law. It certainly does not correspond to the type of certain selling arrangements under the free movement of goods. Nor does it call to mind the case law where the Court found restrictions too remote or insubstantial to warrant their scrutiny under the fundamental freedoms, as discussed later in this book. Finally, road traffic rules or land planning regulations in Member States would hardly ever constitute an obstacle to market access, such as is the case with certain selling arrangements. This, however, means that these rules would be *fully* and (in practice) *unconditionally* exempt from the scope of application of the Services Directive.

### 4.4.3 *Other distinctions between market access and domestic regulation in EU law*

With EU services law, we can examine whether different rules apply based on the qualification of a measure as either affecting access to a services market or as affecting the exercise of the freedom within the market.[55] In secondary law, a distinction between access and exercise is not unknown. Thus the passport directives in the field of insurance, banking and financial services distinguished between authorization requirements and conditions of operation.[56] Snell, in contrast, has argued against making a distinction between rules of access and those of exercise.[57]

In *Alpine Investments* and in other case law, as already mentioned, the criterion was the 'direct impediment to access'. This has been held to represent, as a matter of principle and in 'freedom-neutral' language, a shift from a domestic regulation standard to a market access model (of the Table 4.2 column 2 type, notably).[58] Moreover, in other cases the

[55] Barnard, *The Substantive Law of the EU*, pp. 276–7.

[56] See V. Hatzopoulos, 'Forms of mutual recognition in the field of services', in I. Lianos and O. Odudu (eds.), *Regulating Trade in Services: Trust, Distrust and Economic Integration* (Cambridge University Press, 2012), pp. 59–98 at p. 72.

[57] J. Snell, 'The notion of market access: a concept or a slogan?' (2010) 47 *Common Market Law Review* 437–72 at 445.

[58] See Case C-442/02, *CaixaBank* [2004] ECR I-8961. AG Tizzano in his opinion in this case at para. 54 cites among others Case C-415/93, *Bosman* [1995] ECR I-4921, and Case

Court found measures that 'substantially affect market access' to be caught by Article 49 TFEU, subject to the full list of mandatory requirements.[59] Under the freedom of establishment, such 'all-or-nothing' market access standards can also be observed, although showing even less consistency than with services.[60] Thus, in some cases, the Court seemed to decide exclusively based on a consideration of the relevance of a national measure for impeding market access.

Moreover, a number of other important cases under both freedoms have concerned national measures that are relevant for having market access.[61] First, this concerns flat-out prohibitions of the provision of a certain service, such as with monopolies.[62] It also includes cases on Member State laws laying down criteria for the lawful provision of services, such as requirements of having an establishment[63] or a residence[64] in the host Member State, or a condition of minimum share capital.[65] Authorization and registration requirements such as with professional bodies[66] or documentation requirements[67] fall within the same category. All these measures apply before service providers are allowed to enter the market of a Member State.

However, a full graduation of the services and establishments regime from the combined standard I in Table 4.1 to the market access standard or even the combined standard II in Table 4.2 is not discernible. This would require that *all* cases caught under Articles 49 and 56 TFEU

C-190/98, *Graf* [2000] ECR I-493 as further cases in support of this view. See also the annotation by Spaventa, 'Annotation to Case C-442/02, Caixa-Bank', 1158.

59 Da Cruz Vilaça, 'On the application of Keck', pp. 33ff; Roth, 'The European Court of Justice's case law', p. 16. See also AG Tizzano in Case C-429/02, *Bacardi France* [2004] ECR I-6613, para. 62. He states that the general prohibition on restrictions 'also precludes national provisions which, even if they apply without distinction, are capable of directly affecting access to the market in services in the other Member State'.

60 See Barnard, *The Substantive Law of the EU*, p. 302.

61 See Case 71/76, *Thieffry* [1977] ECR 765, paras. 24–6; Joined Cases 110 and 111/78, *van Wesemael* [1979] ECR 35, para. 30; Case 220/83, *Commission* v. *France* [1986] ECR 3663, para. 17; Case C-101/94, *Commission* v. *Italy* [1996] ECR I-2691, para. 17.

62 Case C-275/92, *Schindler* [1994] ECR I-1039.

63 Case C-131/01, *Commission* v. *Italy* [2003] ECR I-1659, para. 42.

64 Case C-355/98, *Commission* v. *Belgium* [2000] ECR I-1221, para. 23.

65 Joined Cases C-357/10 to C-359/10, *Duomo* [2012] not yet published in the Official Journal.

66 Case C-131/01, *Commission* v. *Italy* [2003] ECR I-1659, para. 27; Case C-264/99, *Commission* v. *Italy (Register of Undertakings)* [2000] ECR I-4417, para. 14; Case C-58/98, *Corsten* [2000] ECR I-7919, para. 34.

67 Case C-298/99, *Commission* v. *Italy* [2002] ECR I-3129, para. 71.

only relate to national non-discriminatory measures that have an effect on market access. However, the Court has also qualified domestic regulations of Member States as violations of the freedoms without them having any apparent relevance for market access. Among others, this jurisprudence concerns national limitations of the transmission time allocated to TV advertising,[68] the regulation of television advertisements[69] and the protection of workers.[70]

### *4.4.4 Conclusion*

The jurisprudence of the Court cannot be read to award, in general, any different treatment based on the qualification of a measure as affecting access to the market or as affecting the exercise of the freedom.[71] There is no full (column 2 or 3) market access standard with services in EU law.[72] The Court, instead, alternates the combined standard I (Table 4.1) with the combined standard II (Table 4.2). Since there is no clear rationale between applying either of the two models in case law, this arguably does not foster transparency and consistency of the law in this area. Moreover, there is little evidence with services (or establishments) of the existence of a certain kind of measure that is considered as market access-neutral per se, comparable to the category of certain selling arrangements with goods.

## 4.5 Do the fundamental freedoms have a 'blind spot'?

In theory, several roads can be taken for distinguishing national regulations on services. One way discussed above would be to transpose the concept of certain selling arrangements and product requirements to the field of services. This would mean distinguishing national measures according to their effect on market access. Another perspective would be to distinguish the addressees of national measures. This would mean looking at whether Member State rules target private persons or economic operators. Third, we might distinguish three different categories of disturbances of the common market on services. Recall that in

68 Case C-6/98, *ARD* [1999] ECR I-7599.

69 Joined Cases C-34, C-35 and C-36/96, *De Agostini* [1997] ECR I-3843.

70 Joined Cases C-369 and 376/96, *Arblade* [1999] ECR I-8453.

71 Barnard, *The Substantive Law of the EU*, pp. 276–7.

72 See the similar logic at N. Maydell, 'The Services Directive and existing Community law', in F. Breuss, G. Fink and S. Griller (eds.), *Services Liberalisation in the Internal Market* (Vienna, New York: Springer, 2008), pp. 21–124 at p. 50. But see Joined Cases C-369/96 and C-376/96, *Arblade* [1999] ECR I-8453, paras. 33 and 80.

*Gebhard* the Court referred to 'national measures liable to hinder or make less attractive' the exercise of the free movement of services and the freedom of establishment. In *Säger* the Court held that the free movement of services is disturbed by measures 'liable to prohibit or otherwise impede the activities of a provider of services'.[73] This suggests that the prohibition of a certain activity is the top offender. This would be followed by national measures that put up an impediment to trade, such as by impairing market access. Third, the least objectionable interference by a Member State with Union law would be the reduction of the attractiveness of cross-border activities.

The test of 'economic attractiveness' represents a different regulatory principle than a test of impediment. While the latter protects market access in particular, the former acknowledges that in the taking-up of a business a Member State may be hampered by *any* kind of regulation in the host state, without it necessarily being an obstacle to market access. Notably, these rules do not exclusively address commercial operators; instead, they concern the whole population, including private actors engaging in a non-commercial activity.

On the one hand, this may concern the existence of divergent rules between the home state and the host state. In other words, the simple fact that the laws of the home state differ from the laws of the host state might reduce the appetite for cross-border trade in the Union. Examples of this would be different speed or exhaust emissions limits for cars, different leasing and renting rules, or different land planning rules. On the other hand, this would concern national regulations that might be called the 'rules of the game'. An example would be non-discriminatory tax rules. Here again, we could inquire whether these rules make it less attractive for foreign providers to enter the market.

We would argue that there are already traces of this criterion of attractiveness in the *Gebhard* and *Säger* cases mentioned above. Moreover, the Court arguably applied this standard in two other cases, where it found an insufficient degree of 'unattractiveness' with regard to certain national measures. The *Viacom* case concerned a municipal tax on advertising.[74] The Court ruled that

> the levying of such a tax is not on any view liable to prohibit, impede or otherwise make less attractive the provision of advertising services to be

[73] On both see Chapter 3.

[74] Case C-134/03, *Viacom Outdoor II* [2005] ECR I-1167.

carried out in the territory of the municipalities concerned, including the case in which the provision of services is of a cross-border nature on account of the place of establishment of either the provider or the recipient of the services.[75]

This was thus about a non-discriminatory national regulation that did not affect market access in the same way that the advertising rule at issue in *Gourmet* made it more difficult for foreign suppliers to enter the target market. Even though the Court did not qualify the tax as a restriction, thus not requiring justification on grounds of public interest, the element of deterrence was put into focus.

In *Mobistar* the Court explained why such a domestic regulation might escape the prohibition under the free movement of services. In this case the Court had to assess a national tax on mobile and personal communications infrastructures. The Court found that 'measures, the only effect of which is to create additional costs in respect of the service in question and which affect in the same way the provision of services between Member States and that within one Member State, do not fall within the scope of Article 59 of the Treaty'.[76] This means that the tax concerned did not even qualify as a restriction. Provided that it is non-discriminatory, it falls outside of the scope of the Treaty, just as selling arrangements fall outside the Treaty under Article 34 TFEU.

It has been argued that *Viacom* and *Mobistar* should be seen as representing some *qualitative de minimis* approach to the application of the freedoms concerned.[77] Restrictions to Union trade that are too insubstantial or remote should not need to be justified.[78] This might be called a blind spot of the freedoms, an intentional lacuna in the scope of application of the Treaty freedoms. However, in contrast to the goods regime, with services and establishments it is not a *defined* blind spot for domestic regulations. While this case law exempts the 'lower' end

[75] Case C-134/03, *Viacom Outdoor II* [2005] ECR I-1167, para. 38.

[76] Joined Cases C-544/03 and C-545/03, *Mobistar* [2005] ECR I-7723, para. 31.

[77] See also D. Edward and N. Nic Shuibhne, 'Continuity and change in the law relating to services', in A. Arnull, P. Eeckhout and T. Tridimas (eds.), *Continuity and Change in EU Law* (Oxford University Press, 2009), pp. 243–59 at pp. 256–7. See A. Biondi, 'Recurring cycles in the internal market: some reflections on the free movement of services', in A. Arnull, P. Eeckhout and T. Tridimas (eds.), *Continuity and Change in EU Law: Essays in Honour of Sir Francis Jacobs* (Oxford University Press, 2007), pp. 228–42 at p. 239, on the *Deliège* case and the 'inherent' test, where analogy is also made to concepts familiar from competition law.

[78] See also Case C-190/98, *Graf* [2000] ECR I-493.

on a scale of 'freedom spoilers' from the application of the Treaty, it does not exempt a specific category of domestic regulations such as are exempted under Article 34 TFEU.[79]

However, it might be too early to safely classify this case law as an example of the combined standard II mentioned above. While the Court in both *Viacom* and *Mobistar* does not openly apply the market access test, a second look at the latter case in particular might raise doubts. Recall that the Court there argued that the national rule would 'affect in the same way the provision of services between Member States and that within one Member State'.[80] Does this not imply that, should a national rule be an obstacle to cross-border trade in the sense of impairing market access, it would be caught irrespective of its insubstantive nature?[81] Snell has argued against the notion that an impediment to market access must be direct in order to qualify as a restriction.[82] He also discounts the concept of a substantial hindrance of market access, making entry into a national market significantly less attractive, for being impracticable and not supported by all case law.[83]

In a recent case the Commission has tried to base its argument on cost differentials that would be incurred by foreign lawyers because of 'additional costs resulting from the application of the Italian system of fees' that would also lead 'to a reduction in profit margins and therefore a loss of competitiveness'.[84] The Court replied that regulatory divergence and the costs of adaptation to the different rules in the host state as such do not qualify as being restrictive.

In this regard, it must be borne in mind at the outset that rules of a Member State do not constitute a restriction within the meaning of the EC Treaty solely by virtue of the fact that other Member States apply less strict, or more

[79] Referring to Joined Cases C-267 and 268/91, *Keck and Mithouard* [1993] ECR I-6097 by ways of comparison with these cases is thus not fully apposite. But see Biondi, 'Recurring cycles in the internal market', p. 240. See also V. Hatzopoulos and U. Do, 'The case law of the ECJ concerning the free provision of services: 2000–2005' (2006) 43 *Common Market Law Review* 923–91 at 959, who herald the *Mobistar* approach as the 'better' *Keck* approach accommodating the post-*Keck* case law such as *Gourmet* and signalling a convergence between the goods and services regimes.

[80] Joined Cases C-544/03 and C-545/03, *Mobistar* [2005] ECR I-7723.

[81] See Hatzopoulos and Do, 'The case law of the ECJ', 945, who seem to distinguish *Viacom* on these grounds from *Mobistar*.

[82] Snell, 'The notion of market access', 451–5.

[83] Snell, 'The notion of market access', 455–60.

[84] Case C-565/08, *Commission v. Italy (Maximum Fee Tariffs)* [2011] ECR I-2101, para. 48.

commercially favourable, rules to providers of similar services established in their territory.[85]

What the Court found decisive is whether service providers are 'deprived of the opportunity of gaining access to the market of the host Member State under conditions of normal and effective competition',[86] which would be for the Commission to demonstrate.[87]

There seem to be generally stricter standards applying to tax measures that are unfavourable to non-residents. It was in this quite specific context that the Court found that 'the articles of the Treaty concerning the free movement of goods, persons, services and capital are fundamental Community provisions and any restriction, even minor, of that freedom is prohibited'.[88]

What we can conclude, therefore, is that the higher costs of operating in a certain market are not a relevant criterion. This concerns both cases of regulatory divergence and cases where national rules are assessed on their own. It seems that any difference in regulation between Member States can only be an issue if it affects market access.

## 4.6 The fault-lines of the debate on discrimination in EU (services) law

### 4.6.1 *Introduction*

The language of discrimination is prone to misunderstandings because of a confusion of standards and concepts. First, this concerns the question of what kind of measures fall under discrimination. This is the conceptual conundrum and does not only involve an understanding of what is meant by de facto, indirect or material discrimination, which are conspicuously opaque concepts. It moreover requires an understanding of what falls under the category of direct discrimination. This is not only important under the GATS, which sharply distinguishes market access from national treatment and from non-discriminatory domestic regulations. It is also highly pertinent in EU law, where different

[85] Case C-565/08, *Commission* v. *Italy (Maximum Fee Tariffs)* [2011] ECR I-2101, para. 49.

[86] Case C-565/08, *Commission* v. *Italy (Maximum Fee Tariffs)* [2011] ECR I-2101, para. 51.

[87] On this and preceding cases, see C. Kuhn, *Die Verwirklichung des freien Dienstleistungsverkahrs im Spannungsfeld von wirtschaftlicher Handlungsfreiheit und Sozialgestaltung: Inhalt und Grenzen des grundfreiheitlichen Liberalisierungsauftrags am Beispiel der Dienstleistungsrichtlinie* (Baden-Baden: Nomos, 2013), pp. 85–8.

[88] Case C-34/98, *Commission* v. *France (Social Security)* [2000] ECR I-995, para. 49. See also, recently, Case C-498/10, *X NV* [2012] not yet published in the Official Journal, para. 30.

justification regimes are attached to this distinction. Second, confusion on discrimination arises because the applicable standards for affirming the existence of discrimination can apply either at the qualification stage, that is the definitional stage, or at the justification stage.[89] A way of complicating matters further is to argue that the public policy interests that could be applied at the justification stage are already relevant for finding discrimination at the definitional stage, alluding to the *tertium comparationis*.[90] Yet another way of framing this issue is to argue based on discriminatory as opposed to protectionist intent.[91]

We will start by exploring the situation in the goods regime.

### *4.6.2 Distinctly and indistinctly applicable measures*

When referring to measures coming under Article 34 TFEU, those that are distinctly applicable are commonly distinguished from those that are indistinctly applicable. The former term is interchangeable with the notion of open discrimination and thus refers to measures providing a different treatment for nationals of a Member State and foreigners respectively. In contrast, indistinctly applicable measures have been defined as those 'which in law apply to both national and foreign products but in fact have a particular burden on the imported goods'.[92] Recall that indirectly discriminatory measures have been defined above as imposing the same burden in law but a different burden in fact. The definition of indistinctly applicable measures under the goods regime thus comes very close to the concept of indirect discrimination as defined above for the services regime.[93] Moreover, indistinctly

[89] See G. de Búrca, 'Unpacking the concept of discrimination in EC and international trade law', in C. Barnard and J. Scott (eds.), *The Law of the Single European Market: Unpacking the Premises* (Oxford and Portland, Oregon: Hart Publishing, 2002), pp. 181–95 at p. 191 and V. Hatzopoulos, *Regulating Services in the European Union* (Oxford University Press, 2012), p. 111 respectively. In German legal terminology, this translates as *Tatbestandsebene* and *Rechtfertigungsebene*.

[90] See N. Diebold, 'Standards of non-discrimination in international economic law' (2011) 60(4) *International and Comparative Law Quarterly* 831–65 at 840.

[91] See C. Hilson, 'Discrimination in Community free movement law' (1999) 24 *European Law Review* 445–62.

[92] Barnard, *The Substantive Law of the EU*, p. 105. See also H. Jarass, 'A unified approach to the fundamental freedoms', in M. Andenas and W.-H. Roth (eds.), *Services and Free Movement in EU Law* (The Hague: Kluwer, 2002), pp. 141–62 at p. 146.

[93] Arguably, however, indistinctly applicable might also include situations of double burden, which are not considered (indirectly) discriminatory in the other freedoms where the *Säger* test of equivalence applies to them.

Table 4.3 Distinctly and indistinctly applicable measures

| **Distinctly applicable measures** | **Indistinctly applicable certain selling arrangements** | |
|---|---|---|
| Equals direct discrimination | Indirectly discriminatory | Same in law and in fact |
| | Measure having equivalent effect | No equivalent effect |
| Closed list of justifications | Open list of justifications | Exempted |

applicable measures concerning trade in goods may equally be justified on case law-based, non-exhaustive reasons.

Under the free movement of goods, the notion of non-discriminatory national measures only comes into play in the context of the *Keck* jurisprudence. As explained above, certain selling arrangements must be applied in a non-discriminatory manner. As stated by the Court in *Keck*, the condition of non-discrimination is not fulfilled when selling arrangements do not affect foreign products '*in the same manner, in law and in fact*'.[94] If a certain selling arrangement falls foul of this test, it comes under Article 34 TFEU, is qualified as an indistinctly applicable measure and hence invokes the full open list of mandatory requirements. However, this essentially means that indirectly discriminatory selling arrangements are treated as indistinctly applicable measures having equivalent effect. This is summarized in Table 4.3.

This is a terminological and conceptual conundrum on fundamental concepts that seems to entangle even some of the most able minds. This is what AG Geelhoed considered the appropriate sequence of analysis in the case *Commission* v. *Austria* on a traffic ban with respect to certain categories of trucks in Austria:

> Next it must be determined whether or not the contested measure is discriminatory in character. This is important for determining which grounds can be invoked for justifying it. According to the Court's general approach to the possibility of justifying restrictions to intra-Community trade, only measures which are indistinctly applicable to national goods and goods imported from other Member States can be justified on grounds of imperative requirements relating to the general interest, including the protection of the environment.

[94] Joined Cases C-267 and 268/91, *Keck and Mithouard* [1993] ECR I-6097, para. 16 (emphasis added).

If the measure must be deemed to be indirectly discriminatory, it can only be justified on the grounds listed in Article 30 EC.[95]

First, using the term indirectly discriminatory would only have been apposite if the case had concerned a certain selling arrangement, which was not the case. Second, since, as mentioned, indirectly discriminatory measures are essentially the same as indistinctly applicable measures, and are also subjected to the same regime of justification, the distinction by AG Geelhoed and the conclusion based on it is flawed.

It is thus no surprise that the concept of discrimination has been deemed too slippery when applied to indistinctly applicable measures.[96] However, to refuse to do so would ignore the circular logic of the concepts used under Article 34 TFEU. In the following section we will explain what might be the root of this confusion.

### 4.6.3 *One-step or two-step review of discrimination?*

The assessment of whether a measure constitutes discrimination requires a very different examination than that to establish if it constitutes a restriction. Before asking for justification, measures should technically always first be judged against an external point of reference (the *tertium comparationis*) to examine objective reasons for the different treatment of like situations or the equal treatment of different situations. If this leads to a finding of discrimination, the measure would be, in a second step, subject to justification.[97] The Court, however, does not proceed in such manner. Objective justification is the substitute for imperative reasons justifying the measure as such, not an additional first part of the inquiry.[98] Thus, while the *tertium comparationis* is an essential feature of any common examination of the existence of discrimination, it is not normally used by the Court in a methodical manner.[99] Instead, when examining discrimination in EU law, there is

[95] Case C-320/03, *Commission* v. *Austria* [2005] ECR I-9871, para. 89.

[96] See Roth, 'The European Court of Justice's case law', p. 5.

[97] See S. Griller, 'Effizienzgebot und Diskriminierungsverbot als Verwaltungsprinzipien in der Rechtsprechung des EuGH?', in H. Bauer and C. Calliess (eds.), *Verfassungsprinzipien in Europa* (Societas Iuris Publici Europaei, 2008), vol. IV, pp. 291–322 at p. 291.

[98] See Case C-147/03, *Commission* v. *Austria (Conditions of Access to University Education)* [2005] ECR I-5969. For a more correct approach, see Case C-29/95, *Pastoors* [1997] ECR I-285, paras. 19–20.

[99] See J. Scott, 'Mandatory or imperative requirements in the EU and the WTO', in C. Barnard and J. Scott (eds.), *The Law of the Single European Market: Unpacking the Premises* (Oxford and Portland, OR: Hart Publishing, 2002), pp. 269–93 at p. 283:

an immediate consideration of the regulatory policies pursued by the Member State. In other words, the assessment of restrictions by applying mandatory requirements of the public interest is often not different from the assessment of the objective justification of discriminatory measures under EU law.

Wilsher has thus analysed an important question in discussing the appropriate comparator when assessing discrimination, arguing that we should distinguish between market equivalence, regulatory equivalence and status equivalence.[100] In his view, market equivalence would require us to compare the products or services in economic terms, while regulatory equivalence compares them in terms of the regulatory means chosen by other Member States.

A problem with this analysis is that it confounds first- and second-level scrutiny. In other words, it suggests that a test that would lead to a finding that there is no discrimination because the products concerned are not comparable is the same as the test to ascertain whether a discriminatory measure can be justified by some regulatory policy objective. While Wilsher's observation that the fact the Court normally does not look at the likeness of products in economic terms is apposite,[101] we would suggest that we should, on dogmatic terms, not confuse this test with the justification of national measures. Selling arrangements are a different matter because here the first-level scrutiny is also the last step, leading to a finding that the measure in issue is not in breach of the Treaty. Here, however, it would in turn topple the established discourse to speak of a *tertium comparationis* with regard to a measure that is considered not discriminatory by definition (if it were, it would not qualify as a selling arrangement).

### 4.6.4 *Indirect discrimination*

We would argue that exploring the concept of indirect discrimination lies at the heart of resolving many complexities of the fundamental freedoms.[102] The principle of indirect discrimination is defined by the Court regularly in the following or similar words:

'This understanding of objective justification as operating as a means of assessing whether there is discrimination, rather than whether the indirect justification may be justified.'

[100] Wilsher, 'Does Keck discrimination make any sense?', 5.

[101] Exceptions are the case law under ex Art. 90 and cases such as Case 391/92, *Commission* v. *Greece (Formula Milk Monopoly)* [1995] ECR I-1621.

[102] See Scott, 'Mandatory or imperative requirements', p. 275.

According to settled case-law, the principle of equal treatment prohibits not only overt discrimination based on nationality but also all covert forms of discrimination which, by applying other distinguishing criteria, lead in fact to the same result.[103]

This different burden in fact could be because of the effect a national measure takes on foreigners as opposed to residents. However, it could also exist because of the way a national rule is drafted. In *O'Flynn* the Court thus stated that indirect discrimination does not only arise where there is a risk that national measures may operate to the particular detriment of foreigners, but also when nationality-neutral conditions in national laws affect essentially foreigners or can be more easily satisfied by nationals of the host Member State than by nationals of other Member States.[104] This second strand of the finding by the Court points to the classics of indirect discrimination, namely residency requirements and language requirements.[105] With respect to such rules, however, the discriminatory burden is rather a result of a part of the regulation provided in the national rule than it is because of the effects the rule may take when applied. Thus we may question whether the tenet of the *same burden in law* but a different burden in fact mentioned above really holds true here, when the wording of the rule is already the basis of indirect discrimination. This of course has a lot to do with the definition of direct discrimination that distinguishes based on the nationality of a service provider or the origin of a product. If the national rule requires an establishment or residence, the Court may qualify this as indirectly discriminatory and allow the open list of justifications, and might only be stricter on the proportionality test.[106]

In some cases the Court was quite clear in applying the *Cassis* regime to indirectly discriminatory measures.[107] In other cases this was only implicit in the reasoning of the Court. Thus, in the above-quoted

[103] Case C-147/03, *Commission* v. *Austria (Conditions of Access to University Education)* [2005] ECR I-5969, para. 41. Further on Art. 18 TFEU, see Case 152/73, *Sotgiu* [1974] ECR 153, para. 11; Case C-209/03 *Bidar* [2005] ECR I-2119, para. 51. On Arts. 49 and 56 TFEU, see Case 22/80, *Boussac* [1980] ECR 3427; Case C-3/88, *Commission* v. *Italy* [1989] ECR I-4035, para. 8.

[104] See Case C-237/94, *O'Flynn* [1996] ECR I-2617, para. 18; Case C-147/03, *Commission* v. *Austria (Conditions of Access to University Education)* [2005] ECR I-5969, paras. 41–8.

[105] See Case 152/73, *Sotgiu* [1974] ECR 153, para. 11; Case C-281/98, *Angonese* [2000] ECR I-4139. See also Case C-209/03, *Bidar* [2005] ECR I-2119, para. 51.

[106] See Barnard, *The Substantive Law of the EU*, p. 375 with references.

[107] Case 120/78, *Rewe-Zentral* [1979] ECR 649; Case C-388/01, *Commission* v. *Italy (Admission to Museums)* [2003] ECR I-721, paras. 19 and 21 respectively.

enforcement case against Austria for indirectly discriminating against foreign students, the Court, without further explanation, considered justifications based on international conventions and on safeguarding the homogeneity of the Austrian higher or university education system.[108] Notably, it did so immediately following the reproduction of a submission by the Commission, arguing that a discriminatory measure may only be justified based on the Treaty derogations.[109] In an enforcement case against Italy for providing that only companies in which all or a majority of the shares are directly or indirectly in public or state ownership may conclude agreements for the development of data processing systems for the public authorities, the Court also considered a justification that was not explicitly based on the Treaty derogations.[110] In contrast, in *Josemans* the Court qualified the prohibition of non-residents to visit Dutch-style 'coffee shops' as indirectly discriminatory.[111] In this case the Court seemed to locate the accepted reason of justification of 'combating drug tourism and the accompanying public nuisance' within the derogations of public order and public health, following a reference to a claim by the Commission that the measure at issue was discriminatory.[112]

### *4.6.5 The justification regime*

The freedoms are grounded on Article 18 TFEU and the prohibition of discrimination enshrined therein underpins the whole common market.[113] One would thus assume that discrimination under Article 18 TFEU is reviewed by the same standard as under the freedoms. This has also repeatedly been claimed by the Court. However, in its case law on Article 18 TFEU, the ECJ does not distinguish between open and indirect discrimination when it comes to the possible justification of Member State measures.[114] Under this provision, all forms of discrimination

[108] Case C-147/03, *Commission* v. *Austria (Conditions of Access to University Education)* [2005] ECR I-5969, paras. 53 *et seq.*

[109] Case C-147/03, *Commission* v. *Austria (Conditions of Access to University Education)* [2005] ECR I-5969, para. 51.

[110] Case C-3/88, *Commission* v. *Italy* [1989] ECR I-4035, paras. 10–11. Contrast this with the Opinion of AG Mischo, para. 33, who applied the general derogations and explicitly rejected reliance on the specific derogations.

[111] C-137/09, *Josemans* [2010] ECR I-13019, para. 58.

[112] See C-137/09, *Josemans* [2010] ECR I-13019, paras. 62 and 65 respectively.

[113] Roth, 'The European Court of Justice's case law', p. 15.

[114] See W. Frenz, *Handbuch Europarecht: Europäische Grundfreiheiten* (Heidelberg: Springer, 2004), vol. I, p. 1112. Conversely, under Art. 90 EC, direct discrimination can never be salvaged in the absence of express derogations, while indirect discrimination can

must be justified by 'objective circumstances' in order to be compatible with Article 18 TFEU.[115] These objective reasons invoked by the Court under Article 18 TFEU are also non-exhaustive, as with the mandatory requirements under the freedoms.

This is different in other areas of EU law. The generally held view seems to be that under the *Gebhard* test, which is widely recognized to be the most authoritative general statement by the ECJ on the test applicable to the freedoms in general, as a first step it must be asked whether a national measure is directly discriminatory.[116] As a second step, it must be assessed whether the national measure in issue is either non-discriminatory or indirectly discriminatory. In this second step the measures may be justified by the full list of imperative reasons recognized by the Court.[117] This means that, when it comes to the stage of justifying the respective national measure, indirectly discriminatory rules are deemed to fall under the same regime as non-discriminatory restrictions. However, as we will see, the case law of the Court is ambiguous on this.

The claim by the Court that the treatment of discrimination under Article 18 TFEU is analogous to its scrutiny under the more specific non-discrimination provisions under the freedoms is thus only apposite with regard to cases of indirect discrimination.[118] For cases of direct discrimination, in contrast, the treatment is different, since there is no closed list of public policy reasons as with other forms of discrimination under the freedoms.

be defended on the basis of objective justification. See Barnard, *The Substantive Law of the EU*, pp. 54–5.

[115] Case C-28/04, *Tod's* [2005] ECR I-5781, para. 28. See also Case C-398/92, *Mund & Fester* [1994] ECR I-467, paras. 16 and 17, and Case C-29/95, *Pastoors* [1997] ECR I-285, para. 19. See S. Griller, 'The new Services Directive of the European Union: hopes and expectations from the angle of a (further) completion of the internal market', General Report, in H. F. Koeck and M. M. Karollus (eds.), *The New Services Directive of the European Union*, Féderation Internationale pour le Droit Européen (FIDE), XXIII Congress Linz 2008 (Vienna: Congress Publications, 2008), vol. III, pp. 379–423 at note 30.

[116] See G. Davies, *European Union Internal Market Law*, 2nd edn (London: Cavendish, 2003), p. 131.

[117] See the discussion by Scott, 'Mandatory or imperative requirements', pp. 275–81, at which time this apparently was still less clear, with cases cited showing how the Court had, at times, treated indirect discrimination in the same way as direct discrimination. See Case 152/73, *Sotgiu* [1974] ECR 153, for an example of this.

[118] Note that there is some ambiguity, however, on the precise role of objective justification in discrimination cases outside the freedoms. See Scott, 'Mandatory or imperative requirements', pp. 282–4.

There are two ways to address this inconsistency. The first would be to apply the regime on direct discrimination to cases of indirect discrimination, limiting the reasons of justification for the latter. By the second approach, the regime on restrictions and indirect discriminations would also be applied to direct discrimination, thereby abandoning the exhaustive list of requirements of the public interest. We have already mentioned examples for such a standard under the freedoms in cases that have mainly concerned justifications pertaining to taxation and to the environment.[119] In support of the second approach, it has been argued that it makes little sense to distinguish between restrictions and discriminatory measures when the drafting of the national law makes all the difference.[120] If a condition of establishment were imposed on all service providers, technically this would make the measure non-discriminatory. Alternatively, if the requirement is imposed on foreign providers only, the rule would be qualified as discriminatory.[121] Thus it is indeed only a matter of drafting that decides whether a national measure falls under the full list of justifications, or rather confines the Member States to three narrowly construed grounds in the Treaty to save the measure.[122]

While this is a valid example, it is submitted that it could also be invoked in support of the first approach mentioned above. Although the first drafting option ('establishment for all') is non-discriminatory at face value, it could arguably just as well be qualified as being indirectly discriminatory. In effect, it is more to the detriment of providers from other Member States than those of the host state. In other words, despite its superficially equal application, the nationality-neutral legislative option serves the same offensive objective as the openly discriminatory variant.[123] We would argue that it is more consistent with the logic of the Treaty to grant the broad list of derogations only to these Member State measures that comprise no such discriminatory element.

[119] See Chapter 3. See also Craig and de Búrca, *EU Law*, p. 803, who mention Case C-415/93, *Bosman* [1995] ECR I-4921 concerning the free movement of workers.

[120] See Roth, 'The European Court of Justice's case law', p. 12; Kingreen, 'Fundamental freedoms', pp. 575–6.

[121] See Roth, 'The European Court of Justice's case law', p. 12.

[122] See also Frenz, *Handbuch Europarecht*, p. 171.

[123] See Case 193/80, *Commission* v. *Italy* [1981] ECR 3019, para. 20: 'The answer to that argument must be that, first, even if the system established by the Italian legislation applies to national and imported products alike, its effects are still protective in nature. It has been drafted in such a way that it allows only wine-vinegar to enter Italy, closing the frontier to all other categories of vinegar of agricultural origin.'

Both indirect and direct discrimination embody the 'unholy' idea of unequal treatment. Thus it would be more consistent to sanction indirect discrimination in the same way as direct discrimination under the freedoms.[124] Member States should be granted the full plethora of policy excuses only for restrictions that, from this perspective, are the least objectionable measures.

Having said this, we are fully aware that at times there may be a fine line between (indirect) discrimination and non-discriminatory measures. Any distinction would have to rely heavily on considerations of the aim of the pertinent Member State measure, since it is there that the discriminatory element would be situated. So far, however, references only to regulatory purpose, as opposed to legislative intent, have occurred in the Court's case law.[125] Moreover, such modification of the fundamental architecture of the common market law would undermine the whole process of the gradual development from the discrimination standard to the restrictions standard by the Court.[126] Finally, this convergence of the regime on indirect discriminations with the regime on direct discriminations would also reverberate under Article 34 TFEU. As we have shown, the Court now does not distinguish between indirectly discriminatory measures having equivalent effect on the one hand, and certain selling arrangements that affect market access on the other hand.

## 4.7 Conclusion

In this chapter we have tried to deconstruct the regulatory standards employed by the Court in the field of services, for which we also had to make incursions into the free movement of goods. We have shown that a standard that is based on non-discrimination is alternated with a standard that is based on considerations of market access in the case law of the Court. This two-pronged regulatory standard is obfuscating

[124] Compare the Commission's submission in Case C-147/03, *Commission* v. *Austria (Conditions of Access to University Education)* [2005] ECR I-5969, paras. 49–50: 'to concede that the Austrian legislation may be justified by grounds other than those expressly provided for by the Treaty would render meaningless, according to the Commission, the concept of indirect discrimination as it results from Case 152/73, *Sotgiu* [1974] ECR 153, that is discrimination which, although based on an apparently neutral criterion, in fact leads to the same result as discrimination on the grounds of nationality.'

[125] See Roth, 'The European Court of Justice's case law', p. 11.

[126] Similarly, see Frenz, *Handbuch Europarecht*, p. 171.

important principles such as *Keck*. It is therefore probably a good thing that the case law under Articles 49 and 56 TFEU exempting certain non-discriminatory national measures from the prohibition of restrictions is neither (openly) based on considerations of market access, nor emulates the category of certain selling arrangements under the goods regime.

We have also shown that the clarity of the non-discrimination standard in EU law is tainted on three important grounds. First, the *tertium comparationis* is normally not considered by the Court in a methodical manner, with policy interests instead playing a role in the first step of the analysis. Second, what is commonly understood by the concept of indirect discrimination is mashed with the concept of indistinctly applicable measures under the free movement of goods, and is inconsistent in case law where the discriminatory element is already built into the national rule. For these reasons we have argued for a common standard with regard to indirect discrimination and direct discrimination, respectively. Third, we have shown that discrimination is treated differently in terms of available justification under the *lex generalis* of Article 18 TFEU when compared with the more specific non-discrimination provisions of the fundamental freedoms.

We will pick up many of the themes discussed in this chapter in Chapter 8, where we will also continue and deepen the comparisons with WTO law, as, clearly, both market access and non-discrimination (aka national treatment) are well-established concepts. In the following chapter, instead of regulatory standards engineered by case law, we will look at different approaches to the regulation of services by means of secondary law in the EU.

# 5 *Variatio delectat*? Different regulatory approaches for different services

## 5.1 Introduction

We would suggest that two different perspectives can be distinguished when looking at the regulatory approach represented by a certain secondary law regime in the Union. First, one could inquire whether a directive is a horizontal legal act as opposed to a sectoral or vertical legal act. For a long time sector-specific legislation has dominated Union activity in the area of services and establishments. Directives have been passed in the fields of financial services,[1] electronic commerce,[2] broadcasting,[3] industry and trade,[4] foodstuffs[5] and hairdressers.[6] Only with the adoption of the strategy for the single market in 2001 did the

[1] See e.g. Directive 2004/39/EC of the European Parliament and the Council of 21 April 2004 on markets in financial instruments, OJ 2004 No. L145/1.

[2] Directive 2000/31/EC of the European Parliament and the Council of 8 June 2000 on certain legal aspects of information society services, in particular electronic commerce, in the internal market, OJ 2000 No. L178/1.

[3] Directive 97/36/EC of the European Parliament and the Council of 30 June 1997 on the coordination of certain provisions laid down by law, regulation or administrative action in Member States concerning the pursuit of television broadcasting activities, OJ 1997 No. L202/60.

[4] Council Directive 64/427/EEC of 7 July 1964 laying down detailed provisions concerning transitional measures in respect of activities of self-employed persons in manufacturing and processing industries falling within ISIC Major Groups 23–40 (Industry and small craft industries), OJ English special edition, Series I, Vol. 1963–1964, p. 148.

[5] Council Directive 68/366/EEC of 15 October 1968 laying down detailed provisions concerning transitional measures in respect of activities of self-employed persons in the food manufacturing and beverage industries (ISIC Major Groups 20 and 21), OJ English special edition, Series I, Vol. 1968 (II), p. 509.

[6] Council Directive 82/489/EEC of 19 July 1982 laying down measures to facilitate the effective exercise of the right of establishment and freedom to provide services in hairdressing, OJ 1982 No. L218/24.

Commission modify its approach and start to enact horizontal directives, such as Directive 2005/36/EC discussed below.[7]

Second, we could ask which regulatory instruments are used in an EU law measure. Under this criterion, we will therefore look at whether a Union directive provides for full harmonization, partial harmonization or minimum harmonization. Moreover, we will discuss whether a legal act contains rules on market access, rules on mutual recognition, administrative provisions, or all of these instruments. We will show that the Services Directive marks the culmination of a steady expansion of the completeness of secondary law in this respect.

Finally, as we will see below with regard to SGEI, there can be areas where the regulatory approach consists of an interpretation of the Treaties by having resort, among others, to Union soft law. This must be distinguished from areas where there has not been any legislative activity, which places the task of regulation in the hands of the ECJ, such as with gambling and private security services, both of which we have discussed briefly above.[8]

In this chapter we will discuss selected examples for different approaches to services regulation in the EU. As we will show, these approaches are often difficult to pin down and are as varied as the areas concerned themselves.

## 5.2 Minimum coordination: posting of workers

Directive 96/71/EC regulates the third mode of cross-border service provision as defined under the GATS.[9] Posted workers are employed in one Member State, but sent by the employer on a temporary basis to carry out work in another Member State. Thus, in contrast to service providers *stricto sensu*, they remain employed in their state of origin. Contrary to providers seeking an establishment in another Member State, their migration is only of a temporary nature. Article 1(3) of Directive 96/71/EC regulates the following three cases of such posting: (a) workers who

[7] Directive 2005/36/EC of the European Parliament and the Council of 7 September 2005 on the recognition of professional qualifications, OJ 2005 No. L255/22.

[8] V. Hatzopoulos, *Regulating Services in the European Union* (Oxford University Press, 2012), pp. 184–90, refers to the approach in these areas as judge-made regulation as a substitute to legislation.

[9] Directive 96/71/EC of the European Parliament and the Council of 16 December 1996 concerning the posting of workers in the framework of the provision of services, OJ 1997 No. L18/1.

are posted on the account and under the direction of the undertaking making the posting, which has an employment relationship with the posted worker;[10] (b) workers who are posted to another establishment or undertaking belonging to the same group as the undertaking making the posting; and (c) postings undertaken by a temporary employment agency, which has an employment relationship with the worker.[11] In this last case the worker works under the control and direction of the user undertaking.[12]

According to Article 3 Directive 96/71, Member States must provide in regulations or collective agreements that posted workers benefit, at a minimum, from the following:

- host state laws regarding minimum pay, including overtime;
- maximum work and rest periods;
- minimum paid annual holidays;
- conditions of the supply of workers by temporary employment undertakings;
- rules on health and safety at work; and
- working conditions of pregnant women and young people.

It is thus the laws of the *host* state that are meant to govern the fundamentals of the work relationship of the posted worker.[13] These host state rules, however, were only meant to set the minimum standard and should not prevent more favourable terms and conditions of employment, as stated in Article 3(7) of Directive 96/71/EC.

In terms of the regulatory approach employed, this is difficult to qualify. Can we call this minimum harmonization? Recital 13 of Directive 96/71/EC states that 'the laws of the Member States must be coordinated in order to lay down a nucleus of mandatory rules for minimum protection to be observed in the host country by employers who post workers to perform temporary work in the territory of a Member State where the services are provided'. The standards that are imposed here are not uniform European standards but national law standards in certain mandatory fields relating to work conditions and salaries. In *Laval* the Court pointed out that Directive 96/71/EC 'did not harmonize the

[10] See Case C-113/89, *Rush Portuguesa* [1990] ECR I-1417, para. 15.

[11] Joined Cases C-307/09, C-308/09 and C-309/09, *Vicoplus* [2011] ECR I-453, para. 46.

[12] Joined Cases C-307/09, C-308/09 and C-309/09, *Vicoplus* [2011] ECR I-453, para. 47.

[13] See S. Deakin, 'Regulatory competition after Laval' (2008) *Cambridge Yearbook of European Legal Studies* 581–609 at 594.

material content of those mandatory rules for minimum protection'.[14] One might, therefore, rather speak of minimum coordination in the present case. At the same time, case law has also injected a strong element of mutual recognition. Article 3(10) of the Directive provides that Member States are not precluded from applying terms and conditions of employment 'in the case of public policy provisions' on matters other than those referred to in the above-mentioned Article 3.[15] The requirement of a written contract or document established pursuant to Directive 91/533 was therefore found to have the effect of making undertakings that post workers 'subject to an obligation to which they are already subject in the Member State in which they are established'.[16]

However, the regulatory autonomy of the host Member State has never fully extended to administrative requirements connected to the entry and the taking up of the work in the host state. Thus the Court ruled, among other things, that Member States may not require the provider to have a representative resident in the Member State of posting, and that the Member State of posting may not require prior authorization.[17] In contrast, the host state requirement to submit a declaration by the time the work starts at the latest,[18] as well as the obligation to keep certain social documents at the workplace, has been deemed reasonable.[19]

Moreover, recent case law has cast into doubt the safeguarding of host state work-related regulatory standards. First, only those matters listed in Article 3 of the Directive enjoy isolation from the prohibition of restrictions.[20] Cases such as *Mazzoleni* and *Portugaia Construçoes* made the application of higher minimum wages dependant on whether this

[14] Case C-341/05, *Laval* [2007] ECR I-11767, para. 60.

[15] Hatzopoulos, *Regulating Services in the European Union*, p. 205.

[16] See Case C-319/06, *Commission* v. *Luxemburg* [2008] ECR I-4323, para. 41, with regard to Directive 91/533/EEC on an employer's obligation to inform employees of the conditions applicable to the contract or employment relationship, OJ 1991 No. L288/32.

[17] See European Commission, Communication, Guidance on the posting of workers in the framework of the provision of services, COM(2006)159 final. But see Deakin, 'Regulatory competition after Laval', 595–7 on the stricter standard apparently applied in the *Laval* case.

[18] Containing information on the workers who have been posted and the location and duration of the posting, and confirms that posted workers from third countries are in a lawful situation in the country in which the service provider is established.

[19] See European Commission, Communication, Guidance on the posting of workers in the framework of the provision of services, COM(2006)159 final.

[20] See Case C-319/06, *Commission* v. *Luxemburg* [2008] ECR I-4323, para. 26.

was necessary and proportionate, and whether it contributed significantly to the social protection of the workers.[21] The rule that workers posted from other Member States can be subjected to certain mandatory protective standards without being challenged as restrictions to the free movement of workers has thus been qualified. Hatzopoulos has also pointed in particular to the *Laval* and *Rüffert* cases as another strike against the minimum host state standards imposed by the Directive, by finding that Member States cannot make the provision of services in their territory conditional upon the observance of standards that 'go beyond the mandatory rules for minimum protection'.[22] However, we would submit that the 'presumption of regime portability' that has been observed as a consequence of this case law, and which would 'fly in the face of the express Directive's provisions', still remains subject to many more conditions than in other situations coming under the free movement rules. Barnard has stressed in this respect that Directive 96/71/EC was primarily a measure to facilitate the free movement of services and not a measure to realize social policy objectives.[23]

In order to address prevalent circumvention of the rules on posting of workers, the Commission has tabled a proposal for a Directive on the enforcement of Directive 96/71/EC.[24] This would establish a general common framework of appropriate provisions, measures and control mechanisms necessary for better and more uniform implementation, application and enforcement in practice of Directive 96/71/EC. Member States would be required to work in close cooperation and provide each other with mutual assistance, especially by replying to reasoned requests for information and carrying out checks, inspections and investigations through competent authorities. Similar to the rules of the Services Directive, the proposal would provide checks and controls by the authorities of the host Member State at the request of the competent authorities of the Member State of establishment.[25]

21 Case C-165/98, *Mazzoleni* [2001] ECR I-2189; Case C-164/99, *Portugaia Construçoes* [2002] ECR I-787. See also Hatzopoulos, *Regulating Services in the European Union*, pp. 201–2.

22 Case C-341/05, *Laval* [2007] ECR I-11767; Case C-346/06, *Rüffert* [2008] ECR I-1989. See Hatzopoulos, Regulating Services, p. 205.

23 C. Barnard, *The Substantive Law of the EU: The Four Freedoms*, 3rd edn (Oxford University Press, 2010), p. 372.

24 Proposal for a Directive of the European Parliament and of the Council on the enforcement of Directive 96/71/EC concerning the posting of workers in the framework of the provision of services, 1 March 2012, COM(2012)131 final.

25 Art. 7(4) of the Proposal, COM(2012)131 final.

## 5.3 Mutual recognition: professional qualifications

The common narrative is that mutual recognition has made its official entry into EU law with the *Cassis de Dijon* judgment by the ECJ in 1979, followed by the Commission Communication in 1980, followed by the introduction of the so-called New Approach in 1985.[26] If we understand mutual recognition as a regulatory instrument requiring some degree of referral to the legal or factual situation in the home state,[27] Directive 2005/36/EC is a paradigmatic example.[28]

The professional qualifications regime is not about access to another Member State market in general, but about the specific issue of the right of a foreign service provider to 'take along' the professional title as proof of professional standards and quality. It applies to 'regulated professions', which is defined broadly as any 'professional activity' requiring specific professional qualifications, such as a professional title.[29] The definition of 'regulated profession' is a matter of EU law.[30] According to Article 3(1)(a) of Directive 2005/36/EC, it refers to 'a professional activity or group of professional activities, access to which, the pursuit of which, or one of the modes of pursuit of which is subject, directly or indirectly, by virtue of legislative, regulatory or administrative provisions to the possession of specific professional qualifications'. Establishing registers for court experts does not regulate a profession in this sense.[31]

Although the term of regulated profession is a Union law concept, the scope of application of Directive 2005/36/EC must be assessed for each Member State separately. It depends entirely on the host state whether a certain profession is regulated and whether it thus constitutes a 'regulated profession' in the meaning of the Directive. Annex II provides for a long and multilingual list of professions regulated in individual

[26] Case 120/78, *Rewe-Zentral* [1979] ECR 649. See V. Hatzopoulos, 'Forms of mutual recognition in the field of services', in I. Lianos and O. Odudu (eds.), *Regulating Trade in Services: Trust, Distrust and Economic Integration* (Cambridge University Press, 2012), pp. 59–98 at p. 59.

[27] See further, M. Klamert, 'Of empty glasses and double burdens: approaches to regulating the services market à propos the implementation of the Services Directive' (2010) *Legal Issues of Economic Integration* 111–32.

[28] OJ 2005 No. L255/22. Even its parts on 'automatic recognition' refer the host state to the amount of time the applicant has spent in a certain profession in the home state. See Art. 16–20 in conjunction with Annex IV of Directive 2005/36/EC.

[29] See Art. 3(1)(a) Directive 2005/36/EC.

[30] See Case C-586/08, *Rubino* [2009] ECR I-12013, para. 23 and the case law cited.

[31] Joined Cases C-372/09 and C-373/09, *Peñarroja* [2011] ECR I-1785, para. 30.

Member States. In areas not covered by the Directive, the Court applies the principle of equivalence, discussed above. Professions that are not regulated, as is the case with tax advisers in several Member States,[32] thus apply the case law regime following *Gebhard* and *Vlassopoulou*.[33] This principle had itself been inspired by EU secondary law preceding Directive 2005/36/EC.[34]

The regime set up by the Directive comprises both self-employed and employed activities in another Member State, and thus transcends the Treaty distinction between the free movement of workers and the freedom of establishment. It therefore already realized what was done much later by the Services Directive with a much broader scope. Under Directive 2005/36/EC, mutual recognition is employed either to compensate for the lack of approximation of national rules for some professions or to complement the minimum harmonization of Member State laws and regulations of some other professions.

Title II concerns the provision of services abroad involving a temporary and occasional activity in the host state, which must fall short of constituting an establishment within the meaning of Article 56 TFEU.[35] The Directive grants professional service providers access to the market of the host Member State on the basis of the professional title they hold in their home state. For this, their qualifications do not need to be recognized by the host state. However, the Directive in this respect imposes certain information and documentation obligations on foreign service providers when they enter the host state for the first time.[36] In the case of temporary movement of service providers under Title II, Article 5(3) Directive 2005/36/EC subjects the provider to the 'professional rules of a professional, statutory or administrative nature which are directly linked to professional qualifications'. This includes host state rules on 'serious professional malpractice' and disciplinary provisions. Under Title III for establishments, mutual recognition is

[32] C. Stumpf, 'Aktuelle Entwicklungen im europäischen Dienstleistungs- und Niederlassungsrecht' (2006) *Deutsche Zeitschrift für Wirtschafts- und Insolvenzrecht* 99–107 at 105. It is only regulated in Germany, Austria and Belgium.

[33] Case C-234/97, *Bobadilla* [1999] ECR I-4773. Barnard, *The Substantive law of the EU*, pp. 328–9.

[34] Case No. C-340/89 *Vlassopoulou* [1991] ECR I-2357, para. 14. See also P. Craig and G. de Búrca, *EU Law: Cases and Materials*, 5th edn (Oxford University Press, 2011), pp. 811–12. When it was adopted in 2005, Directive 2005/36/EC replaced three general and twelve sectoral directives on the recognition of professional qualifications in the Union.

[35] See Art. 5(1)–(2) Directive 2005/36/EC.

[36] Art. 7 Directive 2005/36/EC.

coupled with compensatory measures if there are substantial differences between the standards of the home state and the host state.[37] Such measures are not provided for certain industrial activities, crafts and commercial activities listed in the Directive. In this case, however, mutual recognition is dependent on certain periods of practical experience in the home state.

Thus, while the scope of application of the Directive is determined by the regulation of a profession in the host state, the fact of regulation in the *home* state is relevant under its Article 5(1)(b) regarding the free provision of services as well as for the applicable system of recognition under Title III for established service providers. For professions in the health sector, in contrast, mutual recognition is paired with minimum harmonization of training requirements.[38] Even without requiring full legal integration in the host state, as in the case of established service providers under Title III, Directive 2005/36/EC thus foresees the application of the laws of the *host* state, though these are restricted to matters connected to professional qualification.[39] Under the freedom of establishment, this is not so explicitly regulated in the Directive, but ensues from the general rule of its Article 4(1).[40]

In principle, Directive 2005/36/EC also applies to lawyers as regards their professional title. The mechanisms provided under the specific Directive 98/5/EEC do not exclude the right to apply for recognition under the former regime. In such a case, however, the host state may require an aptitude test.[41] Thus the *Koller* case concerned a national from Austria holding a degree from an Austrian university representing the 'completion of a cycle of post-secondary studies lasting more than three years', who also held an equivalent degree issued in another Member State after additional training of less than three years giving him access to the profession of lawyer in the other Member State, where he also actually practised.[42] Since this was considered a diploma in the meaning of ex Directive 89/49/EEC, he could not be denied the opportunity to take the aptitude test on the ground that he has not

[37] Art. 14 Directive 2005/36/EC.

[38] Nurses responsible for general care, dental practitioners, veterinary surgeons, midwives, architects, pharmacists and doctors.

[39] See F. Lemor, 'Auswirkungen der Dienstleistungsrichtlinie auf ausgesuchte reglementierte Berufe' (2007) *Europäische Zeitschrift für Wirtschaftsrecht* 135–9 at 136.

[40] 'under the same conditions as its nationals'.

[41] Case C-359/09, *Ebert* [2011] ECR I-269, para. 33.

[42] Case C-118/09, *Koller* [2010] ECR I-13627, para. 36.

completed the period of practical experience required by the Austrian legislation.[43]

In addition and specifically, the provision of services *stricto sensu* in another Member State by a lawyer is governed by Directive 77/249/EEC.[44] This instrument grants the right to practise under the home state title on a temporary basis in the host state while being subject to the laws and regulations of the latter. It does away with familiar restrictions such as establishment or registration with a bar or court. In addition, Article 4 of Directive 77/249 requires the observance of the professional ethics rules of the lawyer's home state. For the permanent migration of lawyers in the Union, Directive 98/5[45] provides for the gradual integration of the foreign lawyer into the host state even absent any kind of additional examination.[46] This starts with the right to practise under the home state title under Article 4 of the Directive,[47] and may lead to the full admission to the profession of lawyer in the host state after practising 'effectively and regularly' for three years in the host state under Article 10 of Directive 98/5.[48] In any event, the home state rules on professional ethics must be adhered to in addition to host state rules.[49] In contrast to the regime under Directive 77/249 mentioned above, Member States may therefore set up rules relating to organization, qualifications, professional ethics, supervision, liability and membership of the bar under the condition of non-discrimination.[50]

## 5.4 'Hybrid negative harmonization': the Services Directive

### 5.4.1 *Regulatory approach*

It has commonly been claimed that the Services Directive constitutes a horizontal legal act because it covers a broad range of different

[43] Case C-118/09, *Koller* [2010] ECR I-13627, paras. 38–41.
[44] Council Directive 77/249/EEC of 22 March 1977 to facilitate the effective exercise by lawyers of freedom to provide services, OJ 1977 No. L78/17.
[45] Directive 98/5/EC of the European Parliament and of the Council of 16 February 1998 to facilitate practice of the profession of lawyer on a permanent basis in a Member State other than that in which the qualification was obtained, OJ 1998 No. L77/36.
[46] Barnard, *The Substantive Law of the EU*, p. 328.
[47] Art. 4 Directive 98/5/EC.
[48] Case C-359/09, *Ebert* [2011] ECR I-269, paras. 30–2.
[49] Case C-225/09, *Jakubowska* [2010] ECR I-12329, para. 57.
[50] Case C-359/09, *Ebert* [2011] ECR I-269, para. 41

sectors.[51] Indeed, the Services Directive purports to apply to all service sectors and to all kinds of services, a claim already indicated by its name.[52] In spite of this claim, however, the Directive foresees several exceptions from its scope of application. It excludes non-economic services of general interest entirely,[53] and services of general economic interest such as the energy sector are exempted from some of its most central rules,[54] as is discussed in detail in Chapter 6. It applies to business-to-consumer constellations as well as to business-to-business services, it applies to services irrespective of the mode of their provision and it also applies to the consumption of services. Going beyond the definition of services contained in primary law, it even covers the provision of services by a commercial presence in another Member State. It thus aligns its scope of application to the system of the GATS, where commercial presence is one mode for providing services, as we have explained above.

The wisdom in providing for generally full coverage coupled with 'negative listing' of services not covered, instead of enumerating all service sectors that fall under its scope of application ('positive listing'), could be questioned. In view of the actual scope of application of the Services Directive, positive listing would have been far from unworkable since, as we have shown, the number of services covered is rather limited. One advantage of such an approach would be an increase of transparency for citizens because it would be much clearer whether a certain activity comes under the Services Directive. The counterargument would be that such positive listing would forestall developments in the service industry, since new business models and market niches would not automatically be covered but would require an amendment

[51] See A. Hatje, 'Services Directive: a legal analysis', in F. Breuss, G. Fink and S. Griller (eds.), *Services Liberalisation in the Internal Market* (Vienna, New York: Springer, 2008), pp. 1–20 at pp. 5 and 12; S. Griller, 'The new Services Directive of the European Union: hopes and expectations from the angle of a (further) completion of the internal market', General Report, in H. F. Koeck and M. M. Karollus (eds.), *The New Services Directive of the European Union*, Féderation Internationale pour le Droit Européen (FIDE), XXIII Congress Linz 2008 (Vienna: Congress Publications, 2008), vol. III, pp. 379–423; C. Barnard, 'Unravelling the Services Directive' (2008) *Common Market Law Review* 323–94 at 323.

[52] Art. 2(1) Directive 2006/123/EC.

[53] Art. 2(2)(a) Directive 2006/123/EC.

[54] Art. 17(1)(b) and (c) Directive 2006/123/EC.

to the Directive to be covered.[55] Indeed, the services sector is evolving more dynamically than other sectors,[56] and political compromises behind the sectoral coverage of the Services Directive could be difficult to unpack.

In the WTO, the debate on negative vs positive listing is of course much more developed, where the negative list or top-down approach is contrasted with the positive list or bottom-up approach to regulation. Similar to the EU, in the GATS discussion negative listing refers to an approach where all sectors are covered by an agreement unless explicitly exempted by reservation lists. Bottom-up conversely means that the sectors where governments are willing to make binding commitments must be determined at the outset. The GATS has been described as a hybrid featuring 'a voluntary, positive, choice of sectors, sub-sectors and/or modes of supply in which governments are willing to make binding commitments together with a negative list of non-conforming measures to be retained in scheduled areas'.[57]

### *5.4.2 Regulatory nature*

Hatzopoulos has called the regulatory technique used in the Services Directive 'hybrid' because it features 'rules on harmonization, mutual recognition, administrative cooperation and more'.[58] Indeed, as we will discuss in detail in the next chapter, the Services Directive stands out for not merely including rules to facilitate market access and rules on mutual recognition, but it also comprises extensive prescriptions on administrative cooperation. The instruments it provides for reaching its goals are thus remarkably diverse.[59] This arguably makes the Services Directive the most 'complete' regulatory instrument in the history of EU legislation in the field of services. The only explanation provided in

[55] S. Korte, 'Mitgliedstaatliche Verwaltungskooperation und private Eigenverantwortung beim Vollzug des europäischen Diensteistungsrechts' (2007) *Neue Zeitschrift für Verwaltungsrecht* 501–7 at 503.

[56] See Rec. 33 Services Directive: 'wide variety of ever-changing activities'.

[57] A. Mattoo and P. Sauvé, 'Regionalism in services trade', in A. Mattoo, R. M. Stern and G. Zanini, *A Handbook of International Trade in Services* (Oxford University Press, 2008), pp. 221–86 at p. 253, who have noted that, while the negative list approach has faced strong opposition when GATS was negotiated, it has been adopted in a large number of regional trade agreements.

[58] Hatzopoulos, *Regulating Services in the European Union*, p. 242.

[59] Barnard, 'Unravelling the Services Directive', 392.

the Directive itself for adopting such broad coverage is that it 'establishes a general legal framework which benefits a wide variety of services', but at the same time takes 'into account the distinctive features of each type of activity or profession and its system of regulation'.[60]

The Services Directive thus boasts 'differentiation inside', purporting to take due account of sectoral disparities. It does so not only concerning the sectors it covers in the first place, but also regarding the regulatory instruments used for the various restrictions to trade in services. Recital 7 of the Directive claims that barriers that may be dismantled quickly are treated differently from barriers where this is not possible. For the latter services, the Services Directive provides the instruments of 'evaluation, consultation and complementary harmonisation'.[61]

However, it has been questioned whether the Services Directive can be qualified as a harmonization measure at all. The legal bases for enacting secondary law in the field of services and establishments are Articles 50(1) and 53(1) TFEU.[62] While Article 53(1) TFEU speaks of the 'coordination' of Member State laws,[63] Article 53(2) TFEU provides the mandate for measures of mutual recognition.[64] Thus, while the powers of the Community legislator are certainly broad under this mandate,[65] in previous directives based on Article 53(1) TFEU their harmonizing character has always been expressly emphasized.[66] The harmonizing

[60] Rec. 7 Directive 2006/123/EC.

[61] Rec. 7 Directive 2006/123/EC.

[62] According to these provisions, the Council may adopt directives by qualified majority voting, in order to put into effect as well as to coordinate the mentioned freedoms at issue. With unanimity, it must decide only if a legislative act involves amendments to national law with respect to training and to the conditions of access for natural persons in at least one Member State.

[63] 'For the same purpose, the Council shall, acting in accordance with the procedure referred to in Article 251, issue directives for the coordination of the provisions laid down by law, regulation or administrative action in Member States concerning the taking-up and pursuit of activities as self-employed persons.' Coordination here must be considered the equivalent to harmonization as provided under Art. 114 TFEU. See Klamert, 'Of empty glasses and double burdens'.

[64] 'In order to make it easier for persons to take up and pursue activities as self-employed persons, the Council shall, acting in accordance with the procedure referred to in Article 251, issue directives for the mutual recognition of diplomas, certificates and other evidence of formal qualifications.'

[65] For a different perspective, see G. Davies, 'The Services Directive: extending the country of origin principle and reforming public administration' (2007) *European Law Review* 232–45 at 237.

[66] See Recitals 2 and 5 Directive 2000/46/EC on the taking up, pursuit of and prudential supervision of the business of electronic money institutions, OJ 2000 No. L275/39; Recitals 7 and 47 Directive 2006/48/EC of the European Parliament and the

nature of the Services Directive is less of a problem with the substantial provisions on administrative cooperation contained in the Services Directive, discussed in the next chapter. The Union as a matter of principle is not competent to harmonize national administrative law.[67] It thus cannot force Member States to change the organization of their administration, such as by requiring them to set up new institutions. However, if Member State administrative law impedes the functioning of the Treaty freedoms, it comes within the scope of the legislative competence of the Union.[68] It is this line of case law that justifies the wide-ranging administrative rules contained in the Services Directive.[69]

However, matters are more intricate with regard to Article 16 Services Directive, which deviates from the case law on the justifications available to the Member State, as we will explain in the following chapter. Article 3(3) prescribes that 'Member States shall apply the provisions of this Directive in compliance with the rules of the Treaty on the right of establishment and the free movement of services'. This exhorts the secondary law nature of the Directive, which must be in line with primary law. While some have questioned whether the Services Directive, read as a whole, is a harmonization measure, but have expressed fewer doubts in respect of Article 16(1) and (3),[70] others have stressed that in

Council of 14 June 2006 relating to the taking up and pursuit of the business of credit institutions, OJ 2006 No. L177/1. Other service-related legislation such as on telecommunications or on gas and electricity has been based on the general harmonization mandate provided in what is now Article 114 TFEU. See Directive 2002/21/EC of the European Parliament and the Council of 7 March 2002 on a common regulatory framework for electronic communications networks and services, OJ 2002 No. L108/33; Directive 2003/54/EC of the European Parliament and the Council of 26 June 2003 concerning common rules for the internal market in electricity, OJ 2003 No. L176/37, and Directive 2003/55/EC of the European Parliament and the Council of 26 June 2003 concerning common rules for the internal market in natural gas, OJ 2003 No. L176/57.

67 See Case 96/81, *Commission* v. *Netherlands* [1990] ECR 1791, para. 12. However, see Commission Recommendation 97/344/EC of 22 April 1997 on improving and simplifying the business environment for business start-ups, OJ 1997 No. L145/29, Rec. 48.

68 Case C-128/89, *Commission* v. *Italy* [1990] ECR I-3239. For the cooperation duties of national administrative bodies resulting from EU law, see G. Sydow, *Verwaltungskooperation in der Europäischen Union* (Tübingen: Mohr Siebeck, 2004), pp. 23ff.

69 See U. Schliesky, 'Von der Realisierung des Binnenmarktes über die Verwaltungsreform zu einem gemeineuropäischen Verwaltungsrecht? Die Auswirkungen der geplanten EU-Dienstleistungsrichtlinie auf das deutsche Verwaltungsrecht' (2005) *Deutsches Verwaltungsblatt* 887–95 at 890.

70 See Barnard, 'Unravelling the Services Directive', 367.

any case it is of a different kind to what is familiar from the legislation of goods.[71] Hatzopoulos has even vehemently denied the harmonizing nature of the Services Directive.[72] Those who had no doubts of such nature were still in disagreement on whether the Services Directive achieves full harmonization,[73] or only minimum harmonization in a specific area.[74]

While this is not the place to engage in this debate, we can conclude that the Services Directive is in many ways a novelty. Whether it has been successful will probably become evident not too far in the future, when the Court might topple the envisaged thrust of the Directive in much the same manner as it has done for the Posting of Workers Directive discussed above.

## 5.5 Soft law and case law: services of general economic interest

Examples of soft law that are relevant in the services context are numerous, ranging from handbooks such as the one on the implementation of the Services Directive, to interpretative communications following important decisions by the ECJ.[75]

With SGEI, which we have already discussed above, the Union has de facto adopted yet another regulatory approach. Instead of directives or regulations that would harmonize the conditions for imposing PSOs or would demarcate the border between Member State and Union competence to regulate on SGEI, the regime on the Union side

[71] See Klamert, 'Of empty glasses and double burdens'. See also Barnard, 'Unravelling the Services Directive', 383: 'This is not harmonization as we know it.'

[72] V. Hatzopoulos, 'Legal aspects in establishing the internal market for services', *College of Europe Research Papers* (2007), p. 22: 'Such an interpretation could be valid only if we admitted that the Directive fully harmonises the free provision of services – a claim which is certainly not true.' For doubts as to the legality of the Directive because it would not make free movement easier as required by the legal basis, see Griller, 'The new Services Directive of the European Union', pp. 411–13.

[73] See W.-H. Roth, 'Freier Dienstleistungsverkehr und Verbraucherschutz' (2007) *Verbraucher und Recht* 161–72 at 171, affirming this for the consumer protection rules of Directive 2006/123.

[74] See also D. Schiek, 'The European social model and the Services Directive', in U. Neergaard, R. Nielsen and L. Roseberry (eds.), *The Services Directive: Consequences for the Welfare State and the European Social Model* (Copenhagen: Djof, 2008), pp. 25–62 at pp. 58ff.

[75] For many examples, see Hatzopoulos, *Regulating Services in the European Union*, pp. 348–9.

is a combination of soft law and case law. We will now briefly describe this approach, which makes the regulation of SGEI very different from other services.

Parts of the Treaty regime on SGEI are concerned with the question of whether they are covered by the competition law rules or the rules on state aid, as we have shown above. Thus Article 106 TFEU is the basis for a complicated rule-exception-exception regime that has been complemented by case law, such as *Altmark* in particular.

Another part of the Treaty provisions on SGEI, in contrast, is concerned with the question of who is responsible for defining the difference between SGEI and other public services that are exempted from the mentioned regime altogether. With public services, classification is decisive. While market services fall within the competence of the Union, services in the exercise of public authority are largely a matter for the Member States.[76] Before the Lisbon Treaty, Article 16 EC conferred on Member States the right to provide, to authorize and to fund SGEI, recognizing the role of SGEI for economic, social and territorial cohesion. However, the Court has never expressly relied upon this provision.[77]

Secondary law before the Lisbon Treaty has been confined to the important yet very specific sectors of network industries, with a number of directives on liberalizing the postal, energy and telecommunications sectors, which were initially based on ex Article 86 TFEU but were later based on what is now Article 114 TFEU.[78] A framework directive on SGEI has often been called for and has been on the Commission agenda, but has never materialized.[79] The Services Directive does not

[76] U. Neergaard, 'Services of general economic interest: the nature of the beast' in M. Krajewski, U. Neergaard and J. van de Gronden (eds.), *The Changing Legal Framework for Services of General Interest in Europe: Between Competition and Solidarity* (The Hague: TMC Asser, Kluwer, 2009), pp. 17–50 at p. 19.

[77] It may have informed the application of what is now Art. 106(2) TFEU. See M. Ross, 'Article 16 E.C. and services of general interest: from derogation to obligation' (2000) 25(1) *European Law Review* 22–38.

[78] The liberalization of telecommunications, postal and energy services has been called the first transformation by M. Krajewski, 'Conclusion', in M. Krajewski, U. Neergaard and J. van de Gronden (eds.), *The Changing Legal Framework for Services of General Interest in Europe: Between Competition and Solidarity* (The Hague: TMC Asser, Kluwer, 2009), pp. 499–506 at p. 500. Cf. M. Krajewski, *Grundstrukturen des Rechts öffentlicher Dienstleistungen* (Heidelberg: Springer, 2011).

[79] See J. van de Gronden, 'The EU and WTO law on free trade in services and the public interest: towards a framework Directive on Services of General Economic Interest?', in J. van de Gronden (ed.), *EU and WTO Law on Services: Limits to the Realisation of General Interest Policies within the Services Markets?* (The Hague: Kluwer, 2008), pp. 247–80 at

aim at abolishing service-providing monopolies, nor does it deal with the liberalization of SGEI as such.[80] Article 1 Services Directive grants to the Member States the freedom to determine what they consider an SGEI to be. This includes the competence to decide which services belong to this category, how to organize and how to finance them. Moreover, the applicability of the Directive's rules is limited to activities that are open to competition.[81]

The Commission entered into this legal vacuum by issuing a great number of Communications. These documents contain statements on the division of labour between the Member States and the Union. Thus it was declared that SGEI represent a shared responsibility between the Union and its Member States.[82] It was, however, also mentioned that EU law has an impact on the instruments for the delivery and the financing of SGEI.[83] This professed sharing of the burden of regulating SGEI is further undermined by the growing tendency of the Commission to avail itself of the authorization enacted in Article 106(3) TFEU to specify the meaning and extent of the exception under Article 106(2) TFEU, and to establish binding rules as to the effective monitoring and implementation of the underlying criteria.[84]

More important yet, and also more problematic, are policy papers and communications issued by the European Commission that set out to define terms such as SGI, SGEI, public services and universal services. These papers have been qualified as general policy statements on the one hand, but also as a soft form of legislation on the other hand.[85]

pp. 276–9, with further references. See also S. Rodrigues, 'Towards a general EC framework instrument related to SGEI? Political considerations and legal constraints', in M. Krajewski, U. Neergaard and J. van de Gronden (eds.), *The Changing Legal Framework for Services of General Interest in Europe: Between Competition and Solidarity* (The Hague: TMC Asser, Kluwer, 2009), pp. 255–66. See European Parliament, Resolution of 14 March 2007 on social services of general interest in the European Union, P6_TA(2007)0070, Recital G, stating that 'there is an urgent need to clarify the concepts in question and the legal framework' within which they operate.

80 See Art. 1(2) Directive 2006/123/EC.

81 See Rec. 8 Directive 2006/123/EC.

82 See European Commission, White Paper on services of general interest, COM(2004)374, section 2.3.

83 See White Paper on services of general interest, COM(2004)374, 16.

84 See, most recently, European Commission, Communication, Towards a single market act for a highly competitive social market economy, 50 proposals for improving our work, business and exchanges with one another, COM(2010)608 final.

85 U. Neergaard, 'The Commission's soft law in the area of services', in E. Szyszczak *et al.* (eds.), *Developments in Services of General Interest* (The Hague: TMC Asser, Springer, 2011), pp. 37–59 at p. 52.

A Green Paper by the Commission from 2003 stated that the broader notion of SGI is derived 'in Community practice' from that of SGEI and would cover both market and non-market services.[86] Since then, SGI have been at the centre of various specific Commission documents,[87] emphasizing that those services are assumed to reflect Europe's model of society.[88] NESGI have been qualified as either being activities governed by solidarity such as education and statutory social security schemes or strategic services of the state such as police, justice or the diplomatic service, which are also known as activities of public authority.[89] While NESGI largely evade the application of EU law, as we will discuss below, their concrete organization by national authorities can be reviewed under the most fundamental rules of EU law, in particular the principle of non-discrimination.[90]

Social services of general interest (SSGI) are another category, which has so far appeared exclusively in soft law documents.[91] SSGI must be located somewhere in between SGEI and SGI, and may refer to economic or non-economic services.[92] They have been divided into statutory and complementary social security schemes, irrespective of their organization (mutual or occupational organization) on the one hand, and other essential services directly provided to those in need on the other hand. This latter category has been classified further into the four sub-groups of social assistance, offers for reintegration into society and

[86] It was not entirely evident to what kind of practice it is concretely referring.

[87] See European Commission, Communication on services of general interest in Europe, COM(2000)580, OJ 2001 No. C17/4; European Commission, Report to the Laeken European Council, COM(2001)598; European Commission, Green Paper on Services of General Interest, COM (2003)270; European Commission, White Paper on services of general interest, COM(2004)374.

[88] European Commission, Communication accompanying the Communication on 'A single market for 21st century Europe', Services of general interest, including social services of general interest: a new European commitment, COM(2007)725, p. 3.

[89] European Commission, Communication, COM(2007)725, p. 5.

[90] See also European Commission, Communication, COM(2007)725, para. 2.1.

[91] See the documents mentioned above, as well as European Commission, Staff Working Document, Biennial Report on social services of general interest, SEC(2008)2179/2; European Commission, Communication, Implementing the Community Lisbon Programme: Social services of general interest in the European Union, COM (2006)177, para. 11, p. 4; European Commission, Staff Working Document, SEC(2006)516.

[92] See also J. van de Gronden, 'Social services of general interest and EU law', in E. Szyszczak *et al.* (eds.) *Developments in Services of General Interest*, Legal Issues of Services of General Interest (The Hague: TMC Asser, 2011), pp. 123–51.

into the labour market, long-term care and social housing.[93] It has been argued that the red line running through the Commission's soft law is that SSGI are subject to a modernization process that should inject internal market and competition law into SSGI schemes.[94]

With this proliferation of soft law, the Commission has been accused of walking a tightrope between subsidiarity and the adoption of a European perspective on almost every aspect, which would affect legal certainty.[95] Treaty provisions and soft law coexist without the '"in-between" layer in the shape of directives'.[96] The Court has shown some ambivalence in dealing with this rather unsatisfactory situation. Thus in the *BUPA* decision the Court both relied upon a Commission Communication on SGEI,[97] while at the same time dismissing these papers as being not binding.[98] According to *BUPA*, Member States must show that 'certain minimum criteria common to every SGEI' are satisfied, notably 'the presence of an act of the public authority entrusting the operators in question with an SGEI mission and the universal and compulsory nature of that mission'.[99] Failure to do so may 'constitute a manifest error of assessment, in which case the Commission is required to make a finding to that effect, failing which the Commission itself makes a manifest error'.[100] In its recent case law, in contrast, the Court gave ample room for the Member States to determine the substance

[93] Given their explicit, separate exclusion from Directive 2006/123/EC, it must be assumed that the Union concept of SSGI does not cover health services, which would make them a (sub)category of its own. See also European Commission, Proposal for Directive of the European Parliament and of the Council on the application of patients' rights in cross-border healthcare, COM(2008)414. The proposal itself neither addresses the question of defining health services nor does it include any reference to the concepts of SGI, SGEI and SSGI.

[94] Van de Gronden, 'Social services of general interest and EU law', p. 149.

[95] Neergaard, 'The Commission's soft law in the area of services', pp. 56–8.

[96] Neergaard, 'The Commission's soft law in the area of services', p. 57.

[97] Case T-289/03, *BUPA* [2008] ECR II-81, para. 165.

[98] Case T-289/03, *BUPA* [2008] ECR II-81, para. 187. This contradiction has also been noted by M. Ross, 'The value of solidarity in European public services law', in M. Krajewski, U. Neergaard and J. van de Gronden (eds.), *The Changing Legal Framework for Services of General Interest in Europe: Between Competition and Solidarity* (TMC Asser: Kluwer, 2009), pp. 81–99 at p. 90.

[99] Case T-289/03, *BUPA* [2008] ECR II-81, para. 172. See Neergaard, 'Services of general economic interest', pp. 36–7.

[100] Case T-289/03, *BUPA* [2008] ECR II-81, para. 172. See European Commission, Communication on services of general interest in Europe, COM(2000)580, OJ 2001 No. C17/4, point 22.

and mode of implementation of SGEI.[101] It adopted a more flexible standard of review under which it considered a variety of objectives.[102] On the other hand, in its *GEMO* judgment, delivered a few weeks after the *Altmark* decision, the Court qualified the mere provision of the public service as state aid, instead of its financing.[103]

We would argue that soft law and case law that send out mixed signals on this issue are hardly a sound basis for such redrawing of competence boundaries. A consequence of this approach is also that what constitutes an SGEI may vary from one Member State to another, compromising the endeavour of establishing Union-wide legal certainty in this matter. Moreover, it cannot be assessed a priori whether a certain service is an SGI, but this requires a case-by-case analysis.[104] Thus the Court clarified that SGI include national education and statutory social security schemes that are publicly funded, because a Member State, 'in establishing and maintaining such a system, is not seeking to engage in gainful activity, but is fulfilling its duties towards its own population in the social, cultural and educational fields'.[105] This means conversely that should a Member State finance its higher education predominantly by fees and private funding, this would disqualify a service as an SGI. The same is true with regard to cultural, social and health services, if they are aimed at making economic profit.

Article 14 TFEU has now added that the underlying principles and conditions to guarantee the functioning of SGEI shall be defined by regulations. In practice, this limitation as to the legal instrument to be used will arguably make it rather difficult to adopt a more harmonized approach to the regulation of SGEI in the absence of a broad consensus among the Member States. Moreover, a Protocol annexed to the Lisbon Treaty introduced the notion of SGI into primary law.[106] At the same

[101] See among others Case C-67/96, *Albany International* [1999] ECR I-5751; Case C-320/91, *Corbeau* [1993] ECR I-2533; Case C-340/99, *TNT Traco* [2001] ECR I-4109; Case C-475/99, *Ambulanz Glöckner* [2001] ECR I-8089; Cases C-147/97 and C-148/97, *Deutsche Post* [2000] ECR I-825; Case C-209/98, *FFAD* [2000] ECR I-3743.

[102] See Case C-67/96, *Albany* [1999] ECR I-5751, para. 107.

[103] See Case C-126/01, *GEMO* [2003] I-13769, para. 33.

[104] European Commission, Communication, COM(2007)725, p. 5.

[105] Case C-109/92, *Wirth* [1993] ECR I-6447, para. 15.

[106] See also Art. 36 of the Charter of Fundamental Rights of the EU, which recognizes access to SGEI as one of the fundamental rights of the EU without, however, creating any new rights. See the explanations on Art. 36 by the Secretariat of the Convention on the Future of the European Union.

time, as already mentioned, the Services Directive states that Member State competence to define SGEI will not be touched. Thus the new legal regime under the Lisbon Treaty can be said to prolong the 'schizophrenic' state of play with regard to public services.

## 5.6 Conclusion

This chapter has shown that harmonization can take many forms and that it can go hand in hand with mutual recognition. The Services Directive in particular has proven, at some peril to EU law orthodoxy, that various regulatory approaches and instruments can be combined into one single measure, making it a singularly 'complete' regulatory instrument. This novel approach, however, has made it difficult to classify the Services Directive in terms of its nature. In the following chapter we will take a closer look at the Services Directive in substantive terms.

Directive 2005/36/EC on the recognition of qualifications, while at first glance a clear representation of the mutual recognition approach, also complements this approach with minimum harmonization. Directive 96/71 on posted workers, in turn, cannot really be called a (minimum) harmonization rule, because it does not really harmonize the relevant national laws. It rather represents a form of minimum coordination, which has, however, been remodelled by the Court of Justice in a more unifying mould.

The field of SGEI shows that the absence of regulation and the simultaneous need for regulatory guidance can produce a regime that is based on soft law and case law, which both try to make sense of the balancing act that SGEI are in view of the 'signals' sent by the Member States. While the current state is certainly not conducive to legal certainty and transparency, SGEI also show that a horizontal legal framework is not always preferable. In spite of advantages such as producing a set of clear-cut and consolidated principles, we strongly doubt that this could outweigh the difficulty of covering within a single piece of horizontal legislation the various distinct aspects of this category of services. In general, we would thus argue that if one would want a horizontal measure on SGEI, it would have to be a 'framework' directive, leaving the specificities of the diverse SGEI for a separate body of legislation.

The measures discussed above clearly do not give a full picture of the variety of regulatory approaches that exist in the EU. However, they are some of the most prominent ones in the field of services and they arguably go a long way in showing that approaches in the EU are varied, often difficult to classify, and may appear in all kinds of combinations.

# 6 The Services Directive: innovation and fragmentation

## 6.1 Introduction

Directive 2006/123/EC has been qualified as perhaps the single most important act of secondary law on the common market.[1] It submits the freedom of establishment and the freedom to provide services to a novel statutory regime.[2] We will show that, in particular, the rules on service providers and recipients in more than one way recast the current regime under the Treaty. Even the rules on established service providers, which were meant to reflect faithfully previous case law, might change Union law in a fundamental manner. In addition, the Directive introduces potentially momentous and innovative rules on administrative cooperation, such as single points of contact and a screening mechanism for national law.

The Services Directive was conceived at the Lisbon Extraordinary European Council of 23–4 March 2000 as a cornerstone of the European Union's strategy to become the most competitive and dynamic knowledge-based economy in the world by the year 2010. Consequently, the Commission submitted a paper called Internal Market Strategy for Services in order to assess whether 'there are unjustifiable and preventable barriers preventing services being bought or sold across borders', and to develop 'legislative measures to dismantle remaining barriers

[1] Directive 2006/123/EC of the European Parliament and the Council of 12 December 2006 on services in the internal market, OJ 2006 No. L376/36 (references to Articles in this chapter refer to this Directive unless indicated otherwise). Parts of this chapter draw on M. Klamert, 'Way to go? More on the Services Directive and the Fundamental Freedoms' (2009) *Zeitschrift für Öffentliches Recht* 335–55.

[2] Arts. 9–15 and 16–21.

and prevent the emergence of new ones'.[3] This was followed by a Commission report on 'The State of the Internal Market for Services'.[4] It is this report on which the Services Directive builds and to which it seeks to respond.[5] The Services Directive is based on the acknowledgment that barriers to trade in services cannot be tackled by applying the Treaty freedoms alone.[6] The Commission proposal[7] had also foreseen the so-called country of origin principle in the central provision of Article 16, discussed below. This would have subjected service providers to their home state laws. This draft (by the then responsible commissioner Bolkestein) and the public fears it has caused had even been one of the reasons for the rejection of the Constitutional Treaty, especially in France. Only by abandoning this principle could the Directive eventually be adopted in 2006.[8] It has been shown that the Central and Eastern European Member States that had been strongly in favour of this principle had been bought off with a more comprehensive screening regime for national restrictions, discussed below.[9]

In this chapter we will, among other things, show that the Services Directive is fraught with exemptions of various kinds. This concerns, above all, several service sectors that are either exempted entirely from the scope of the Directive, or are exempted from Article 16 in particular. These sectors exempted from the scope of application of the Services Directive continue to come under the Treaty regime of Articles 49 and 56 TFEU.[10] Thus any sectoral fragmentation in the Services Directive

[3] European Commission, An Internal Market Strategy for Services, COM(2000)888.

[4] European Commission, Report, The State of the Internal Market for Services, COM(2002)441.

[5] See Recital 3: 'The report from the Commission on "The State of the Internal Market for Services" drew up an inventory of a large number of barriers which are preventing or slowing down the development of services between Member States.'

[6] See Rec. 6.

[7] European Commission, Proposal for a Directive of the European Parliament and of the Council on services in the internal market, COM(2004)2 final.

[8] See also J. Flower, 'Negotiating European legislation: The Services Directive' (2006–2007) *Cambridge Yearbook of European Legal Studies* 217–38; and K. Nicolaïdis and S. K. Schmidt, 'Mutual recognition "on trial": the long road to services liberalization' (2007) *Journal of European Public Policy* 717–34.

[9] M. Dagnis Jensen and P. Nedergaard, 'From "Frankenstein" to "toothless vampire"? Explaining the watering down of the Services Directive' (2012) 19(6) *Journal of European Public Policy* 844–62.

[10] See also C. Barnard, 'Unravelling the Services Directive' (2008) *Common Market Law Review* 323–94 at 343. But see A. Biondi, 'Recurring cycles in the internal market: some reflections on the free movement of services', in A. Arnull, P. Eeckhout and T. Tridimas (eds.), *Continuity and Change in EU Law: Essays in Honour of Sir Francis Jacobs* (Oxford University Press, 2007), pp. 228–42 at p. 235, who deplores a 'repatriation

leads to a corresponding fragmentation in primary law and in the scope of application of other secondary law that is relevant for the services sector.

## 6.2 Scope of application

### *6.2.1 Introduction*

The Services Directive covers non-established service providers (what we will refer to also as services *stricto sensu*) in its Chapter IV, and established service providers in Chapter III. It thus realizes the much-debated extension of the definition of services to encompass all activities that are closely related from an economic perspective. Whether the Services Directive only regulates situations involving at least two Member States or whether it also applies to purely internal situations will be discussed in Chapter 7 on the implementation of the Services Directive.

According to Article 4, providers of services[11] and natural or legal persons established in a Member State in the meaning of Article 49 TFEU (ex-Article 43 EC) are covered by the Directive.[12] This excludes branches of companies established in third countries.[13] However, Recital 33 empowers Member States to include third country nationals who are receiving services within their respective territory.

### *6.2.2 Key concepts*

The general definition of services in Article 4(1) refers to what is now Article 57 TFEU (ex-Article 50 EC).[14] As we have already discussed above, Article 57 TFEU defines services as any service for remuneration unless it falls under the free movement of persons, thus the freedom of establishment. Concerning establishments, the Services Directive does not engage in facilitating their freedom in general, but only as far as 'access

of powers to the national legislator' in view of the many exemptions in the Services Directive.

11 'Any natural person who is a national of a Member State, or any legal person, as referred to in Article 48 of the Treaty, established in a Member State, who offers or provides a service.'

12 'The actual pursuit of an economic activity, as referred to in Article 43 of the Treaty, by the provider for an indefinite period and a stable infrastructure from where the business of providing services is actually carried out.'

13 See Rec. 36.

14 'Any self-employed economic activity, normally provided for remuneration, as referred to in Article 50 of the Treaty.'

to a service activity or the exercise thereof' is concerned.[15] Hence, also under Chapter III the definition of the term 'service activity' is decisive. However, since Article 4(1) in combination with Article 57 TFEU specifically exclude services coming under the freedom of establishments, the term 'service activity' would deprive Chapter III of the Directive of any scope of application. As this cannot have been intended, the term 'service activity' under Chapter III must have a meaning distinct from the general definition under Article 4. Chapter III thus applies to economic activities falling under the freedom of establishment in the meaning of the TFEU, but which at the same time represent a service activity from an economic perspective.[16]

As regards the coverage of national measures, requirements are defined in Article 4(7) as 'any obligation, prohibition, condition or limit provided for in the laws, regulations or administrative provisions of the Member States or in consequence of case-law, administrative practice, the rules of professional bodies, or the collective rules of professional associations or other professional organisations, adopted in the exercise of their legal autonomy'. This resembles the concept of restriction used by the Court, which refers to measures 'liable to hinder or make less attractive the exercise of fundamental freedoms'.[17] Recital 9 states that the Services Directive does not apply to requirements that 'do not specifically regulate or specifically affect the service activity but have to be respected by providers in the course of carrying out their economic activity in the same way as by individuals acting in their private capacity'.[18] Recital 9 mentions road traffic rules, rules concerning the development or use of land, town and country planning, building standards and administrative penalties imposed for non-compliance with such rules. We would argue that this might have made sense under the Commission proposal where it would have been apposite to exclude the

[15] Arts. 9(1) and 14.

[16] See, e.g., Rec. 5: 'It is therefore necessary to remove barriers to the freedom of establishment for providers in Member States'. Read this in conjunction with Rec. 36: 'The concept of "provider" should cover any natural person who is a national of a Member State or any legal person engaged in a service activity in a Member State, in exercise either of the freedom of establishment.'

[17] See Chapters 3 and 4. Case C-55/94, *Gebhard* [1995] ECR I-4165, para. 37.

[18] Compare the definition of the coordinated field in Art. 4(9) of the Commission proposal, COM(2004)2 final ('any requirement applicable to access to service activities or to the exercise thereof'). See also Rec. 43 of the Commission proposal, COM(2004)2 final.

mentioned areas of law from the country of origin principle.[19] Instead, the reference to road traffic rules is an exemption demanded by the UK for political reasons.[20] What is important with these 'rules of a general nature' is that they are not meant to exempt rules such as planning laws in general, but only depending on their actual effect.[21]

### 6.2.3 *Sectoral coverage*

While Recital 33 lists some of the sectors covered, there is no official, exhaustive list of sectors. Article 2(1) states that the Directive 'shall apply to services supplied by providers established in a Member State'. This is qualified, however, by a variety of exemptions and derogations in Articles 2(2) and 3 unprecedented for an act of secondary law, explaining why the Services Directive is better known for what it does *not* regulate, than for the services it actually covers.[22] This negative listing approach to the sectoral scope of application of the Services Directive complicates the assessment of the actual scope of the Services Directive. Whether this is an apposite approach from a policy perspective will be discussed in Chapter 8. Suffice to note that the sectoral scope of application of the Services Directive results from what is not exempted from its scope of application.[23] Here we can distinguish between business-to-business services, services addressed to both consumers and entrepreneurs, and consumer services covered by the Services Directive. Important examples for the first category are the

[19] After all, a German lorry driver could hardly be subject to German traffic rules, including driving on the right side of the road, when operating in the UK.

[20] Barnard, 'Unravelling the Services Directive', 336–7.

[21] See European Commission, *Handbook on Implementation of Services Directive* (hereafter *Implementation Handbook*) (2007), available at http://ec.europa.eu/internal_market/services/docs/services-dir/guides/handbook_en.pdf, at p. 14. The Handbook specifically provides that 'the actual effect of the requirements in question needs to be assessed to determine whether they are of a general nature or not. Thus, when implementing the Directive, Member States need to take account of the fact that legislation labelled as "town planning" or "building standards" may contain requirements, which specifically regulate service activities and are thus covered by the Services Directive. For instance, rules on the maximum surface of certain commercial establishments, even when contained in general urban planning laws, would come under the Services Directive and, as a result, will be covered by the obligations in the establishment chapter of the Directive.'

[22] V. Hatzopoulos, 'Que reste-t-il de la directive sur les services?' (2007) *Research Papers in Law*, College of Europe, p. 12, has called this 'négativisme ambiant'.

[23] For the following compare European Commission, Single Market News, 'Grünes Licht für die Dienstleistungsrichtlinie', No. 44, January 2007, pp. 8–9; Rec. 33 Services Directive.

sectors of management consultancy, certification and testing, advertising, recruitment services and sales agents. Under the second category fall legal and tax services, real estate services, construction including architects, trade, the organization of trade fairs, the leasing of motor vehicles and travel agencies. Finally, services catering for consumers coming under the Services Directive are, among others, tourism including tour guides, leisure and recreational services, and sports centres and amusement parks. Among others, important exceptions are services by public notaries exempted both by Article 2 and Article 17.

### *6.2.4 Exemptions from the scope of application*

Article 1 provides that the Services Directive must not affect measures to protect or promote cultural or linguistic diversity or media pluralism, the exercise of fundamental rights and collective bargaining rights.[24] We would argue that in order not to affect the freedom of Member States to take such measures, they must be deemed outside the scope of application of the substantive provisions of the Services Directive.

Article 2(3) Services Directive excludes tax law from the Directive's scope of application. Article 1(6), using different language, exempts matters of labour law as well as social security legislation. Article 1(5) excludes Member State 'rules of criminal law'.[25] Article 2(2) Services Directive excludes a number of services from its scope of application that are already governed by a specific secondary law regime. Thus, it exempts non-economic services of general interest, which are discussed in detail in Chapters 3 and 8. Article 2(2)(b) exempts financial services 'such as banking, credit, insurance and re-insurance, occupational or personal pensions, securities, investment funds, payment and investment advice, including the services listed in Annex I to Directive 2006/48/EC'. Article 2(2)(c) exempts electronic communication services in view of the new regulatory framework in this area.[26]

In Article 2(d), the Services Directive excludes 'services in the field of transport, including port services, falling within the scope of Title V

[24] The difference between a prohibition to deal with certain aspects of Member State law and the pledge that the Services Directive would not affect national matters is not clear. Hatzopoulos, 'Que reste-t-il?', p. 13, has suggested that the latter phrasing is stronger, but has not elaborated in which way precisely. The French wording of 'n'affecte pas' and 'ne s'applique pas', indeed, seem a bit more distinct and their correlation in English is all but obvious.

[25] See Rec. 12 and 14 Services Directive.

[26] Cf. Rec. 19 Services Directive.

of the Treaty'. Recital 21 adds that this includes urban transport, taxis, ambulances and port services. In contrast, services that are not predominantly dedicated to transportation, such as driving schools, removal services, car rental services, funeral services, aerial photography as well as other commercial activities in ports or airports (shops and restaurants), are fully covered by the Directive.[27]

The exclusion of healthcare services in Article 2(f), 'whether or not they are provided via healthcare facilities, and regardless of the ways in which they are organised and financed at national level or whether they are public or private', has been read in a broad manner by the Court.[28] The exception pertains to services provided by 'health professionals to patients, to assess, maintain or restore their state of health'.[29] Thus services offered to the health professional himself or to a hospital such as administration services, accounting, cleaning, the provision and maintenance of medical equipment, as well as contributions by medical research centres, are covered by the Directive, as are complementary wellness or relaxation services that are not essentially designed to maintain, assess or restore the health of patients.[30]

Article 2(j) exempts 'social services relating to social housing, childcare and support of families and persons permanently or temporarily in need which are provided by the State, by providers mandated by the State or by charities recognised as such by the State'. This therefore requires two cumulative conditions to be fulfilled, namely regarding the nature of the activities carried out and the status of the service provider.[31] As to the latter condition, any private provider, acting without mandate from the state, such as private nannies or private household support services, escape the exclusion and are fully covered by the Services Directive.[32] Furthermore, services of temporary work agencies, audio-visual services,[33] gambling services,[34] services connected

[27] See European Commission, *Implementation Handbook*, p. 11.

[28] See Case C-57/12, *Femarbel* [2013] not yet published in the Official Journal, paras. 36–41, with respect to day-care and night-care centres for the elderly, whereby the Court relied heavily on the Commission's *Implementation Handbook*.

[29] Rec. 22 Services Directive.

[30] European Commission, *Implementation Handbook*, p. 12.

[31] Case C-57/12, *Femarbel* [2013] not yet published in the Official Journal, paras. 42–50, again referring to the Implementation Handbook in support of its interpretation.

[32] European Commission, *Implementation Handbook*, p. 13.

[33] See Art. 2(2)(g) Services Directive: 'including cinematographic services, whatever their mode of production, distribution and transmission, and radio broadcasting'.

[34] See Art. 2(h) Services Directive: 'which involve wagering a stake with pecuniary value in games of chance, including lotteries, gambling in casinos and betting transactions'.

with the exercise of official authority, private security services and services provided by notaries and bailiffs are also excluded.

Finally, Article 3(2) contains a broad exemption for international private law rules (conflict of laws rules), specifically mentioning 'rules governing the law applicable to contractual and non-contractual obligations'. This seems to be mainly an attempt to preserve national consumer protection standards.[35]

### 6.2.5 *The partial exemption of services of general economic interest*

According to Article 1 Services Directive, it does not concern the liberalization[36] of services of general economic interest, or affect the freedom of Member States to define services of general economic interest. Moreover, Article 2(2) Services Directive exempts SGI as well as certain SGEI such as transport, telecommunication and healthcare services.[37]

With regard to SGI, this would not have been necessary given the fact that the Treaty rules only apply to commercial services offered for remuneration, as we have explained above.[38] It also exempts certain SSGI such as 'social services relating to social housing, childcare and support of families and persons permanently or temporarily in need which are provided by the State, by providers mandated by the State or by charities recognised as such by the State'.[39] One reason for the

[35] '[Those] which guarantee that consumers benefit from the protection granted to them by the consumer protection rules laid down in the consumer legislation in force in their Member State.' But see the interpretation by S. Griller, 'The new Services Directive of the European Union: hopes and expectations from the angle of a (further) completion of the internal market', General Report, in H. F. Koeck and M. M. Karollus (eds.), *The New Services Directive of the European Union*, Féderation Internationale pour le Droit Européen (FIDE), XXIII Congress Linz 2008 (Vienna: Congress Publications, 2008), vol. III, pp. 379–423.

[36] Liberalization has to be understood in this context as the opening up to free market competition.

[37] See European Parliament, Resolution on the impact and consequences of the exclusion of health services from the Directive on services in the internal market, 23.05.2007, P6_TA(2007)201.

[38] See also J. van de Gronden, 'The EU and WTO law on free trade in services and the public interest: towards a framework directive on Services of General Economic Interest?', in J. van de Gronden (ed.), *EU and WTO Law on Services: Limits to the Realisation of General Interest Policies within the Services Markets?* (The Hague: Kluwer, 2008), pp. 247–80 at p. 267.

[39] Art. 2(j) Services Directive. Critical of this specific exclusion, S. Wernicke, 'Taking stock: the EU institutions and SGEI', in M. Krajewski, U. Neergaard and J. van de Gronden (eds.), *The Changing Legal Framework for Services of General Interest in Europe: Between Competition and Solidarity* (The Hague: TMC Asser, Kluwer, 2009), pp. 69–79 at p. 73

reduced scope of application of the Services Directive on SGEI might be found in the pertinent jurisprudence of the ECJ.[40]

This means, however, that all SGEI not mentioned in this list are indeed covered by the Services Directive. In turn, those SGEI actually covered by the Services Directive are exempted under Article 17(1) Services Directive from the prohibition of restrictions in Article 16, as already mentioned. Article 17 lists the postal, energy, gas, water and waste disposal sectors as examples for SGEI that are already regulated by secondary law.[41] Exempted SGEI not yet covered by specific Union legislation continue to fall under the Treaty regime.[42] As we will discuss below, the rule of priority in Article 3 Services Directive for other acts of secondary law only applies in the event of a norm conflict between the Services Directive and another legal act. In order to avoid legal uncertainty with regard to the legality of Member State measures that are allowed under such sectoral regimes, but that would equally fall under the prohibition in Article 16 Services Directive, the exemption in Article 17(1) Services Directive actually makes sense.[43]

Conversely, this means that all other rules of Chapter IV, such as on the rights of recipients of services (Articles 19–21 Services Directive), fully apply to SGEI. Moreover, SGEI not generally exempted from the Services Directive, which are provided through an establishment, come fully under the scope of application of the Directive. However, Chapter III takes account of the specifics of SGEI in two places. While the list of explicitly banned requirements in Article 14 Services Directive is fully applicable, the obligation under Article 15 Services Directive for (other) requirements is qualified by Article 15(4). Thus the conditions of non-discrimination, necessity and proportionality stipulated by Article 15 only apply to SGEI to the extent that this would 'not obstruct the performance, in law or in fact, of the particular task assigned to them'. This

40 See Hatzopoulos, 'Que reste-t-il?', pp. 15–17.

41 There is explicit reference to Directive 97/67/EC of the European Parliament and the Council of 15 December 1997 on common rules for the development of the internal market of Community postal services and the improvement of quality of service, OJ 1998 No. L15/14; Directive 2003/54/EC of the European Parliament and the Council of 26 June 2003 concerning common rules for the internal market in electricity, OJ 2003 No. L176/37; and Directive 2003/55/EC of the European Parliament and the Council of 26 June 2003 concerning common rules for the internal market in natural gas, OJ 2003 No. L176/57.

42 See Art. 3(3) Services Directive. Under the Commission proposal, COM(2004)2 final, an exhaustive list of SGEI had been exempted.

43 For a different perspective without reference to Art. 3 Services Directive, see van de Gronden, 'The EU and WTO law on free trade in services', pp. 270–1.

wording is identical to Article 106(2) TFEU, which means that any SGEI benefiting from the derogation under Article 15(4) Services Directive must be clearly defined and explicitly entrusted through an act of public authority, in addition to the other requirements set up by Article 106(2) TFEU, discussed below.[44] Article 9(3) Services Directive provides for an exemption regarding the obligations applying to the introduction of authorization schemes in Article 9(2), if aspects related to such schemes are governed directly or indirectly by other Union law instruments.[45] Directive 2006/12/EC, which obliges Member States to subject certain activities relating to wastewater to authorization regimes, would be an example of such an instrument in a non-exempted sector. Since, however, this Directive refrains from imposing concrete rules such as the conditions for granting an authorization, its duration or the procedure to be applied, the exemption, arguably, does not apply and Member States have to ensure that authorization schemes under the Waste Directive comply with the conditions imposed by Article 9(1).

Finally, the Services Directive subjects all SGEI not generally exempted to the Directive's rules on administrative cooperation and on the quality of services.

Thus the Directive arguably widens the gap between national claims to autonomy and the reality of extensive Union law regulation in this field. By adding to an already patchy regime, the Services Directive compounds the lack of clarity and legal certainty with regard to the regulation of SGEI within the Union. At the same time, however, the Services Directive does not provide substantive horizontal rules with regard to SGEI. The only exception is for those SGEI that are provided by establishments, in which case, however, the Article 106(2)-like exception under Article 15(4), as well as the justification regime under Article 9(1) Services Directive, will considerably diminish its impact.[46]

[44] By contrast, full applicability of Art. 14 Services Directive on SGEI suggests that Art. 106(2) TFEU is not applicable. In other words, any authorization requirement prohibited by Art. 14 cannot be justified by invoking the general interest.

[45] The justification regime in Art. 9 Services Directive is of course also applicable and might be quite relevant to SGEI. See van de Gronden, 'The EU and WTO law on free trade in services', p. 271.

[46] See, however, van de Gronden, 'The EU and WTO law on free trade in services', p. 272, who has argued that the application of Art. 9 Services Dirctive instead of Art. 106(2) TFEU will affect Member States' recourse to SGEI.

## 6.3 The rules on established service providers

### *6.3.1 Blacklisted national measures*

Article 14 provides a list of national measures that are prohibited without further qualification, that is they cannot be justified. All of these measures have been qualified as discrimination or restriction in case law.[47] As regards discriminatory measures, Article 14 prohibits requirements that are based directly or indirectly on nationality or, in the case of companies, on the location of the registered office. This includes, in particular, nationality or residence requirements for the provider, his staff, persons holding the share capital, or members of the provider's management or supervisory bodies.

Moreover, Article 14 blacklists the following non-discriminatory national measures:

- requirements for not having establishments or for being registered with professional bodies or associations in more than one Member State;
- restrictions on the freedom to choose between a principal or a secondary establishment, regarding the location of the principal establishment, or regarding the form of establishment;
- conditions of reciprocity with the Member State in which the provider already has an establishment;
- case-by-case application of an economic needs test or a test of appropriateness in relation to economic planning objectives unless these serve overriding reasons relating to the public interest;
- undue direct or indirect influence of competing operators in the granting of authorizations or in the adoption of other decisions of the competent authorities;
- obligations to provide or participate in a financial guarantee or to take out insurance from a provider or body established in their territory;
- obligations to have been pre-registered in national registers or to have previously exercised the activity for a given period in a Member State's territory.

This recalls the blacklisting in the Unfair Commercial Practices Directive[48] and might provide food for developments in case law such

[47] See European Commission, *Implementation Handbook*.

[48] Directive 2005/29/EC of the European Parliament and the Council of 11 May 2005 concerning unfair business-to-consumer commercial practices in the internal market, OJ 2005 No. L149/22.

as those handed down on its basis. This case law has arguably demonstrated that blacklists of prohibited national provisions can significantly reduce the leeway of all actors.[49] Thus national authorities may feel inclined to take a more conservative position as regards the legality of national law in the face of an EU rule that does not allow for discretion. Similarly, national lower courts might feel in a safer position to take a firm stance when the Union instrument leaves little doubt as to the standard that has to be applied. Further blacklisting is foreseen under Article 16(1) for services *stricto sensu*, discussed later.

### *6.3.2 Restrictions*

#### 6.3.2.1 Introduction

In addition to the unconditionally prohibited measures mentioned above, the Services Directive's section on establishments regulates national authorization regimes on the one hand, and the already familiar category of requirements on the other hand. The term authorizations, in contrast to requirements as we have defined them above, refers to national administrative procedures for obtaining a decision on the access to or the exercise of a service activity, such as schemes for licences, approvals, concessions and memberships with professional bodies.[50] This kind of national measures had not been specifically identified in case law before the Services Directive. Authorizations must be considered to be the more specific term compared to the broad definition of requirements.

#### 6.3.2.2 Requirements

Article 15 provides that certain national measures may only be adopted if they satisfy the criteria of 'necessity' and proportionality. Necessity is the term used by the Services Directive to refer to the condition of justification by an overriding reason relating to the public interest discussed below. This concerns the following non-discriminatory restrictions:

- quantitative or territorial restrictions, in particular in the form of limits fixed according to population or of a minimum geographical distance between providers;
- an obligation on a provider to take a specific legal form;

[49] See Case C-428/11, *Purely Creative Ltd* [2012] not yet published in the Official Journal.
[50] Art. 4(6). Cf. Rec. 39.

- requirements which relate to the shareholding of a company;[51]
- requirements reserving access to particular providers by virtue of the specific nature of the activity, unless provided under other Union legal acts;
- a ban on having more than one establishment in the territory of the same Member State;
- requirements fixing a minimum number of employees;
- fixed minimum and/or maximum tariffs with which the provider must comply;
- an obligation on the provider to supply other specific services jointly with his service.

In addition, these Article 15 measures are subject to a screening procedure discussed below.

### 6.3.2.3 Authorizations

Authorization schemes are subject to a two-tier test of legality under the Directive. In the first step, their introduction into the national legal order is considered; in the second step, their application is subjected to certain rules. Article 9(1) stipulates that in order to be introduced in the first place, an authorization scheme must satisfy the conditions of justification, proportionality and non-discrimination. In addition to these criteria, Article 10(2) provides that the authorities of a Member State must apply such schemes in a clear and objective manner. The Court recently ruled in the *Yellow Cab* decision in a similar vein.[52] In this case the national legislation provided that an application for authorization had to be carried out by the competent national authority on the sole basis of the statements made by a direct potential competitor.[53]

Moreover, authorization schemes must be notified in a timely manner and transparent. According to Article 10(4), authorizations must also be valid nationwide, subject, however, to exceptions for overriding public reasons.[54]

[51] Joined Cases C-357/10 to C-359/10, *Duomo* [2012] not yet published in the Official Journal, para. 37, on the requirement on participants in a procedure for the award of a concession to have a fully paid-up share capital of a certain amount.

[52] Case C-338/09, *Yellow Cab* [2010] ECR I-3297, para. 53. See also Case C-470/11, *SIA Garkalns* [2012] not yet published in the Official Journal, para. 43.

[53] Case C-338/09, *Yellow Cab* [2010] ECR I-3297.

[54] Joined Cases C-128/10 and C-129/10, *Naftiliaki Etaireia Thasou AE* [2011] ECR I-1885.

Article 11(1) provides that authorizations, in general, must be granted for an unlimited period.[55] Article 13 prescribes that the actual administration of such schemes is transparent and expedient. Should the promised time for processing an application for an authorization be exceeded, the Directive orders that authorization shall be granted *ex lege*.[56]

Article 10(3) Services Directive, which only applies in the part on establishments, states the following:

> The conditions for granting authorisation for a new establishment shall not duplicate requirements and controls which are equivalent or essentially comparable as regards their purpose to which the provider is already subject in another Member State or in the same Member State.

Recall that in *Säger*, discussed above, the Court held that

> the freedom to provide services may be limited only by rules which are justified by imperative reasons relating to the public interest and which apply to all persons or undertakings pursuing an activity in the State of destination, in so far as that interest is not protected by the rules to which the person providing the services is subject in the Member State in which he is established.[57]

However, the Court continued to examine whether the pertinent requirement of a lawyer qualification for the cross-border provision of patent renewal services was justified and proportionate (which it was not). In *Säger*, therefore, whether the British provider already had a licence under UK law was not decisive. In contrast, in Article 10(3) there is no reference to objective reasons of justification. Double burdens seem to be banned entirely, at least under Part III of the Services Directive, without any possibility of justifying them.

### 6.3.3 *Justification*

As we have seen above, both the authorizations in Article 9(1) and requirements in Article 14(3) can be justified by overriding reasons of the public interest. Article 4(8) defines these reasons as those 'recognised as such in the case law of the Court of Justice', and provides an illustrative list of the following fourteen reasons:

- public policy;
- public security;

[55] Art. 11(1)(a)–(c) provides certain exceptions to that principle.
[56] But see Art. 13(4).
[57] Case C-76/90, *Säger* [1991] ECR I-4221, para. 15.

- public safety;
- public health;
- preserving the financial equilibrium of the social security system;
- the protection of consumers, recipients of services and workers;
- fairness of trade transactions;
- combating fraud;
- the protection of the environment and the urban environment;[58]
- the health of animals;
- intellectual property;
- the conservation of the national historic and artistic heritage;
- social policy objectives;
- cultural policy objectives.[59]

Further reasons on whose basis national measures may be justified are mentioned in Recital 40:

- the maintenance of order in society;
- the prevention of unfair competition;
- the protection of creditors;
- safeguarding the sound administration of justice;
- road safety;
- the need to ensure a high level of education, the maintenance of press diversity and the promotion of the national language;
- veterinary policy.

In Chapter 3 we observed that case law often makes no differentiation between the express derogations provided in the Treaty such as public health and public policy on the one hand, and the mandatory requirements such as environmental protection and consumer protection on the other hand. This unification of the justifications regime in the common market is now also reflected in the Services Directive. When we compare the reasons for justification provided in the Directive with the ones applying under the Treaty regime discussed in Chapter 5, we must note that there is no precise match. However, this discrepancy is irrelevant, since the list in Article 4(8) Services Directive is not exhaustive. We must also note that this arrangement in the Services Directive first acknowledges the practice of the Court of finding new reasons of justification in its case law and, second, provides a cross-reference to this case

[58] This includes town and country planning. See Rec. 40.
[59] Including safeguarding the freedom of expression of various elements, in particular social, cultural, religious and philosophical values of society. See Rec. 40.

law in order to be able to apply the Directive. This entails that, at least with respect to the justifications regime, situations falling under the Services Directive are treated equally to situations coming under the Treaty freedoms.[60] That such synchronicity is not self-understood will be shown below in the section on fragmentation. However, does this also signify, conversely, that whenever the Court is asked to interpret the Services Directive on possible justifications of national measures within its scope of application, the Court's findings would also apply in the areas covered by the freedom of establishment or the freedom to provide services outside of the Services Directive, such as concerning establishments that are not providing services? If that were the case, it would be another (rare) example of the interpretation of primary law in the light of secondary law.

### 6.3.4 *Conclusion*

National authorization schemes and requirements with regard to service activities conducted through an establishment in the host state have in common that they may be justified by a non-exhaustive list of overriding reasons of the public interest. While the Services Directive distinguishes between the introduction and the administration of authorization schemes, it is more casuistic and more prohibitive regarding requirements by barring some of the most 'notorious' examples. The system of regulation for established services providers under the Services Directive is summarized in Table 6.1.

## 6.4 The rules on services

### 6.4.1 *Introduction*

The centre of the debate on the Services Directive has always been Article 16(1) on the freedom to provide services. As mentioned above, in the 2004 Commission proposal, Article 16 still stipulated the so-called country of origin principle. Opinions had differed widely on whether this principle would have been the legal cornerstone essential for

[60] See AG Cruz Villalón in Joined Cases C-357/10 to C-359/10, *Duomo* [2012] not yet published in the Official Journal, para. 39: 'This list is, however, simply by way of example: it seems clear that the intention of the Directive was not to limit the list of overriding reasons relating to the public interest to those expressly mentioned in Article 4, but to refer to a generic category which the case-law has always regarded as open.'

Table 6.1 Regulation of established service providers in the Services Directive

| Authorization schemes | Requirements |
|---|---|
| 'any procedure ... to obtain ... access to a service activity or the exercise thereof' | 'any obligation, prohibition, condition or limit' |
| *Introduction*<br>'Overriding reason' + proportionality + non-discrimination (Article 9) | *Discriminatory*<br>'Blacklisting' (Article 14) |
| *Application*<br>Article 9 + procedural requirements and equivalence (Article 10) | *Non-discriminatory*<br>'Necessity' + proportionality + screening (Article 15) |

producing the economic effects projected, or whether it would rather have driven Europe into a race to the bottom on social and labour standards.[61] Following strong pressure from a very assertive European Parliament during the co-decision procedure, this country of origin principle was replaced by a rule titled 'freedom to provide services' in Article 16.[62] This is complemented by a blacklist of certain national measures under Article 16(2).

It has been argued that this change in the wording of Article 16(1) is only semantic,[63] or that it merely provides a qualification of the Commission's country of origin principle.[64] In contrast, it has been

[61] See the accounts by Anon., 'The Services Directive proposal: striking a balance between the promotion of the internal market and preserving the European social model?' (2006) 43 *Common Market Law Review* 307–11, and C. Calliess, *Die Dienstleistungsrichtlinie: Von der grundfreiheitlichen Deregulierung zur europäischen Re-Regulierung?* (Bonn: Zentrum für Europäisches Wirtschaftsrecht, 2007), pp. 3–5. For an account of the discussion on the legality of this country of origin principle, see R. Craufurd Smith, 'Old wine in new bottles? From the "country of origin principle" to "freedom to provide services" in the European Community Directive on services in the internal market' (2007) *Mitchell Working Paper Series* 13.

[62] Griller, 'The new Services Directive', p. 319.

[63] Craufurd Smith, 'Old wine in new bottles?', 23. Had she referred to Art. 31 Services Directive in conjunction with Art. 16 Services Directive to make such point, this would have some force, but would still not be convincing, as has been explained.

[64] In this sense, e.g., W.-H. Roth, 'Freier Dienstleistungsverkehr und Verbraucherschutz' (2007) *Verbraucher und Recht* 161–72; Craufurd Smith, 'Old wine in new bottles?', 23.

suggested that Article 16 now provides for a 'qualified country of *destination* principle'.[65] This is not the place to assess the differences between the abandoned country of origin principle and the rule eventually adopted in Article 16. Suffice to note here that there are good arguments why the regime under the Commission's proposal would have differed considerably from the regime under current Article 16.[66] We will return to these questions in Chapter 8.

Article 19 provides the corresponding rule with regard to service *recipients*, prohibiting Member States from imposing requirements on a recipient that restrict the use of a service supplied by a provider established in another Member State. This concerns the Member State where the recipient is established or where it resides and the state that the recipient visits temporarily to receive a service.

### 6.4.2 *The freedom to provide services in Article 16(1)*

#### 6.4.2.1 The wording of Article 16(1) and the relevance of Article 16(3)

The main part of Article 16(1) has the following wording:

> Member States shall not make access to or exercise of a service activity in their territory subject to compliance with any requirements which do not respect the following principles:
>
> (a) non-discrimination: the requirement may be neither directly nor indirectly discriminatory with regard to nationality or, in the case of legal persons, with regard to the Member State in which they are established;
> (b) necessity: the requirement must be justified for reasons of public policy, public security, public health or the protection of the environment;
> (c) proportionality: the requirement must be suitable for attaining the objective pursued, and must not go beyond what is necessary to attain that objective.

Article 16(3) seems to express the same regulatory principle, in perhaps a more affirmative manner. It provides that Member States 'to which the provider moves shall not be prevented from imposing

[65] See M. Möstl, 'Wirtschaftsüberwachung von Dienstleistungen im Binnenmarkt' (2006) *Die öffentliche Verwaltung* 281–7 at 287 (emphasis added).

[66] See on this M. Klamert, 'Of empty glasses and double burdens: approaches to regulating the services market à propos the implementation of the Services Directive' (2010) *Legal Issues of Economic Integration* 111–32.

requirements', under the condition that they are justified by the four reasons of Article 16(1)(b), and that they are (also otherwise) in accordance with paragraph 1. The only distinct meaning of Article 16(3) could lie in the reference to the Member State 'to which the provider moves', which would exclude the cross-border and passive modes of services provision. While there is no apparent reason for such distinction, it is also pointless given that the remainder of the provision does not go beyond what is provided by Article 16(1) Services Directive.[67] One could argue that Article 16(3) is a case of bad drafting.[68]

### 6.4.2.2 The justifications regime under Article 16

Article 16(1)(b) reduces Member State regulatory autonomy by foreclosing recourse to most of the imperative requirements the Court has developed in its case law to compensate for the creation of the prohibition of restrictions beyond the strict wording of the Treaty.[69] Precisely how many have been abolished depends on the relevance of Articles 1 and 2 for the construction of Article 16 Services Directive.[70] As already mentioned, Article 1 provides that the application of the Services Directive must not produce certain regulatory outcomes. In particular, it must not 'affect' measures to protect or promote cultural or linguistic diversity or media pluralism, or the exercise of fundamental rights and collective bargaining rights. Under the Treaty freedoms, all three objectives have been allowed as mandatory requirements by the Court. In the Services Directive, we would argue, such national measures fall out of even its scope of application. Should the prohibition of regulatory implications in Article 1 merely constitute additional reasons of justification, they would still be subject to the test of proportionality. In contrast, if they are exempted entirely, Article 16 does not apply to them.

In any case, instead of broadening the range of reasons available to Member States for justifying discriminatory measures, as discussed in

67 Confusion is also deplored by Hatzopoulos, 'Que reste-t-il?', p. 14.

68 C. S. Buchinger, A. Michner and C. Müller, *Die Dienstleistungsrichtlinie: Ein Erfolg der österreichischen Präsidentschaft 2006* (Vienna: Verlag Österreich, 2007), p. 75. For a different perspective, see Griller, 'The new Services Directive', pp. 409ff.

69 See, among many others, N. Maydell, 'The Services Directive and existing Community law', in F. Breuss, G. Fink and S. Griller (eds.), *Services Liberalisation in the Internal Market* (Vienna, New York: Springer, 2008), pp. 21–124 at pp. 47ff.

70 For a Member State-friendly reading, see Griller, 'The new Services Directive', pp. 410–12.

Chapter 5, the Services Directive could be said to align the justifications for non-discriminatory measures with those applying to discriminatory measures. Recall that, in a number of cases on the free movement of goods, the Court has also allowed recourse to environmental reasons to justify discriminatory measures.

Moreover, there is a striking parallel between the justifications in Article 16, and the four reasons that had been contained in Article 17(17) of the Commission proposal. The latter provision had been an exemption from the country of origin principle and had only applied to 'indispensable' Member State measures.[71] Hence interests that now save national requirements from being deemed unlawful would 'only' have prevented the application of the laws of the host state under the Commission proposal.[72]

Another question concerns the approach the Court will choose for the interpretation of these four reasons of justification, that is whether they will be construed narrowly, such as the Treaty-based derogations with regard to discriminatory measures, or whether they will rather be construed in more liberal terms, such as with the case law-based mandatory requirements under the freedoms. For the public health justification, the Services Directive itself implies a broader interpretation. Although Recital 41 refers to 'the concept of "public policy" as interpreted by the Court of Justice', the Recital adopts a much broader meaning 'relating to human dignity, the protection of minors and vulnerable adults and animal welfare' in protecting against 'a genuine and sufficiently serious threat affecting one of the fundamental interests of society'.[73] This corresponds to the fact that animal welfare is also listed as an overriding reason under Article 4(8), as shown above. There have also been attempts already to read Article 24(2) for commercial communications of the Directive as *lex specialis* to Article 16(2).[74]

[71] 'specific requirements of the Member State to which the provider moves, that are directly linked to the particular characteristics of the place where the service is provided and with which compliance is indispensable for reasons of public policy or public security or for the protection of public health or the environment'. See Rec. 43 of the Commission proposal.

[72] It is doubtful whether it would also have exempted these measures from Art. 56 TFEU.

[73] See C. Barnard, *The Substantive Law of the EU*, 3rd edn (Oxford University Press, 2010), p. 404.

[74] See Opinion of AG Mazák in Case C-119/09, *Société fiduciaire* [2011] ECR I-2551, paras. 62–4. See later at note 131.

In *Commission* v. *Portugal (Construction)*, the Court noted that 'the general obligation set out in Article 16(1) of Directive 2006/123, according to which the Member States are to ensure access to and exercise of a service activity within their territory by making that access or exercise subject only to non-discriminatory and objectively justified requirements, stems directly from Article 49 EC'.[75] Hatzopoulos has argued that this would infer that exceptions to this rule should also stem directly from the Treaty and thus provide for the open list of overriding reasons of general interest.[76] This, however, may be reading too much into this passage, since this note by the Court was in response to the claim by Portugal that there had been no harmonization of the exercise of construction activities before the Services Directive and that the obligations contained therein could not have flown directly from the Treaty.[77] In another case, *Duomo*, while the Court did not touch on this issue, the AG was all the more blunt in this respect, doubting 'the exhaustive nature of the Article 16(1)(b) list, or even its compatibility with the provisions of the Treaty and, essentially, the very validity of the Directive on this point'.[78] This may therefore become a contested issue in proceedings to come before the Court in the future.

Note that Article 16(1)(a) prohibits discriminatory measures, including those of an indirect nature.

### 6.4.2.3 The limited relevance of Article 16(1)

We would argue that the practical importance of the new regime under Article 16 may be rather limited, for the following reasons.

First, some of the traditionally most 'offensive' service sectors, such as private security,[79] health, audio-visual services[80] and gambling,[81] are exempted from the Services Directive.[82] The same applies to the posting

[75] Case C-458/08, *Commission* v. *Portugal* [2010] ECR I-11599, para. 88.

[76] V. Hatzopoulos, 'The Court's approach to services (2006–2012): from case law to case load?' (2013) 50 *Common Market Law Review* 459–502 at 462.

[77] See Case C-458/08, *Commission* v. *Portugal* [2010] ECR I-11599, para. 78.

[78] Opinion of AG Cruz Villalón in Joined Cases C-357/10 to C-359/10, *Duomo* [2012] not yet published in the Official Journal, para. 55.

[79] Art. 2(2)(k). Case C-65/05, *Commission* v. *Greece* [2006] ECR I-10341.

[80] Art. 2(2)(g). Case C-250/06, *United Pan-Europe Communications Belgium* [2007] ECR I-11135.

[81] Case C-65/05, *Commission* v. *Greece* [2006] ECR I-10341 would probably have been thrown out by Art. 2(2)(h).

[82] See also V. Hatzopoulos, *Regulating Services in the European Union* (Oxford University Press, 2012), p. 182.

of workers[83] and tax matters.[84] Second, for service providers without establishment, the rules that primarily count are those on whether they are allowed temporarily to render their consulting, hairdressing or tourist guide services, thus market access. Such host state restrictions are unlikely to 'survive' the blacklist of Article 16(2) discussed below, which catches the bulk of the most notorious restrictions.[85] The situation is not fundamentally different if we consider national rules on the exercise of a service activity. The act of the provision of services is unlikely to be subject to substantial regulation either by the host or by the home state.[86]

An example for such rules is the hypothetical case of a German 'star hairdresser' providing services to clients at the Salzburg Festival and remaining subject to German laws on the 'quality and extent' of the service, on the liability for damages and on marketing activities.[87] With regard to the first aspect, we doubt that even a legal system such as the German system would regulate which scissors a hairdresser is allowed to use or how long the haircut should take. Tort law was exempted from the country of origin principle in the Commission's proposal, and is now excluded from the scope of the Services Directive.[88] Finally, as we will discuss later in detail, the Services Directive does not affect the application of Directive 2005/36/EC on the recognition of professional qualifications.[89] Thus, on all these counts, either there would be

[83] Art. 3(1)(a). Case C-346/06, *Rüffert* [2008] ECR I-1989; Case C-490/04, *Commission* v. *Germany* [2007] ECR I-6095.

[84] Art. 2(3). Case C-290/04, *FKP Scorpio Konzertproduktionen* [2006] ECR I-9461.

[85] For recent cases, see Case C-257/05, *Commission* v. *Austria (Kesselprüfstelle)* [2006] ECR I-134. Cf. the cases mentioned by Barnard, 'Unravelling the Services Directive', 364ff.

[86] An exception, admittedly, are national pricing regulations, which however only exist for heavily regulated professions. See Joined Cases C-94/04 and C-202/04, *Cipolla* [2006] ECR I-11421 for such restriction for lawyers' fees. See S. Evans, 'The Services Directive: (too) great expectations? An initial overview of the rights and obligations under the Services Directive', in J. van de Gronden (ed.), *EU and WTO Law on Services: Limits to the Realisation of General Interest Policies within the Services Markets?* (The Hague: Kluwer, 2008), pp. 7–29 at p. 17.

[87] W. Schroeder, 'Der Binnenmarkt für Dienstleistungen: Zwischen Herkunftslandprinzip und sozialpolitischer Gestaltungsfreiheit', in S. Griller (ed.), *Die europäische Wirtschaftsverfassung de lege lata et ferenda* (Vienna, New York: Springer, 2007), pp. 379–423 at p. 118.

[88] Art. 3(2).

[89] See Art. 5(3) Directive 2005/36/EC of the European Parliament and the Council of 7 September 2005 on the recognition of professional qualifications, OJ 2005 No. L255/22.

little national regulation to be caught under Article 16(1), or pertinent national measures would fall under a separate regime in any case.

Thus it should not come as a surprise that very few cases decided under the Treaty freedom would have fallen under Article 16, had the Services Directive already been in force at their occurrence.[90] The only situations conceivable where Article 16 would be of relevance and Member States would be shorthanded with reasons to justify national restrictions concern services cases where there is no establishment involved but where there nonetheless exists substantive host state law. We could think here of the (cross-border) use of equipment such as for bungee jumping,[91] mobile plants such as a merry-go-round, or the only temporary use of infrastructure such as in a restaurant or a serving of wine.[92] This would not constitute an establishment under Chapter III of the Services Directive and would therefore come under Article 16(1). Under national law, these cases would come under (light) regulation in the case of the mobile plant, as regarding safety and quality regulations, and would probably fall under normal regulation in the case of commercial infrastructure, as regarding opening hours, among other things.[93]

Thus, while Article 16 of the adopted Services Directive arguably is fundamentally different from the country of origin principle foreseen in the Commission proposal,[94] this change from home state to host state rule matters little for non-established service providers regulated by Article 16. While this does not diminish the regulatory importance of Article 16(1), we should thus be aware that its actual impact might pale in comparison to the discussion it has caused. The much more effective measure in this context may be the blacklist in Article 16(2). Having said that, in the following section we will briefly look at the

[90] See G. Davies, 'Trust and mutual recognition in the Services Directive', in I. Lianos and O. Odudu (eds.), *Regulating Trade in Services: Trust, Distrust and Economic Integration* (Cambridge University Press, 2012), pp. 99–120 at p. 112, who has argued that Art. 16 of the Services Directive is not such a big change to the Treaty regime because the Court is often striking down national law and consumer protection has never played a big role in justifying national measures.

[91] Note that national requirements in this context would fall under Art. 16(2)(f), which provides for a derogation within the blacklist of Art. 16(2) for equipment-related requirements 'necessary for health and safety at work'.

[92] See L. Albath and M. Giesler, 'Das Herkunftslandprinzip in der Dienstleistungsrichtlinie: eine Kodifizierung der Rechtsprechung?' (2006) *Europäische Zeitschrift für Wirtschaftsrecht* 38–42 at 41.

[93] At least in Austria under the Industrial Code (*Gewerbeordnung*).

[94] See Klamert, 'Of empty glasses and double burdens'.

discussion on the legality of the Services Directive that has centred on Article 16(1).

### 6.4.2.4 The legality of Article 16(1)

Article 3(3) prescribes that 'Member States shall apply the provisions of this Directive in compliance with the rules of the Treaty on the right of establishment and the free movement of services'. This is an expression of the secondary law nature of the Services Directive. However, as explained above, Article 16(1) deprives the Member States of a number of reasons to justify the legality of their national laws and regulations that have been developed by the Court. We have noted earlier that this has already raised doubts as to the validity of the Services Directive.[95]

There are two fundamentally opposed ways of assessing a potential conflict between EU primary law and its interpretation by the Court on the one hand, and an act of secondary law on the other hand. The first position relies on the competence of the EU to abolish obstacles to the free movement of persons and services, which legitimizes any legislative act pursuing this objective.[96] More narrowly, it has been submitted that this would require that such an act comes within the ambit of the relevant legal basis in the Treaty.[97] This leads us back to the discussion above on the regulatory approach used in the Services Directive and the kind of measures Article 56 TFEU allows the Union to enact. Others have argued that the Court has the power 'to interpret the Treaty in accordance with internationally recognized canons of interpretation', thus political institutions must 'work within the bounds of that interpretation unless and until the Treaty itself is amended by those who have the power to amend it'.[98] In the present context, this would mean that if the Court has introduced a certain number of mandatory requirements, this could only be changed by amending the respective Treaty provisions.

[95] See AG Cruz Villalón in Joined Cases C-357/10 to C-359/10, *Duomo* [2012] not yet published in the Official Journal, para. 55.

[96] C. Calliess, 'Europäischer Binnenmarkt und europäische Demokratie: Von der Dienstleistungsfreiheit zur Dienstleistungsrichtlinie - und wieder Retour?' (2007) *Deutsches Verwaltungsblatt* 336–46 at 345.

[97] Griller, 'The new Services Directive', pp. 411–13. For a critical assessment of the legality of the Services Directive, see Klamert, 'Of empty glasses and double burdens'.

[98] D. Edward, Editorial Comment, 'Will there be honey still for tea?' (2006) *Common Market Law Review* 623–7 at 627.

As mentioned, this is not the place to discuss these difficult and fundamental issues fully.[99] However, the discussion shows to what extent the Services Directive has touched on the foundations of EU law.

### *6.4.3 The Article 16(2) blacklist*

Article 16(2) bans the following national requirements imposed on providers or recipients of services within the scope of the Services Directive:

(a) requirement of establishment;
(b) authorization or registration requirements, unless provided in other Union legal acts;
(c) a ban on the provider setting up a certain form or type of infrastructure in their territory, including an office or chambers, which the provider needs in order to supply the services in question;
(d) the application of specific contractual arrangements between the provider and the recipient which prevent or restrict service provision by the self-employed;
(e) an obligation on the provider to possess an identity document issued by its competent authorities specific to the exercise of a service activity;
(f) requirements, except for those necessary for health and safety at work, that affect the use of equipment and material that are an integral part of the service provided;
(g) restrictions on the freedom to provide the services referred to in Article 19.

This exhaustive list of explicitly prohibited national measures cannot be justified.[100] As under the Article 14 blacklist on establishments, these measures have been declared unlawful by the Court in its case law preceding the Services Directive.[101] Article 16(2) measures do not fall under the screening obligation discussed below. This makes compliance with Article 16(2) purely a matter of implementation.

[99] For such a discussion, see M. Klamert, *The Principle of Loyalty in EU Law* (Oxford University Press, 2014), pp. 117–225.

[100] Whether national measures listed in Art. 16(2) really are unjustifiable and thus compare to the unqualified blacklisting in Art. 14 Services Directive is disputed by Barnard, 'Unravelling the Services Directive', 364.

[101] European Commission, *Implementation Handbook*, pp. 53–5.

### 6.4.4 *Safety measures under Article 18*

Any national measure with the exception of the blacklisted measures in Article 16(2) may be defended by Member States for reasons relating to the safety of a service. By way of derogation from Article 16(1), Article 18 grants the host state the right to impose requirements on the service provider for safety reasons on a 'case-by-case' basis.[102] It must be noted that safety measures are inherently discriminatory because they only target specific service providers from other Member States.[103] Article 18(3) provides that these rules 'shall be without prejudice to provisions, laid down in Community instruments, which guarantee the freedom to provide services or which allow derogations therefrom'. We would argue that this hardly signifies the supremacy of conflicting provisions in the Services Directive itself.[104] This would make Article 18 pointless because every safety measure would need to comply with Article 16 and its prohibition of discrimination.[105] Article 18 should rather apply alongside other rules such as Article 16 in particular.

To be permissible, safety measures must meet four cumulative conditions: (1) an envisaged measure must not have been subject to harmonization; (2) the safety measure must guarantee a higher level of protection compared to a measure taken by the home state of the service provider; (3) the home state must have breached its duty of mutual cooperation pursuant to Article 35 discussed below; and (4) the safety measure must be proportional.

It has been noted that Member States will hardly invoke the more prohibitive Article 18 if they can justify measures under Article 16.[106] However, as we will show below, discrimination is prohibited under Article 16. Safety measures are thus a form of discrimination allowed under the Services Directive under certain conditions.

[102] The Services Directive here, following its internal logic, does not use the defined term requirements, but speaks of 'measures'.

[103] This specific meaning of 'case-by-case' derogation only ensues from European Commission, *Implementation Handbook*, p. 74.

[104] See European Commission, *Implementation Handbook*, p. 59, where the meaning of Art. 18(3) is rather located with reference to other Union acts such as Directive 2000/31/EC of the European Parliament and the Council of 8 June 2000 on certain legal aspects of information society services, in particular electronic commerce, in the internal market, OJ 2000 No. L178/1 specifically.

[105] See Hatzopoulos, 'Que reste-t-il?', pp. 14–15, who negates a distinct role of Art. 18 measures.

[106] Barnard, 'Unravelling the Services Directive', 370. See also Craufurd Smith, 'Old wine in new bottles?', 21.

Table 6.2 Regulation of non-established services providers in the Services Directive

| General prohibition | Blacklisting | Safety measures |
|---|---|---|
| Public policy, security and health, environment + non-discrimination + proportionality<br>No screening | Exhaustive list<br>No justification<br>No screening | Four conditions<br>Target specific providers<br>Screening applies |

### 6.4.5 *Conclusion*

Similar to the complex rules for established service providers in Chapter III of the Services Directive, Articles 16 to 18 are not a showcase of transparency. This holds true even when we leave aside for the moment the exemptions provided under Article 17, which are discussed in Chapter 8. The system of regulation for non-established services providers under the Services Directive is summarized in Table 6.2.

## 6.5 The bigger picture on rules on services and establishments under the Services Directive

If we compare the regimes under the Services Directive on establishments and on services *stricto sensu*, the most striking difference is that requirements under the former may be justified by the full range of public reasons, whereas requirements for services *stricto sensu* can be upheld, invoking a much shorter list of reasons. What both regimes have in common is that national measures must not be discriminatory and must be proportional. The exceptions here are safety measures, which are *per definitionem* discriminatory. On the other hand, safety measures, as with Article 15 requirements, are imposed on established service providers in that they come under a screening mechanism. While Article 39(5) obliges Member States to report to the Commission all national requirements whose application would violate Article 16 and provide reasons for their justification, this regime is not comparable to the screening discussed below.

Finally, we must note that the 'test of equivalence' provided in Article 10(3) for authorization schemes is stipulated neither for requirements

Table 6.3 Regulatory standards under the Services Directive

| Combined standard I | Combined standard II |
| --- | --- |
| Targets both discriminatory and non-discriminatory measures | Targets discriminatory measures; targets non-discriminatory measures only when they affect market access |
| Closed list of justifications for discriminatory measures; open list for non-discriminatory measures | Closed list of justifications for discriminatory measures; open list for non-discriminatory measures |

in the chapter on establishments, nor for requirements in the chapter on services. This is striking as this test has been prominently applied in the *services* context in *Säger*, and in the Treaty regime it arguably applies to any case of double burden under both Article 49 and Article 56 TFEU. If we consider the *Säger* test an integral part of the proportionality test under the Treaty regime as discussed above, it could also be located within Articles 15(3)(c) and 16(1)(c). However, this would arguably make Article 10(3) redundant because proportionality is also prescribed in Article 10(2)(c).

If we look at the rules of the Services Directive from the perspective of the regulatory approach they represent, it is useful to recall the discussion in Chapter 4 on the principles of EU law on services. There we have argued that the Court alternates the application of the combined standard I and the combined standard II, as juxtaposed in Table 6.3, which provides a synthesis of Tables 4.1 and 4.2 from Chapter 4.

Recall that a full graduation of the services and establishments regime to a market access approach would require that *all* cases relate only to national non-discriminatory measures that have an effect on market access.

With regard to services *stricto sensu*, the Services Directive now prohibits the most notorious obstacles to market access such as requirements to have an establishment or to obtain an authorization. In fact, the large majority of the blacklisted Member State requirements in Article 16(2) concern market access. However, the reference to 'access to or exercise of a service activity' in Article 16(1) leaves no doubt as to its applicability both to measures affecting market access and to measures affecting the exercise of the service within the host state. It has therefore been correctly noted that the Services Directive does not make a distinction between the exercise of services or the access to their provision.[107]

Regarding established service providers, the distinction in the Services Directive between authorizations and requirements is not explicitly reflected in the Treaty law regime. In spite of reference again to 'access to a service activity or the exercise thereof' in Articles 4(6) and 9(1) of the Services Directive, authorization schemes arguably rather concern market access than domestic regulation. In contrast, the category of requirements is much broader and encompasses both access-related measures of Member States as well as domestic regulations. There is no indication that such requirements for established service providers are now only subject to scrutiny if they impair market access.

Thus the Directive does, in general, not represent a radical modification of the picture under the current case law. If the Services Directive does not support the adoption of a full market access approach, which would target non-discriminatory measures only when they affect market access and apply the open list of justifications to them,[108] we would propose that the Court should be consistent in either applying combined approach I or combined approach II when applying the Services Directive. Moreover, in such event this should be applied with regard to both services *stricto sensu* and established service providers.

However, there is one important exception from the statement above about the impact of the Services Directive on the current regime on services. Recall that the Court under the Treaty regime distinguishes between openly discriminatory measures, indirectly discriminatory measures and non-discriminatory measures by applying the open list of mandatory requirements only to the second and third category of measures. There is no such distinction in central places in the Services Directive. In Chapter III on establishments, Article 14(1) explicitly prohibits 'discriminatory requirements based directly or indirectly on nationality' without the possibility of justification. Article 15(3)(a) provides that Member States shall verify that requirements satisfy the condition of '(a) non-discrimination: requirements must be neither directly nor indirectly discriminatory according to nationality nor, with regard to companies, according to the location of the registered office'.[109]

[107] J. Snell, 'The notion of market access: a concept or a slogan?' (2010) 47 *Common Market Law Review* 437–72 at 446.

[108] See the second column of Table 6.3.

[109] Curiously, discrimination is not so defined with respect to authorizations, where the Services Directive plainly speaks of 'discrimination' in Arts. 9(1)(a) and 10(2)(a).

Similarly, Article 16 prohibits any requirements that do not respect the principle of '(a) non-discrimination: the requirement may be neither directly nor indirectly discriminatory with regard to nationality or, in the case of legal persons, with regard to the Member State in which they are established'. In general, the Services Directive thus establishes the same treatment for indirectly discriminatory measures as for directly discriminatory national measures.

More specifically, these provisions put an end to the possibility currently existing under the Treaty regime of justifying openly discriminatory measures against establishments by at least a narrow list of derogations. This only remains possible in sectors not falling under the Services Directive. Hence, the commonly shared view that Chapter III on established service providers 'amounts to a simple recitation of existing Article 49 case law' with 'no adjustment in the scope of host state regulatory competence'[110] is not correct with respect to open discrimination.

Moreover, the same applies to indirectly discriminatory measures, which are also unconditionally prohibited within the scope of the Services Directive. This means that they can no longer be justified either by the open list of mandatory requirements currently applying under the Treaty regime or by any other reason of the public interest.[111] The Services Directive thus disconnects the standard of review applying to indirect discrimination from the standard applying to non-discriminatory measures. This supports our arguments above regarding the close relation between the two forms of discrimination in the common market. However, the limitation of Member State autonomy this entails would warrant a clearer definition of indirect discrimination in the Services Directive. It also raises, again, questions regarding equal treatment in view of the fact that discrimination in sectors not covered by the Services Directive are currently subject to a different, more permissive regime.

[110] S. Weatherill, 'Promoting the consumer interest in an integrated services market' (2007) *Mitchell Working Paper Series* 7; similarly see Barnard, 'Unravelling the Services Directive', 359; Roth, 'Freier Dienstleistungsverkehr und Verbraucherschutz', 169; G. Davies, 'The Services Directive: extending the country of origin principle and reforming public administration' (2007) *European Law Review* 232–45 at 234.

[111] The argument by J. Snell, 'Freedom to provide services in the case law and in the Services Directive: problems, solutions, and institutions', in U. Neergaard, R. Nielsen and L. Roseberry (eds.), *The Services Directive: Consequences for the Welfare State and the European Social Model* (Copenhagen: Djof, 2008), pp. 171–97 at p. 190, that this prohibition of indirect discrimination does not really matter since such measures

## 6.6 Screening

### *6.6.1 Introduction*

The Services Directive foresees several reporting obligations in its Article 39.[112] For established service providers, authorization schemes and requirements must be identified and their lawfulness must be justified. The same applies to national requirements for services deemed to fall under the prohibitions of Articles 16(1) and 16(3) Services Directive. Any changes of requirements as well as new requirements must also be reported and justified vis-à-vis the European Commission.[113] Similar duties are imposed with regard to multidisciplinary activities. Moreover, pursuant to Article 16(4) Services Directive, the Commission was required to submit a report on the application of Article 16 Services Directive specifically by 28 December 2011 and propose, if necessary, further harmonization measures.

The Services Directive's reporting duties shall operate in addition to the technical reports on the performance of the goods, services and capital markets regularly produced by the European Commission. They, on the other hand, seem to be outside the general monitoring measures under the 'Internal Market Scoreboard' to follow up on the implementation of common market directives.

### *6.6.2 Requirements and safety measures*

The most 'intrusive' screening instrument concerns non-discriminatory requirements restricting the freedom of establishment. Article 15(6) provides that Member States may only introduce such requirements listed under Article 15(2) if the conditions of necessity and proportionality are met. Such national measures must be notified and justified to the Commission, which examines their lawfulness and conveys them to the other Member States. Within a period of three months from receipt of a notification, the Commission must request the Member State to refrain from adopting the requirement concerned, or, if already adopted, to repeal it. This deadline is no standstill obligation, and Article 15(7) explicitly stipulates that such notification

are subjected to a full list of reasons of objective justification in the first place before being qualified as indirect discriminations is only valid in theory, but not in the light of case law. See Chapter 4.

[112] This section draws on M. Klamert, 'Die Notifizierungspflichten der Dienstleistungsrichtlinie: ein Fall für den EuGH?' (2008) *Deutsches Verwaltungsblatt* 829–32.

[113] Arts. 15(5)(b) and 39(1).

does not prevent a Member State from adopting the requirements in question.

A similar procedure is provided with regard to safety measures under Article 18. Recall that safety measures may be taken against specific service providers by the host state under certain conditions. On request of the host Member State, the provider's home state is obliged to act appropriately against a service considered unsafe. If these countermeasures taken by the home Member State are deemed inadequate by the host state, it may unilaterally adopt safety measures under the conditions of Article 18. However, according to Article 35(4) this is subject to a standstill obligation of fifteen working days between notification and adoption by the host state. The Commission, to which the intended adoption must be notified and justified, must decide 'as a matter of urgency' on the lawfulness of these measures. If it considers them unlawful, the Commission can ask the Member State either to give up on the safety measures or to terminate them. According to Article 35(5), the standstill obligation has no bearing on the Commission's decision.

Screening thus gives the Commission a say if a Member State plans to introduce new, potentially restrictive measures. However, the Commission cannot directly influence the behaviour of Member States because the Services Directive does not provide for specific sanctions in the event that Member States do not comply with the decisions of the Commission on the legality of the notified measures. The decision requesting the Member State to comply is not more than what it appears to be, that is a request without sanction in case of disobedience. Moreover, as already mentioned, Member States are not prevented under the Services Directive from introducing notified national measures without having to wait for the decision of the Commission on their legality.

Table 6.4 summarizes the different screening rules for requirements and safety measures respectively.

### 6.6.3 *The potential of screening*

Notification duties are well known to play a prominent role in enforcing Union law. Thus Directive 98/34/EC on technical standards provides for a system of prior inspection for standards and for technical regulations on industrial, agricultural and fishing products.[114] Under this Directive,

[114] Directive 98/48/EC of the European Parliament and the Council of 20 July 1998 laying down a procedure for the provision of information in the field of technical standards

Table 6.4 Screening rules in the Services Directive

| Requirements | Safety measures |
|---|---|
| Notification of new Article 15 requirements when necessary and proportional | Notification of new safety measures when home Member State has not taken appropriate measures |
| Notification does not stop Member State | Standstill obligation of Member State of 15 working days after notification |
| EU has 3 months to decide on legality | EU must decide on legality as matter of urgency |
| EU decision on request to refrain or repeal | EU decision on request to refrain or repeal |

a technical regulation is understood to be any technical specification or other requirement relating to a product, the observance of which is compulsory for its marketing or use.[115] Standards are defined as any technical specification approved by a recognized standardization body for repeated or continuous application, with which compliance is not compulsory.[116] The Services Directive requires every Member State to notify and justify to the Commission the introduction or amendment of technical regulations. This notification triggers a standstill period of up to six months if the Commission finds that the draft rules may impede the free movement of goods, and of up to eighteen months should the Commission want to act or has already acted in the same area.

There is an explicit link between the Services Directive and the Technical Standards Directive. Pursuant to Article 15(7) of the Services Directive, the notification of a draft national law in accordance with the Technical Standards Directive fulfils the obligation of notification under the former. Moreover, there are several analogies to screening under the Services Directive. As discussed, the screening rights of the Commission do not have an immediate effect on Member State action.

and regulations, OJ 1998 No. L217/18. Directive 98/48/EC extends the application of the information procedures introduced by Directive 98/34/EC to information society services but not to radio and television broadcasting services which are covered by Directive 89/552/EEC (television without frontiers).

[115] Art. 1. Directive 98/48/EC.

[116] Art. 1 Directive 98/48/EC.

We would argue, however, that they might have indirect effects for the following reasons.

First, screening does not rule out action by the Commission to enforce the implementation of the Services Directive, of which the duty of notification is one aspect.[117] This is comparable to the case law on Regulation 2679/98,[118] which aims at eliminating obstacles to trade put up by private parties.[119] This Regulation provides for an early warning mechanism through national contact points. The Court decided that this procedure was not a condition the Commission needed to satisfy before starting the pre-litigation procedure under Article 260 TFEU, and that it therefore does not restrict the Commission's powers.[120] Thus any decision in the screening process does not prejudice the right of the Commission to bring an enforcement action before or at the same time as a decision under the Services Directive. The Commission's decision on the lawfulness of a notified measure might, however, bind the Court in an eventual enforcement action, or might at least constitute a formal notice under the Article 260 TFEU procedure. The latter has been the case with the 'detailed opinions' pursuant to Directive 83/189, which has been the precursor of the Technical Standards Directive.[121]

Second, in a number of very controversial judgments the Court has ruled that the prohibition to adopt a national measure without prior notification under Articles 8 and 9 of Directive 83/189 has direct effect.[122] In the words of the Court in *CIA Security*:

As already found in paragraph 41 of this judgment, the directive has, precisely, a more general aim of eliminating or restricting obstacles to trade, to inform other States of technical regulations envisaged by a State, to give the Commission and the other Member States time to react and to propose

[117] See the reference to the infringement procedure in Rec. 75, which, however, only refers to obligations to abolish national requirements and to evaluation. See also Barnard, 'Unravelling the Services Directive', 359.

[118] Council Regulation (EC) No 2679/98 of 7 December 1998 on the functioning of the internal market in relation to the free movement of goods among the Member States, OJ 1998 No. L337/8.

[119] Case C-265/95, *Commission* v. *France* [1997] ECR I-6959.

[120] Case C-320/03, *Commission* v. *Austria* [2005] ECR I-9871.

[121] A. J. Gil Ibañez, *The Administrative Supervision and Enforcement of EC Law: Powers, Procedures, and Limits* (Oxford and Portland, OR: Hart Publishing, 1999), p. 118.

[122] Case C-443/98, *Unilever Italia* [2000] ECR I-7535; Case C-194/94, *CIA Security* [1996] ECR I-2201. C. P. Craig and G. de Búrca, *EU Law: Texts and Materials*, 5th edn (Oxford University Press, 2011), pp. 207–10.

amendments for lessening restrictions to the free movement of goods arising from the envisaged measure and to afford the Commission time to propose a harmonizing directive. Moreover, the wording of Articles 8 and 9 of Directive 83/189 is clear in that those articles provide for a procedure for Community control of draft national regulations and the date of their entry into force is made subject to the Commission's agreement or lack of opposition.[123]

This has been distinguished by the Court from the notification duty provided in Article 3(2) of the Waste Directive 75/442.[124] Notification under the Waste Directive requires the Member States to inform the Commission of certain waste-reducing measures. However, since it does not confer supervisory powers to the Union, it has not been awarded direct effect by the Court.[125] While Hatzopoulos has noted that the Services Directive for the first time foresees a notification obligation for national measures affecting services, it would be much more limited in scope and intensity than the system for goods, and it would be contestable whether the *CIA Security* case law would be extended to the Services Directive.[126]

However, we would argue that screening in the Services Directive bears more resemblance to notification under the Technical Standards Directive than to notification under the Waste Directive. The reasoning in *CIA Security* on the general aim of notification and on the conferral of controlling powers to the Union can also be applied to screening under the Services Directive. Screening therein is rather a control instrument than a mere information obligation. However, the lack of an effective standstill period in the Services Directive might differentiate screening from supervision under the Technical Standards Directive enough to deny the former direct effect.

Finally, yet another option has been proposed by AG Villalon in his Opinion in the *Duomo* case.[127] He argued that, because of Article 15(6), national measures should already have been evaluated under the Directive before the deadline for its transposition expired. While the AG noted the absence of a standstill clause, he based this claim on

[123] Case C-194/94, *CIA Security* [1996] ECR I-2201, para. 50.

[124] Council Directive 75/442/EEC of 15 July 1975 on waste, OJ 1975 No. L194/39.

[125] Case C-380/87, *Enichem Base* [1989] ECR 2491, paras. 20–1.

[126] V. Hatzopoulos, 'Forms of mutual recognition in the field of services', in I. Lianos and O. Odudu (eds.), *Regulating Trade in Services: Trust, Distrust and Economic Integration* (Cambridge University Press, 2012), pp. 59–98 at p. 65.

[127] Joined Cases C-357/10 to C-359/10, *Duomo* [2012] not yet published in the Official Journal.

the *Inter-Environnement Wallonie* case law, requiring Member States to refrain from taking any measures 'liable seriously to compromise the attainment of the result prescribed' by a directive.[128] This, however, was not endorsed by the Court, who decided the case based on the Treaty provisions.

## 6.7 Quality of services

In Chapter V the Services Directive provides for rules intended 'to safeguard the interests of consumers by improving the quality of the services of the regulated professions in the internal market'.[129] While these will not be discussed in full detail here, let us mention the following points.

Among others, Article 22 requires certain information on providers and their services, such as on the name of the provider, their legal status, address and contact details, details of their registration, where the activity is subject to an authorization scheme, the particulars of the relevant competent authority or the single point of contact, where it is a regulated activity the competent professional body, the professional title and the Member State in which that title has been granted, general conditions and clauses used, the existence of an after-sales guarantee, the price of the service, the main features of the service, and information on insurance or guarantees referred to in Article 23(1).[130] This information must be easily accessible, also in electronic form, and must be supplied on the provider's own initiative.

Article 22(3) requires the provider to supply additional information at the request of the recipient, such as a reference to the applicable professional rules, information on multidisciplinary activities and partnerships, and on pertinent codes of conduct.

Article 24(1) provides that 'Member States shall remove all total prohibitions on commercial communications by the regulated professions'.

128 Joined Cases C-357/10 to C-359/10, *Duomo* [2012] not yet published in the Official Journal, paras. 21–23.

129 Case C-119/09, *Société fiduciaire* [2011] ECR I-2551, para. 28.

130 Art. 23(1) calls on Member States ('may') to ensure that providers whose services present a direct and particular risk to the health or safety of the recipient or a third person, or to the financial security of the recipient, subscribe to professional liability insurance appropriate to the nature and extent of the risk, or provide a guarantee or similar arrangement which is equivalent or essentially comparable as regards its purpose. Equivalent measures taken in the home state of the provider must be accepted by the host state.

Furthermore, according to Article 24(2), professional rules on commercial communications must be 'non-discriminatory, justified by an overriding reason relating to the public interest and proportionate'. AG Mazak had pointed out that this conflicts with the limitation to the four reasons mentioned in Article 16(1)(b), and that therefore Article 24(2) must be considered *lex specialis* in relation to Article 16(1)(b).[131] According to the Court, Article 24(1) prohibits total prohibitions on commercial communications by the regulated professions, including a ban on any unsolicited personal contact that could be regarded as touting for clients or a concrete proposal of commercial services by qualified accountants ('canvassing'), without allowing for justification.[132] In contrast, Member States retain the right to lay down prohibitions relating to the content or methods of commercial communications as regards regulated professions, if these rules are justified and proportionate for the purposes of the independence, dignity and integrity of the profession, as well as the professional secrecy necessary in its practice.[133]

Article 25 requires Member States to ensure that providers are not made subject to requirements that oblige them to exercise a given specific activity exclusively or that restrict the exercise jointly or in partnership of different activities. Under certain conditions, this does not apply to the regulated professions, or to providers of certification, accreditation, technical monitoring, testing services or trial services.

Finally, Article 26 obliges Member States, in cooperation with the Commission, to take accompanying measures to encourage providers to take action on a voluntary basis in order to ensure the quality of service provision, by measures such as the certification or assessment of their activities by independent or accredited bodies, by encouraging professional bodies to cooperate at Union level and by encouraging the development of independent assessments, such as by consumer associations.

## 6.8 Administrative provisions

### *6.8.1 Introduction*

Perhaps the greatest impact of the Services Directive lies in its provisions on administrative simplification in Chapter II, with the key

[131] Opinion of AG Mazák in Case C-119/09, *Société fiduciaire* [2011] ECR I-2551, paras. 62–4.
[132] Case C-119/09, *Société fiduciaire* [2011] ECR I-2551, paras. 27 and 45.
[133] Case C-119/09, *Société fiduciaire* [2011] ECR I-2551, para. 30.

requirement to establish points of single contact, and on administrative cooperation in Chapter VI. This comprises rules affecting the institutional set-up of Member States for the interaction between service providers and service recipients, certain changes in the substantive administrative law of the Member States, the cooperation between Member States and specific rules on implementation. These rules apply both to established service providers and to non-established providers, that is they are cutting across the separate regimes in Chapters III and IV.

### 6.8.2 *Information and administration*

Points of single contact, whose realization has proven most intricate, will be discussed separately in Chapter 7 on the implementation of the Services Directive. Suffice to note here that they complement SOLVIT, the online network for resolving problems between Member States as a result of the application of EU law by national authorities. Member States must also ensure that administrative procedures relating to the access to or the exercise of a service activity can easily be completed from across borders.[134] As the title of Article 8 shows, this primarily should concern procedures by electronic means, but could also be satisfied by any other procedures that can be completed from across borders without physical contact.[135]

Under the heading 'simplification of procedures', Article 5(3) provides for an unconditional duty of mutual recognition for documents related to a pertinent administrative procedure. Thus national requirements to submit documents in original, certified copies or translations are explicitly prohibited. Member States may, however, impose additional criteria if this is provided for in certain other Union law acts that are listed under Article 5(4),[136] or if it is justified by an 'overriding reason

[134] See Art. 8 and Rec. 52. Article 8(2) exempts 'the inspection of premises on which the service is provided or of equipment used by the provider' and the 'physical examination of the capability or of the personal integrity of the provider or of his responsible staff' from the obligation to facilitate cross-border completion of the relevant procedures.

[135] This might comprise a combination of the already existing Internal Market Information (IMI)-System (primarily authority-to-authority communication) and the SOLVIT System (primarily citizen-to-authority communication).

[136] Art. 5(4) lists inter alia certain articles of Directive 2005/36/EC and Directive 98/5/EC of the European Parliament and of the Council of 16 February 1998 to facilitate practice of the profession of lawyer on a permanent basis in a Member State other than that in which the qualification was obtained, OJ 1998 No. L77/36.

relating to the public interest'.[137] Article 7(1) provides for rights of service providers and service recipients to certain information. Member States must make available information on national requirements, contact details of authorities and conditions for accessing relevant public registers and databases.[138]

### 6.8.3 *Mutual assistance, cooperation and supervision*

Article 28 foresees the establishment of liaison points, which shall handle all communication and requests for information and consultation between the Member States. They shall also inform the Commission when Member States fail to comply with their obligations in this respect. Similarly, Member States must inform the Commission and all other states about any service activity 'that could cause serious damage to the health or safety of persons or to the environment'.[139] Article 33 requires mutual information on disciplinary or administrative actions, criminal sanctions or decisions concerning fraudulent insolvency. This cooperation is processed through the Internal Market Information System (IMI).[140]

While mutual assistance and effective cooperation are straightforward instruments, supervision is a complex system of rule-exception. Article 30 provides for the supervision by the Member State of establishment should a provider temporarily move to another Member State. Thus the home state is both competent and obliged to supervise the service provider and the services delivered in another Member State. If this control requires on-site measures, the host state must act on behalf of the home state.[141] This makes home state control the principal rule

137 See the definition in Art. 4(8).

138 See Art. 7(2)–(6) for details.

139 Art. 32: 'Alert mechanism'.

140 This is comparable to Decision 3052/95, which requires Member States to inform each other via notification to the Commission about restrictive national measures amounting to a direct or indirect general prohibition or refusal of marketing authorization, among others. See Decision No. 3052/95/EC of the European Parliament and the Council of 13 December 1995 establishing a procedure for the exchange of information on national measures derogating from the principle of the free movement of goods within the Community, OJ 1995 No. L321/1. One might also think of Directive 2001/95/EC on product safety, which allows Member States to take restrictive measures if a product poses a serious threat calling for quick action. Directive 2001/95/EC of the European Parliament and the Council of 3 December 2001 on general product safety, OJ 2002 No. L 11/4. The exchange of information in such cases is carried out via the information system RAPEX.

141 Note that this obligation is no one-way street and the host Member State may equally request the state of establishment to undertake necessary checks, inspections and investigations (Art. 29(2)).

of supervision under the Services Directive. The host state may only supervise the service provider if this is done in a non-discriminatory and proportionate manner.[142] In addition, Article 31 provides for the supervision by the home state in the event of the temporary movement of the provider. This gives the home state the right to supervise the provider's compliance with home state laws should the provider operate in another Member State. The reason for this is, we would argue, that the home state should not be prevented from enforcing its pertinent national rules such as regarding the provider's commercial establishment if the provider is (also or exclusively) active abroad. We can therefore see this as an exception to the Services Directive's general rules on mutual assistance.

The host state is exclusively competent to supervise compliance with those national requirements that are not prohibited under the Services Directive. However, this supervision by the host state is limited to the issue of compliance with the restriction it is allowed to apply.[143]

## 6.9 Fragmentation/relation to other secondary law

### *6.9.1 Introduction*

There has already been substantial fragmentation between the intensity of the regulation of different service sectors before the arrival of the Services Directive because of the fact that some service sectors, such as transport and financial services, are exhaustively harmonized while the majority of sectors in the EU are subject to case law and/or the Services Directive.[144] As regards primary law, the level of fragmentation depends on the extent the Services Directive harmonizes the law in the field concerned. The reason is that the Treaty rules on freedoms cease to apply in fields that have been harmonized by secondary law.[145] As we have shown above, the Services Directive is highly fragmented in its treatment of services *stricto sensu* on the one hand and of established service providers on the other hand. This concerns both the standard of scrutiny applied to national laws and the application of the screening procedure.

[142] Art. 31(3) and (4). [143] Art. 31(2).

[144] See Hatzopoulos, *Regulating Services in the European Union*, p. 351, who calls this 'unevenness between fields'.

[145] See Case 5/77, *Tedeschi* [1977] ECR 1555, para. 35; Case C-5/94, *Hedley Lomas* [1996] ECR I-2553, para. 18.

Sectors exempted from the scope of application of the Services Directive continue to come under the Treaty regime of Articles 49 and 56 TFEU.[146] Any sectoral fragmentation in the Services Directive thus leads to a corresponding fragmentation in primary law and in the scope of application of other secondary law that is relevant for the services sector. As to the relationship to other acts of secondary law, Article 3(1) Services Directive provides that in the case of a conflict with a provision of another Union law act 'governing specific aspects of access to or exercise of a service activity in specific sectors or for specific professions', the other act's provision prevails over the Services Directive.[147]

Specifically, Article 17 excludes certain matters that are completely or partly regulated by other secondary law acts from the application of Article 16(1), thus from the main provision for services *stricto sensu*.[148] The rationale for retaining Article 17 after the deletion of the country of origin principle in Article 16(1) has been doubted.[149] Moreover, there is a conspicuous overlap between matters generally exempted in Article 3 and matters specifically exempted under Article 17.[150] The double exemption of Directive 96/71/EC seems especially

[146] See also Barnard, 'Unravelling the Services Directive', 343. But see Biondi, 'Recurring cycles in the internal market', p. 235, who deplores a 'repatriation of powers to the national legislator' in view of the many exemptions in the Directive.

[147] The non-exhaustive list of secondary law concerned includes Directive 96/71/EC on the posting of workers, Regulation 1408/71 on the application of social security schemes, Directive 89/552 on television broadcasting activities, and the Professional Qualifications Directive 2005/36.

[148] This concerns various services of general economic interest, such as postal services covered by Directive 97/67, services in the electricity sector covered by Directive 2003/54, in the gas sector covered by Directive 2003/55, water distribution and supply services and wastewater services, and the treatment of waste. Moreover, it exempts matters covered by Regulation 259/93 as regards the shipment of waste, matters covered by the data protection Directive 95/46, matters covered by the Lawyers Directive 77/249, and the activity of judicial recovery of debts. With regard to matters covered by Directive 2004/38, Art. 17 exempts formalities concerning the free movement of persons and their residence. With regard to third country nationals who move to another Member State in the context of the provision of a service, Art. 17 does not apply to the possibility for Member States to require visa or residence permits for third country nationals who are not covered by the mutual recognition regime provided for in Art. 21 of the Schengen Agreement. Finally, Art. 17 exempts copyright, neighbouring rights and rights covered by Directives 87/54 and 96/9, acts requiring the involvement of a notary; matters covered by Directive 2006/43 on statutory audit of annual accounts and consolidated accounts, and the registration of vehicles leased in another Member State.

[149] Hatzopoulos, 'Que reste-t-il?', p. 14.

[150] See Arts. 3(1)(a) and 17(2), and Arts. 3(2) and 17(5) respectively.

futile since the Services Directive also exempts labour law, collective agreements and social security matters in several places and in a very general manner.[151] Moreover, the exemption for services of temporary work agencies in Article 2(2)(e) is also of direct relevance for the posting of workers. The minimum standards required under the Posting of Workers Directive thus do not fall under the scope of the Services Directive in any case. Similarly, the exemption of notaries in Article 2 as well as in Article 17 Services Directive can be seen as bearing witness to the extent of lobbying that this profession has put to the fore.

We will now briefly explain that this double exemption might be rationalized with regard to professional qualifications and lawyers.[152] At the same time we will illustrate how complex the regime on various services has become with the adoption of the Services Directive.

### *6.9.2 The relationship between Article 3 and Article 17 Services Directive*

Article 17 Services Directive leaves other provisions under Chapter IV such as those on the freedom to *receive* services fully applicable. What is more, these exemptions also do not affect other parts of the Services Directive such as Chapter III on establishments and the provisions on administrative cooperation. Thus, when attorneys or notaries provide their services through an establishment in another Member State, Articles 9 to 15, among others, fully apply to them.

Article 17(6) exempts matters covered by Title II of Directive 2005/36/EC from the application of Article 16 and thus from the key prohibition of restrictions on the freedom to provide services.[153] Directive 2005/36/EC grants professional service providers access to the market of the host Member State on the basis of the professional title they hold in their home state. For this, their qualifications do not need to be recognized by the host state. However, in this respect the Services Directive imposes certain information and documentation obligations on foreign

[151] Art. 1(6) and (7) Services Directive. See also Art. 16(3). See Griller, 'The new Services Directive', 399–403.

[152] See Barnard, 'Unravelling the Services Directive', 324.

[153] Title II concerns the provision of services abroad involving a temporary and occasional activity in the host state, which must fall short of constituting an establishment within the meaning of Article 56 TFEU. See Art. 5(1)–(2) Directive 2005/36/EC of the European Parliament and the Council of 7 September 2005 on the recognition of professional qualifications, OJ 2005 No. L255/22.

service providers when they enter the host state for the first time.[154] In the case of temporary movement, Article 5(3) Directive 2005/36/EC subjects service providers to the 'professional rules of a professional, statutory or administrative nature which are directly linked to professional qualifications'.[155]

A conflict requires the existence of contradictory rules. In other words, a regulatory conflict between the Services Directive and Directive 2005/36/EC can only arise if compliance with rules of both Directives is not possible without violating one of the respective rules. Thus no conflict exists between the decision to let a foreign architect practise as an architect in another Member State, while the Services Directive governs Member State rules on company registration and minimum fees.[156] Conversely, when Article 5(2) Directive 2005/36/EC allows Member States to demand from service providers proof of two years' practice in their home state where a profession is not regulated in the home state, this arguably would constitute a requirement under Article 16 Services Directive and would thus require justification.[157] The same applies to certain administrative provisions the host state can impose on foreign providers under Directive 2005/36/EC.[158] Between these provisions and the Services Directive no clear-cut situation of conflict arises because Article 16 does not prohibit Member States from imposing such conditions, but instead submits them to a further standard of review.

In this respect, the specific exemption in Article 17(6) Services Directive therefore makes sense as an addition to the general conflict rule in Article 3 Services Directive. It clarifies that the test of Article 16 does not apply to the conditions host states may establish under Directive 2005/36/EC. This specific exemption in Article 17(6) is furthermore relevant in connection with the 'blacklisted' requirement in the Services Directive 'to obtain an authorization from their competent authorities

[154] Art. 7 Directive 2005/36/EC.

[155] This includes host state rules on 'serious professional malpractice' and disciplinary provisions. A third reference to Directive 2005/36 is provided in Art. 5(4) Services Directive, which excludes the mutual recognition provision in Art. 5(3) Services Directive for documents mentioned in Arts. 7(2) and 50 Directive 2005/36/EC.

[156] See Barnard, 'Unravelling the Services Directive', p. 347.

[157] This seems to be the position of F. Lemor, 'Auswirkungen der Dienstleistungsrichtlinie auf ausgesuchte reglementierte Berufe' (2007) *Europäische Zeitschrift für Wirtschaftsrecht* 135–9 at 138.

[158] See Art. 7 Directive 2005/36/EC.

including entry in a register or registration with a professional body or association in their territory'.[159] Article 6(a) Directive 2005/36/EC, in contrast, states that, while the host state may not demand of service providers *stricto sensu* 'authorisation by, registration with or membership of a professional organisation or body', Member States are permitted to provide 'for automatic temporary registration or pro forma membership', in order to facilitate the application of its professional rules with respect to the foreign service provider. The exemption in Article 17(6) Services Directive thus clarifies that such temporary registration does not qualify as a prohibited requirement under Article 16(2). However, in this case there may be some redundancy because Article 16(2)(b) Services Directive only applies 'except where provided for in this Directive or other instruments of Community law'.[160] In any case, non-burdensome requirements under Article 6(a) Directive 2005/36/EC can be imposed on foreign service providers without violating the Services Directive.

In principle, Directive 2005/36/EC also applies to lawyers as regards their professional title. The provision of services *stricto sensu* in another Member State by a lawyer is governed by Directive 77/249/EEC.[161] Article 4 of Directive 77/249/EEC requires the observance of the professional ethics rules of the lawyer's home state. For the permanent migration of lawyers in the Community, Directive 98/5/EC[162] provides for the gradual integration of the foreign lawyer into the host state even absent any kind of additional examination.[163] Prescribing the application of host state laws connected to the qualification and the corresponding right

[159] Art. 16(2)(b) Services Directive. See Chapter 4.

[160] See European Commission, *Implementation Handbook*, pp. 53–5.

[161] Council Directive 77/249/EEC of 22 March 1977 to facilitate the effective exercise by lawyers of freedom to provide services, OJ 1977 No. L78/17. This instrument grants the right to practise under the home state title on a temporary basis in the host state while being subject to the laws and regulations of the latter. It prohibits familiar restrictions such as establishment or registration with a bar or court.

[162] Directive 98/5/EC of the European Parliament and of the Council of 16 February 1998 to facilitate practice of the profession of lawyer on a permanent basis in a Member State other than that in which the qualification was obtained, OJ 1998 No. L77/36.

[163] See Barnard, 'Unravelling the Services Directive', 328. This starts with the right to practise under the home state title (and home state rules of professional ethics in addition to host state rules), and leads to the acquisition of full host state rights after 'effectively and regularly' practising for three years in the host state. See Arts. 4 and 10 Directive 98/5/EC.

## Table 6.5 Overview of the degree of sectoral fragmentation following the entry into force of the Services Directive

| **Applicable Regime** / **Sector** | **Directive 2006/123/EC (SD)** | **Directive 2005/36/EC (PQD)** | **Other secondary law** |
|---|---|---|---|
| Architects | Applicable but conflict with PQD | Applicable | None |
| Audio-visual | Article 2 | Not applicable (de facto)[1] | Directive 2010/13/EU on audio-visual media services[2] |
| Auditors (statutory) | Applicable | Not applicable (Article 2 (3)) | Directive 2006/43/EC[3] |
| Construction | Applicable but conflict with Posting of Workers Directive | Applicable | Posting of Workers Directive 96/71/EC[4] |
| Consultancy | Applicable | Not applicable (de facto) | None |
| Crafts | Applicable but conflict with PQD | Applicable | None |
| Electronic commerce/Online | Applicable but see other secondary law | Not applicable (de facto) | Directive 2000/31/EC on electronic commerce[5] |
| Electronic communications | Applicable but see other secondary law | Not applicable (de facto) | Framework Directive 2002/21/EC,[6] Authorisation Directive 2002/20/EC,[7] Universal Services Directive 2002/22/EC,[8] Access Directive 2002/19/EC[9] |
| Energy | Article 17 | Not applicable (de facto) | Electricity Directive 2009/72/EC,[10] Gas Directive 2009/73/EC[11] |
| Financial/Insurance | Article 2 | Not applicable (Art. 2 (3)) | Directive 2006/48/EC,[12] Directive 2002/92/EC,[13] Directive 2004/39/EC,[14] Directive 2002/65/EC,[15] Directive 2002/83/EC[16] |

Table 6.5 (*Cont.*)

| | | | |
|---|---|---|---|
| Health care professionals | Article 2 | Applicable | None |
| Health insurance | Article 2 | Not applicable (de facto) | Patient Mobility Directive 2001/24/EU[17] |
| Lawyering | Article 17 | Partly not applicable (Art. 2 (3)), partly applicable | Directives 98/5/EC[18] and 77/249/EEC[19] |
| Notaries and bailiffs | Article 17 | Not applicable | None |
| Pharmacy | Article 2 (under the title health) | Applicable | None |
| Postal | Article 17 | Not applicable (de facto) | Directive 97/67/EC[20] |
| Private security | Article 2 | Not applicable (de facto) | None |
| Social | Article 2 | Not applicable (de facto) | None |
| Tax advisers | Applicable | Applicable in some MS | None |
| Temporary work agencies | Article 2 | Not applicable (de facto) | Posting of Workers Directive 96/71/EC[21] |
| Tourism (tour guides, travel agencies) | Applicable | Not applicable (de facto) | |
| Trade/Retail | Applicable | Not applicable (de facto) | |
| Transport | Article 2 | Not applicable (Art. 2 (3)) | Directive 96/26/EC[22] |

Table 6.5 (*Cont.*)

| | | | |
|---|---|---|---|
| Waste (including shipment) | Article 17 | Not applicable (de facto) | Waste Directive 2008/98/EC[23] |
| Water | Article 17 | Not applicable (de facto) | |

[1] De facto refers to the fact that the applicability of Dir. 2005/36/EC depends on whether the relevant profession is regulated in the host state.
[2] Directive 2010/13/EU of the European Parliament and the Council of 10 March 2010 on the coordination of certain provisions laid down by law, regulation or administrative action in Member States concerning the provision of audio-visual media services, OJ 2010 No. L95/1.
[3] Directive 2006/43/EC of the European Parliament and the Council of 17 May 2006 on statutory audits of annual accounts and consolidated accounts, OJ 2006 No. L157/87.
[4] Directive 96/71/EC of the European Parliament and the Council of 16 December 1996 concerning the posting of workers in the framework of the provision of services, OJ 1997 No. L18/1.
[5] Directive 2000/31/EC of the European Parliament and the Council of 8 June 2000 on certain legal aspects of information society services, in particular electronic commerce, in the internal market, OJ 2000 No. L178/1.
[6] Directive 2002/21/EC of the European Parliament and the Council of 7 March 2002 on a common regulatory framework for electronic communications networks and services, OJ 2002 No. L108/33.
[7] Directive 2002/20/EC of the European Parliament and the Council of 7 March 2002 on the authorisation of electronic communications networks and services, OJ 2002 No. L108/21.
[8] Directive 2002/22/EC of the European Parliament and the Council of 7 March 2002 on universal service and users' rights relating to electronic communications networks and services, OJ 2002 No. L108/51.
[9] Directive 2002/19/EC of the European Parliament and the Council of 7 March 2002 on access to, and interconnection of, electronic communications networks and associated facilities, OJ 2002 No. L108/7.
[10] Directive 2009/72/EC, OJ 2009 No. L211/55.
[11] Directive 2009/73/EC, OJ 2009 No. L211/94.
[12] Directive 2006/48/EC of the European Parliament and the Council of 14 June 2006 relating to the taking up and pursuit of the business of credit institutions, OJ 2006 No. L177/1.
[13] Directive 2002/92/EC of the European Parliament and the Council of 9 December 2002 on insurance mediation, OJ 2003 No. L9/3.
[14] Directive 2004/39/EC of the European Parliament and the Council of 21 April 2004 on markets in financial instruments, OJ 2004 No. L145/1.
[15] Directive 2002/65/EC of the European Parliament and the Council of 23 September 2002 concerning the distance marketing of consumer financial services, OJ 2002 No. L271/16.
[16] Directive 2002/83/EC of the European Parliament and the Council of 5 November 2002 concerning life assurance, OJ 2002 No. L345/1.
[17] Directive 2011/24/EU of the European Parliament and the Council of 9 March 2011 on the application of patients' rights in cross-border healthcare, OJ 2011 No. L88/45.
[18] Directive 98/5/EC, OJ 1998 No. L77/36.
[19] Council Directive 77/249/EEC, OJ 1977 No. L78/17.
[20] Directive 97/67/EC, OJ 1998 No. L15/14.
[21] OJ 1997 No. L18/1.
[22] Council Directive 96/26/EC of 29 April 1996 on admission to the occupation of road haulage operator and road passenger transport operator and mutual recognition of diplomas, certificates and other evidence of formal qualifications intended to facilitate for these operators the right to freedom of establishment in national and international transport operations, OJ 1996 No. L124/1.
[23] Directive 2008/98/EC of the European Parliament and the Council of 19 November 2008 on waste, OJ 2008 No. L312/3.

to hold a title in Article 4 of Directive 77/249/EEC would not necessarily conflict with the examination of such Member State measures under Article 16 Services Directive. In principle, however, and apart from Article 16 Services Directive, which is excluded without further qualification, the Lawyers Directives coexist with the Services Directive.

The latter only prevails in the case of a conflict, which would need to be argued for each provision of the respective directives. Yet this also means that there are now not three regimes applicable to lawyers but four – a state of affairs that, we submit, does not really foster legal clarity.

Table 6.5 provides an overview of the degree of sectoral fragmentation following the entry into force of the Services Directive.

## 6.10 Conclusion

It has been argued that the Services Directive is not of great substantive import and is primarily a 'communicative measure' as it provides for increased communication between national authorities in the Member States.[164] This assessment may overstate both its virtues and its vices. The primary tool for creating transparency and communication in the Services Directive, namely the points of single contact, have proven difficult to implement and often fall short of the intended one-stop-shop concept, as we will discuss in Chapter 7. On the other hand, we would argue that what is often forgotten when discussing the Services Directive is its introduction of blacklists to EU law on services and establishments. These blacklists might change the way national authorities, courts and the ECJ approach national law in this field considerably.

What we have also noted above, however, is that Article 16 of the Services Directive, in spite of all the controversy it has caused and the difficulty in assessing the standard it prescribes, might have little practical impact. With regard to the screening mechanism in the Services Directive, we have again seen the ball in the field of the Court, which could follow some precedents that would breathe life into these rules beyond the implementation phase, as discussed in Chapter 7.

The Services Directive is fraught with exemptions of various kinds. Above all, this concerns several service sectors that are either exempted

[164] Davies, 'Trust and mutual recognition in the Services Directive', pp. 100–1 and 106, noting that there is nothing in EU law that prevents national authorities and courts from taking conservative and free-movement unfriendly positions, and that EU law cannot thus guarantee free movement rights. At the same time, however, he claims that the Directive, while no longer referring to the country-of-origin principle, essentially maintains this powerful principle in substance.

entirely from the scope of the Services Directive, or are exempted in particular from its Article 16. We have given an overview of the regulation of the most important sectors. This is meant to show that the Services Directive, at least when it comes to a sectoral perspective, has further complicated the Union regime on services instead of providing for 'harmonization'.

# 7 The implementation of the Services Directive: a Herculean effort with poor results?

*Marcus Klamert and Georg Adler*

## 7.1 Introduction

The deadline for implementation of the Services Directive 2006/123/EC expired on 28 December 2009.[1] In late 2010 there was a lot of hand-wringing in view of the poor progress[2] made by a number of Member States regarding this – as the Council called it – 'unique opportunity to modernise and simplify Member States' regulatory frameworks'.[3] The delay is not really a surprise since the Services Directive demands considerable modifications to national legal orders, both in substantive as well as in procedural respects. According to the European Commission, the implementation of the Services Directive would necessitate a differentiated methodical approach encompassing the amendment of existing sectoral and horizontal laws as well as the adoption of new

Georg Adler, Attorney at Law, Vienna, and Lecturer at the Institute for European and International Law, Vienna University of Economics and Business.

[1] Directive 2006/123/EC of the European Parliament and the Council of 12 December 2006 on services in the internal market, OJ 2006 No. L376/36 (Arts. in this Chapter refer to this Directive unless indicated otherwise).

[2] The Council stated in May 2010 that it observed a 'significant delay' in the drafting of the required changes to sector-specific legislation in seven Member States (Austria, Cyprus, Greece, Ireland, Luxembourg, Portugal and Slovenia). See European Commission, Information note after the meeting of the Competitiveness Council on 24–25 September 2009 titled 'Implementation of the Services Directive: Making the Internal Market for Services Work Better', 9475/10, May 2010, p. 4.

[3] See European Commission, Information note after the meeting of the Competitiveness Council on 24–25 September 2009 titled 'Implementation of the Services Directive: Making the Internal Market for Services Work Better', 6817/10, 26 February 2010, p. 2.

sectoral and horizontal provisions.[4] In most countries it required about 300 such amendments to existing laws.[5]

By the end of May 2012, almost two and a half years after the end of the implementation deadline, all Member States officially had transposed the Services Directive.[6] Regarding the choice of a horizontal or vertical implementation instrument, most Member States decided on a horizontal approach. Thus twenty-five Member States adopted horizontal implementation laws,[7] while only two Member States chose a more vertical transposition approach by including the provisions of the Services Directive in various substantive legal acts.[8] However, fundamental differences can be noticed in respect of the concrete design as well as the scope of application of the transposition laws because Member States made use of the manifold implementation options the Services Directive offers.

In this chapter, after a discussion of the pertinent requirements of the Services Directive, we will focus on the implementation approach adopted by Austria and Germany. These Member States are of particular interest because both have a federal structure, while at the same time the two states have chosen entirely different transposition concepts, as we will show.

[4] See European Commission, *Handbook on Implementation of Services Directive* (hereafter *Implementation Handbook*) (2007), available at http://ec.europa.eu/internal_market/services/docs/services-dir/guides/handbook_en.pdf, p. 8.

[5] By means of so-called 'omnibus laws'. See European Commission, Information note, 6817/10, 26 February 2010, p. 3. For the UK, see the list in M. Trybus and A. Berger, 'The implementation of the Services Directive in the United Kingdom', in U. Stelkens, W. Weiß and M. Mirschberger (eds.), *The Implementation of the EU Services Directive: Transposition, Problems, Strategies* (The Hague: TMC Asser, 2012), pp. 633–65 at pp. 636–44. See also V. Hatzopoulos, 'The Court's approach to services (2006–2012): from case law to case load?' (2013) 50 *Common Market Law Review* 459–502 at 461.

[6] See European Commission, Press Release, 31 May 2012, IP/12/534. On 27 October 2011 the Commission decided to refer Germany, Austria and Greece to the Court of Justice for failing to fully transpose the Services Directive and asked the Court to impose penalty payments on these three Member States. Procedures had been opened against Germany, Austria and Greece. Germany and Austria notified the Commission of the adoption of their final transposition measures in January and April 2012 respectively. The proceedings against these two Member States were therefore closed on 26 January and 26 April 2012. On 31 May 2012 the European Commission decided to terminate the infringement proceedings against Greece for failing to fully transpose the Services Directive.

[7] Austria, Belgium, Bulgaria, Czechoslovakia, Cyprus, Denmark, Estonia, Finland, Greece, Hungary, Ireland, Italy, Latvia, Lithuania, Luxembourg, Malta, Netherlands, Poland, Portugal, Romania, Slovakia, Slovenia, Spain, Sweden, United Kingdom.

[8] France and Germany.

## 7.2 Requirements of the Services Directive from an implementation perspective

### *7.2.1 Introduction*

We would identify four main problems that have arisen with regard to the implementation of the Services Directive.

First, and probably foremost from a practical perspective, is the issue of compliance with the duty of setting up points of single contact in each Member State. The establishment of these administrative 'one-stop-shops' constitutes the most significant amendment required by the Services Directive not only in legal but also in practical terms. A wide variety of solutions to this have been chosen across the Union.[9]

The second issue is whether the Services Directive also mandates an application to service transactions internal to each Member State.[10] The Commission clearly envisaged that Member States would not in any case make a distinction between implementing rules applicable to foreign providers and those addressing only their nationals.[11] Indeed, it would seem somewhat artificial to prohibit nationals from addressing the mentioned points of single contact once they have been designated for the territory of a Member State. However, whether this requirement can be derived from the Services Directive will be discussed further below.

Third, and also of particular interest, is the implementation approach with respect to Article 13(4) Services Directive, according to which an authorization is granted if the authority fails to respond within a fixed period made public in advance.[12]

Finally, we submit that the most intricate issue from a dogmatic point of view is how properly to implement Article 16 Services Directive and the other general prohibitions of restrictions the Directive provides for in Articles 9, 10 and 15.

We will start by addressing these issues in turn in a general manner, before addressing them under the specific perspective of the implementation in Germany and Austria.

[9] See the Commission's website at http://ec.europa.eu/internal_market/eu-go/.

[10] On this see G. Davies, 'The Services Directive: extending the country of origin principle and reforming public administration' (2007) *European Law Review* 232–45 at 241–3.

[11] European Commission, *Implementation Handbook*, p. 16.

[12] This time period may be extended once by the competent authority for a limited time.

### *7.2.2 Points of single contact*

The administrative law principle of accumulation applies to situations that fall under different substantive law requirements, which have all to be fulfilled cumulatively. This phenomenon exists in all Member States of the EU. Thus, before being allowed to establish their businesses in a Member State, service providers regularly will have to apply for a substantial amount of licences. The extent of this challenge increases in states based on a federal structure, as providers often have to apply for licences at different state levels. In such constellations, lifting barriers to the functioning of the internal market appears to be of particular difficulty because the competences of different authorities often result from the constitutional distribution of legislative and executive competences among different territorial communities.[13] Windoffer's example of a French real estate broker that has to fulfil eighteen 'formalities' before being allowed to open an establishment in Germany brings the complexity, length and legal uncertainty of administrative procedures to the fore.[14] Taking into account, furthermore, that a potential provider of cross-border services also has to face numerous cultural and linguistic hurdles in other Member States, it is small wonder that providers are deterred from entering new markets. These challenges resulting from the fundamental difficulties in accessing service activities and exercising them affect small and medium-sized companies in particular.

In order to simplify administrative procedures, the Services Directive seeks to abolish administrative barriers by ensuring that each provider has a single point through which he can complete all procedures and formalities.[15] The idea behind the points of single contact is 'one-stop government'. Because of the establishment of points of single contact, providers would only have to contact one single institution for the fulfilment of all requirements concerning access to and exercise of service activities under the scope of the Services Directive. However, the concept of the points of single contact does not oblige each Member State

[13] H. Mayer, *Genehmigungskonkurrenz und Verfahrenskonzentration* (Vienna: Signum, 1985), pp. 2, 25; K. Stöger, 'Der einheitliche Ansprechpartner im Bundesstaat: Ein Blick über die Grenze', in C. Jabloner *et al.* (eds.), *Vom praktischen Wert der Methode: Festschrift Heinz Mayer zum 65. Geburtstag* (Vienna: Manz, 2011), pp. 755–73 at p. 756.

[14] A. Windoffer, 'Das System des einheitlichen Ansprechpartners', in S. Leible (ed.), *Die Umsetzung der Dienstleistungsrichtlinie: Chancen und Risiken für Deutschland* (JWV Jenaer Wiss. Verl.-Ges, 2008), pp. 25–42 at pp. 26ff.

[15] Recs. 43 and 48.

to set up a single, physical, centralized agency for its entire territory. In fact, the points of single contact are 'single' only as far as the perspective of the individual service provider is concerned.[16] The provider must be able to complete all formalities and procedures required for service activities through the same entity, particularly relating to authorizations.[17] In addition to this, the Services Directive emphasizes that no interference with competences among the national authorities[18] is required, and allows for the establishment of points of single contact as a mere supporting institution for the provider. However, amendments in respect of the domestic allocation of competences are not prohibited per se.[19] Thus it remains within a certain Member State's discretion whether to entrust already established bodies, chambers or entirely newly created institutions with the exercise of these duties.

### 7.2.3 *Applicability to purely internal situations*

In contrast to Chapter IV of the Services Directive, which explicitly refers to cross-border services,[20] other parts such as Chapter III do not contain such a reference, raising the question of whether the rules of the Services Directive also apply to purely internal situations in the Member States.[21] Some authors have supported this view based on the unclear substance of the Services Directive, and the fact that it purports to regulate the entire services sector of a Member State.[22] We

[16] U. Schliesky, 'Von der Realisierung des Binnenmarktes über die Verwaltungsreform zu einem gemeineuropäischen Verwaltungsrecht? Die Auswirkungen der geplanten EU-Dienstleistungsrichtlinie auf das deutsche Verwaltungsrecht' (2005) *Deutsches Verwaltungsblatt* 887–95 at 891.

[17] This had already been pointed out in the Commission proposal, COM(2004)2 final.

[18] Compare Art. 6(2), which states that 'the establishment of points of single contact shall be without prejudice to the allocation of functions and powers among the authorities within national systems'.

[19] The wording that procedures and formalities can be accomplished through points of single contact replaces the version of a single point of contact contained in the 'Bolkestein' draft. Member States are given the discretion to grant points of single contact decision-making authority or to establish them only as 'processing' units. See C. S. Buchinger, A. Michner and C. Müller, *Die Dienstleistungsrichtlinie: Ein Erfolg der österreichischen Präsidentschaft 2006* (Vienna: Verlag Österreich, 2007), p. 65.

[20] Compare Art. 16(1): 'Member States shall respect the right of providers to provide services in a Member States other than that in which they are established.'

[21] See G. Adler and T. Kröll, 'Austrian Report', in U. Stelkens, W. Weiß and M. Mirschberger (eds.), *The Implementation of the EU Services Directive: Transposition, Problems and Strategies* (The Hague: TMC Asser, Springer, 2012), pp. 65–87 at pp. 68.

[22] C. Böhret, D. Grunow and J. Ziekow, 'Der Vorschlag zu einer Richtlinie des Europäischen Parlamentes und des Rates über Dienstleistungen im Binnenmarkt:

would argue, in contrast, that the Services Directive covers only transnational situations for the following reasons. First, the fact that some chapters of the Services Directive do not explicitly state their scope of application does not imply that these parts of the Services Directive are applicable to purely internal situations. Second, the position within the system of the Treaty of Article 47 TEU, which constitutes the legal basis of the Services Directive together with Article 55 TEU, argues against a broader scope. This Treaty provision is located within the same chapter as Article 43 TEU, which explicitly refers solely to cross-border situations. Moreover, in its case law the ECJ has so far refused to apply the fundamental freedoms to purely internal situations. In *Uecker and Jacquet* the Court put this as follows:

> It has consistently been held that the Treaty rules governing freedom of movement and regulations adopted to implement them cannot be applied to cases which have no factor linking them with any of the situations governed by Community law and all elements of which are purely internal to a single Member State.[23]

Before the ECJ, this issue is likely to be decided following a claim of reverse discrimination. While this, at first sight, could serve as an argument of the application of the Services Directive to internal situations,[24] we should note that some Member State laws, such as those of Austria, protect their citizens against being the victim of reverse discrimination.[25]

### 7.2.4 *Tacit authorization*

The Services Directive also seeks to eliminate delays, costs and dissuasive effects arising from unnecessary or excessively complex and burdensome procedures, in particular because of indeterminate or excessively long periods before a response is given by the administration.[26] While Article 13(1) Services Directive contains general criteria concerning requirements of procedural laws, paragraph 2 obliges the Member States to grant efficient authorization procedures, which, in particular, shall not impose excessive costs. Article 13(3) Services Directive obliges

Regelungsgehalt – Problemfelder – Akteurspositionen' (Speyerer Forschungsberichte, No. 241, 2006), p. 239.

[23] Joined Cases C-64/96 and C-65/96, *Land Nordrhein-Westfalen* v. *Kari Uecker and Vera Jacquet* v. *Land Nordrhein-Westfalen* [1997] ECR I-3171, para. 16.

[24] Compare the explanations below on Austria and the points of single contact.

[25] See e.g. Austria Constitutional Court decision, VfSlg 14.963/1997.

[26] Rec. 43.

Member States to provide quick and, in any event, reasonable periods for authorization procedures and formalities. The time considered reasonable for a concrete authorization procedure may vary from case to case depending on the complexity of the procedure and the issues involved.[27] However, the conditions have to be made public in advance, whereas the competent authority may extend time periods only once for a limited time. In this connection, Article 13(4) Services Directive entails a fundamental amendment relating to national authorization schemes by introducing the so-called *lex silencio positivo*. This means that in the event of failure to respond to an application within the time limit that has been set or that has been extended,[28] authorization will be deemed granted. The broad scope of application of this rule constitutes a novelty in most Member States.[29] Deviations are possible only where justified by overriding reasons relating to the public interest, including a legitimate interest of third parties.

### *7.2.5 Article 16 Services Directive*

We have already discussed Article 16 of the Directive at length in Chapter 6. Recall that this provision belongs to the 'cornerstones [sic] of the Services Directive',[30] and stipulates that services falling within the scope of the Services Directive and not coming under the exemptions of Article 17 Services Directive must not be restricted by Member States unless this is justified. Recall further that Article 16(2) Services Directive contains a 'blacklist' of measures that cannot be justified under EU law, as well as that paragraph 3 is not very clear on what it adds to this regime.[31]

It seems that the Commission has assumed that Member States would implement Article 16 Services Directive in a horizontal 'framework

[27] European Commission, *Implementation Handbook*, p. 28.

[28] The period has to run only from the time when all documentation has been submitted. Compare Art. 13(3).

[29] Before the adoption of the Services Directive, the instrument of tacit authorization as a general rule appears to have been used by only four Member States, namely Hungary, Italy and to some extent Romania and Spain. However, most Member States were already familiar with that system and had already used it in specific administrative laws. See U. Stelkens, W. Weiß and M. Mirschberger, 'General comparative report', in U. Stelkens, W. Weiß and M. Mirschberger (eds.), *The Implementation of the EU Services Directive: Transposition, Problems and Strategies* (The Hague: TMC Asser, Springer, 2012), pp. 3–61 at p. 35.

[30] European Commission, *Implementation Handbook*, p. 28.

[31] See Chapter 6.

law'.[32] Many Member States, such as Poland, Spain and the United Kingdom, have indeed informed the Commission of passing such laws of cross-sectoral coverage, while most of these countries, in addition, undertook adaptations in the substantive laws. Only a few Member States such as Austria, Germany and the Netherlands adapted their substantive laws solely in this connection.

## 7.3 Implementation in Germany

### *7.3.1 Introduction*

As already mentioned, the implementation of a one-stop government constitutes a particular challenge for Member States based on a federal structure.[33] German administrative law consists of a general codification of procedures at federal and state level on the one hand, and an almost innumerable amount of substantive law regulating specific fields of administration on the other hand. The latter provides substantive standards and/or special procedural rules, completing or derogating the general regimes. For the transposition process, in addition to the competences for enacting procedural laws[34] and substantive laws,[35] the competences for passing organizational laws[36] also had to be taken into account.[37] These competence areas are divided between federal and state level.[38]

For the implementation of the Services Directive, the German legislator refrained from adopting a separate horizontal implementation bill at the federal level, but instead decided on inclusion in already existing laws at federal and state level. It is hardly surprising that the coordination of the implementation proved to be rather complex and resulted

[32] European Commission, *Implementation Handbook*, p. 8.

[33] Against the background of the constitutional distribution of competences, the establishment of a centralized point of contact was recognized to be a risk for federal states' administrative structures. See T. von Danwitz, *Europäisches Verwaltungsrecht* (Berlin: Springer, 2008), p. 500.

[34] Arts. 30, 84 German Basic Law (*Grundgesetz*, GG).

[35] Whether the competence for bringing a substantive law into accordance with the objectives of the Services Directive is left to the federal or the state legislator depends on the constitutional distribution of competences. See J. Ziekow and A. Windoffer, 'Kommentar zu Art. 6', in M. Schlachter and C. Ohler (eds.), *Europäische Dienstleistungsrichtlinie: Handkommentar* (Baden-Baden: Nomos, 2008), paras. 28 *et seq.*

[36] Art. 84(1) GG; Ziekow and Windoffer, 'Kommentar zu Art. 6', para. 6.

[37] Stöger, 'Der einheitliche Ansprechpartner im Bundesstaat', p. 763.

[38] Arts. 30, 70–4 and 83–91(e) GG.

in the adoption of a multitude of different laws, such as two acts[39] and four regulations[40] at federal level, and a remarkable amount of implementation acts at state level.[41] The bodies responsible for implementation were the Federal Ministry of Economics and Technology together with the Conference of Ministers of Economic Affairs, which is an assembly of the heads of the respective departments at state level.

### 7.3.2 *Points of single contact*

Because of the allocation of competences between federal and state level and because of the absence of a clause allocating competence in favour of the federal level, the concrete establishment of the points of single contact took place at regional level. However, the federal laws are also of relevance in this connection, as we will show below. As we have already mentioned, organizational, procedural and substantive law competences had to be taken into consideration within the implementation process.

The organizational competence for the establishment of the points of single contact mainly lies with the state governments.[42] The states are competent for the actual organizational establishment of points of single contact and their scope of application. Thus each of the states adopted a separate law, making extensive use of their competences and leading to a highly heterogeneous transposition in regard of the organizational structure of the points of single contact. Concerning the establishment of the points of single contact in the different states, approaches range from choosing administrative and urban districts,[43] chambers[44] and private companies[45] to perform this function,

[39] See the 4th Act for the Changing of Administrative Procedures of 11 December 2008, BGBl I 2008/58, 2418; Act for the Implementation of the Services Directive in Trade Law and in other Laws of 17 July 2009, BGBl I 2009/44.

[40] Regulation on Information Obligations for Service Providers of 12 February 2010, BGBl I 2010/11; Regulation for Transposing the Services Directive in the Area of Environmental Law and to Change Environmental Rules, BT-Drs 17/862; Regulation for Adopting Trade Regulations to the Services Directive of 9 March 2010, BGBl I 2010/11.

[41] In each of the sixteen states at least two implementation acts were adopted.

[42] Ziekow and Windoffer, 'Kommentar zu Art. 6', para. 22.

[43] See e.g. s. 1 of the Act on the Point of Single Contact of Lower Saxony.

[44] See e.g. s. 2 of Hamburg's Act on the Realisation of the Tasks of the Point of Single Contact.

[45] In the city-state of Bremen, the Wirtschaftsförderung Bremen GmbH (WFB) fulfils the duty of a point of single contact.

or creating special institutions under public law.[46] Basic procedural provisions concerning the points of single contact were inserted in the federal Administrative Procedures Act (*Verwaltungsverfahrensgesetz*, VwVfG).[47] Section 71(a) VwVfG provides for the application of that section whenever a law refers to the handling of an administrative procedure through a point of single contact. This general procedural law rule enables the respective substantive law legislators at federal level and the procedural and substantive law legislators at state level to 'opt in'. As the substantive design of the points of single contact follows a common approach regarding a harmonized field of responsibility,[48] most state law provisions are in fact more or less identical to the procedural provisions at federal level.

In particular, this concerns the question of the applicability of the points of single contact also to purely internal situations. It can be argued that Sections 71(a) to 71(e) VwVfG allow for the application of the points of single contact also to purely internal situations. The (federal or state) legislators responsible for the substantive law aspects must establish the concrete rules on the points of single contact, and in that they can deviate from the general procedural law provisions at federal and state level. However, the resolution of the above-mentioned Conference of Ministers of Economic Affairs postulated the inclusion also of purely internal situations,[49] and most states decided to follow a common approach on this. The only exemption in this connection is Bavaria, which explicitly rendered the points of single contact only applicable for cross-border situations.[50]

Because of the manifold implementation laws at federal and state level in Germany, the identification of the competent points of single contact appears rather complex from a dogmatic view.[51] This complex legislative design is combined with a plurality of points of single contact of various natures.[52] Thus one might argue that the one-

[46] See s. 1 of the Act on the Establishment of the Point of Single Contact of the province of Schleswig-Holstein.

[47] Section 71(a)–(e) VwVfG.

[48] See Bund-Länder-Ausschuss Dienstleistungswirtschaft, Anforderungsprofil für 'Einheitliche Ansprechpartner' (2007), p. 3.

[49] Compare the *Beschluss* of the Wirtschaftsministerkonferenz of 4 to 5 June 2007 in Eisenach (point 2).

[50] S. 1 of the Bavarian Act on Points of Single Contact. The situation provided in Saxony is unclear: see s. 1 of the Act on Points of Single Contact of Saxony.

[51] Stöger, 'Der einheitliche Ansprechpartner im Bundesstaat', p. 763.

[52] In total, there are around 150 points of single contact in Germany.

stop government required under the Services Directive has not been achieved. However, from the practical view of a service provider, the establishment of a central homepage with a subsection covering all German points of single contact makes the identification of the competent points of single contact rather easy. Problems may arise, however, when a service provider seeks to establish his business in more than one state, so that various points of single contact would have to be contacted. We would submit that this approach undermines the requirement that a potential service provider must have the impression of handling all formalities covered by the Services Directive through one single contact point. In this context it must also be noted that the subpages of many states that can be accessed from the central homepage, such as Thüringen, Brandenburg, Niedersachsen and Bayern, are only available in German.

In spite of this critique, Germany's overall implementation of the Services Directive is commendable. Besides the fact that most of the requirements of the Services Directive were implemented in time, the strong role of the states in establishing the points of single contact should lead to competition between them and, thus, should produce overall positive effects for service providers.[53] Service providers will make their decision on where to establish their business depending on the procedures and formalities they have to cope with, and thus not least on the basis of whether there is a comprehensive one-stop government available in a certain state.[54] As a result, the active role of the German states in comparison to other Member States and the ensuing inter-state competition could have positive implications for Germany from the business perspective.

### 7.3.3 *Tacit authorization*

Prior to the Services Directive, Germany had not provided for a general requirement concerning the duration of administrative procedures. Thus the German legislator had to implement the requirements of Article 13 Services Directive. According to the newly inserted §42a VwVfG, an authorization is deemed to be granted after the expiration of the defined decision period, which essentially amounts to three months. However, the provision does not apply automatically, but

[53] Stöger, 'Der einheitliche Ansprechpartner im Bundesstaat', p. 770.

[54] A. Luch and S. Schulz, 'Die Umsetzungsgesetzgebung der Bundesländer zur Einrichtung Einheitlicher Ansprechpartner nach Art. 6 DLR' (2010) *Gewerbearchiv* 225–30 at 230.

requires a reference in substantive laws and adequate substantiation by the applicant.

The advantage of this approach lies in the flexibility of the legislator that is competent for the respective substantive law at state level, as he or she may also assess whether and how far a one-to-one transposition is required and reasonable. Whether this opting-in approach for the state legislator is in accordance with the requirements of the Services Directive depends on how far the competent legislators according to the German allocation of competences refer to the minimum requirements provided for in §42a VwVfG in all fields encompassed by the Services Directive.[55] German scholars have submitted that the tacit authorization has a similar character as an authorization granted under ordinary procedural rules.[56] This would make all provisions concerning the nullity, revocability and other matters of administrative acts (§§35–53 VwVfG) also applicable to tacit authorizations. Thus it would also be possible to impose additional conditions on the fictitious authorization at a later stage without affecting the authorization itself.[57]

### 7.3.4 *Article 16 Services Directive*

The Commission has opined that Article 16 Services Directive, in principle, does not require Member States to remove existing requirements, but merely obliges them to refrain from applying them to service providers established in other Member States.[58] A removal would only be necessary with regard to provisions designed specifically for service providers established in other Member States. However, in our opinion this approach taken by the Commission does not protect Member States from additionally having to rectify their national laws in a clear and transparent manner. According to the case law by the ECJ, mere administrative practice does not constitute an adequate measure of

[55] M. Krajewski, 'Anforderungen der Dienstleistungsrichtlinie an Genehmigungsregelungen und ihre Umsetzung im deutschen Recht' (2009) *Neue Zeitschrift für Verwaltungsrecht* 929–35 at 933.

[56] See, among others, H. Jäde, 'Die verwaltungsverfahrensrechtliche Genehmigungsfiktion' (2009) *Umwelt- und Planungsrecht* 169–73 at 169.

[57] M. Mirschberger, 'German Report', in U. Stelkens, W. Weiß and M. Mirschberger (eds.), *The Implementation of the EU Services Directive: Transposition, Problems and Strategies* (The Hague: TMC Asser, Springer, 2012), pp. 225–83, referring to BT-Drs. 16/10493, p. 16.

[58] See European Commission, *Implementation Handbook*, p. 36.

transposition.[59] In other words, the mere fact that a Member State's administrative practice is in accordance with the requirements of the Services Directive does not mean that the Treaty would not require another level of compliance.

The German legislator apparently followed the latter approach. Thus German substantive laws were screened on their accordance with the requirements of the Services Directive and, where indicated, brought into compliance. Of foremost importance in this connection was the insertion of §4 into the German Trade, Commerce and Industry Regulation Act (*Gewerbeordnung*, GewO). Its paragraph 1 refers to requirements under the GewO, which are not applicable to service providers established in other Member States. Thus authorization obligations for running the business of an auctioneer or agent are not applicable in transnational situations. However, paragraph 2 states that these benefits do not apply when providers establish themselves in another Member State only in order to avoid the application of the requirements mentioned under paragraph 1. Albeit that ECJ case law as well as the Services Directive allow Member States to retain the right to prevent providers from abusing the fundamental freedoms,[60] we would argue that this German provision could be contrary to the internal market because the inherent idea of a single market is the opportunity for companies to set up branches in other Member States. In any case, the German authorities will have to assess a potential misuse in the light of the objectives pursued by the Services Directive.[61]

## 7.4 Implementation in Austria

### *7.4.1 Introduction*

As with other states that are based on a federal structure, the wide scope of the Services Directive constituted a particular challenge for the Austrian implementation process, because it affected competences at federal, state as well as at local level.[62] The Commission does not

[59] Case C-131/88, *Commission* v. *Germany* [1991] ECR I-825.

[60] E.g. Case 33/74, *van Binsbergen* [1974] ECR 1299; Case C-61/89, *Bouchoucha* [1990] ECR I-3551.

[61] C-206/94, *Paletta II* [1996] ECR I-2357.

[62] The Federal Ministry for Economics, Family and Youth served as the coordinating institution. All legislation documents – the draft, the initiative by the Austrian government, and the parliamentary procedures – can be accessed at http://www.parlament.gv.at/PG/DE/XXIV/I/I_00317/pmh.shtml.

differentiate whether an infringement is caused by the federal state or by the states and always holds the federal state accountable. According to an agreement governed by constitutional law between the states and the federation on the rights of participation of the states and the communes in matters of European integration, the states are liable towards the federal state for all costs caused to the federation because of breaches of EU law.

In a first step, the different territorial entities had to screen their procedural and substantive laws with the requirements of the Services Directive by 31 August 2008. In the case of non-compliance with the prescriptions of the Services Directive, the respective laws and regulations had to be amended.[63] For reasons of efficiency, the government draft sought to implement the Services Directive's provisions concerning the points of single contact as well as procedural laws and the provisions concerning administrative cooperation by a horizontal act at federal level that would allow the federal legislator to regulate fields that, according to the constitution, fall under the legislative powers of the federal states.

Thus Section 1 of the draft government bill[64] provided for a competence clause ('*Kompetenzklausel*') covering the adoption by the federal legislator and requiring a two-thirds majority in parliament. Due to political reasons entirely unrelated to the Services Directive, the transposition laws could not be passed by 28 December 2009. However, in spite of the absence of a legally binding transposition, the Services Directive was effectively implemented and put into force. In particular, points of single contact were established and made operational. However, it was clear that such a merely de facto implementation of the Services Directive would not qualify as a formal transposition measure. In October 2011, twenty-two months after the expiration of the transposition deadline, the Commission decided to refer Austria, among other Member States, to the ECJ because it had only partially transposed the Services Directive.[65] The Commission withdrew the infringement claim as the Austrian transposition law came into force on 22 November

[63] E.g., the province of Styria adopted a law amending the provincial laws on accreditations, elevators, construction, construction products, mountain and skiing guides, electricity organization, prostitution, dancing schools and administrative acts. See the Official Journal of Styria, 2010/7. The state of Upper Austria amended its laws on sports, caretakers, camping sites and childcare, among others. See Official Journal of Upper Austria, 2010/30.

[64] 317dB XXIV GP.

[65] European Commission, Press Release, 27 October 2011, IP/11/1283. In addition to this, Germany and Greece were referred to the ECJ.

2011. The Austrian parliament had dropped the competence clause and, thus, could adopt the Austrian Services Act with only a simple majority, instead of the higher threshold required for constitutional laws. Consequently, the states had to adopt separate laws for transposing the procedural law provisions contained in the Services Directive, particularly concerning the points of single contact, tacit authorization and the administrative cooperation applicable equally at state level.[66]

### *7.4.2 Points of single contact*

As already mentioned, there was a lively discussion about the implementation of the Services Directive in general. The transposition of the points of single contact was a point of particular controversy. Not only were existing authorities and newly created institutions considered in this context, but mandating the responsible institutions for the respective professions, such as chambers of commerce, bar associations and architectural associations, was also discussed. In the end, the provinces prevailed and the points of single contact were located at the highest administrative entity at the province level (*Ämter der Landesregierungen*), thus with already existing institutions at state level.[67] The assignment at the state level seems to have advantages,[68] because the states exercise the larger part of administrative competences as a result of the constitutional principle of indirect federal administration.[69]

The transposition was twofold because of the elimination of the competence clause in Section 1 of the Austrian Services Act: in the Austrian Services Act on the one hand and in the state laws on the other hand as far as state competences were concerned. Consequently, there were ten almost identical laws (one at federal state level, nine at state level) concerning the points of single contact. Under these Austrian laws, points of single contact constitute mere mail administration centres that do

[66] The provinces already anticipated the necessity of adopting separate laws. Thus both Styria and Upper Austria adopted laws on Points of Single Contact.

[67] In every state there is one Amt der Landesregierung (i.e. nine overall). This provides assistance to the state government (its Members) and to the respective state governor. The Amt der Landesregierung is not a public authority as such.

[68] S. Börger, 'Anlagengenehmigungsverfahren und die Dienstleistungsrichtlinie', in F. Merli and S. Greimel, *Optimierungspotentiale bei Behördenverfahren* (Vienna: Linde, 2009), pp. 121–39 at p. 130.

[69] According to the principle of indirect federal administration, the states and the communities also execute most matters covering a large range of issues that the Austrian Constitution assigns to the federal states in legislation.

not decide on the merits of a case. In other words, the points of single contact act functionally for the competent authorities.[70]

The scope of applicability of the points of single contact also caused a dispute, in relation to two questions in particular: first, whether the points of single contact would be applicable not only to citizens of other Member States but also to Austrian citizens and, second in the affirmative, whether purely internal situations would be covered as well. Concerning the first issue, we would submit that the points of single contact have a broad scope, considering that §2 Austrian Services Act and all state laws implementing the points of single contact for their areas of competence refer to services providers in European Economic Area countries.[71] With regard to the second question, §2 Austrian Services Act and all state laws[72] explicitly state that they only cover services in the sense of Article 50 EC (now Article 57 TFEU).[73] Here it appears already clear from the wording itself that the scope of the Austrian Services Act and the state laws is coherent with that of the Services Directive, so that purely internal situations are not covered.[74] Consequently, Austrians may only rely upon the points of single contact in transnational situations.[75] This leads to the problem of reverse discrimination, which has already been discussed above. In the present case, the problem cannot be solved by interpreting the provision in a way that is in conformity with the Austrian Constitution.[76] The result, namely the different treatment between transnational and purely internal situations under the Austrian Services Act, remains an issue

[70] With regard to claims brought against the points of single contact, compensation must be divided between those units in proportion to their competence areas. See 317dB XXIV GP, 11.

[71] See Stöger, 'Der einheitliche Ansprechpartner im Bundesstaat', p. 764.

[72] See e.g. s. 1 of the Act on Points of Single Contact of Upper Austria.

[73] S. 2 in connection with s. 5 para. 2 Austrian Services Act.

[74] This opinion is also supported by the parliamentary procedures, which refer to the fact that the Services Directive only requires that points of single contact are competent for transnational situations. However, the history of the legislation process makes clear that the original intention of the legislator was to make the Austrian Services Act applicable to national as well as to transnational situations. The draft implementation act (32/ME XXIV GP) foresaw their provision not only in the Austrian Services Act, but also in s. 20a of the general administrative procedural law, the AVG. However, this approach met with resistance from the states and from some ministries. See also on this, Adler and Kröll, 'Austrian report', pp. 68ff.

[75] See also, in favour of the applicability of the Austrian Services Act for purely internal situations, Stöger, 'Der einheitliche Ansprechpartner im Bundesstaat', p. 765.

[76] Austrian Constitutional Court, VfSlg 11.036/1986.

that has to be addressed under Austrian law. According to settled case law by the Austrian Constitutional Court, reverse discrimination has to be justified objectively to be in accordance with the constitutional principle of equal treatment. The respective provision has to be eliminated in a separate procedure when it is challenged before the Constitutional Court. This, however, is not a result of the internal market rules.

### 7.4.3 *Tacit authorization*

Prior to the implementation of the Services Directive, the Austrian General Administrative Procedure Act (*Allgemeines Verwaltungsverfahrensgesetz*, AVG) did not contain a general rule enabling the settling of an application via tacit (fictitious) authorization. Only in specific cases did substantive administrative laws provide for this possibility.[77] The risk of an excessively long duration of procedures, nevertheless, has been addressed by Section 73(1) AVG requiring the competent authority to make a decision within a period of six month after receipt of an application.[78] In cases where the competent authority does not act accordingly, the concerned party is allowed to submit an application for 'devolution' according to Section 73(2) AVG, referring the case to a higher federal or state authority for decision on the merits.[79]

The Austrian Services Act implements the authorization scheme of Article 13 Services Directive in Section 12 Austrian Services Act by establishing an 'opting-in' clause that is combined with 'opting-out' aspects. This means that the basic provision establishing the tacit authorization is only applicable if the competent substantive law legislator adopts it. Moreover, the legislator may deviate from the specifics of the provision, such as concerning the period in which the competent authority is obliged to issue a notification.[80] In any case, the Services Directive only

[77] For example, the Austrian Act on Associations (BGBl I Nr. 66/2002 idF BGBl I Nr. 45/2008), provides in s. 13(2) that the application for the foundation of a voluntary association according to that law is deemed granted if the authority does not prohibit the activity within six weeks after receipt of the application. The voluntary association is deemed to be founded with expiry of the veto period.

[78] Furthermore, s. 18 AVG obliges the competent authorities to handle matters in an efficient and cost-saving manner towards all parties and participants.

[79] Basically, this is three months from receipt of the application, although the competent authority may extend this period once because of the complexity of the case. See Adler and Kröll, 'Austrian report', pp. 79ff.

[80] Compare Art. 13(4) Services Directive. Particularly in connection with the three-month period, it makes sense to leave the choice of a deviating period to the substantive law legislator as it is more qualified to assess the necessity thereof for the concrete procedure. See RV 317 BlgNR XXIV. GP 14.

allows a deviation from the three-month period in situations where mandatory requirements exist (e.g. in some multiparty proceedings). Pursuant to Section 12(4) Austrian Services Act, where the competent authority does not respond to the filed application within the set or the extended deadline, a tacit (fictitious) authorization is granted to the service provider. However, the competent authority must issue confirmation as soon as possible, which all parties are entitled to obtain within four weeks. This provision equally constitutes an 'opting-out' clause, since the federal or state legislator competent for the respective substantive administrative law may deviate therefrom.[81]

As already mentioned, the Austrian legislator set up the points of single contact as mere mail processing centres, passing on each application to the competent authority. The points of single contact are neither competent to check the application on defaults or its completeness nor to decide on the merits. The respective authority is obliged to return any incomplete or faulty applications to the applicants for revision. According to Section 12(3) Austrian Services Act, the three months decision period of the competent authority starts with the receipt of a written application free from defaults. In contrast, if the application is delivered over the points of single contact, the decision period of the competent authority starts with the third day after delivery.[82]

As far as the effects of a tacit authorization are concerned, the latter constitutes a substitute for the authorization normally granted in the form of a formal decision (*Bescheid*). It settles the filed application in a formal and substantive way so that the legal effects of a tacit authorization and of a formal decision (*Bescheid*) are equivalent. In the case of a tacit authorization, it is not possible to prescribe conditions or limitations.[83] The provisions of the AVG about the *ex officio* modification or repeal of formal decisions and about the reopening of the procedure also apply to tacit authorizations.[84]

### *7.4.4 Article 16 Services Directive*

Austria demonstrates that the fact of notifying the Commission of a horizontal implementation law does not necessarily mean that the full body of the Services Directive, including its Article 16 or the other

[81] In relation to s. 73 AVG, s. 12 draft Austrian Services Act constitutes a *lex specialis*.
[82] Section 6(4) Austrian Services Act.
[83] RV 317 BlgNR XXIV. GP 14.
[84] Section 12(5) Austrian Services Act.

general prohibitions of restrictions, would be imposed directly on national authorities. While the horizontal Austrian Services Act mainly regulates the points of single contact and other procedural matters, Articles 9, 10, 15 and 16 Services Directive have not been specifically implemented. Implementation of these provisions in Austria, but also in Germany and France, which have not even claimed to have passed a horizontal framework law, must logically mean that Austria would abstain from sustaining or enacting national law contrary to the mentioned prohibitions.

When considering the manifold matters provided in various substantive laws that were seen to be in conflict with the requirements of the Services Directive,[85] one becomes aware of the obvious risk that a passive implementation entails. It is unlikely that the screening could cover all substantive laws so that all provisions not in accordance with Article 16 Services Directive could be found and revoked.

## 7.5 A comparative view of the implementation of Article 16

We would argue that both the proactive transposition of Article 16 in particular into national law such as in the UK, as well as the adoption of a passive position on implementation such as in Austria or the Netherlands,[86] raises questions.[87] On both accounts, it must be noted that since Articles 49 and 56 TFEU have been found by the ECJ to possess direct effect, it would arguably be incoherent not to hold the same of the corresponding provisions in the Services Directive, including its

[85] Approximately sixty substantive laws were affected and amendments were carried out, particularly at the state level. For example, the authorization procedures for the opening of dancing schools were abolished and replaced by a simple notification. Other examples are the elimination of the ban on multiple ownership for ski schools and of the needs test for burial facilities. For a more detailed survey compare Milieu Ltd, Services Directive: Assessment of Implementation Measures in Member States: National Report for Austria, Part I (2011), pp. 6ff, available at http://ec.europa.eu/internal_market/services/docs/services-dir/mileu-study/at-national-report-part_I_en.pdf.

[86] S. Prechal, S. de Vries and F. van Doorn, 'The implementation of the Services Directive in the Netherlands', in U. Stelkens, W. Weiß and M. Mirschberger (eds.), *The Implementation of the EU Services Directive: Transposition, Problems, Strategies* (The Hague: TMC Asser, 2012), pp. 435–74 at p. 444.

[87] The following draws on M. Klamert, 'Of empty glasses and double burdens: approaches to regulating the services market à propos the implementation of the Services Directive' (2010) *Legal Issues of Economic Integration* 111–32.

Article 16. A 'copy-and-paste' solution should likely see the duty of consistent interpretation in heavy demand and national courts struggling with all the ambiguities the Services Directive offers. On the other hand, this approach respects the rule that Community directives must be implemented by an active and assertive legislative act satisfying the 'five tests of adequacy'.[88] Two of these five standards that the Court imposes on national implementation measures – clarity/precision and publicity/transparency – are particularly significant 'where the directive in question is intended to accord rights to nationals of other Member States'.[89] A provision having direct effect is *per definitionem* qualified to accord such rights. Writing Article 16 Services Directive in particular into national law would not only raise the awareness of providers from other Member States but also of national authorities regarding the changes that this provision brings for their regulatory autonomy.

In addition to raising doubts in respect of this transparency standard,[90] the alternative, passive approach to implementation, such as seen in Austria, produces the following 'anomaly'. Assume that the one-off screening does manage to abolish all existing prohibited requirements, yet a Member State continues to introduce new measures in breach of the general prohibitions of restrictions in the Services Directive. Instead of invoking Articles 49 and 56 TFEU before their national courts, EU citizens would have to rely on the Services Directive's prohibitions that, as mentioned previously, largely correspond to the Treaty with the exception of Article 16 Services Directive. What would then be the benefit of having Articles 9, 10 and 15 written into the Services Directive? EU citizens, it is submitted, would not be better off than under the Treaty freedoms. The Services Directive would provide the identical remedy

[88] See further M. Klamert, 'Judicial implementation of directives and anticipatory indirect effect: Connecting the dots' (2006) *Common Market Law Review* 1251–75 at 1263. The fact that the Treaty freedoms do not require implementation should not distract from this. For a contrasting view see S. Evans, 'The Services Directive: (too) great expectations? An initial overview of the rights and obligations under the Services Directive', in J. van de Gronden (ed.), *EU and WTO Law on Services: Limits to the Realisation of General Interest Policies within the Services Markets?* (The Hague: Kluwer, 2008), pp. 7–29 at p. 26.

[89] Case 29/84, *Commission v. Germany* [1985] ECR 1661, para. 23.

[90] W.-H. Roth, 'Die Dienstleistungsrichtlinie und der Verbraucherschutz', in S. Leible (ed.), *Die Umsetzung der Dienstleistungsrichtlinie: Chancen und Risken für Deutschland* (Jena: JWV, 2008), pp. 205–35 at p. 212, has argued for the legality and the usefulness of 'doubling' Treaty rules in secondary law on grounds of transparency. We would question an increase of transparency without the implementation of the secondary law into national law.

against national restrictions/requirements already available under the Treaty. Citizens would still need to rely on Community law before national courts instead of relying on a provision of their national law. The only real change would be the ongoing notification obligation vis-à-vis the Commission discussed in Chapter 6. This, it is true, might be more effective in ensuring compliance with these prohibitions than to have them 'only' in the Treaty.[91] However, as already explained, recurrent notification is only foreseen under Articles 15 and 16 and is supposed to result in an infringement procedure at best, without any direct empowerment of individual service providers. We submit that, both on grounds of transparency and for the benefit of the rights of individuals, an active form of implementation is preferable, in spite of the problems mentioned that this may cause in the future.

## 7.6 Conclusion

In substantive terms, the efforts by those Member States analysed more closely in this chapter have been truly sizeable on the basis of the screening obligation during the implementation phase. In this respect, the Services Directive, which has been called the first EU text aimed at regulatory reform at the Member State level,[92] has indeed had a substantial impact on domestic regulation in the Member States.

At the same time, however, the impact of the Services Directive on national administrative systems, which has been considered the greatest potential of the Services Directive in the literature,[93] might fall short in practice. We have seen that, while Germany went beyond what was strictly required for the implementation of the Services Directive, Austria adopted a minimum approach, as did other Member States

[91] Roth, 'Die Dienstleistungsrichtlinie und der Verbraucherschutz', p. 212.

[92] V. Hatzopoulos, 'Forms of mutual recognition in the field of services', in I. Lianos and O. Odudu (eds.), *Regulating Trade in Services: Trust, Distrust and Economic Integration* (Cambridge University Press, 2012), pp. 59–98 at p. 93.

[93] G. Davies, 'Trust and mutual recognition in the Services Directive', in I. Lianos and O. Odudu (eds.), *Regulating Trade in Services: Trust, Distrust and Economic Integration* (Cambridge University Press, 2012), pp. 99–120 at pp. 100–1, 106, noting that there is nothing in EU law that prevents national authorities and courts from taking conservative and free-movement unfriendly positions, and that thus EU law cannot guarantee free movement rights. At the same time, however, he claims that the Services Directive, while no longer referring to the country-of-origin principle, essentially maintains this powerful principle in substance.

such as the Netherlands.[94] It has also been shown that the hopes of the Commission that the Services Directive would foster cooperation and the exchange of best practices have largely not materialized to date.[95] However, results are also uneven in this respect, since in the Netherlands the Services Directive has brought the first rules on transnational administrative assistance with the transposition of Chapter VI of the Services Directive.[96]

Finally, the Services Directive also seems to be a reflection of a profoundly different perspective on EU law between Member States such as Germany in particular and the United Kingdom. While in Germany the Services Directive has kept commentators busy for years and where transposition has been intense and intricate, the United Kingdom placed focus on the screening exercise, but seemed to have no theoretical or legislative problems by simply transposing the Services Directive almost verbatim.[97] Therefore, on several levels the Services Directive gives food for thought on how to nudge states to adopt substantive and procedural change on a larger scale in a certain area of regulation.

In the next chapter we will return to many of the concepts and principles that we have discussed in previous chapters. We will thus again switch from a 'micro' view on services regulation, namely the implementation of EU secondary law, to the bigger picture both in terms of level of abstraction and analytical scope.

[94] Prechal *et al.*, 'The implementation of the Services Directive in the Netherlands', p. 436.
[95] Stelkens *et al.*, 'General comparative report', p. 48.
[96] Prechal *et al.*, 'The implementation of the Services Directive in the Netherlands', p. 466.
[97] See Trybus and Berger, 'The implementation of the Services Directive in the United Kingdom', pp. 644 and 664–5. Compare the lack of any doctrinal references in this chapter with the list of references acompanying the contribution on Germany by M. Mirschberger in the same volume.

# 8 Principles of services law in the EU and the WTO: comparing the comparable

## 8.1 Introduction

In previous chapters we have seen that an important issue in EU law is the balance the Court of Justice strikes between adopting a market access approach on the one hand, and an approach based on tackling any regulation in the Member States that could be perceived as burdensome for foreigners on the other hand. We have also discussed the choice between prohibiting only discriminatory measures and also prohibiting non-discriminatory measures of the Member States. While a focus on market access is more concerned with the breaking down of barriers between the markets of the individual Member States and thus with market integration, the focus with domestic regulation is rather on the *deregulation* of national legal regimes.[1] As already mentioned in the Introduction, in both the EU and the GATS we see a delicate balancing exercise between limiting the reach of its rules for fostering the integration of the Member State markets, or venturing deeper into the regulatory prerogatives of its members.[2] We would argue that

The author acknowledges the contribution of Kathrin Blanck-Putz, Team Leader, DG MARKT, European Commission, Brussels, in the writing of section 8.3.

[1] This holds true irrespective of whether the standard of scrutiny adopted under the domestic regulation approach follows a non-discrimination model or seeks to abolish all kinds of barriers to trade.

[2] The fact that in the context of EU law reference is not commonly made to domestic regulation, but instead to restrictions or obstacles to trade, should not detract from acknowledging this fundamental shared problem. It is thus a misrepresentation of EU law to state that it does not accord much weight to the difference between market access and domestic regulation. For such a view, however, see J. Pauwelyn, 'Rien ne va plus? Distinguishing domestic regulation from market access in GATT and GATS' (2005) *World Trade Review* 131–70 at 141.

the underlying problems in EU law are readily comparable with those prevalent in the WTO regime.

In the literature on services, the regulatory approaches of non-discrimination, mutual recognition and harmonization have been distinguished.[3] Others have distinguished between host state rule, home state rule and harmonization.[4] However, rarely have these different standards and concepts been clearly set apart. Thus, in the debate on the Services Directive, home state rule has been discussed under the term country of origin principle. At the same time, under the name 'home state regulation', it has also been associated with the *Cassis* case law by Wilsher, who has argued that *Cassis* has created the 'rebuttable presumption that goods lawfully sold in other Member States have been adequately regulated to meet host state standards'.[5] Similarly, Diebold has claimed that the *Cassis* rule was 'generally referred to as principle of origin'.[6]

Similar ambiguity exists with the concept of mutual recognition. Thus Article 16 of Directive 2006/123/EC has been qualified as a case of mutual recognition, because it would limit the grounds for justification of national 'requirements'.[7] Recall, however, that Article 16 is titled 'Freedom to provide services' and by its wording represents a prohibition of restrictions. In a similar vein, in the area of media and e-commerce, an 'internal market' clause stipulating that Member States must ensure freedom of reception and must not restrict retransmission on their territory has been called 'an extended application of the mutual recognition principle and the application of the law of the country of

[3] M. Krajewski, *National Regulation and Trade Liberalization in Services: The Legal Impact of the General Agreement on Trade in Services (GATS) on National Regulatory Autonomy* (The Hague: Kluwer, 2003), p. 6.

[4] K. Armstrong, 'Mutual Recognition', in C. Barnard and J. Scott (eds.), *The Law of the Single European Market: Unpacking the Premises* (Oxford and Portland, OR: Hart Publishing, 2002), pp. 225–67 at pp. 228–30. See also M. Poiares Maduro, *We the Court* (Oxford and Portland, OR: Hart Publishing, 2002), pp. 108–10.

[5] Case 120/78, *Rewe-Zentral* [1979] ECR 649. D. Wilsher, 'Does Keck discrimination make any sense? An assessment of the non-discrimination principle within the European Single Market' (2008) 33 *European Law Review* 3–22 at 6 and 14, who has also claimed that the Court has given the job of regulation to the home state, only ensuring that the host state does not unjustifiably discriminate against the home state's regulatory standards.

[6] N. Diebold, 'Standards of non-discrimination in international economic law' (2011) 60(4) *International and Comparative Law Quarterly* 831–65 at 850.

[7] In this sense, M. Möstl, 'Preconditions and limits of mutual recognition' (2010) 2 *Common Market Law Review* 405–36 at 414.

origin'.[8] We will argue that, technically speaking, mutual recognition is not reregulation, since no new laws are applied in the host state. For the same reason, we will show that it is not a conflict of laws clause, because the host state authorities do not apply home state laws; they merely recognize them. Finally, it is important to see that mutual recognition does not lead to deregulation, because in most of its representations, regulatory standards are retained by the host state. Thus, as explained in Chapter 5, Directive 2005/36/EC makes mutual recognition dependant on certain minimum criteria, and allows Member States to impose compensatory measures, such as adaptation tests.[9]

Hence there seems to be some degree of conceptual confusion as to when we should speak of home state rule, host state rule or mutual recognition, which we will address in this chapter. We will also discuss market access and discrimination from a comparative perspective, allowing us to discuss the different issues relating to the various forms of discriminatory treatment in EU and in WTO law, among others. We will also deal with the regulatory approach to what we call differential regulation and double burdens in the conceptual 'nirvana' between the market access standard and the discrimination standard. We will see that, with regard to most of these concepts, we can detect some interesting analogies between EU law and WTO law.

We will, however, start with a comparative analysis of what is referred to as the sectoral and horizontal approaches to liberalizing services, and of the way both regimes exempt certain undertakings and services from their scope of application.

## 8.2 The sectoral and horizontal approaches compared

Recall that the Services Directive is characterized by a proclaimed broad coverage coupled with a wide array of exempted sectors. In defence of this approach, it has been argued that the objectives of the Lisbon Strategy in the EU could not have been attained by relying only on

[8] See M. van Huffel, 'The legal framework for financial services and the internet', in N. Nic Shuibhne (ed.), *Regulating the Internal Market* (Cheltenham and Northampton: Edward Elgar, 2006), pp. 144–80 at p. 157. On these 'second generation' mutual recognition instruments, see V. Hatzopoulos, 'Forms of mutual recognition in the field of services', in I. Lianos and O. Odudu (eds.), *Regulating Trade in Services: Trust, Distrust and Economic Integration* (Cambridge University Press, 2012), pp. 59–98 at pp. 73–4.

[9] Möstl, 'Preconditions and limits of mutual recognition', 423–33.

time-consuming sectoral legislation.[10] However, we would question the sense in providing a comprehensive regulation for precisely those sectors included within the scope of application of the Services Directive, as well as the soundness of a 'negative listing' approach in general, for the following reasons.

First, to continue the previous practice of sectoral directives would, arguably, have avoided attracting the amount of public attention that has so heavily influenced and slowed the process of law-making. It is certainly easier not having to deal with most lobby groups at once, as was the case with the Services Directive. Including the construction sector and the trade sector, on the other hand, has raised some of the most controversial and complex issues with regard to the Services Directive, such as on its relationship with the Posting of Workers Directive, or on labour and social security standards in general. A much conjured-up image in this context has been the plumber from Poland operating abroad under home state laws, who, particularly in France, has been perceived as crowding out more expensive domestic providers. We would argue that devising sectoral regimes for these matters might have made the Union legislator's life a lot easier. However, in such cases the Services Directive's coverage would hardly have justified its proud title, which would have meant utter defeat for the ambitions of the Commission, after already seeing the regulatory heart of its proposal (the country of origin principle discussed below) being abandoned in the co-decision procedure.

Second, a horizontal approach only appears apposite if the sectors concerned are homogenous to some degree. Conversely, sectoral harmonization would seem better suited when different service sectors require heterogeneous rules. In this light, the array of sectors regulated by the Services Directive seems rather the result of a survival of the 'least lobbied' than a selection made in view of the regulatory needs of the sectors covered.[11] While advisory services on the one hand and leisure and recreational services on the other are without doubt of a different nature, they arguably do not justify separate legislation. An entirely different matter is the construction sector, which

[10] C. Barnard, 'Unravelling the Services Directive' (2008) *Common Market Law Review* 323–94 at 327 mentions eighty-three sectors requiring regulation, not counting financial services.

[11] While a large number of services have been excluded because of prior regulation elsewhere, such as financial services, some have been opted out for purely political reasons, such as social services.

is characterized by labour-intensiveness and a propensity for work abroad. It could be argued that, with a more homogenous coverage, the Services Directive might have produced more ambitious rules, and might also have encompassed some other important sectors exempted from the Directive, such as notaries, in exchange for a lesser number of sectors. This might have been achieved by adopting only the rules on administrative cooperation and administrative simplification in a horizontal measure.[12] Thus it at least makes sense that the energy sector is not covered by the Services Directive, since the specifics of this market and the special rules required as a result could hardly have fitted with the rules apposite for the other sectors.

The debate on the sectoral approach versus the horizontal approach for regulating the services sector also exists in the GATS context. The multilateral negotiations on national treatment and market access on telecommunications and on financial services initiated a debate over the efficacy of this sectoral approach as compared to a horizontal, cross-sectoral approach. It has been argued that a general approach to negotiations will economize on negotiation efforts, will lead to the creation of disciplines for all services sectors, and reduces the likelihood of negotiations being captured by sectoral interest groups.[13] However, negotiations over a specific sector, as opposed to a multi-sectoral approach, can potentially oblige some members to make more significant new commitments, whereas a general elimination of government-imposed barriers to guarantee market access would not necessarily pave the way for attaining full liberalization in that sector, or would not even be immediately possible considering the economic structure of a given country.[14] Moreover, one could also argue that negotiating on a sectoral basis has the advantage that some specific sectoral empirical evidence can be used and exchanged between negotiators. Sectoral-based negotiations also take into account the demands and concerns of individual regulators in a specific sector.

Hence it can also be argued that in the WTO there is better potential within sectoral agreements to achieve significant liberalization when

[12] See also S. Griller, 'Two steps forward, how many back? Concluding remarks', in F. Breuss, G. Fink, and S. Griller (eds.), *Services Liberalisation in the Internal Market* (Vienna, New York: Springer, 2008), pp. 225–41 at pp. 232–3.

[13] See P. Low and A. Mattoo, 'Is there a better way? Alternative approaches to liberalization under GATS', in P. Sauvé and R. Stern (eds.), *GATS 2000: New Directions in Services Trade Liberalization* (Washington DC: Brookings, 2000), pp. 449–72 at p. 463.

[14] This applies more prominently to developing countries.

the conditions are right and the ability of any one country to liberalize its own regulations is facilitated.[15] This shows that the issues underpinning the choice of the proper regulatory approach (sectoral or horizontal) are highly comparable in the EU and the WTO.

## 8.3 Exemptions compared

As we have seen throughout this book, several factors can limit the scope of EU law with regard to services, or can exempt certain services from falling under the Treaty rules or under parts of the Treaty. The first is remuneration. An economic activity must be undertaken for consideration.[16] Another important factor is whether a service provider qualifies as an undertaking. If this is not the case, the provider concerned will not fall under the competition law rules, or under the free movement rules of the TFEU, as will be shown below. The nature of the entity providing services is therefore instrumental in limiting the scope of EU law. The third factor is the nature of the service concerned. Services that are rendered in the general interest, be it a non-economic or economic interest, may equally not fall under the free movement rules. What is more important here is, however, that they may also be exempted from the competition law regime. We will now take a closer look at these criteria from a comparative perspective.

Recall that, according to Article 51 TFEU and Article 62 TFEU, free movement rules do not apply to activities connected with the exercise of official authority, whereas Article 106(2) TFEU exempts SGEI from, above all, competition law under the complex regime discussed in Chapter 3. While services claimed to be rendered in official authority are often challenged under the free movement rules mainly because they discriminate against providers from other Member States, SGEI are challenged because their provision is connected with the conferral of special rights by the state. In the WTO, recall that Article I:3(b) GATS exempts services 'supplied in the exercise of governmental authority'.[17] As stipulated by Article I:3(c), these encompass 'any service which is supplied neither on a commercial basis, nor in

[15] See also Competition Bureau Canada, Competition Policy Considerations in the GATS Negotiations, 2001.

[16] Case 36/74, *Walrave* [1974] ECR 1405, para. 4.

[17] Art. I:3(b) GATS. Moreover, as set out in the WTO, GATS, Annex on Air Transport Services, measures affecting air traffic rights and services directly related to their exercise are also explicitly excluded from the GATS.

competition with one or more service suppliers'. This means, first, that both in WTO law and in EU law, SGEI such as those in the network industries on the one hand, and governmental services/services in official authority on the other hand, fall under different regimes. Under WTO law, public services would only be exempted if they could be characterized by the absence of a commercial basis as well as of competition. Under EU law, by contrast, they are governed by Article 106(2) TFEU.[18]

A parallel to SGEI exists under the GATS only in the Annex on Telecommunications and the Reference Paper on Telecommunications. The Annex's Article 5(e) requires WTO Members to ensure that no condition is imposed on access to and use of public telecommunications transport networks and services other than those necessary to safeguard a certain number of objectives in the general interest, such as general availability. Paragraph 3 of the Reference Paper states that each WTO Member has the right to define the kind of universal service obligation it wishes to maintain, provided that these obligations are administered in a 'transparent, non-discriminatory and competitively neutral manner and are not more burdensome than necessary'.[19] Based on case law of the AB on the concept of necessity in a different context, it has been noted that while the DSB could be placed in the difficult position of assessing the importance of the public service obligations in a particular WTO Member, such weighing has so far never been undertaken.[20] It has also been noted that Article 5(e)(i) of the Annex can be seen as being functionally equivalent to Article 106(2) TFEU.[21] Although it has been cautioned that the case law in the EU may not have an impact on the interpretation of the GATS,[22] the similarities here are still striking.

[18] For a slightly different perspective, see M. Krajewski, 'Public services and trade liberalization: mapping the legal framework' (2003) 6(2) *Journal of International Economic Law* 341–67 at 350.

[19] See M. Krajewski, 'Universal service provisions in international agreements of the EU', in Erika Szyszczak *et al.* (eds.), *Developments in Services of General Interest* (TMC Asser, Springer, 2011), pp. 231–50 at pp. 237–41, on the complex issues this provision raises for WTO Members. Krajewski also points to the EU proposal for a Reference Paper on Postal and Courier Services, which contains an analogous clause.

[20] Krajewski, 'Universal service provisions', pp. 237–8.

[21] Krajewski, 'Universal service provisions', p. 238.

[22] See also E. H. Leroux, 'What is a "service supplied in the exercise of governmental authority" under Article I:3(b) and (c) of the General Agreement on Trade in Services?' (2006) 30(3) *Journal of World Trade* 345–85 at 359ff.

As to the GATS criterion of a commercial basis, one could think of looking at how similar issues are dealt with under EU law. Under the GATS, while commercial service supply may refer to activities 'engaged in work designed for the market' without a direct necessity to make a profit, it may also be understood as including the objective of financial gain.[23] The concept of 'commercial' also appears in another context in Article XXVIII(d) GATS, which defines it as 'any type of business or professional establishment'. Based on this definition, some authors have claimed that commercial activity under the GATS would imply a profit-seeking motivation.[24] It has been argued that qualifying as 'commercial' any activity without a profit-oriented element would mean to virtually diminish the coverage of Article I:3(b) and (c) GATS.[25] In contrast, others have adopted a broader perspective by requiring 'an element of economic behavior' for considering an activity as commercial.[26]

Under EU law, any activity 'consisting in offering goods and services on a given market is an economic activity'.[27] The Court has classified entities as undertakings depending on the economic nature of the activity exercised and regardless of the entity's legal status and the way in which it is financed.[28] Thus the maintenance of air navigation safety[29] and the protection of the environment[30] have been exempted, because these activities involve the exercise of official authority aiming at regulating the market instead of participating in it. In a different strand of case law, the Court has exempted activities from the Treaty

[23] See Penguin English Dictionary (London: Penguin, 2000).

[24] See Krajewski, 'Public services and trade liberalization', 351; Leroux, 'What is a "service supplied in the exercise of governmental authority"?', 349. See e.g. WTO Appellate Body Report, *Canada–Measures Relating to Exports of Wheat and Treatment of Imported Grain*, WT/DS276/AB/R, adopted 27 September 2004, paras. 137–51.

[25] Leroux, 'What is a "service supplied in the exercise of governmental authority"?', 354.

[26] R. Adlung 'Public services and the GATS' (2006) 9(2) *Journal of International Economic Law* 455–85 at 463. Such broader view could point to the fact that even a railway monopolist might take into account alternative transport services such buses, taxis or airlines when setting its prices.

[27] Joined Cases C-180–184/98, *Pavlov* [2000] ECR I-6451, para. 75. Conversely, this means that activities that are not concerned with offering goods or services and/or for whose offering no market exists fall outside of the free movement and competition law rules.

[28] See Opinion of AG Poiares Maduro in Case C-205/03 P, *FENIN* [2006] ECR I-6295, paras. 10–32, who has argued that the underlying conditions under which relevant activities are supplied are decisive, and not whether competitive markets exist or not, and that the Court would look at the 'nature, the aim and the rules which govern an activity'.

[29] Case C-364/92, *SAT Fluggesellschaft* [1994] ECR I-43.

[30] Case C-343/95, *Calì* [1997] ECR I-1547.

rules if they are pursued either under specific conditions or for a specific purpose. Thus the Court exempted an institution offering a social security scheme with compulsory membership because of its social objective based on the principle of solidarity and because the benefits bear no relation to the amount of the contribution.[31] However, in other judgments a sectoral pension fund[32] and a public employment agency[33] were both considered undertakings for the purpose of competition law, despite the fact that the fund was not profit-oriented and despite the pursuit of a social objective.[34] We have also seen that in borderline cases the Court differentiates whether institutions are privately or publicly financed.[35] We have also seen that the understanding of what constitutes remuneration has been broadened to include triangular situations and indirect remuneration.[36]

As to the second condition for applying Article I:3(b) and (c) GATS, that services are provided in the absence of competition, we have to note that, under EU law, the competition situation is not an explicit criterion for delimiting exempted and covered services and service providers. SGEI can be exempted even if there is competition in the market, the condition being that the provider offering the SGEI is not too privileged compared to the other market participants. This explains the benchmarks for compensation and the transparency of the process of discharging special rights or obligations. Under the GATS, while there is no dispute settlement practice on the concept of the absence of competition, there are various references to the concept of competition in the GATS and the Annex on Financial Services.[37] Moreover, several decisions by WTO dispute settlement bodies have applied Article III:2 GATT

[31] See Joined Cases C-159/91 and C-160/91, *Poucet* [1993] ECR I-637, para. 18.

[32] Case C-67/96, *Albany* [1999] ECR I-5751, para. 87.

[33] Case C-41/90, *Höfner* [1991] ECR I-1979, para. 22. See also Case C-55/96, *Job Centre* [1997] ECR I-7119.

[34] On the latter count, there are some parallels in EU free movement case law regarding the scope of application of Art. 56 TFEU. Thus, in its *Freskot* decision, the Court exempted a Greek institution conducting a compulsory insurance scheme covering insurable risks. See Case C-355/00, *Freskot AE* v. *Elliniko Dimosio* [2003] ECR I-5263, para. 59. See J. van de Gronden, 'Social services of general interest and EU law', in E. Szyszczak *et al.* (eds.) *Developments in Services of General Interest*, Legal Issues of Services of General Interest (The Hague: TMC Asser, 2011), pp. 123–51 at p. 127.

[35] Case 263/86, *Humbel* [1988] ECR 5365, paras. 17–19.

[36] See Chapter 3.

[37] See e.g. Arts. IX (certain business practices may restrain competition) and XVII (conditions of competition) of the GATS; Annex on Financial Services, para. 1(c) (in competition with a public entity).

dealing with 'directly competitive or substitutable products', as well as with the concept of 'like' products.[38] The ambiguity of this concept in the GATS can be illustrated by the example of a public and a private hospital that compete with each other since they both provide medical care and are targeting the same market. In 1998 the WTO Secretariat acknowledged the existence of an inherent competitive relationship between private and publicly owned hospitals.[39] In 2001, conversely, it stated that 'the co-existence of governmental and private services in the same industry does not mean that they are in competition in the sense of Article I:3(c) and therefore does not invalidate the exclusion from the GATS of the public sector'.[40] Similarly, the field of higher education is prone to conflicting interpretations. The hybrid nature of most higher education systems, where the same university or institute can be publicly funded and at the same time offer commercial education programmes, risks blurring the GATS boundaries and extending its scope of application to all forms of providing higher education.

In conclusion, we would argue that the case law in the EU on what constitutes an undertaking and what qualifies as remuneration could inspire the interpretation of what constitutes a commercial activity under the GATS. SGEI, in contrast, will be difficult to transplant to the GATS, apart from explicit rules such as on telecommunication. The criterion of the absence of competition is too rigid to accommodate any meaningful distinction based on whether a service is provided in the interest of the public.

## 8.4 Home state rule and host state rule

### *8.4.1 Home state rule*

The Commission proposal for the Services Directive would have established the most absolute form of home state rule to date.[41] It

[38] See e.g. WTO Panel Report, *Japan–Taxes on Alcoholic Beverages*, WT/DS8/R, WT/DS10/R, WT/DS11/R, adopted 1 November 1996, paras. 6.22 and 6.28; WTO Appellate Body Report, *United States–Transitional Safeguard Measure on Combed Cotton Yarn from Pakistan*, WT/DS192/AB/R, adopted 5 November 2001.

[39] Background Note on Health and Social Services, 1998, S/C/W/50, para. 39.

[40] WTO, Special Study Nr. 6 on Market Access, 2001, p. 124.

[41] The following builds on and expands parts of M. Klamert, 'Of empty glasses and double burdens: approaches to regulating the services market à propos the implementation of the Services Directive' (2010) *Legal Issues of Economic Integration* 111–32.

would have been of a different nature than what has previously been deemed to represent a country of origin principle in EU secondary law.[42] Under regimes such as the E-commerce Directive 2000/31/EC, the Audiovisual Media Services Directive 2010/13/EU or the Credit Institutions Directive 2006/48/EC,[43] host state authorities would not have been required to apply the laws of the state of establishment of the service provider.[44] Only the version of Article 16 proposed by the Commission would have prescribed such home state rule as a matter of principle.[45]

Host state rule gives rise to specific concerns. The first is that the host state courts would have to apply a foreign legal order.[46] However, this is not very different from the parties to a contract choosing a foreign law to be applied to any dispute between them. Second, service providers might establish in the state with the most advantageous legal regime and then 'export' this regime when operating in another Member State

[42] Art. 3(2) Directive 2000/31/EC, OJ 2000 No. L178/1: 'Member States may not, for reasons falling within the coordinated field, restrict the freedom to provide information society services from another Member State.' This is qualified by para. 4, which allows for derogations 'necessary' for reasons of (further defined) public policy, public health, public security, and 'the protection of consumers, including investors'. Compare A. Lopez-Tarruella, 'A European Community regulatory framework for electronic commerce' (2001) *Common Market Law Review* 1343–55. See also the country of transmission principle in Directive 89/552/EEC, OJ 2007 No. L332/27.

[43] Directive 2006/48/EC, OJ 2006 No. L177/1. See E. Lomnicka, 'The home country control principle in the financial services directives and the case law', in M. Andenas and W.-H. Roth (eds.), *Services and Free Movement in EU Law* (The Hague: Kluwer, 2002), pp. 295–319 at pp. 298–303.

[44] See N. Maydell, 'The Services Directive and existing Community law', in F. Breuss, G. Fink and S. Griller (eds.), *Services Liberalisation in the Internal Market* (Vienna, New York: Springer, 2008), pp. 21–124 at p. 114.

[45] But see R. Craufurd Smith, 'Old wine in new bottles? From the "country of origin principle" to "freedom to provide services" in the European Community Directive on services in the internal market' (2007) *Mitchell Working Paper Series* 10–11; See S. Weatherill, 'Promoting the consumer interest in an integrated services market' (2007) *Mitchell Working Paper Series*, 5.

[46] See S. Griller, 'The new Services Directive of the European Union: hopes and expectations from the angle of a (further) completion of the internal market', General Report, in H. F. Köck and M. M. Karollus (eds.), *The New Services Directive of the European Union*, Féderation Internationale pour le Droit Européen (FIDE), XXIII Congress Linz 2008 (Vienna: Congress, 2008), vol. III, pp. 379–423 at pp. 228–30. See also A. Hatje, 'Services Directive: a legal analysis', in F. Breuss, G. Fink and S. Griller (eds.), *Services Liberalisation in the Internal Market* (Vienna, New York: Springer, 2008), pp. 1–20 at pp. 15–16, and the critical remarks in V. Hatzopoulos, *Regulating Services in the European Union* (Oxford University Press, 2012), pp. 241–3.

('home-state-shopping').[47] Moreover, host state rule requires a careful definition of a measure's scope of application, because within this field the host state would be deprived of regulatory and supervisory powers. Thus, under the country of origin principle in the Commission proposal for the Services Directive, the laws of the Member State of origin would only have applied in the coordinated field. This field would have been 'any requirement applicable to access to service activities or to the exercise thereof'.[48] Thus, within this broad field, foreign law would had to have been applied in the host state by host state authorities, extending the regulatory autonomy and supervisory power of the home state.

Even in this radical form, the borders with host state rule can be blurred. Article 17(17) of the Commission's proposal exempted requirements of the host state 'that are directly linked to the particular characteristics of the place where the service is provided and with which compliance is indispensable for reasons of public policy or public security or for the protection of public health or the environment'. For some national requirements, therefore, host state rules would have applied, subject to a standard of review.

We would argue that there is nothing comparable in WTO law, since home state rule does clearly represent the most direct threat to the regulatory autonomy of a state. This is despite the fact that goods, when they are traded across borders, also export the legal regime under which they have been produced. With goods, however, this 'export' is achieved by mutual recognition, as discussed below. With regard to services and establishments, mutual recognition only applies with regard to qualifications. Note that mutual recognition does not require that host state courts apply a foreign legal order, and therefore avoids one of the problems mentioned above.

### *8.4.2 Host state rule*

Host state rule is a notion rarely used in the EU law context. It implies that the laws of the state where a service provider operates decide on the regulatory standards to be applied to it. As with home state rule, borders may be blurred here. However, host state rule should be the rule

[47] See G. Davies, 'The Services Directive: extending the country of origin principle and reforming public administration' (2007) *European Law Review* 232–45 at 238–9; Craufurd Smith, 'Old wine in new bottles?', 13.

[48] Art. 4(9). See also Rec. 21 Services Directive.

and not the exception to deserve such a name. This would mean that, in order to have host state rule, the host state laws would have to be deemed lawful unless successfully challenged. Conversely, if they were considered unlawful as a matter of principle unless they can be justified, this would not constitute host state rule in our understanding.

We would argue that the restrictions approach in EU Treaty law on services as well as Article 16 Services Directive must be qualified as rather representing host state rule, for the following reasons. First, in spite of the very broad definition of restrictions under the Treaty regime and perhaps the even broader definition of requirements under the Services Directive, there is a blind spot in the scope of application of both regimes.[49] This means that some national laws are not qualified as restrictions or requirements and thus are not considered illegal unless justified.[50] Second, we would argue that authorities in the Member States would not assume the illegality of national laws unless this has been adjudicated by the Court or there is clear precedence.[51] This means that in practice there is a 'bias' for the legality of home state law.[52] If this were different and if Member State authorities on their own initiative were to set aside obstacles to the trade in services, there would not have been a perceived need for the Services Directive's reporting and notification duties.[53] In other words, if the restrictions approach really was *not* host state rule, it would have to be claimed that host state authorities would apply foreign law to service providers operating in their territory, unless their national laws were deemed justified. We would doubt, however, that Austrian authorities apply Hungarian rules on the provision of accountancy services to Hungarian service providers operating in Austria; or that the British industrial code is applied to British maintenance workers rendering their services in Austria. The restrictions approach under the

[49] See also W-H. Roth, 'Die Dienstleistungsrichtlinie und der Verbraucherschutz', in S. Leible (ed.), *Die Umsetzung der Dienstleistungsrichtlinie: Chancen und Risken für Deutschland* (Jena: JWV, 2008), pp. 205–35 at p. 216.

[50] See Chapter 4.

[51] See, for instance, the empirical research on 'contained compliance' by L. Conant, *Justice Contained: Law and Politics in the European Union* (Ithaca: Cornell University Press, 2002), pp. 68–73.

[52] See also L. Albath and M. Giesler, 'Das Herkunftslandprinzip in der Dienstleistungsrichtlinie: eine Kodifizierung der Rechtsprechung?' (2006) *Europäische Zeitschrift für Wirtschaftsrecht* 38–42.

[53] See also Rec. 6 of the Services Directive, where the failure of the Treaty restrictions approach is stated as a reason to propose the Services Directive.

fundamental freedoms as well as under the Services Directive therefore represents host state rule rather than home state rule. As we will discuss below, however, mutual recognition injects some element of home state rule into this.

In order to apply analogous considerations to the GATS, we would have to argue based on the hypothesis that the draft DDR were annexed to the GATS.[54] Only in this event would the DDR be directly binding on all WTO Members, irrespective of whether they have scheduled sectoral commitments. Under the DDR, the necessity test would apply to all non-discriminatory national measures on licensing and qualifications in all sectors. This would extend the current standstill obligation under Article VI:5 GATS to all sectors and would not impose its current prerequisite of nullification or impairment and the lack of reasonable expectations. Even in this hypothetical situation, the GATS would thus remain limited to obstacles to trade connected with licenses and qualifications, while there is no such constraint on the kind of national measures subjected to the restrictions approach in EU law. Even in such a case, however, EU law would be different, because qualification requirements are subject to mutual recognition and harmonization under Directive 2005/36/EC,[55] or are subject to the test of equivalence in the case of licensing requirements.

## 8.5 Mutual recognition as the missing link

### *8.5.1 Introduction*

Mutual recognition has become increasingly fashionable in recent times from a governance perspective.[56] From an economic perspective, recognition of standards reduces the costs of entry for foreign suppliers by avoiding investments in education and training, enabling them to operate in another market.[57] Nicolaïdis has distinguished between

[54] This may seem a rather unrealistic prospect now, but in the long term it might not be completely implausible.

[55] Directive 2005/36/EC of the European Parliament and the Council of 7 September 2005 on the recognition of professional qualifications, OJ 2005 No. L255/22.

[56] See, among many others, S. K. Schmidt, 'Mutual recognition as a new mode of governance' (2007) *Journal of European Public Policy* 667–81 at 671.

[57] J. A. Marchetti and P. C. Mavroidis, 'I now recognize you (and only you) as equal: an anatomy of (mutual) recognition agreements in the GATS', in I. Lianos and O. Odudu (eds.), *Regulating Trade in Services: Trust, Distrust and Economic Integration* (Cambridge University Press, 2012), pp. 415–44 at p. 419.

'pure' and 'managed' mutual recognition.[58] Mutual recognition has been classified (1) based on its origin – that is EU or WTO law, (2) based on the legal instruments used – pure mutual recognition without any regulatory instrument organizing it, non-binding standards, secondary legislation, (3) based on the degree of harmonization, and (4) based on the way it is used by economic operators – as a sword to gain market access or as a shield to avoid a burden.[59]

While these categories overlap considerably, they illustrate the variety of rules that can be labelled under mutual recognition. The fact that mutual recognition can be as binding or flexible as required has been considered its main advantage.[60] At the same time, however, this reveals a difficulty in defining the core characteristics of this principle. In the following section, we will briefly discuss the role of mutual recognition in the respective treaty regimes, before we explore the nature of mutual recognition and its relationship with the harmonization standard, a relationship that has been discussed in the context of both EU and WTO law.

### *8.5.2 Mutual recognition in the GATS and the EU Treaty*

In the EU Treaties, mutual recognition in the services context is mentioned in Article 53(1) TFEU, which provides the mandate for enacting directives for the mutual recognition of diplomas, certificates and other evidence of formal qualifications. This provision has been interpreted broadly as allowing 'any measures concerning the access to and exercise of a self-employed activity'.[61] However, while this makes sense in the context of the definition of the scope of EU competences, it does not provide any clarity on what defines mutual recognition as a regulatory standard.

Mutual recognition in the WTO in general, with the exception of the SPS Agreement,[62] and in the GATS specifically, has not played a

[58] K. Nicolaïdis, 'Trusting the Poles? Constructing Europe through mutual recognition' (2007) *Journal of European Public Policy* 682–98 at 688.

[59] Hatzopoulos, 'Forms of mutual recognition in the field of services', pp. 70–2.

[60] Hatzopoulos, 'Forms of mutual recognition in the field of services', pp. 98.

[61] A. Randelzhofer and U. Forsthoff, 'Art. 47 para. 19', in E. Grabitz and M. Hilf (eds.), *Das Recht der Europäischen Union* (Munich: Beck, 2001).

[62] The SPS Agreement requires Members to allow plant and animal products that conform to the Codex Alimentarius unless they can defend their own stricter standard. See P. Holmes, 'The WTO and the EU: some constitutional comparisons', in G. de Búrca and J. Scott (eds.), *The EU and the WTO: Legal and Constitutional Issues* (Oxford and Portland, OR: Hart Publishing, 2002), pp. 59–80 at p. 69.

role comparable to the one it has had in EU law to date. This is despite predictions that the 'logic of Cassis-style "mutual recognition" or functional parallelism' would inevitably emerge under the GATT as well as part of the necessity test.[63] Mutual recognition has been referred to in relation to Article XVI GATS as comprising an obligation of mutual recognition of services originating in other WTO Members.[64] Article VII GATS permits the conclusion of recognition agreements, which becomes pertinent when a WTO Member unilaterally or bilaterally recognizes foreign qualifications and licenses, on which there has, however, been only insubstantial activity.[65] Article VI:4 GATS provides for procedural obligations for WTO Members that make specific commitments on professional services. Only the Accountancy Disciplines and the draft DDR contain a substantive obligation of mutual recognition for qualifications held by foreigners. Should such a general obligation become binding under the GATS by the adoption of the DDR, this would render recognition agreements superfluous and might be a powerful tool for liberalizing markets. We would even argue that the prevention of regulatory duplication would be the most logical first step in rendering the provision of services less burdensome and, thus, in fulfilling the mandate in Article VI:4 GATS.

### *8.5.3 The nature of mutual recognition*

It has been argued that mutual recognition would normally not be possible without limiting it to products/services from countries with largely equivalent standards,[66] or some underlying form of minimum approximation of substantive standards.[67] It has also been argued that if the notion of mutual recognition were to have any distinct meaning, it should require some degree of referral to the legal or factual situation in the home state.[68] Without an obligation of the host state to consider regulatory decisions or factual aspects of home state rule and

[63] See J. H. H. Weiler, 'Epilogue: Towards a common law of international trade', in J. H. H. Weiler (ed.), *The EU, the WTO, and the NAFTA* (Oxford University Press, Collected Courses of the Academy of European Law, 2001), pp. 201–32 at p. 221.

[64] Hatzopoulos, 'Forms of mutual recognition in the field of services', p. 70. See also J. Trachtman, 'Embedding mutual recognition at the WTO' (2007) 14(5) *Journal of European Public Policy* 780–99.

[65] Marchetti and Mavroidis, 'I now recognize you (and only you) as equal', pp. 421, 427 *et passim*.

[66] Holmes, 'The WTO and the EU', p. 69.

[67] Möstl, 'Preconditions and limits of mutual recognition', 415.

[68] Armstrong, 'Mutual recognition', p. 231 has called this 'other-regarding'.

recognize them as being equivalent or at least 'functionally equivalent' to its own standards, it has been found hard to speak of mutual *recognition.*[69] Thus, even in its parts on 'automatic recognition', Directive 2005/36/EC requires the host state to consider the amount of time the applicant has spent in a certain profession in the home state.[70]

As mentioned above, mutual recognition has been associated with both general prohibitions as such, and with market access guarantees more specifically. Thus it has often been argued that the *Cassis* case has introduced mutual recognition into EU law.[71] We would respond that from there it is only a small step to arguing that Articles VII or XVI GATS are based on the principle of mutual recognition. After all, judging only by the regulatory approach they represent, there is little difference between the *Cassis* principle and market access under the GATS. The differences are rather in the enforcement sphere, where clearly the direct effect of EU law has a decisive impact for the benefit of economic operators, as explained in Chapter 2.

We would not support an understanding that equates mutual recognition with home state rule or the country of origin principle.[72] As has been foreseen in the Commission proposal for the Services Directive 2006/123/EC, as explained above, home state rule and the country of origin principle requires the application of foreign law, leaving no room for the host state to examine and/or recognize decisions taken by the home state. In contrast, mutual recognition does not reallocate regulatory power in the sense of imposing the law to be applied in the host state.[73] This is also made clear in the Services Directive. Recall that its Article 10(3) provides that 'conditions for granting authorisation for a new establishment shall not duplicate requirements and controls which are equivalent or essentially comparable as regards their purpose to which the provider is already subject in another Member

[69] See Armstrong, 'Mutual recognition', p. 230: 'Mutual recognition requires that the regulatory history of a product, service or worker acquired in the home state cannot be ignored when it comes to considering what legitimate regulatory controls may be applied in the host state.'

[70] Arts. 16–20 in conjunction with Annex IV of Directive 2005/36/EC.

[71] Case 120/78, *Rewe-Zentral* [1979] ECR 649.

[72] For such a view, see C. Barnard, *The Substantive Law of the EU: The Four Freedoms*, 3rd edn (Oxford University Press, 2010), p. 381.

[73] This is also submitted by Möstl, 'Preconditions and limits of mutual recognition', 282–3. See also M. Cornils, 'Artikel 10 Voraussetzungen für die Erteilung der Genehmigung', in M. Schlachter and C. Ohler (eds.), *Europäische Dienstleistungsrichtlinie* (Baden-Baden: Nomos, 2008), para. 14.

State or in the same Member State'. Recital 61 of the Services Directive expounds that this should not require the application of home state laws in the host state.[74]

However, it can be said that mutual recognition represents a link between home state and host state rule for cases of double burden. By preventing the duplication of tests in the host state to which a service provider had already been subjected in its home state, this principle injects an element of home state rule into a host state rule approach.[75] Consider the test of equivalence applied in cases such as *Säger*, according to which a host state burden serving the same regulatory standard whose compliance has already been required by the home state must not be applied.[76] This test prescribes that the home state's tests and licenses must be recognized by the host state. This is commonly referred to as a case of double burden and is discussed more specifically below. In such a constellation, the test of equivalence entails that the home state retains a quasi-regulatory, extraterritorial role. After all, the recognition of standards of another Member State inevitably constitutes a loss of regulatory autonomy.[77]

### *8.5.4 The relationship between mutual recognition and harmonization*

Three views can be distinguished on the way mutual recognition relates to harmonization in EU law. The first view sees mutual recognition as a substitute if harmonization is not possible. Thus it has been argued that

[74] Rec. 61 Directive 2006/123/EC: 'The provision relating to the non-duplication of conditions for the granting of an authorisation should not prevent Member States from applying their own conditions as specified in the authorisation scheme. It should only require that competent authorities, when considering whether these conditions are met by the applicant, take into account the equivalent conditions which have already been satisfied by the applicant in another Member State. This provision should not require the application of the conditions for the granting of an authorisation provided for in the authorisation scheme of another Member State.'

[75] Emphasised by C. Calliess, 'Europäischer Binnenmarkt und europäische Demokratie: Von der Dienstleistungsfreiheit zur Dienstleistungsrichtlinie – und wieder Retour?' (2007) *Deutsches Verwaltungsblatt* 336–46 at 341.

[76] Case C-76/90, *Säger* [1991] ECR I-4221, para. 15: 'in so far as that interest is not protected by the rules to which the person providing the services is subject in the Member State in which he is established'. On this and the forerunner Joined Cases 110 and 111/78, *van Wesemael* [1979] ECR 35, see J. Snell, 'Free movement of services and the Services Directive: the legitimacy of the case law', in J. van de Gronden (ed.), *EU and WTO Law on Services: Limits to the Realisation of General Interest Policies within the Services Markets?* (The Hague: Kluwer, 2008), pp. 31–54 at pp. 37–8.

[77] Möstl, 'Preconditions and limits of mutual recognition', 407.

when substantive harmonization is not available, mutual recognition is adopted on the basis of secondary law.[78] Another view has presented mutual recognition as an instrument of last resort if harmonization has failed.[79] Weiler has also emphasized the limitations of mutual recognition with regard to its market impact, which would ultimately require the intervention of the legislator.[80]

Fourth, and most critically, mutual recognition has been presented as a harbinger of harmonization. Davies has thus argued that mutual recognition enables trade and by doing so, it would create a situation in which harmonization is 'politically necessary and possible'.[81] Successful mutual recognition would thus gradually lead to harmonization.[82] It has been suggested that this makes mutual recognition a 'dangerous toy', as it makes harmonization difficult to avoid at a certain stage of economic integration.[83] We would argue that this might perhaps be true for the mutual recognition of goods. However, even there the empirical evidence presented by Davies is thin, pointing to the rules on alcohol levels that were harmonized after the *Cassis* judgment.[84] On this basis, Zúñiga Schroder has cautioned parties to trade agreements from seeking a similar level of integration as the EU.[85]

For services, it seems that mutual recognition is rather less 'dangerous' in terms of luring Member States into eventually accepting harmonization that they would initially have eschewed. We can think here of professional qualifications, the mutual recognition clause in Article 5(3) Services Directive and other recent legal acts such as Directive

[78] See Möstl, 'Preconditions and limits of mutual recognition', 406, also pointing to the new field of application in the area of freedom, security and justice. He makes the pertinent remark that, while mutual recognition in the internal market supports economic freedom, mutual recognition in the area of freedom, security and justice, such as with the European arrest warrant, curtail the freedom of individuals. See *ibid.*, 409.

[79] See Hatzopoulos, *Regulating Services in the European Union*, p. 269, on the area of financial services.

[80] Weiler, 'Epilogue: Towards a Common Law of International Trade', pp. 223–5.

[81] G. Davies, 'Is mutual recognition an alternative to harmonization? Lessons on trade and tolerance of diversity from the EU', in F. Ortino and L. Bartels (eds), *Regional Trade Agreements and the WTO Legal System* (Oxford University Press, 2006), pp. 265–80 at p. 271.

[82] Davies, 'Is mutual recognition an alternative to harmonization?', 271.

[83] Davies, 'Is mutual recognition an alternative to harmonization?', 275–6.

[84] Davies, 'Is mutual recognition an alternative to harmonization?', 271. See H. Zúñiga Schroder, *Harmonization, Equivalence and Mutual Recognition of Standards in WTO Law* (Alphen/Rijn: Kluwer Law International, 2011), p. 162, who also points to foodstuffs.

[85] Zúñiga Schroder, *Harmonization, Equivalence and Mutual Recognition of Standards*, p. 171.

2011/24/EU.[86] In all these cases, harmonization has not really been an option because of the unwillingness of Member States to fully align their national education systems, their administrative procedures, or issues as mundane as medical prescriptions. Other areas in the services field are even further away from embracing mutual recognition, let alone harmonization, such as gambling or SGEI. The reasons are that services are largely provided by natural persons, and their qualification, necessary authorizations and the conditions under which they operate are the subject of regulation.[87] However, these matters do not easily allow for standardization, certification[88] or harmonization because the underlying national rules are not primarily technical but political, such as the nature of the educational system.[89]

Thus we would argue that mutual recognition might be the only politically viable way for liberalization of services, and might not necessarily be an antechamber to harmonization.

## 8.6 Market access

### *8.6.1 Introduction*

We would suggest that a comparison of the different regulatory approaches in the EU and the WTO, and those based on discrimination or market access in particular, must acknowledge the differences that exist between general prohibitions with a strong inherent balancing element on the one hand, and prohibitions based on blacklists on the other hand. Examples of the former can be found in both EU law, with the prohibition of discriminations and the prohibition of restrictions based on the Treaty, and in the Services Directive, as well as in the GATS where Article VII provides for national treatment and Article XVII for a prohibition of the denial of market access in scheduled sectors. Article XVI looks like a blacklist of national measures that violate market access, but is open to justification under Article XII GATS. A true blacklist has been introduced in Articles 14 and 16 Services Directive in the sense that measures listed there cannot be justified by public interest objectives. We have stated earlier that this is one of the substantive

[86] Directive 2011/24/EU of the European Parliament and the Council of 9 March 2011 on the application of patients' rights in cross-border healthcare, OJ 2011 No. L88/45.

[87] Hatzopoulos, 'Forms of mutual recognition in the field of services', p. 63, has called such rules 'non-incorporated'.

[88] The 'new approach' with goods.

[89] See in a similar vein, Hatzopoulos, *Regulating Services in the European Union*, pp. 274–8.

changes in the Services Directive and potentially more momentous than might generally be assumed.

The *US–Gambling* case, discussed below, is a good illustration of how the approaches to regulating services may be different in the WTO and the EU, but how the underlying issues may however be quite similar.[90] We will start by comparing whether national measures are scrutinized rather by their form or their effect.

### 8.6.2 *Form and effect in EU and WTO law*

As previously explained, the GATS prohibits an exhaustive list of measures under Article XVI once sectors have been committed. Thus, in contrast to EU law, market access in the WTO is a formal and narrow notion, primarily depending on a measure's form and not its effects.[91] If we keep this difference in mind, this does not in our opinion make a comparison between EU law and WTO law inappropriate, or even dangerous, as has been submitted by Snell.[92]

Under EU law, the form of a national measure matters little because EU law does not clearly define what constitutes an impediment to market access. In this context, rules preventing market access, such as a total ban of imports or a total ban of a product on the one hand, have been distinguished from those rules that have an unequal impact on market access.[93] One result of this is that in EU law there are no defined categories of measures that must be interpreted and applied to the facts of a case. Instead, under EU law the qualification of a national measure as a restriction to market access must be assessed on a case-by-case basis. As already discussed, this is even more pertinent in the services regime, where the equivalent to selling arrangements and product requirements is missing. Thus, under EU law the effect of a national measure is decisive for an assessment of relevance for market access.[94] Recall that in *Alpine Investment* the Court qualified a prohibition of cold calling as a restriction of the freedom to provide services, arguing that it 'directly affects access to the market in services in the other Member States and is thus capable of hindering intra-Community

[90] For a different perspective, see J. Snell, 'The notion of market access: a concept or a slogan?' (2010) 47 *Common Market Law Review* 437–72.
[91] Snell, 'The notion of market access', 441.
[92] Snell, 'The notion of market access', 443.
[93] Snell, 'The notion of market access', 447–8.
[94] Snell, 'The notion of market access', 442.

trade in services'.[95] Similarly, in the case on the ban of canvassing by qualified accountants, the Court held that this could 'affect professionals from other Member States more, by depriving them of an effective means of penetrating the national market in question'.[96]

On the other hand, this does not mean that the Court necessarily compares the effect of the pertinent measure on market access for domestic providers with the effect the measure has on providers from other Member States, as it did in the *Gourmet* case under the free movement of goods. In cases that apply the restrictions approach, the Court may use the language of market access simply to qualify a national measure as restriction. Thus the Court has recently handed down a preliminary ruling case on a national law conferring exclusive rights to organize horse race betting.[97] The Court noted that 'any restriction concerning the supply of games of chance over the internet is more of an obstacle to operators established outside the Member State concerned', because it deprives those operators of a 'means of marketing that is particularly effective for directly accessing that market'. Consequently, however, the Court of Justice did not reason specifically in terms of market access, but simply examined the justifications brought forward by the Member State concerned.

Yet more recent case law has buttressed the impression that bans on the remote supply of services should be treated as restrictions on market access. In *Ker-Optika* the Court examined the second *Keck* criterion of market access with regard to the pertinent prohibition of the sale of contact lenses by mail order by arguing:

> It is clear that the prohibition on selling contact lenses by mail order deprives traders from other Member States of a particularly effective means of selling those products and thus significantly impedes access of those traders to the market of the Member State concerned.[98]

Reid has therefore correctly pointed to the analogous decisions in *DocMorris* as supporting the view that a ban of remote supply of gambling services should be treated as a restriction on market access.[99]

[95] Case C-384/93, *Alpine Investments* [1995] ECR I-1141, para. 38.
[96] Case C-119/09, *Société fiduciaire* [2011] ECR I-2551, para. 43.
[97] Case C-212/08, *Zeturf* [2011] ECR I-5633, para. 74.
[98] Case C-108/09, *Ker-Optika* [2010] ECR I-12213, para. 54.
[99] Case C-322/01, *DocMorris* [2003] ECR I-14887. See E. Reid, 'Regulatory autonomy in the EU and WTO: defining and defending its limits' (2010) 44(4) *Journal of World Trade* 877–901 at 898.

As we will see next, this is exactly the result adopted by the AB in *US–Gambling*.

### 8.6.3 *A comparative view of* US–Gambling

Recall that Antigua and Barbuda had brought a complaint against the USA regarding measures against online gambling at different federal levels affecting the cross-border supply of gambling and betting services. The central argument for deciding this case in favour of Antigua and Barbuda was that the category of 'limitations on the number of service suppliers whether in the form of numerical quotas, monopolies, exclusive service suppliers or the requirements of an economic needs test' in Article XVI GATS was interpreted to also prohibit *zero* quotas, that is a complete ban on the provision of a certain service.[100] Thus the US laws were considered a violation of market access in a sector in which the USA had made commitments.[101] While we might simply agree with the decision of the AB because of the special character of the GATS,[102] we would suggest that the finding of the AB is also apposite when adopting a comparative perspective.

The AB has been criticized for mistaking the effect of a domestic regulation with its form in this case.[103] It has been argued that by confusing a prohibition of online gambling with a numerical quota, *any* non-discriminatory measure taken by a WTO Member would have to be deemed to affect market access, including requirements such as a driving test for taxi drivers.[104] However, it should be considered that not every national measure that is non-discriminatory leads to the complete ban of a certain services activity. Licensing requirements and qualification requirements such as driving tests are examples of non-discriminatory measures that do not close off the market, but 'merely' reduce the number of market participants.[105]

[100] WTO Appellate Body Report, *United States–Measures Affecting the Cross-Border Supply of Gambling and Betting Services (US–Gambling)*, WT/DS285/AB/R, adopted 20 April 2005, paras. 225–34.

[101] On this issue, see the discussion of judicial activism in Chapter 2.

[102] See also L. van den Hende, 'GATS, dispute settlement and concerns about WTO Members' regulatory autonomy: the need for a practical interpretation of the GATS following *US-Gambling*', in D. Horovitz, D. Moulis and D. Steger (eds.), *Ten Years of WTO Dispute Settlement* (London: International Bar Association, 2007), pp. 259–78 at pp. 259–78.

[103] Pauwelyn, 'Rien ne va plus?', 159–61.

[104] But see Pauwelyn, 'Rien ne va plus?', 160, 166.

[105] This could also be argued with respect to economic needs tests if they were not mentioned in Art. XVI GATS.

In criticisms of the finding in *US–Gambling*, a distinction between quantitative and qualitative measures has also been relied on, presenting the argument that only quantitative measures should come under Article XVI GATS, while qualitative non-discriminatory measures should be governed by Article VI GATS.[106] It has been claimed that the qualitative nature of limiting access by one (the cross-border) mode lies in the policy preference that is expressed for the provision by other modes such as commercial presence in the present context.[107] We would argue that there is no difference between the total ban of a mode of providing a certain service on the one hand, and a numerical quota greater than zero on the other hand. A complete prohibition is no more a qualitative regulation than a numerical quota. Both measures primarily reduce the number of market participants; that they may additionally influence the choice of mode to use to enter a market is a subordinate effect.

The fallacy of this thought is illustrated by imagining the case of a sector where services are predominantly provided by one mode and the other modes are not alternatives from an economic perspective. If this one economically viable mode were banned, we would argue that this would have to qualify as relevant for market access. This argument can be made even in the gambling context. With gambling, the costs of market entry are higher in terms of commercial presence compared to the cross-border option, because it is clearly more expensive to build a casino than to open a shop on the Internet.[108] Prohibiting online gambling may therefore lead to more establishments by foreign providers, but it is at the same time bound to reduce the number of foreign providers entering the market. This point can also be made from the EU law perspective: it could hardly be argued that the prohibition of cold calling in a case such as *Alpine Investment* does *not* concern market access, because direct marketing by regular mail was still allowed in the Netherlands, when the latter is much less effective for market entry.

We may see the *US–Gambling* case from yet another comparative perspective, if we consider the repercussions of qualifying a national

[106] D. Prévost, 'Services and public policy regulation in WTO law: the example of the US-Gambling case', in J. van de Gronden (ed.), *EU and WTO Law on Services: Limits to the Realisation of General Interest Policies within the Services Markets?* (The Hague: Kluwer, 2008), pp. 215–46 at p. 243, arguing that the AB blurred the line between these two provisions. See also Pauwelyn, 'Rien ne va plus?', 162.

[107] Pauwelyn, 'Rien ne va plus?', 164–5.

[108] This seems to be the underlying assumption by Pauwelyn, 'Rien ne va plus?', 165.

measure as *not* impairing market access under the GATS and EU law. Counterintuitively, these may potentially be even smaller in EU law than in WTO law. Under the GATS, such a measure would be exempted from the scope of Article XVI, meaning that it could only be covered by Article VI GATS on domestic regulation. Under this provision, the measure concerned would not be prohibited under the current legal status of the disciplines on the one hand, and in view of the high threshold for coming under the standstill obligation of Article VI:5 GATS on the other hand. We would submit, however, that the 'price' for exempting a measure from the reach of Article XVI GATS is not much greater than in EU law. Under the latter regime, a measure that is not affecting market access would be entirely unassailable unless it is discriminatory, while under the GATS it might in the future still come under the DDR once they are formally integrated. Moreover, even though the standstill obligation in Article VI:5 GATS is difficult to apply, it is more than what would apply under the freedom to provide services or the Services Directive. We would thus have to conclude that the GATS, at least potentially, is stricter on regulating impairments to market access in scheduled sectors compared to the EU law regime. Note, however, that this is arguably more than compensated for by defining measures affecting access to the market for foreign providers under Article XVI GATS so narrowly.

Nonetheless, under the GATS we would also have to accept that a ban on providing online services that is not qualified as a measure prohibited by Article XVI GATS would most likely survive the review under Article VI GATS.[109] However, this would lead to the curious outcome that, whereas WTO Members that completely ban a certain activity in a committed sector would only fall under Article VI GATS, a quota of 95 per cent would be prohibited under Article XVI GATS. This means that in order to prevent the nullification of the initial commitment to market access in a given sector, the only effective approach is to subject complete bans under Article XVI GATS.

### *8.6.4 Conclusion*

Thus, both from a comparative perspective and from a systematic perspective, the finding of the AB in *US–Gambling* makes sense. In contrast, the market access approach should arguably be less about the rule itself and much more about its (deterrent) effect. Among other things,

[109] See also Pauwelyn, 'Rien ne va plus?', 167.

this entails that only with the latter approach is it apposite to examine whether there are other means of entering the relevant market that are equally or even more effective than the one closed off by a national measure, as the Court did in *DocMorris*.[110]

## 8.7 Non-discrimination

### *8.7.1 Introduction*

The most striking difference between non-discrimination in the EU and the WTO is, from an EU perspective, that WTO law distinguishes between MFN treatment and national treatment, and, from a WTO perspective, that there is no MFN treatment in the relations between the EU and third countries.[111] As regards the different forms of discrimination, the GATS outlaws both directly discriminatory measures as well as indirectly discriminatory measures.[112] Both types of discrimination are subject to Article XVII GATS and may only be justified by the general exceptions under Article XIV GATS. In the GATS there is a clear systematic exclusivity between discriminatory measures regulated by Article XVII GATS on the one hand, and domestic regulation provided in Article VI GATS on the other hand.

Under EU Treaty law, as explained, findings of direct discrimination in the context of services have been based on a narrow interpretation of the concept of direct discrimination. A residence requirement was not seen as directly discriminatory.[113] Different justification regimes apply to openly discriminatory measures on the one hand, and to indirectly discriminatory measures and non-discriminatory measures on the other hand. The Services Directive, as we have argued above, completely forbids any form of discrimination within its scope of application. This severity in the treatment of open discrimination in the EU has also been noted in the WTO context, where it has been

[110] See E. Spaventa, 'Annotation to Case C-442/02, Caixa-Bank France v. Ministère de l'Économie, des Finances et de l'Industrie' (2005) 42(4) *Common Market Law Review* 1151–68. See also Chapter 4.

[111] See M. Cremona, 'Neutrality or discrimination? The WTO, the EU and External Trade', in G. de Búrca and J. Scott (eds.), *The EU and the WTO: Legal and Constitutional Issues* (Oxford and Portland, OR: Hart Publishing, 2002), pp. 151–84 at p. 153 on the first point, and pp. 166–7 in particular on the second argument.

[112] Möstl, 'Preconditions and limits of mutual recognition', 405.

[113] See E. Spaventa, 'On discrimination and the theory of mandatory requirements' (2002) 3 *Cambridge Yearbook of European Legal Studies* 457–78 at 461.

argued by Hudec that there is no textual basis for a different treatment, yet that there might be some pressure to relax the standard of review for de facto discrimination, in particular through the application of Article XX GATT.[114] If such difference in treatment would occur through the aims and effects test, it should be noted that this does not refer to the justification stage, but to the stage of establishing the breach in the first place. This is where a claim of de facto discrimination might be easier to rebut in WTO law.[115]

In the following section, we will analyse various constellations that have been discussed in the context of discrimination, or in our opinion should be discussed in this context. We will distinguish between different forms of discrimination that are distinct from *de jure*, open or direct discrimination. Note that our primary aim here is to enhance the understanding of the different forms that discrimination may take, and to draw analogies between the treatments accorded to them in the two regimes under examination. We will start by discussing the way the comparator is applied in EU and WTO law.

### *8.7.2 Likeness and the* tertium comparationis

A central divergence in the way discriminatory measures are governed in the EU and the WTO respectively concerns the concept of likeness. Recall that Article XVII GATS provides that formally identical treatment or formally different treatment may be accorded to services or service suppliers. Likeness, therefore, is a precondition for the finding of discrimination under the GATS. In other words, only if services and/or service suppliers are 'like' can there be a violation of a full commitment for national treatment in a sector. Thus discrimination in the GATS is always assessed with a view to the nature of the foreign actor or service concerned.

As already discussed, in *EC–Bananas III* the AB rejected the relevance of the so-called 'aims and effects test' under Article XVII GATS, arguing that the aims and effects of a measure are in no way 'relevant in determining whether that measure is inconsistent with those provisions'.[116] In *China–Audiovisual Products* the AB referred to the *US–FSC* finding that the examination of whether a measure involves 'less

[114] R. E. Hudec, *Essays on the Nature of International Trade Law* (London: Cameron May, 1999), pp. 362–3.

[115] See, using other words, J. Flett, 'WTO space for national regulation: requiem for a diagonal vector test' (2013) 16(1) *Journal of International Economic Law* 37–90 at 57.

[116] WTO Appellate Body Report, *EC–Bananas III*, WT/DS27/AB/R, para. 241. See Chapter 1.

favourable treatment' must be grounded in close scrutiny of the 'fundamental thrust and effect of the measure itself', but not 'on the actual effects of the contested measure in the marketplace'.[117] However, as has been argued by Diebold, the comparator could either be an objective standard interpreting the concept of like products purely on formal grounds, an economic standard looking at competitive relationship or a subjective standard that considers the *tertium* to be the regulatory purpose.[118] Diebold has pointed to *US–Clove Cigarettes*, which in his view has taken into account regulatory context under the likeness analysis under Article 2.1 TBT Agreement, thus reversing previous rejections of the aims and effects test under the GATT and GATS.[119]

In EU law, in contrast, likeness has commonly not been an issue in assessing discriminatory measures imposed by Member States.[120] Consequently, all the complexities we encounter in WTO law on this issue have been absent in EU law. The reason for this divergence, we submit, is twofold. First, in the GATT and GATS the element of likeness is a contractual given, which cannot be ignored, while in the EU the explicit references to discrimination in the Treaties only concern the obligation to award equal treatment to individuals/companies/services of other Member States. Second, under the GATS the scheduling of commitments, including the one on national treatment, is sectoral and subsectoral in nature. It follows that violations of these commitments must equally be assessed against the sector concerned since the commitment to award national treatment only applies to this specific kind of service. Under EU law, in contrast, it suffices to argue that a Member

[117] Appellate Body Report, *China–Measures Affecting Trading Rights and Distribution Services for Certain Publications and Audiovisual Entertainment Products*, WT/DS363/AB/R, adopted 19 January 2010, paras. 7.1130–7.1131.

[118] Diebold, 'Standards of non-discrimination in international economic law', 836–9. On this see also J. H. H. Weiler, 'Law, culture, and values in the WTO: gazing into the crystal ball', in D. Bethlehem *et al.* (eds.), *The Oxford Handbook of International Trade Law* (Oxford University Press, 2009), pp. 750–72, pp. 758–70.

[119] Diebold, 'Standards of non-discrimination in international economic law', 840. See also, similarly, Flett, 'WTO space for national regulation', 60–76, arguing that the aims and effects test is relevant in the context of the less favourable treatment analysis.

[120] See the discussion in G. de Búrca, 'Unpacking the concept of discrimination in EC and international trade law', in C. Barnard and J. Scott (eds.), *The Law of the Single European Market: Unpacking the Premises* (Oxford and Portland, OR: Hart Publishing, 2002), pp. 181–95 at pp. 192–3. However, see Joined Cases C-372/09 and C-373/09, *Peñarroja* [2011] ECR I-1785, para. 50, where the Court mentioned the abolition of any restriction for a provider of services established in another Member State 'in which he lawfully provides similar services'.

State treats individuals/companies/services of other Member States differently from its own nationals/companies/services. In other words, the proof of unequal treatment based on nationality or on equivalent criteria in the case of indirect discrimination is enough to establish a violation of the Treaty. It is, in contrast, immaterial to compare individuals/companies/services under any further element such as their classification or the sector commitments that have been inscribed. This leads to another difference between EU law and WTO law on this issue.

While in WTO law DSBs look for the likeness between individuals/companies/services concerned as a first step in assessing discrimination, the ECJ mostly conducts a one-step test under the title 'objective justification', as discussed above.[121] Thus, while the ECJ is not discussing likeness, it often looks at regulatory intent in a first stage. Cremona has implied that this also explains why the EC in the *Bananas* case had defended its market organization as the pursuit of 'entirely legitimate policies', which might have provided an objective justification if the case had been heard before the ECJ.[122] Under WTO law, it has been proffered that a separate assessment of regulatory intent would require an explicit justification or exception clause, such as exists in Article 36 TFEU.[123] Provisions such as Article XIV GATS were too static and could not accommodate new public policy concerns such as environmental protection or consumer protection, Diebold has argued.[124] However, recall that the ECJ has taken on board environmental protection at least as an additional ground for justification under Article 36 TFEU.[125]

Recent EU case law, however, shows examples of a two-tier test on discrimination. In *Commission* v. *Spain (Shopping Centers)*, the Court firstly held that it is incumbent upon the Commission to prove by providing all factual information that a contested legislation has indirectly discriminatory effects.[126] This would mean in the pertinent case that the Commission would have had to show that large retail

121 See Chapter 4. According to Diebold, the subjective standard, which integrates the assessment of regulatory intent into the examination as to whether there is a discriminatory treatment in the first place is rarely used in WTO dispute settlement. See Diebold, 'Standards of non-discrimination in international economic law', 849.

122 Cremona, 'Neutrality or discrimination?', 155–6.

123 Diebold, 'Standards of non-discrimination in international economic law', 850.

124 Diebold, 'Standards of non-discrimination in international economic law', 850.

125 Diebold's comparison in this respect with the prohibition of restrictions and the open list of justification is not fully apposite in our view. The ECJ has never ascribed to Art. 36 TFEU a flexible nature that would justify the introduction of mandatory requirements.

126 Case C-400/08, *Commission* v. *Spain (Shopping Centers)* [2011] ECR I-1915, paras. 58–9.

establishments were treated differently in Spain from other retail establishments and that that difference constituted a disadvantage for large retail establishments. Moreover, the Commission would have had to show that that difference in treatment works to the advantage of Spanish operators, because Spanish operators favour small and medium-sized establishments while operators from other Member States prefer large retail establishments. Because the figures provided by the Commission did not enable the Court 'to determine with certainty' the number of establishments concerned or the breakdown between Spanish and non-Spanish control of a significant part of the establishments falling within the category of large establishments, the Commission was found to not have adduced conclusive evidence to confirm its claim.[127]

This means that the examination of the existence of discrimination in WTO law is less abridged compared to EU law, if only for reasons inherent to the system of the GATS. It also means that the debate in WTO law is far ahead of the debate on discrimination under EU law.

### *8.7.3 Direct and covert discrimination*

Hatzopoulos has argued that one should distinguish measures that discriminate formally by introducing distinctions and that are directly based on nationality, which should be justifiable under express Treaty derogations.[128] Measures that discriminate formally but indirectly on criteria other than nationality could only be justified by both the open and the closed list of exceptions.[129] This separates indirect discrimination from direct discrimination in terms of justification, although the only difference between them is that the one discriminates based on nationality and the other based on some other formal criterion. Hilson has argued that there must be both discriminatory and protectionist intent for distinctly applicable measures to be unlawful.[130] This language dresses the distinction between the finding of discrimination on the qualification stage and a finding at the justification stage in different language. Hilson has submitted that it should be distinguished between direct discrimination covering both indirect discrimination in law, obvious intentional protectionism 'and possibly also indirect

[127] Case C-400/08, *Commission* v. *Spain (Shopping Centers)* [2011] ECR I-1915, para 60.

[128] Hatzopoulos, *Regulating Services in the European Union*, p. 119.

[129] Hatzopoulos, *Regulating Services in the European Union*, p. 120.

[130] C. Hilson, 'Discrimination in Community free movement law' (1999) 24 *European Law Review* 445–62 at 447.

discrimination in law'.[131] Indirect discrimination, according to Hilson, would comprise measures that do not discriminate in law but discriminate in effect.[132]

What is clear is that *de jure* or direct discrimination requires a reference to nationality in a national law or regulation. However, this means that the requirement to be a resident of the host state in particular only escapes the qualification as being openly discriminatory because of this narrow definition of direct discrimination. Hence it is only the way a rule is drafted – 'residency for all' or 'residency only for foreigners' – that makes a difference, while the effect in both cases is the same. One could argue that only the distinction based on nationality has been singled out by the Treaty as being especially opposed to the very idea of the fundamental freedoms. However, we doubt whether this quite fanciful distinction carries such an important difference in regulatory autonomy, expressed in the nature of public policy interests that can be fielded by a state.

We would suggest calling this category 'disguised' or 'covert' discrimination, to distinguish it from other forms of discrimination discussed below. In addition to residency, we would also argue that this should relate to conditions that have no scope of application in the host state, but primarily aim at discriminating against foreigners. An example of this is the requirement to show a certain right to access higher education in the state issuing the high school diploma, if such condition does not exist in the host state.[133] This category of discrimination has to overcome the objection that the regulatory intent is not decisive in establishing discrimination both under the GATS[134] and, as mentioned above, under EU law. While this may be true, we suggest there is an alternate route that could be taken here.

In a discussion of the scope of Article XVII GATS, it has been suggested that de facto or *de jure* discriminatory measures should be those that could at least in theory be inscribed as limitations under Article XVII GATS on national treatment.[135] This would qualify only those measures

131 Hilson, 'Discrimination in Community free movement law', 450.

132 Hilson, 'Discrimination in Community free movement law', 451.

133 See Case C-147/03, *Commission* v. *Austria (Conditions of Access to University Education)* [2005] ECR I-5969, paras. 49 *et seq.*

134 See P. Eeckhout, 'Constitutional concepts for free trade in services', in G. de Búrca and J. Scott (eds.), *The EU and the WTO: Legal and Constitutional Issues* (Oxford and Portland, OR: Hart Publishing, 2002), pp. 211–35 at pp. 226–31.

135 See the argument by Krajewski, *National Regulation and Trade Liberalization in Services*, p. 113.

as de facto or *de jure* discriminatory, for which a discriminatory effect is foreseeable because the distinguishing criterion 'is apparently and typically more easily fulfilled by domestic service suppliers'.[136] We would submit that this could also apply under EU law for cases of covert discrimination. By relying on the foreseeability of the discriminatory effect and its typical nature, this avoids relying on legislative intent or even regulatory purpose. If a state provides a requirement in its national law, which is nationality-neutral but does not have any application for domestic situations, such as residency, the discriminatory effect is clearly foreseeable and the protectionist purpose is evident.[137]

### *8.7.4 Indirect discrimination and de facto discrimination*

Spaventa has distinguished between different treatment of comparable situations (formal discrimination) and equal treatment of non-comparable situations (material discrimination).[138] According to her, with measures that discriminate indirectly, what matters is neither the form nor the intention, but rather the effect of the rules.[139]

Let us first consider regulatory criteria that require a certain link between the provider and the host state, such as the condition to obtain certain qualifications in the host state, or to be proficient in the host state's language.[140] Such measures equally contain some element of regulation that works to the detriment of foreigners. However, they can be distinguished from covert discrimination by being to a lesser degree predicated by a protectionist attitude in the host state. It may not be foreseeable that the requirement to have a certain qualification is an issue for foreigners. We would refer to this category of measures as indirect discrimination. In this vein, indirectly discriminatory measures have been defined in the literature as measures that encompass 'a regulatory distinction' producing effects 'similar to the effects of measures of clear-cut discrimination'.[141] The example of a new regulatory condition put up by the host state that only applies to one specialized market dominated by foreign companies has been mentioned.[142] While this condition would apply mainly to the detriment of foreigners, it

136 Krajewski, *National Regulation and Trade Liberalization in Services*, p. 113.
137 See Hudec, *Essays on the Nature of International Trade Law*, pp. 385–6.
138 Spaventa, 'On discrimination', 467.
139 Spaventa, 'On discrimination', 467.
140 Similarly Krajewski, *National Regulation and Trade Liberalization in Services*, p. 108.
141 Eeckhout, 'Constitutional concepts for free trade in services', p. 234.
142 Eeckhout, 'Constitutional concepts for free trade in services'.

would neither be typically burdensome for foreigners, nor might the national legislature have been able to foresee this unequal effect. In other words, this condition might be more 'innocent' than covert discrimination as defined above.

There is yet another category of discrimination we may distinguish from indirect discrimination.[143] These relate to national measures that do not formally distinguish between nationals and foreigners, but may nonetheless have the unintended effect of mainly affecting foreign goods/services/providers.[144] This can be defined as de facto discrimination, and has so far mostly been discussed in the WTO context.[145] Residency requirements would therefore not be an example of de facto discrimination.[146] Article XVII:3 GATS provides that formally identical treatment is prohibited when it 'modifies the conditions of competition'. On this basis, the DSB has held that in some cases the application of 'formally identical legal provisions would in practice accord less favourable treatment to imported products and a contracting party might thus have to apply different legal provisions to imported products to ensure that the treatment accorded to them is in fact no less favourable'.[147] In *EC–Bananas III* the allocation of shares of the import licences under the pertinent quota regime was found to have worked to the detriment of the complainants.[148] The decisive element would therefore be that de facto discrimination is characterized by the way the measure is actually applied by national authorities.

A differentiation between de facto discrimination and indirect discrimination both in EU law and in WTO law might improve transparency and comparability of central concepts. It might also help the

[143] For a perspective which does not make this distinction, see W. Zdouc, 'WTO dispute settlement practice relating to the General Agreement on Trade in Services', in F. Ortino and E-U. Petersmann (eds.), *The WTO Dispute Settlement System 1995–2003* (The Hague: Kluwer, 2004), pp. 381–420 at p. 405. See also M. E. Footer and C. George, 'The General Agreement on Trade in Services', in P. F. J. Macrory, A. E. Appleton and M. G. Plummer (eds.), *The World Trade Organization: Legal, Economic and Political Analysis* (New York: Springer, 2005), pp. 799–953 at p. 852.

[144] Eeckhout, 'Constitutional concepts for a free trade in services', p. 232.

[145] See, recently, Flett, 'WTO space for national regulation', 51–7.

[146] See, however, WTO, Council for Trade in Services, Guidelines for the Scheduling of Specific Commitments under the GATS, adopted on 23 March 2001, S/L/92, 28 March 2001, p. 6.

[147] See the GATT Panel Report, *United States–Section 337 of the Tariff Act of 1930*, BISD 36S/345, adopted 7 November 1989, para. 5.11.

[148] WTO Appellate Body Report, *EC–Bananas III*, WT/DS27/AB/R. See Eeckhout, 'Constitutional concepts for free trade in services', 231–2; Hudec, *Essays on the Nature of International Trade Law*, p. 348.

better understanding of the lack of distinction in EU law between the concepts of indistinctly applicable measures on the one hand, and indirectly discriminatory measures on the other hand.[149] As we have shown, both these categories are commonly defined as imposing on foreigners 'the same burden in law but a different burden in fact'. The distinction proposed here is between national measures that provide a certain condition for providers to fulfil under national law that can be identified as being more burdensome for foreigners than for nationals. This would be indirect discrimination. In contrast, a national measure that does not comprise such an element but is nonetheless more burdensome for foreigners because it is applied in this manner would be de facto discrimination.

### *8.7.5 Conclusion: what test for which form of discrimination?*

We propose a more finely tuned distinction between the different forms of discrimination than currently prevails. For this, we suggest distinguishing between several elements that can be applied when examining these different categories: (1) the form of the national measure, (2) the regulatory intent pursued, (3) the typical effect, and (4) the actual effect of a measure under national law. For EU law, we can take inspiration from WTO law, where de facto discrimination covers measures with unintended implications on the conditions of competition on a market. Covert discrimination would typically be residency requirements, since they have the same effect and underlying intent as conditions based on nationality. This is summarized in Table 8.1.

Currently in the EU, all categories except for direct discrimination apply the full range of reasons for justification.[150] We would submit that it would make more sense to treat direct and covert discrimination equally. However, the distinctions explored above also go some way to show that it is a fallacy to reject market access as a useless concept.[151] When Snell inquires that if the main concern was discrimination, 'why not use that term, or another formulation such as "disparate impact",

[149] See S. Enchelmaier, 'Always at your service (within limits): the ECJ's case law on Article 56 TFEU (2006–11)' (2011) 36 *European Law Review* 615–50, who does not distinguish further between direct and indirect discrimination or between distinctly and indistinctly applicable measures.

[150] See Hatzopoulos, *Regulating Services in the European Union*, p. 120.

[151] Snell, 'The notion of market access', 448–9. Snell has doubted the feasibility of having private litigators demonstrating that certain measures favour national products, and expresses a preference for a discrimination standard instead.

Table 8.1 Proposed classification of forms of discrimination

| Categories of discrimination | Direct | Covert | Indirect | De facto |
|---|---|---|---|---|
| **Characteristics** | - formal<br>- protectionist<br>- evident effect | - formal<br>- protectionist<br>- foreseeable effect | - formal<br>- not protectionist<br>- not foreseeable effect | - informal (no criterion)<br>- application has discriminatory effect |
| **Examples** | nationality | residency, criteria not applicable for domestic situations | local testing requirements, local qualifications, language requirements | disadvantageous application, biased administrative practice |

or refer to obstacles to trade instead of to market access',[152] we would not gain much. The different forms of discrimination all embody different degrees of 'protectiveness', thus different degrees of attempting to keep operators and services from other states out. We therefore cannot escape an assessment in terms of market access as well.

The distinction between de facto and indirect discrimination is a fine line to tread. As we have argued, with de facto discrimination what should be decisive is the effect of the national measures on the conditions of competition in a national market. Thus the fact that a certain national law would primarily work against foreign companies or providers in this case is not due to a regulatory distinction, but because of the market conditions and the way the regulation works in the market. This brings de facto discrimination very close to what we call differential regulation and double burdens, which are discussed next.

## 8.8 Differential regulation and double burdens

### *8.8.1 Introduction*

The situations we discuss under these titles have in common that there is normally no intent to discriminate against foreigners. There is also no regulatory element that can be identified as being particularly detrimental to the position of service providers or companies from other Member States, such as is the case with indirect discrimination.

[152] Snell, 'The notion of market access', 468.

However, both with differential regulation and situations of double burden, foreigners have a higher burden of adjusting to the host state rules than operators already in the market. With differential regulation this is because the same activity is regulated in a different manner in the host state than in the home state of the provider.

This will be especially pertinent if the host state rules are stricter than the home state rules. With respect to situations of double burden, the problem for the foreign provider is not so much the difference in regulation, but that a regulatory requirement in the host state duplicates a condition that has already been satisfied by the provider in its home state. As in the case of discrimination, here the same burden in law is imposed on the foreigner, but in fact the legal situation may be more burdensome than for the national of the home state. Where, then, is the line between a non-discriminatory case of differential regulation or double burden on the one hand, and a case of indirect and de facto discrimination on the other hand? We shall start by discussing the more specific case of double burdens.

### *8.8.2 Double burdens*

Double burdens are a particularly intricate matter to classify. Hilson has classified them as indirect discrimination only with regard to product requirements.[153] In contrast, he has qualified (product) selling arrangements as non-discriminatory and as cases of single burden, since they could in fact only be applied in the host state/state of destination.[154] According to Hatzopoulos, double burdens could be justified by showing that the failure of mutual recognition cannot be held against the host state.[155] Measures that neither discriminate nor impose double burdens in his view are legal unless they '"greatly" affect market access, in which case they could be justified again by all available public policy grounds'.[156]

This implies the importance of intent if the only apparent difference between discrimination and double burdens in his view is that the latter measures 'give no indication' that they would protect nationals against free movers.[157] At the same time, Hatzopoulos correctly notes in

[153] See Hilson, 'Discrimination in Community free movement law', 454.
[154] Hilson, 'Discrimination in Community free movement law', 545.
[155] Hatzopoulos, *Regulating Services in the European Union*, p. 120.
[156] Hatzopoulos, *Regulating Services in the European Union*, p. 120.
[157] Hatzopoulos, *Regulating Services in the European Union*, p. 110. See also *ibid.*, p. 111: 'Intent therefore has a role to play.'

passing that intent is not taken into account at the qualification stage but at the justification stage.[158] This, however, ignores one fact that is essential in this very context. At the justification stage, the consideration of regulatory intent disguised in the form of a proportionality test might already come too late, namely in those cases where the qualification of a certain measure as discriminatory or non-discriminatory decides the applicable public policy reasons available for justification.

Double burden cases under EU law are dealt with under the restrictions approach, applying the open list of grounds of public interest for justifying them. Thus qualification or licence requirements constitute a violation of the freedom of establishment or the free movement of services and must be justified.[159] In the *Parodi* case on the requirement for a credit institution already authorized in the home state to obtain an authorization in the host state, the Court summarized that such requirement is illegal unless it:

- is required of every person or company pursuing such an activity within the territory of the Member State of destination;
- is justified on grounds of public interest, such as consumer protection; and
- is objectively necessary to ensure compliance with the rules applicable in the sector under consideration and to protect the interests which those rules are intended to safeguard, and the same result cannot be achieved by less restrictive rules.[160]

Absent of binding disciplines on domestic regulation under Article VI GATS, such an approach to restrictions is missing under the GATS. Under the GATS, double burden situations therefore seem to raise a considerable problem in deciding which is the correct provision to apply.[161]

[158] Hatzopoulos, *Regulating Services in the European Union*, p. 111.

[159] Also under the free movement of goods, double burdens are not dealt with under the title of discrimination. For a different view, see J. Scott, 'Mandatory or imperative requirements in the EU and the WTO', in C. Barnard and J. Scott (eds.), *The Law of the Single European Market: Unpacking the Premises* (Oxford and Portland, OR: Hart Publishing, 2002), pp. 269–93 at p. 276. Instead, they fall under the category of indistinctly applicable national measures, defined as rules, 'which in law apply to both national and foreign products but in fact have a particular burden on the imported goods'. See Barnard, *The Substantive Law of the EU*, p. 105.

[160] Case C-222/95, *Parodi* [1997] ECR I-3899, para. 32.

[161] This has been referred to as 'boxing' (as in boxes, not the sport) by Pauwelyn in a different context.

A fictive case of double burden has been discussed under the (indirect) discrimination discourse in the literature on the GATS.[162] While this might work in the EU, double burdens should not be discussed in terms of discrimination, which requires an assessment of likeness in the GATS, because the likeness discourse does not work in this case for the following reason. Let us assume that a national regulation requires all drivers in the transport services business to have trained in host state schools and hold driving licences of the host state; it has been discussed whether, in such a case, foreign drivers are 'like' host state drivers.[163] The consequences of such examination are clear: if they were found to be like, the host state would have breached its full commitments under Article XVII GATS; if not, the host state requirements would not constitute a discriminatory measure.[164] In the latter case, the requirement would 'only' fall under Article VI GATS, with the above-discussed consequences. However, what does likeness mean when comparing drivers from two different Member States who hold different qualifications? Does it suffice to point to the fact that training standards in the states concerned are different?[165]

We would argue that it should not fall under discrimination if a WTO Member requires service providers to comply with certain non-discriminatory standards for reasons of ensuring road safety. We would suggest referring to Footnote 10 to Article XVII:1 GATS in support of this view. This footnote states that Members must not 'compensate for any inherent competitive disadvantages which result from the foreign character of the relevant services or service suppliers'. We would argue that this applies to cases where qualification standards differ between Members. It does not contradict the GATS if foreign providers have a disadvantage because of the requirement of passing additional tests in the host state. Double burden situations therefore do not come within the ambit of Article XVII GATS. The requirement to have a certain qualification is one of the central examples of a double burden. One could here submit that it might depend whether these qualifications are required with the intent of placing foreign providers at a disadvantage, in which case the discriminatory element would be more apparent. However, this

[162] A. Mattoo, 'National treatment in the GATS: corner stone or Pandora's Box?' (1997) *Journal of World Trade* 107–35 at 128.
[163] Mattoo, 'National treatment in the GATS', 128.
[164] Footer and George, 'The General Agreement on Trade in Services', p. 852.
[165] Footer and George, 'The General Agreement on Trade in Services', p. 852.

would still boil down to the question of whether mutual recognition is granted by the host state, which is a matter that Hatzopoulos discusses squarely under the double burden label.[166] The *Laval* case is a different matter, and discussed by Hatzopoulos as a case of double burden that was wrongly qualified as a case of discrimination by the Court.[167] Here Swedish rules on collective agreements were considered discriminatory because they failed to take into account collective agreements to which the Latvian company posting workers was already subject in Latvia. For the Court it did not matter in this case whether the Latvian service provider was bound in Latvia by labour laws that were equivalent to those applied to the posted workers under Swedish law.[168]

### 8.8.3 *Differential regulation*

Diebold has argued that standards with regard to the 'less favourable treatment' test can either look for whether a group of foreign market actors is disproportionately disadvantaged as compared to a domestic group (asymmetric impact test, disparate impact test), or whether even only one individual foreign actor is treated less favourably than any one domestic operator (diagonal test).[169] The diagonal test would have the strongest deregulating effect, and has thus been compared to the prohibition of restrictions in EU law.[170] This submission blurs the few borders that can be established between the discrimination standard and the restrictions standard. Moreover, Diebold concedes that it is applied neither in WTO nor in EU law.

We would suggest again referring to Footnote 10 to Article XVII GATS, which could be ascribed a more general relevance in assessing differential regulation. '[I]nherent competitive disadvantages' does not refer to any other element of Article XVII:1 GATS and could be read to mean 'inherent in the foreign character of a service or a service provider'.[171]

[166] Hatzopoulos, *Regulating Services in the European Union*, p. 111.

[167] Case C-341/05, *Laval* [2007] ECR I-11767. See Hatzopoulos, *Regulating Services in the European Union*, p. 112.

[168] See O. de Schutter, 'Transborder services and "social dumping"', in I. Lianos and O. Odudu (eds.), *Regulating Trade in Services: Trust, Distrust and Economic Integration* (Cambridge University Press, 2012), pp. 349–80 at p. 372.

[169] Diebold, 'Standards of non-discrimination in international economic law', 842–8. The only comparison between the disparate impact test and EU law drawn by Diebold here is to case law on Art. 110 TFEU on tax discrimination.

[170] Diebold, 'Standards of non-discrimination in international economic law', 853.

[171] For the suggestion of a rather complicated quantitative test based on this footnote, see Zdouc, 'WTO dispute settlement practice', pp. 412–13.

This would exempt competitive disadvantages that arise because of higher adjustment burdens or because of market conditions from the ambit of the non-discrimination rule in GATS.

While it has no provision comparable to Footnote 10, EU law equally does not subject obstacles because of regulatory differences to the discrimination standard.[172] However, because of the broad definition of restrictions under the fundamental freedoms and of requirements under the Services Directive, any obstacle might be qualified as such and thus become subject to the necessity and proportionality test. This principled application of the freedoms also to cases of differential regulation has been made clear in the *Alpine Investments* decision, where the ECJ has explained that 'the fact that one Member State imposes less strict rules than another Member State does not mean that the latter's rules are disproportionate and hence incompatible with Community law'.[173] Conversely, the application of the proportionality test here means that, as a matter of principle, these stricter rules do qualify as restrictions in the first place. In the *Dickinger* case the Court found in a similar vein that the 'mere fact that a Member State has opted for a system of protection which differs from that adopted by another Member State cannot affect the assessment of the need for and proportionality of the relevant provisions'.[174]

The only exceptions are where we can argue for the existence of a blind spot with regard to non-discriminatory measures, thus with respect to laws of a general application in the meaning of Recital 9 Services Directive, or relating to cases such as *Viacom* and *Mobistar* under the Treaty. As explained in Chapter 4, Recital 9 measures that 'do not specifically regulate or specifically affect the service activity but have to be respected by providers in the course of carrying out their economic activity in the same way as by individuals acting in their private capacity', would introduce, tucked away in the Directive's preamble, nothing less than a statutory defined blind spot of application, which is missing so far from the Treaty services regime.[175] However,

[172] This explains why the cases under the free movement of goods, such as *German Beer* and *Cassis de Dijon*, have also not been decided by invoking this concept. See the question posed by Scott, 'Mandatory or imperative requirements', p. 285. On the GATS, see R. Pillai, 'National treatment and WTO dispute settlement' (2002) 1(3) *World Trade Review* 321–43 at 337.

[173] Case C-384/93, *Alpine Investments* [1995] ECR I-1141, para. 51.

[174] Case C-347/09, *Dickinger* [2011] ECR I-8185, para. 46.

[175] See J. Snell, 'Freedom to provide services in the case law and in the Services Directive: problems, solutions, and institutions', in U. Neergaard, R. Nielsen and L.

several arguments also militate against such a reading of Recital 9. First, a recital might not be the right place to introduce such a novel category of domestic regulations. Second, as already argued, we would doubt whether the increase in the 'freedom' of the Member States from having to defend their national law under the freedom to provide services would compensate for the loss of flexibility and for increased legal uncertainty over an additional classification of national measures. Third, note that under the Commission proposal for the Services Directive rules very similar to those mentioned in Recital 9[176] would have been exempted from the country of origin principle; but they arguably would still have come under the regime of Article 56 TFEU. This means, however, that even if we assume that Recital 9 of the Services Directive exempts certain national measures from the scope of application of the Directive, they would continue to fall under the Treaty regime. This would add to the problem of fragmentation raised earlier.

We would argue instead that only those situations of differential legislation that cause nothing more than adjustment costs for the market entrant are exempted under EU law. These costs are 'inherent in the foreign character of a service or a service provider', and must also therefore be deemed exempted from the restrictions standard. Thus they must not be justified, while other rules such as those mentioned in Recital 9 of the Services Directive must be considered as restrictions that are subject to justification in EU law.

## 8.9 Conclusion

We have seen that considerations of market access also have a place in the EU, both as an implicit part of the examination of discriminatory measures that discriminate because of their effect based on a regulatory element or based on the application of a 'neutral' provision of law, as well as under the market access approach in general. We have argued that the market access standard both in the EU and the WTO

Roseberry (eds.), *The Services Directive: Consequences for the Welfare State and the European Social Model* (Copenhagen: Djof, 2008), pp. 171–97 at p. 187.

[176] Compare 'requirements relating to the safety of building sites' to 'building standards and administrative penalties imposed for non-compliance with such rules', and 'authorisations to occupy or use the public highway' to 'road traffic rules'.

should be less about the rule itself and much more about its (deterrent) effect. This would require that economic considerations play a larger role than with discriminatory measures, considering among other things whether there are alternative ways for the service provider or the service to enter the market. From this perspective, the reasoning of the AB in *US–Gambling* makes sense, as does that by the Court in *DocMorris*. We have argued that the GATS might in theory provide for a stricter standard on market access than the EU, yet this is tempered by the narrow corset of Article XVI GATS.[177]

We have shown that discrimination can take very diverse forms. Yet what all these categories discussed have in common is that they follow the logic of unequal treatment. Under EU law, discrimination is the 'original sin', while in WTO law the prohibition of discriminatory measures does not have this higher 'constitutional' rank. We have argued that this is significant in the sense that it should justify a strict standard for discriminatory measures in the EU. As suggested, this could mean that what has been termed covert discrimination is treated equally to direct discrimination in terms of the justifications that are available to Member States.

Double burdens have been qualified as restrictions under EU law, being subject to the principle of mutual recognition in the specific form of the test of equivalence. In contrast, under the GATS they would only come under the rules on domestic regulations, unless they are qualified as discriminatory, which would not be justified in our view, however. The GATS regime on domestic regulations is still very weak, however, and is likely to remain so for the near future. In the EU, mutual recognition has proven a politically and legally viable way for progress in this matter, especially since it is not necessarily an antechamber to harmonization.

An issue that is unresolved in the EU is what we have called differential regulation, which correlates with what has also been discussed under 'blind spots' in the application of the freedoms in Chapter 4. This concerns nothing less than the 'line of defence' for national sovereignty.

[177] For a different perspective, see Reid, 'Regulatory autonomy in the EU and WTO', 900, who has argued that, because domestic regulations under Article VI GATS could be justified by a broader range of justifications than under Articles XVI or XVII GATT, Article XVI GATS would impinge to a greater extent upon regulatory autonomy than is the case in the EU, which would support a narrower interpretation of its scope.

Here no guidance presents itself in EU law, where the Court of Justice seems to hand down varied directions, and a recital in the Services Directive is of unclear relevance. In contrast, in the GATS, in spite of its 'image' of being less 'interventionist', there is at least a footnote that seeks to clarify this issue.

# 9 *Quo vadit?* Conclusions and recommendations

The GATS and EU services law clearly are two different animals. This, however, is mainly owed to the divergent 'organizational' set-up, including the much more cautious approach to treaty interpretation by the DSB compared to the activism by the ECJ, and the divergent effects in national law. There also is little common ground with regard to public services, mainly because of the absence of a comprehensive competition and public procurement regime in the WTO. Apart from this, when we look at the regulatory instruments and standards at its disposal, the WTO and the GATS arguably are not fundamentally different from the EU. Moreover, the superficial view that EU (services) law is more 'mature' compared to the GATS is only partly true.

Thus we have argued for clarification of the non-discrimination standard in EU law by taking cues from WTO law. Non-discrimination in EU law has for the longest time been in the shadow of the more 'glamorous' restrictions standard. Precisely because such restrictions standard has been missing from WTO law, it seems that the concepts underlying non-discrimination have been more fully thought through. In general, we would welcome a more careful theoretical groundwork in the EU with elements such as a one- or a two-tier review of discriminatory measures, or the proper identification of the *tertium comparationis*. There is also a discourse in the WTO on where the limits should be with regard to incursions into the regulatory prerogative of nation states, which in the EU has remained patchy. Conversely, double burdens are an intricate category, where we have shown that WTO law could take inspiration from a fairly sophisticated debate in EU law. Mutual recognition is the recommended solution for these constellations in the services field, as concerns with this approach in relation to the goods regime have been found to be less pertinent here.

With regard to EU law, we have observed the lack of clear-cut regulatory standards. Thus there is no full-fledged home state rule or host state rule, and mutual recognition has as many different faces as monikers in the literature. We have also criticized the fact that the Court alternates a restrictions standard with a market access standard, and sometimes throws in a non-discrimination standard, such as in the *Keck* case, to complete the confusion. Thus the market access standard has been shown not only to seep into the restrictions standard, but equally to be of relevance for some categories of discrimination. The Services Directive has consolidated these standards to some extent by largely outlawing discriminatory measures. Otherwise, after the demise of a radical host state law rule in the Commission draft, the Directive has only moderately modified the non-discrimination and the restrictions standards, and has instead aimed at changing national procedures and institutions. This is something that seems beyond what is feasible in the WTO, whose institutional framework is much less developed when compared to the EU. However, a closer look at the draft disciplines on domestic regulation under Article VI GATS reveals some remarkable parallels with the Services Directive. This also shows that in this respect, in theory, the GATS would not be lagging behind.

Another implication of the Services Directive is the fragmentation of the services regime in the EU. While it aligns its coverage with the GATS modes by covering services *stricto sensu* as well as established service providers, the Directive does not provide for a uniform regulation of these two categories. The difference in treatment between establishments and services, which has partly been overcome by more recent case law of the ECJ, is thus elevated to another level of complexity. Services and establishments are now subject to four distinct legal regimes: (1) Chapter IV of the Services Directive for services *stricto sensu*; (2) Chapter III of the Services Directive for services rendered through an establishment; (3) Article 49 TFEU for establishments not operating in the services business and for those in sectors exempted from the Directive; and (4) Article 56 TFEU for all services *stricto sensu* in sectors exempted from the Services Directive.

Blacklists could be the real achievement of the Services Directive in the long run, bringing legal clarity in an area where this has often been wanting. Most importantly, blacklists abolish the need for a justification regime. Here the Services Directive has led to a rapprochement with WTO law, where blacklists are at the core of the regime on market access. We suggest closely monitoring the application of these lists, which can be very powerful instruments of not merely 'full' harmonization but, arguably beyond that, 'unconditional' harmonization. We also recommend observing the use of notification duties of the Member States provided in the Services Directive, which might be applied forcefully by the Court in analogy to other such duties in secondary EU law. However, overall we find that the legislative experiment of 'codifying' a case law-based regime which is in flux and inconsistent in itself would have warranted a much higher level of care by the EU legislature. Moreover, the implementation of the Services Directive has shown that if Member States are not handed clear rules, they tend to choose the minimum solution, which might considerably diminish the effect of the instrument.

Whereas genuine cross-sectoral regulation has proven elusive in EU law, with even the 'Services' Directive exempting more sectors than it covers, this has been realized in WTO law from the outset. The strength of EU law, however, is that sectoral measures can be as varied as the services themselves, ranging from 'soft regulation' to various forms and degrees of harmonization. The 'best' the WTO can hope for here, in contrast, is negative harmonization by eventually adopting the mentioned disciplines. However, GATS negotiators can be forgiven for being suspicious of regulatory standards such as a prohibition of restrictions that have remained ambiguous even in the EU where they have a long record. Above all, it has proven difficult to distinguish the market access standard, even in the WTO, where rules on market access are expressly provided in contrast to EU law.

Chances are that both the EU and the WTO will develop at a different pace and by using different instruments. However, the fundamental issues with liberalizing markets are comparable, as are most of the regulatory standards. It would therefore be a pity if there were not more cross-fertilization than has hitherto occurred. We would proffer that one needs not ignore the differences between the two regimes in order to acknowledge their similarities. Both regimes speak the same language of market access, discrimination, justification and harmonization, yet seem not to understand each other. That the existing, fundamental differences in philosophy and available instruments obscure the view on these communalities is to be regretted, and we hope that this book can contribute to at least raising awareness of this fact.

# References


Adler, Georg and Thomas Kröll, 'Austrian Report', in Ulrich Stelkens, Wolfgang Weiß and Michael Mirschberger (eds.), *The Implementation of the EU Services Directive: Transposition, Problems and Strategies* (The Hague: TMC Asser, Springer, 2012), pp. 65–87

Adlung, Rudolf, 'GATS commitments on environmental services: "hover through the fog and filthy air"?', in Thomas Cottier, Olga Nartova and Sadeq Z. Bigdeli (eds.), *International Trade Regulation and the Mitigation of Climate Change* (Cambridge University Press, 2009), pp. 274–80

'Public services and the GATS' (2006) 9(2) *Journal of International Economic Law* 455–85

'Services liberalization from a WTO/GATS perspective: in search of volunteers' (2009) Staff Working Paper ERSD

Albath, Lars and Martina Giesler, 'Das Herkunftslandprinzip in der Dienstleistungsrichtlinie: eine Kodifizierung der Rechtsprechung?' (2006) *Europäische Zeitschrift für Wirtschaftsrecht* 38–42

Anon., 'The Services Directive proposal: striking a balance between the promotion of the internal market and preserving the European social model?' (2006) 43 *Common Market Law Review* 307–11

Armstrong, Kenneth, 'Mutual recognition', in Catherine Barnard and Joanna Scott (eds.), *The Law of the Single European Market: Unpacking the Premises* (Oxford and Portland, OR: Hart Publishing, 2002), pp. 225–67

Bacchus, James, 'Appellators: the quest for the meaning of and/or', in Dan Horovitz, Daniel Moulis and Debra Steger (eds.), *Ten Years of WTO Dispute Settlement* (London: International Bar Association, 2007), pp. 19–40

Baelz, Kilian and Teresa Baldwin, 'The end of the real seat theory (Sitztheorie): the European Court of Justice decision in Ueberseering of 5 November 2002 and its impact on German and European company law' (2002) 3 *German Law Journal*, available at www.germanlawjournal.com/index.php?pageID=11&artID=214

Baquero Cruz, Julio, 'Beyond competition: services of general interest and European Community law', in Gráinne de Búrca (ed.), *EU Law and the*

*Welfare State: In Search of Solidarity* (Oxford University Press, 2005), pp. 169–212
Barnard, Catherine, 'Fitting the remaining pieces into the goods and persons jigsaw?' (2001) 26 *European Law Review* 35–59
*The Substantive Law of the EU: The Four Freedoms*, 3rd edn (Oxford University Press, 2010)
'Unravelling the Services Directive' (2008) *Common Market Law Review* 323–94
Barnard, Catherine and Simon Deakin, 'Market access and regulatory competition', in Catherine Barnard and Joanna Scott (eds.), *The Law of the Single European Market: Unpacking the Premises* (Oxford and Portland, OR: Hart Publishing, 2002), pp. 197–224
Bartels, Lorand, 'The legality of the EC mutual recognition clause under WTO law' (2005) 8(3) *Journal of International Economic Law* 691–720
Bauby, Pierre, 'From Rome to Lisbon: SGIs in primary law', in Erika Szyszczak *et al.* (eds.), *Developments in Services of General Interest* (The Hague: TMC Asser, Springer, 2011), pp. 19–36
Bekkedal, Tarjei, 'Article 106 TFEU is dead. Long live Article 106 TFEU!', in Erika Szyszczak *et al.* (eds.), *Developments in Services of General Interest* (The Hague: TMC Asser, Springer, 2011), pp. 61–102
Biondi, Andrea, 'Recurring cycles in the internal market: some reflections on the free movement of services', in Anthony Arnull, Piet Eeckhout and Takis Tridimas (eds.), *Continuity and Change in EU Law: Essays in Honour of Sir Francis Jacobs* (Oxford University Press, 2007), pp. 228–42
Bobjoseph, Mathew, *The WTO Agreements on Telecommunications* (Berne/Frankfurt/Brussels: Peter Lang, 2003)
Böhret, Carl, Dieter Grunow and Jan Ziekow, 'Der Vorschlag zu einer Richtlinie des Europäischen Parlamentes und des Rates über Dienstleistungen im Binnenmarkt: Regelungsgehalt – Problemfelder – Akteurspositionen' (Speyerer Forschungsberichte, No. 241, 2006)
Börger, Stefan, 'Anlagengenehmigungsverfahren und die Dienstleistungsrichtlinie', in Franz Merli and Stefan Greimel (eds.), *Optimierungspotentiale bei Behördenverfahren* (Vienna: Linde, 2009), pp. 121–39
Bovis, Christopher, 'Financing services of general interest in the EU: how do public procurement and state aids interact to demarcate between market forces and protection?' (2005) *European Law Journal* 79–109
Bronckers, Marco, *A Cross-section of WTO Law* (London: Cameron May, 2000)
Bronckers, Marco and Pierre Larouche, 'Telecommunications services', in Patrick F. J. Macrory, Arthur E. Appleton and Michael G. Plummer (eds.), *The World Trade Organization: Legal, Economic and Political Analysis* (New York: Springer, 2005), pp. 989–1040
Buchinger, Stefan, Alois Michner and Christian Müller, *Die Dienstleistungsrichtlinie: Ein Erfolg der österreichischen Präsidentschaft 2006* (Vienna: Verlag Österreich, 2007)
Burri-Nenova, Mira and Sadeq Z. Bigdeli, 'Commentary of GATS Article IX Business Practices' (2008) *SSRN Working Paper Series*

Calliess, Christian, *Die Dienstleistungsrichtlinie: Von der grundfreiheitlichen Deregulierung zur europäischen Re-Regulierung?* (Bonn: Zentrum für Europäisches Wirtschaftsrecht, 2007)

'Europäischer Binnenmarkt und europäische Demokratie: Von der Dienstleistungsfreiheit zur Dienstleistungsrichtlinie – und wieder Retour?' (2007) *Deutsches Verwaltungsblatt* 336–46

Cameron, Kelly, 'Telecommunications and audio-visual services in the context of the WTO: today and tomorrow', in Damien Geradin and David Luff (eds.), *Global Convergence in Telecommunications and Audio-Visual Services* (Cambridge University Press, 2004), pp. 21–33

Cartland, Michel, Gérard Depayre and Jan Woznowski, 'Is something going wrong in the WTO dispute settlement?' (2012) 46(5) *Journal of World Trade* 979–1015

Conant, Lisa, *Justice Contained: Law and Politics in the European Union* (Ithaca: Cornell University Press, 2002)

Cornils, Matthias, 'Artikel 10 Voraussetzungen für die Erteilung der Genehmigung', in Monika Schlachter and Christoph Ohler (eds.), *Europäische Dienstleistungsrichtlinie* (Baden-Baden: Nomos, 2008)

Cossy, Mireille, 'Environmental services and the General Agreement on Trade in Services (GATS): legal issues and negotiating stakes at the WTO', in Christoph Herrmann and Jan Philip Terhechte (eds.), *European Yearbook of International Economic Law* (Heidelberg, Vienna: Springer, 2011), pp. 239–63

Cottier, Thomas and Krista N. Schefer, 'The relationship between World Trade Organization law, national law and regional law' (1998) *Journal of International Economic Law* 83–122

Craig, Paul and Gráinne de Búrca, *EU Law: Texts and Materials*, 5th edn (Oxford University Press, 2011)

Craufurd Smith, Rachael, 'Old wine in new bottles? From the "country of origin principle" to "freedom to provide services" in the European Community Directive on services in the internal market' (2007) *Mitchell Working Paper Series*

Cremona, Marise, 'Neutrality or discrimination? The WTO, the EU and External Trade', in Gráinne de Búrca and Joanna Scott (eds.), *The EU and the WTO: Legal and Constitutional Issues* (Oxford and Portland, OR: Hart Publishing, 2002), pp. 151–84

Da Cruz Vilaça, José Luís, 'On the application of Keck in the field of free provision of services', in Mads Andenas and Wulf-Henning Roth (eds.), *Services and Free Movement in EU Law* (Oxford University Press, 2003), pp. 25–40

Dagnis Jensen, Mads and Peter Nedergaard, 'From "Frankenstein" to "toothless vampire"? Explaining the watering down of the Services Directive' (2012) 19(6) *Journal of European Public Policy* 844–62

Damjanovic, Dragana, 'Annotation to Joined Cases C–22/08 & C–23/08, *Athanasios Vatsouras and Josif Koupatantze* v. *Arbeitsgemeinschaft (ARGE) Nürnberg 900*' (2010) *Common Market Law Review* 847–61

Davey, William J., 'Non-discrimination in the World Trade Organization: the rules and exceptions', in Académie De Droit International (ed.), *Collected Courses of the Academy of International Law* (Leiden, Boston: Martinus Nijhoff, 2011)

Davies, Gareth, *European Union Internal Market Law*, 2nd edn (London: Cavendish, 2003)

'Is mutual recognition an alternative to harmonization? Lessons on trade and tolerance of diversity from the EU', in Federico Ortino and Lorand Bartels (eds), *Regional Trade Agreements and the WTO Legal System* (Oxford University Press, 2006), pp. 265–80

'The Services Directive: extending the country of origin principle and reforming public administration' (2007) *European Law Review* 232–45

'Trust and mutual recognition in the Services Directive', in I. Lianos and O. Odudu (eds.), *Regulating Trade in Services: Trust, Distrust and Economic Integration* (Cambridge University Press, 2012), pp. 99–120

'What does Article 86 actually do?', in Markus Krajewski, Ulla Neergaard and Johan van de Gronden (eds.), *The Changing Legal Framework for Services of General Interest in Europe: Between Competition and Solidarity* (The Hague: TMC Asser Press, Cambridge University Press, 2009), pp. 51–67

Davies, Gareth and Erika Szyszczak, 'Universal service obligations: fulfilling new generations of services of general economic interest', in Erika Szyszczak *et al.* (eds.), *Developments in Services of General Interest* (The Hague: TMC Asser, Springer, 2011), pp. 155–77

Dawes, Anthony, '"Bonjour Herr Doctor": national healthcare systems, the internal market and cross-border medical care within the European Union' (2006) 33(2) *Legal Issues of Economic Integration* 167–82

De Búrca, Gráinne, 'Unpacking the concept of discrimination in EC and international trade law', in Catherine Barnard and Joanna Scott (eds.), *The Law of the Single European Market: Unpacking the Premises* (Oxford and Portland, OR: Hart Publishing, 2002), pp. 181–95

De Meester, Bart, 'The global financial crisis and government support for banks: what role for the GATS?' (2010) 13(1) *Journal of International Economic Law* 27–63

de Schutter, Olivier, 'Transborder services and "social dumping"', in I. Lianos and O. Odudu (eds.), *Regulating Trade in Services: Trust, Distrust and Economic Integration* (Cambridge University Press, 2012), pp. 349–80

De Witte, Bruno, 'Direct effect, supremacy, and the nature of the legal order', in Paul Craig and Gráinne de Búrca (eds.), *The Evolution of EU Law* (Oxford University Press, 1999), pp. 177–213

Deakin, Simon, 'Regulatory competition after Laval' (2008) *Cambridge Yearbook of European Legal Studies* 581–609

Delimatsis, Panagiotis, 'Determining the necessity of domestic regulations in services: the best is yet to come' (2008) *European Journal of International Law* 365–401

Diebold, Nicolas, 'Standards of non-discrimination in international economic law' (2011) 60(4) *International and Comparative Law Quarterly* 831–65

Dougan, Michael, 'Annotation of Case C-390/99, *Canal Satelite Digital* [2002] ECR I-607 and Case C-159/00, *Sapod Audicv EcoEmballages* [2002] ECR I-5031' (2003) 40(1) *Common Market Law Review* 193–218

Edward, David, Editorial Comment, 'Will there be honey still for tea?' (2006) *Common Market Law Review* 623–7

Edward, David and Niamh Nic Shuibhne, 'Continuity and change in the law relating to services', in Anthony Arnull, Piet Eeckhout and Takis Tridimas (eds.), *Continuity and Change in EU Law* (Oxford University Press, 2009), pp. 243–59

Eeckhout, Piet, 'Constitutional concepts for free trade in services', in Gráinne de Búrca and Joanna Scott (eds.), *The EU and the WTO: Legal and Constitutional Issues* (Oxford and Portland, OR: Hart Publishing, 2002), pp. 211–35

Enchelmaier, Stefan, 'Always at your service (within limits): the ECJ's case law on Article 56 TFEU (2006–11)' (2011) 36 *European Law Review* 615–50

Evans, Simone, 'The Services Directive: (too) great expectations? An initial overview of the rights and obligations under the Services Directive', in Johan van de Gronden (ed.), *EU and WTO Law on Services: Limits to the Realisation of General Interest Policies within the Services Markets?* (The Hague: Kluwer, 2008), pp. 7–29

Feketekuty, Geza, 'Assessing and improving the architecture of GATS', in Pierre Sauvé and Robert Stern (eds.), *GATS 2000: New Directions in Services Trade Liberalization* (Washington DC: Brookings, 2000), pp. 85–111

'Competition policy and the WTO: implications or recent developments in the services sector', Paper prepared for the Third Symposium on Competition Policy and the Multilateral Trading System, Geneva, April 1999

Feketekuty, Geza and Robert A. Rogowsky, 'The scope, implication and economic rationale of a competition-oriented approach to future multilateral trade negotiations', in Sven Arndt and Chris Milner, *The World Economy: Global Trade Policy* (London: Blackwell Publishers, 1996), pp. 167–81

Fiedziuk, Natalia, 'Putting services of general economic interest up for tender: reflections on applicable rules' (2013) 50 *Common Market Law Review* 87–114

'Towards a more refined economic approach to services of general economic interest' (2010) 16(2) *European Public Law* 271–88

Flett, James, 'WTO space for national regulation: requiem for a diagonal vector test' (2013) 16(1) *Journal of International Economic Law* 37–90

Flower, Jennifer, 'Negotiating European legislation: the Services Directive' (2006–2007) *Cambridge Yearbook of European Legal Studies* 217–38

Flynn, Leo, 'Coming of age: the free movement of capital case law 1993–2002' (2002) 39 *Common Market Law Review* 773–805

Footer, Mary E. and Carol George, 'The General Agreement on Trade in Services', in Patrick F. J. Macrory, Arthur E. Appleton and Michael G. Plummer (eds.), *The World Trade Organization: Legal, Economic and Political Analysis* (New York: Springer, 2005), pp. 799–953

Francois, Jospeh F. and Ian Wooton, 'Market structure and market access' (2008) World Bank Policy Research Working Paper No. 4151, http://ssrn.com/abstract=965604

'Market structure, trade liberalization, and the GATS' (2001) 17(2) *European Journal of Political Economics* 389–402

Frenz, Walter, *Handbuch Europarecht: Europäische Grundfreiheiten* (Heidelberg: Springer, 2004), vol. I

Frenz, Walter and Phillipp Schleissing, 'The never ending story of "in-house" procurement', in Markus Krajewski, Ulla Neergaard and Johan van de Gronden (eds.), *The Changing Legal Framework for Services of General Interest in Europe: Between Competition and Solidarity* (The Hague: TMC Asser, Kluwer, 2009), pp. 171–87

Gil Ibañez, Alberto J., *The Administrative Supervision and Enforcement of EC Law: Powers, Procedures, and Limits* (Oxford and Portland, OR: Hart Publishing, 1999)

Griller, Stefan, 'Effizienzgebot und Diskriminierungsverbot als Verwaltungsprinzipien in der Rechtsprechung des EuGH?', in Hartmut Bauer and Christian Calliess (eds.), *Verfassungsprinzipien in Europa* (Societas Iuris Publici Europaei, 2008), vol. IV, pp. 291–322

'Judicial enforceability of WTO law in the European Union: annotation to Case C-149/96, Portugal V. Council' (2000) 3(3) *Journal of International Economic Law* 441–72

'The new Services Directive of the European Union: hopes and expectations from the angle of a (further) completion of the internal market', General Report, in Heribert Franz Koeck and Margit Maria Karollus (eds.), *The New Services Directive of the European Union*, Féderation Internationale pour le Droit Européen (FIDE), XXIII Congress Linz 2008 (Vienna: Congress Publications, 2008), vol. III, pp. 379–423

'Two steps forward, how many back? Concluding remarks', in Fritz Breuss, Gerhard Fink and Stefan Griller (eds.), *Services Liberalisation in the Internal Market* (Vienna, New York: Springer, 2008), pp. 225–41

Griller, Stefan and Katharina Gamharter, 'External trade: is there a path through the maze of competences?', in Stefan Griller and Birgit Weidel (eds.), *External Economic Relations and Foreign Policy in the European Union* (Vienna, New York: Springer, 2002), pp. 65–112

Hansen, Jesper L., 'Full circle: is there a difference between the freedom of establishment and the freedom to provide services?', in Mads Andenas and Wulf-Henning Roth (eds.), *Services and Free Movement in EU Law* (The Hague: Kluwer, 2002), pp. 197–210

Hatje, Armin, 'Services Directive: a legal analysis', in Fritz Breuss, Gerhard Fink and Stefan Griller (eds.), *Services Liberalisation in the Internal Market* (Vienna, New York: Springer, 2008), pp. 1–20

Hatzopoulos, Vassilis, 'Forms of mutual recognition in the field of services', in Ioannos Lianos and Okeoghene Odudu (eds.), *Regulating Trade in Services: Trust, Distrust and Economic Integration* (Cambridge University Press, 2012), pp. 59–98

'Legal aspects in establishing the internal market for services', *College of Europe Research Papers* (2007)

'Que reste-t-il de la directive sure les services?' (2007) *Research Papers in Law*, College of Europe

'Recent development of the case law of the ECJ in the field of free movement of services 1994–2000' (2000) *Common Market Law Review* 43–82

*Regulating Services in the European Union* (Oxford University Press, 2012)

'The Court's approach to services (2006–2012): from case law to case load?' (2013) 50 *Common Market Law Review* 459–502

Hatzopoulos, Vassilis and Uyen Do, 'The case law of the ECJ concerning the free provision of services: 2000–2005' (2006) 43 *Common Market Law Review* 923–91

Herrmann, Christoph, 'Bilateral and regional trade agreements as a challenge to the multilateral trading system', EUI Working Papers LAW 2008/09

Herrmann, Christoph, Wolfgang Weiß and Christoph Ohler, *Welthandelsrecht*, 2nd edn (Munich: Beck, 2007)

Hillion, Christophe and Panos Koutrakos (eds.), *Mixed Agreements Revisited: The EU and its Member States in the World* (Oxford and Portland, OR: Hart Publishing, 2010)

Hilson, Chris, 'Discrimination in Community free movement law' (1999) 24 *European Law Review* 445–62

Hoekman, Bernard, 'Liberalizing trade in services: A survey' (2006) Working Paper Series 4030, World Bank, Washington DC, https://openknowledge.worldbank.org/handle/10986/9004

Hoeckman, Bernard and Patrick A. Maeserlin, 'Liberalizing trade in services: reciprocal negotiations and regulatory reform', in Pierre Sauvé and Robert Stern (eds.), *GATS 2000: New Directions in Services Trade Liberalization* (Washington DC: Brookings, 2000), pp. 487–508

Holmes, Peter, 'The WTO and the EU: some constitutional comparisons', in Gráinne de Búrca and Joanna Scott (eds.), *The EU and the WTO: Legal and Constitutional Issues* (Oxford and Portland, OR: Hart Publishing, 2002), pp. 59–80

Howse, Robert, 'Importing regulatory standards and principles into WTO dispute settlement: the challenge of interpreting the GATS Arrangements on Telecommunications', in Ioannos Lianos and Okeoghene Odudu (eds.), *Regulating Trade in Services: Trust, Distrust and Economic Integration* (Cambridge University Press, 2012), pp. 445–69

Howse, Robert and Kalypso Nicolaïdis, 'Democracy without sovereignty: the global vocation of political ethics', in Tomer Broude and Yuval Shany (eds.), *The Shifting Allocation of Authority in International Law: Considering Sovereignty, Supremacy and Subsidiarity – Essays in Honour of Professor Ruth Lapidoth* (Oxford and Portland, OR: Hart Publishing, 2008), pp. 163–91

Hsueh, Ching-wen, 'Direct effect, the WTO compliance mechanism and protection for individuals: lessons from the EC' (2009) 4(2) *Asian Journal of WTO & International Health Law and Policy* 521–55

Hudec, Robert E., *Essays on the Nature of International Trade Law* (London: Cameron May, 1999)

Jackson, John H., 'Status of treaties in domestic legal systems: a policy analysis' (1992) 86 *American Journal of International Law* 315–19

Jacobs, Francis, 'Direct effect and interpretation of international agreements in the recent case law of the Court', in Alan Dashwood and Marc Maresceau (eds.), *Law and Practice of EU External Relations: Salient Features of a Changing Landscape* (Cambridge University Press, 2008), pp. 13–33

Jäde, Henning, 'Die verwaltungsverfahrensrechtliche Genehmigungsfiktion' (2009) *Umwelt- und Planungsrecht* 169–73

Jarass, Hans, 'A unified approach to the fundamental freedoms', in Mads Andenas and Wulf-Henning Roth (eds.), *Services and Free Movement in EU Law* (The Hague: Kluwer, 2002), pp. 141–62

Jones, Kent, *The Doha Blues: Institutional Crisis and Reform in the WTO* (Oxford University Press, 2010)

Karayigit, Mustafa T., 'The notion of services of general economic interest revisited' (2009) 15(4) *European Public Law* 575–95

Kessie, Edwini, 'The Doha Development Agenda at the crossroads: What are the remaining obstacles to the conclusion of the round: Part II', in Christoph Herrmann and Jan Philipp Terhechte (eds.), *European Yearbook of International Economic Law* (Heidelberg: Springer, 2011), pp. 403–15

Kingreen, Torsten, 'Fundamental freedoms', in Armin von Bogdandy and Jürgen Bast (eds.), *Principles of European Constitutional Law* (Oxford and Portland, OR: Hart Publishing, 2005)

Klamert, Marcus, 'Dark matter: competence, jurisdiction and the area largely covered by EU law - Comment on Lesoochranárske' (2012) *European Law Review* 340–50

'Die Notifizierungspflichten der Dienstleistungsrichtlinie: ein Fall für den EuGH?' (2008) *Deutsches Verwaltungsblatt* 829–32

'Judicial implementation of directives and anticipatory indirect effect: Connecting the dots' (2006) *Common Market Law Review* 1251–75

'Of empty glasses and double burdens: approaches to regulating the services market à propos the implementation of the Services Directive' (2010) *Legal Issues of Economic Integration* 111–32

*The Principle of Loyalty in EU Law* (Oxford University Press, 2014)

'Way to go? More on the Services Directive and the Fundamental Freedoms' (2009) *Zeitschrift für Öffentliches Recht* 335–55

Klamert, Marcus and Niklas Maydell, 'Lost in exclusivity: implied non-exclusive external competences in Community law' (2008) *European Foreign Affairs Review* 493–513

'Rechtsfragen der impliziten Außenkompetenz der EG illustriert am Beispiel der Dienstleistungsrichtlinie und der *Minimum Platform on Investment*' (2008) 4 *Europarecht* 589–602

Korte, Stefan, 'Mitgliedstaatliche Verwaltungskooperation und private Eigenverantwortung beim Vollzug des europäischen Diensteistungsrechts' (2007) *Neue Zeitschrift für Verwaltungsrecht* 501–7

Koutrakos, Panos, 'Interpretation of mixed agreements', in Christophe Hillion and Panos Koutrakos (eds.), *Mixed Agreements Revisited: The EU and its Member States in the World* (Oxford and Portland, OR: Hart Publishing, 2010), pp. 116–37

Krajewski, Markus, 'Anforderungen der Dienstleistungsrichtlinie an Genehmigungsregelungen und ihre Umsetzung im deutschen Recht' (2009) *Neue Zeitschrift für Verwaltungsrecht* 929–35

'Conclusion', in Markus Krajewski, Ulla Neergaard and Johan van de Gronden (eds.), *The Changing Legal Framework for Services of General Interest in Europe: Between Competition and Solidarity* (The Hague: TMC Asser, Kluwer, 2009), pp. 499–506

*Grundstrukturen des Rechts öffentlicher Dienstleistungen* (Heidelberg: Springer, 2011)

*National Regulation and Trade Liberalization in Services: The Legal Impact of the General Agreement on Trade in Services (GATS) on National Regulatory Autonomy* (The Hague: Kluwer, 2003)

'Public services and trade liberalization: mapping the legal framework' (2003) 6(2) *Journal of International Economic Law* 341–67

'Services trade liberalisation and regulation: new developments and old problems', in Christoph Herrmann and Jörg Phillip Terhechte (eds.), *European Yearbook of International Economic Law* (Heidelberg, New York: Springer, 2009), pp. 153–78

'Universal service provisions in international agreements of the EU', in Erika Szyszczak *et al.* (eds.), *Developments in Services of General Interest* (TMC Asser, Springer, 2011), pp. 231–50

Krallmann, Andreas, 'WTO dispute settlement: the establishment of "binding guidance" by the Appellate Body in US Stainless Steel and recent dispute settlement rulings', in Christoph Herrmann and Jan Philipp Terhechte (eds.), *European Yearbook of International Economic Law* (Heidelberg: Springer, 2011), pp. 417–46

Kuhn, Christoph, *Die Verwirklichung des freien Dienstleistungsverkahrs im Spannungsfeld von wirtschaftlicher Handlungsfreiheit und Sozialgestaltung: Inhalt und Grenzen des grundfreiheitlichen Liberalisierungsauftrags am Beispiel der Dienstleistungsrichtlinie* (Baden-Baden: Nomos, 2013)

Lang, Andrew T. F., 'GATS', in Daniel Bethlehem *et al.* (eds.), *The Oxford Handbook of International Trade Law* (Oxford University Press, 2009), pp. 157–85

Lang, Craig, 'Annotation of the *DocMorris* case' (2005) *Common Market Law Review* 189–204

Lemor, Florian, 'Auswirkungen der Dienstleistungsrichtlinie auf ausgesuchte reglementierte Berufe' (2007) *Europäische Zeitschrift für Wirtschaftsrecht* 135–9

Leroux, Eric H., 'What is a "service supplied in the exercise of governmental authority" under Article I:3(b) and (c) of the General Agreement on Trade in Services?' (2006) 30(3) *Journal of World Trade* 345–85

Lester, Simon and Mercurio, Bryan, *World Trade Law: Text, Materials and Commentary* (Oxford and Portland, OR: Hart Publishing, 2008)

Lomnicka, Eva, 'The home country control principle in the financial services directives and the case law', in Mads Andenas and Wulf-Henning Roth (eds.), *Services and Free Movement in EU Law* (The Hague: Kluwer, 2002), pp. 295–319

Lopez-Tarruella, Aurelio, 'A European Community regulatory framework for electronic commerce' (2001) *Common Market Law Review* 1343–55

Louis, Frédéric and Anne Vallery, 'Ferring revisited: the Altmark case and state financing of public service obligations' (2004) 27(1) *World Competition* 53–74

Low, Patrick and Aaditya Mattoo, 'Is there a better way? Alternative approaches to liberalization under GATS', in Pierre Sauvé and Robert Stern (eds.), *GATS 2000: New Directions in Services Trade Liberalization* (Washington DC: Brookings, 2000), pp. 449–72

Luch, Anika and Sönke Schulz, 'Die Umsetzungsgesetzgebung der Bundesländer zur Einrichtung Einheitlicher Ansprechpartner nach Art. 6 DLR' (2010) *Gewerbearchiv* 225–30

Luff, David, 'Current international trade rules relevant to telecommunications services', in Damien Geradin and David Luff (eds.), *Global Convergence in Telecommunications and Audio-visual Services* (Cambridge University Press, 2004), pp. 34–51

Lynskey, Orla, 'The application of Article 86(2) EC to measures which do not fulfil the Altmark criteria' (2007) 30(1) *World Competition* 153–68

Marchetti, Juan A. and Petros C. Mavroidis, 'I now recognize you (and only you) as equal: an anatomy of (mutual) recognition agreements in the GATS', in Ioannos Lianos and Okeoghene Odudu (eds.), *Regulating Trade in Services: Trust, Distrust and Economic Integration* (Cambridge University Press, 2012), pp. 415–44

'The genesis of the GATS (General Agreement on Trade in Services)' (2011) 22(3) *The European Journal of International Law* 689–721

Matsushita, Mitsuo, 'Some thoughts on the Appellate Body', in Patrick F. J. Macrory, Arthur E. Appleton and Michael G. Plummer (eds.), *The World Trade Organization: Legal, Economic and Political Analysis* (New York: Springer, 2005), pp. 1389–403

Matsushita, Mituso, Thomas J. Schoenbaum and Petros C. Mavroidis, *The World Trade Organization: Law, Practice and Policy* (Oxford University Press, 2003)

Mattoo, Aaditya, 'National treatment in the GATS: corner stone or Pandora's Box?' (1997) *Journal of World Trade* 107–35

Mattoo, Aaditya and Pierre Sauvé, 'Regionalism in services trade', in Aaditya Mattoo, Robert M. Stern and Gianni Zanini, *A Handbook of International Trade in Services* (Oxford University Press, 2008), pp. 221–86

Mattoo, Aaditya and Sasha Wunsch-Vincent, 'Preempting protectionism in services: the GATS and outsourcing', Peter G. Peterson Institute for International Economics, January 2004

Mavroidis, Petros, 'Highway XVI re-visited: the road from non-discrimination to market access in GATS' (2007) *World Trade Review* 1–23
Maydell, Niklas, 'The Services Directive and existing Community law', in Fritz Breuss, Gerhard Fink and Stefan Griller (eds.), *Services Liberalisation in the Internal Market* (Vienna, New York: Springer, 2008), pp. 21–124
Mayeda, Graham, 'Developing disharmony? The SPS and TBT Agreements and the impact of harmonization on developing countries' (2004) 7(4) *Journal of International Economic Law* 737–64
Mayer, Franz C., 'Art 19 EUV', in Eberhard Grabitz, Meinhard Hilf and Martin Nettesheim (eds.), *Das Recht der Europäischen Union* (Munich: Beck, 2011)
Mayer, Heinz, *Genehmigungskonkurrenz und Verfahrenskonzentration* (Vienna: Signum, 1985)
Mirschberger, Michael, 'German Report', in Ulrich Stelkens, Wolfgang Weiß and Michael Mirschberger (eds.), *The Implementation of the EU Services Directive: Transposition, Problems and Strategies* (The Hague: TMC Asser, Springer, 2012), pp. 225–83
Möstl, Markus, 'Preconditions and limits of mutual recognition' (2010) 2 *Common Market Law Review* 405–36
'Wirtschaftsüberwachung von Dienstleistungen im Binnenmarkt' (2006) *Die öffentliche Verwaltung* 281–7
Müller-Graff, Peter-Christian, 'Protectionism or reasonable national regulation?', in Stefan Griller (ed.), *At the Crossroads: The World Trading System and the Doha Round* (Vienna, New York: Springer, 2008), pp. 147–67
Neergaard, Ulla, 'Services of general economic interest: the nature of the beast', in Markus Krajewski, Ulla Neergaard and Johan van de Gronden (eds.), *The Changing Legal Framework for Services of General Interest in Europe: Between Competition and Solidarity* (The Hague: TMC Asser, Kluwer, 2009), pp. 17–50
'The Commission's soft law in the area of services', in Erika Szyszczak *et al.* (eds.), *Developments in Services of General Interest* (The Hague: TMC Asser, Springer, 2011), pp. 37–59
Neven, Damien J. and Joseph Weiler, 'One bad apple? A comment on Japan: Measures Affecting the Importation of Apples – AB-2003-4', in Dan Horovitz, Daniel Moulis and Debra Steger (eds.), *Ten Years of WTO Dispute Settlement* (London: International Bar Association, 2007), pp. 235–57
Nicolaïdis, Kalypso, 'Trusting the Poles? Constructing Europe through mutual recognition' (2007) *Journal of European Public Policy* 682–98
Nicolaïdis, Kalypso and Susanne K. Schmidt, 'Mutual recognition "on trial": the long road to services liberalization' (2007) *Journal of European Public Policy* 717–34
O'Leary, Síofra and José Fernández-Martín, 'Judicially-created exceptions to the free provision of services', in Mads Andenas and Wulf-Henning Roth (eds.), *Services and Free Movement in EU Law* (The Hague: Kluwer, 2002), pp. 163–96

Ortino, Federico, *Basic Legal Instruments for the Liberalisation of Trade: A Comparative Analysis of EC and WTO Law* (Oxford and Portland, OR: Hart Publishing, 2004)

'The principle of non-discrimination and its exceptions in GATS: selected legal issues', in Mads Andenas and Alexander Kern (eds.), *The World Trade Organization and Trade in Services* (Nijhoff: Brill, 2008), pp. 173–206

Ostry, Sylvia, 'Globalization and the World Trading System: the Deeper Integration Policy Agenda', in Canadian Bar Association and Department of Justice Canada, 14th International Trade Law Seminar, 1996

Pauwelyn, Joost, 'Rien ne va plus? Distinguishing domestic regulation from market access in GATT and GATS' (2005) *World Trade Review* 131–70

Petersmann, Ernst-Ulrich, 'Rights and duties of states and rights and duties of their citizens', in Ulrich Beyerlin *et al.* (eds.), *Recht zwischen Umbruch und Bewahrung: Festschrift für Rudolf Bernhardt* (Berlin: Springer, 1995), pp. 1087–128

Pillai, Rajesh, 'National treatment and WTO dispute settlement' (2202) 1(3) *World Trade Review* 321–43

Poiares Maduro, Miguel, 'Harmony and dissonance in free movement', in Mads Andenas and Wulf-Henning Roth (eds.), *Services and Free Movement in EU Law* (The Hague: Kluwer, 2002), pp. 41–68

*We the Court* (Oxford and Portland, OR: Hart Publishing, 2002)

Potacs, Michael, *Auslegung im öffentlichen Recht: Eine vergleichende Untersuchung der Auslegungspraxis des Europäischen Gerichtshofs und der österreichischen Gerichtshöfe des öffentlichen Rechts* (Baden-Baden: Nomos, 1994)

Prechal, Sascha, Sybe de Vries and Frans van Doorn, 'The implementation of the Services Directive in the Netherlands', in Ulrich Stelkens, Wolfgang Weiß and Michael Mirschberger (eds.), *The Implementation of the EU Services Directive: Transposition, Problems, Strategies* (The Hague: TMC Asser, 2012), pp. 435–74

Prévost, Denise, 'Services and public policy regulation in WTO law: The example of the US-Gambling case', in Johan van de Gronden (ed.), *EU and WTO Law on Services: Limits to the Realisation of General Interest Policies within the Services Markets?* (The Hague: Kluwer, 2008), pp. 215–46

Prosser, Tony, 'Competition law and public services: from single market to citizenship rights? (2005) 11(4) *European Public Law* 543–63

Randelzhofer, Albrecht and Ulrich Forsthoff, 'Art. 47 para. 19', in Eberhard Grabitz and Meinhard Hilf (eds.), *Das Recht der Europäischen Union* (Munich: Beck, 2001)

Reid, Emily, 'Regulatory autonomy in the EU and WTO: defining and defending its limits' (2010) 44(4) *Journal of World Trade* 877–901

Robertson, Viktoria H. S. E., *Perspectiven für den grenzüberschreitenden Dienstleistungshandel: Das EU-Dienstleistungsrecht und sein Verhältnis zum GATS* (Baden-Baden: Nomos, 2012)

Rodrigues, Stéphane, 'Towards a general EC framework instrument related to SGEI? Political considerations and legal constraints', in Markus Krajewski, Ulla Neergaard and Johan van de Gronden (eds.), *The Changing Legal*

*Framework for Services of General Interest in Europe: Between Competition and Solidarity* (The Hague: TMC Asser, Kluwer, 2009), pp. 255–66

Ross, Malcolm, 'Article 16 E.C. and services of general interest: from derogation to obligation' (2000) 25(1) *European Law Review* 22–38

'The value of solidarity in European public services law', in Markus Krajewski, Ulla Neergaard and Johan van de Gronden (eds.), *The Changing Legal Framework for Services of General Interest in Europe: Between Competition and Solidarity* (TMC Asser: Kluwer, 2009), pp. 81–99

Roth, Günther and Peter Hilpold (eds.), *Der EuGH und die Souveränität der Mitgliedstaaten* (Stuttgart: Richard Boorberg, 2008)

Roth, Wulf-Henning, 'Die Dienstleistungsrichtlinie und der Verbraucherschutz', in Stefan Leible (ed.), *Die Umsetzung der Dienstleistungsrichtlinie: Chancen und Risken für Deutschland* (Jena: JWV, 2008), pp. 205–35

'Freier Dienstleistungsverkehr und Verbraucherschutz' (2007) *Verbraucher und Recht* 161–72

'The European Court of Justice's case law in the freedom to provide services: is Keck relevant?', in Mads Andenas and Wulf-Henning Roth (eds.), *Services and Free Movement in EU Law* (The Hague: Kluwer, 2002), pp. 1–24

Rothe, Nicole, 'Freedom of establishment of legal persons within the European Union: an analysis of the European Court of Justice decision in the Überseering case' (2004) *American University Law Review* 1103–41

Sauter, Wolf, 'Services of general economic interest and universal service in EU law' (2008) 2 *European Law Review* 167–93

Schiek, Dagmar, 'The European social model and the Services Directive', in Ulla Neergaard, Ruth Nielsen and Lynn Roseberry (eds.), *The Services Directive: Consequences for the Welfare State and the European Social Model* (Copenhagen: Djof, 2008), pp. 25–62

Schliesky, Ulf, 'Von der Realisierung des Binnenmarktes über die Verwaltungsreform zu einem gemeineuropäischen Verwaltungsrecht? Die Auswirkungen der geplanten EU-Dienstleistungsrichtlinie auf das deutsche Verwaltungsrecht' (2005) *Deutsches Verwaltungsblatt* 887–95

Schmidt, Susanne K., 'Mutual recognition as a new mode of governance' (2007) *Journal of European Public Policy* 667–81

Schroeder, Werner, 'Der Binnenmarkt für Dienstleistungen: Zwischen Herkunftslandprinzip und sozialpolitischer Gestaltungsfreiheit', in Stefan Griller (ed.), *Die europäische Wirtschaftsverfassung de lege lata et ferenda* (Vienna, New York: Springer, 2007), pp. 379–423

Scott, Joanna, 'Mandatory or imperative requirements in the EU and the WTO', in Catherine Barnard and Joanna Scott (eds.), *The Law of the Single European Market: Unpacking the Premises* (Oxford and Portland, OR: Hart Publishing, 2002), pp. 269–93

Sherman, Laura B., '"Wildly enthusiastic" about the first multilateral agreement on trade in telecommunications services' (1991) 51 *Federal Communications Law Journal* 61–110

Skovgaard Olykke, Grith, 'The definition of a contract under Article 106 TFEU', in Erika Szyszczak *et al.* (eds.), *Developments in Services of General Interest* (TMC Asser, Springer, 2011), pp. 103–20

Snell, Jukka, 'Free movement of services and the Services Directive: the legitimacy of the case law', in Johan van de Gronden (ed.), *EU and WTO Law on Services: Limits to the Realisation of General Interest Policies within the Services Markets?* (The Hague: Kluwer, 2008), pp. 31–54

'Freedom to provide services in the case law and in the Services Directive: problems, solutions, and institutions', in Ulla Neergaard, Ruth Nielsen and Lynn Roseberry (eds.), *The Services Directive: Consequences for the Welfare State and the European Social Model* (Copenhagen: Djof, 2008), pp. 171–97

'The notion of market access: a concept or a slogan?' (2010) 47 *Common Market Law Review* 437–72

Snell, Jukka and Mads Andenas, 'Exploring the outer limits: restrictions on the free movement of goods and services', in Mads Andenas and Wulf-Henning Roth (eds.), *Services and Free Movement in EU Law* (The Hague: Kluwer, 2002), pp. 69–140

Spaventa, Eleanor, 'Annotation to Case C-442/02, Caixa-Bank France v. Ministère de l'Économie, des Finances et de l'Industrie' (2005) 42(4) *Common Market Law Review* 1151–68

'On discrimination and the theory of mandatory requirements' (2002) 3 *Cambridge Yearbook of European Legal Studies* 457–78

Stein, Eric, 'Lawyers, judges, and the making of a transnational constitution' (1981) *The American Journal of International Law* 1–27

Stelkens, Ulrich, Wolfgang Weiß and Michael Mirschberger, 'General comparative report', in Ulrich Stelkens, Wolfgang Weiß and Michael Mirschberger (eds.), *The Implementation of the EU Services Directive: Transposition, Problems and Strategies* (The Hague: TMC Asser, Springer, 2012), pp. 3–61

Stewart, Terence P., 'Trade remedy actions by WTO members: a cause for concern or a reflection of improved market access?' (2013) 8(6) *Global Trade and Customs Journal* 159–63

Stöger, Karl, 'Der einheitliche Ansprechpartner im Bundesstaat: Ein Blick über die Grenze', in Clemens Jabloner *et al.* (eds.), *Vom praktischen Wert der Methode: Festschrift Heinz Mayer zum 65. Geburtstag* (Vienna: Manz, 2011), pp. 755–73

Streinz, Rudolf and Christoph Herrmann, 'Der Fall Mangold: Eine "kopernikanische Wende im Europarecht"?' (2007) *Recht der Arbeit* 165–9

Streinz, Rudolf, Christoph Ohler and Christoph Herrmann, *Der Vertrag von Lissabon zur Reform der EU*, 2nd edn (Munich: Beck, 2008)

Stumpf, Cordula, 'Aktuelle Entwicklungen im europäischen Dienstleistungs- und Niederlassungsrecht' (2006) *Deutsche Zeitschrift für Wirtschafts- und Insolvenzrecht* 99–107

Swick, Brenda and Vanessa Gruben, 'Judicial activism and the WTO: the evolution of an unprecedented juridical institution', in Dan Horovitz,

Daniel Moulis and Debra Steger (eds.), *Ten Years of WTO Dispute Settlement* (London: International Bar Association, 2007), pp. 93–112
Sydow, Gernot, *Verwaltungskooperation in der Europäischen Union* (Tübingen: Mohr Siebeck, 2004)
Szyszczak, Erika, 'Cases: financing services of general economic interest' (2004) 67(6) *Modern Law Review* 982–1011
Thouvenin, Jean-Marc, 'The Altmark case and its consequences', in Markus Krajewski, Ulla Neergaard and Johan van de Gronden (eds.), *The Changing Legal Framework for Services of General Interest in Europe: Between Competition and Solidarity* (The Hague: TMC Asser, Kluwer, 2009), pp. 103–15
Trachtman, Joel P., 'Embedding mutual recognition at the WTO' (2007) 14(5) *Journal of European Public Policy* 780–99
'Regulatory jurisdiction and the WTO' (2007) 10(3) *Journal of International Economic Law* 631–51
'Toward open recognition? Standardization and regional integration under Article XXIV of GATT' (2003) 6(2) *Journal of International Economic Law* 459–92
Trebilcock, Michael J., Robert Howse and Antonia Eliason, *The Regulation of International Trade*, 4th edn (London and New York: Routledge, 2013)
Trybus, Martin and Almuth Berger, 'The implementation of the Services Directive in the United Kingdom', in Ulrich Stelkens, Wolfgang Weiß and Michael Mirschberger (eds.), *The Implementation of the EU Services Directive: Transposition, Problems, Strategies* (The Hague: TMC Asser, 2012), pp. 633–65
Van Damme, Isabelle, 'Interpretation, jurisdiction, and applicable law', in Daniel Bethlehem, Donald McRae, Rodney Neufeld and Isabelle Van Damme (eds.), *The Oxford Handbook of International Trade Law* (Oxford University Press, 2009), pp. 298–343
van de Gronden, Johan, 'Social services of general interest and EU law', in Erika Szyszczak *et al.* (eds.) *Developments in Services of General Interest*, Legal Issues of Services of General Interest (The Hague: TMC Asser, 2011), pp. 123–51
'The EU and WTO law on free trade in services and the public interest: towards a framework directive on Services of General Economic Interest?', in Johan van de Gronden (ed.), *EU and WTO Law on Services: Limits to the Realisation of General Interest Policies within the Services Markets?* (The Hague: Kluwer, 2008), pp. 247–80
Van den Bossche, Peter and Werner Zdouc, *The Law and Policy of the World Trade Organization: Text Cases and Materials* (Cambridge University Press, 2013)
van den Hende, Lode, 'GATS, dispute settlement and concerns about WTO Members' regulatory autonomy: the need for a practical interpretation of the GATS following *US-Gambling*', in Dan Horovitz, Daniel Moulis and Debra Steger (eds.), *Ten Years of WTO Dispute Settlement* (London: International Bar Association, 2007), pp. 259–78

van Huffel, Michel, 'The legal framework for financial services and the internet', in Niamh Nic Shuibhne (ed.), *Regulating the Internal Market* (Cheltenham and Northampton: Edward Elgar, 2006), pp. 144–80

Vogenauer, Stefan, *Die Auslegung von Gesetzen in England und auf dem Kontinent: Eine vergleichende Untersuchung der Rechtsprechung und ihrer historischen Grundlagen* (Tübingen: Mohr Siebeck, 2000)

von Danwitz, Thomas, *Europäisches Verwaltungsrecht* (Berlin: Springer, 2008)

Vranes, Erich, 'Der Verhältnismäßigkeitsgrundsatz: Herleitungsalternativen, Rechtsstatus und Funktionen' (2009) 47(1) *Archiv des Völkerrechts* 1–35

'The overlap between GATT and GATS: a methodological mate' (2009) *Legal Issues of Economic Integration* 215–38

*Trade and the Environment: Fundamental Issues in International Law, WTO Law and Legal Theory* (Oxford University Press, 2009)

Weatherill, Stephen, 'Promoting the consumer interest in an integrated services market' (2007) *Mitchell Working Paper Series* 7

Wernicke, Stephan, 'Taking stock: The EU institutions and SGEI', in Markus Krajewski, Ulla Neergaard and Johan van de Gronden (eds.), *The Changing Legal Framework for Services of General Interest in Europe: Between Competition and Solidarity* (The Hague: TMC Asser, Kluwer, 2009), pp. 69–79

Weiler, Joseph H. H., 'Cain and Abel: Convergence and divergence in international trade law', in Joseph H. H. Weiler (ed.), *The EU, the WTO, and the NAFTA* (Oxford University Press, Collected Courses of the Academy of European Law, 2001), pp. 1–4

'Epilogue: Towards a common law of international trade', in Joseph H. H. Weiler (ed.), *The EU, the WTO, and the NAFTA* (Oxford University Press, Collected Courses of the Academy of European Law, 2001), pp. 201–32

'Law, culture, and values in the WTO: gazing into the crystal ball', in Daniel Bethlehem *et al.* (eds.), *The Oxford Handbook of International Trade Law* (Oxford University Press, 2009), pp. 750–72

'The transformation of Europe' (1991) *The Yale Law Journal* 2403–83

Weiß, Wolfgang, 'GATS and domestic regulation: a threat to democracy?', in Stefan Griller (ed.), *At the Crossroads: The World Trading System and the Doha Round* (Vienna, New York: Springer, 2008), pp. 369–83

Wilsher, Daniel, 'Does Keck discrimination make any sense? An assessment of the non-discrimination principle within the European Single Market' (2008) 33 *European Law Review* 3–22

Windoffer, Alexander, 'Das System des einheitlichen Ansprechpartners', in Stefan Leible (ed.), *Die Umsetzung der Dienstleistungsrichtlinie: Chancen und Risiken für Deutschland* (JWV Jenaer Wiss. Verl.-Ges, 2008), pp. 25–42

Wouters, Jan, Dominic Coppens and Bart de Meester, 'The European Union's external relations after the Lisbon Treaty', in Stefan Griller and Jacques Ziller (eds.), *The Lisbon Treaty: EU Constitutionalism without a Constitutional Treaty* (Vienna, New York: Springer, 2008), pp. 143–203

Zarbiyev, Fuad, 'Judicial activism in international law: a conceptual framework for analysis' (2012) 3(2) *Journal of International Dispute Settlement* 247–78

Zdouc, Werner, 'WTO dispute settlement practice relating to the General Agreement on Trade in Services', in Ortino Federico and Ernst-Ulrich Petersmann (eds.), *The WTO Dispute Settlement System 1995–2003* (The Hague: Kluwer, 2004), pp. 381–420

Zhang, Xin, 'Direct effect of the WTO Agreements: national survey' (2003) 9 *International Trade Law & Regulation* 35–46

Ziekow, Jan and Alexander Windoffer, 'Kommentar zu Art. 6', in Monika Schlachter and Christoph Ohler (eds.), *Europäische Dienstleistungsrichtlinie: Handkommentar* (Baden-Baden: Nomos, 2008)

Zúñiga Schroder, Humberto, *Harmonization, Equivalence and Mutual Recognition of Standards in WTO Law* (Alphen/Rijn: Kluwer Law International, 2011)

# Index